Calvin and the Resignification of the World

Calvin's 1559 *Institutes* is one of the most important works of theology that emerged at a pivotal time in Europe's history. As a movement, Calvinism has often been linked to the emerging features of modernity, especially to capitalism, rationalism, disenchantment, and the formation of the modern sovereign state. In this book, Michelle Chaplin Sanchez argues that a closer reading of the 1559 *Institutes* recalls some of the tensions that marked Calvinism's emergence among refugees, and ultimately opens new ways to understand the more complex ethical and political legacy of Calvinism. In conversation with theorists of practice and signification, she advocates for reading the *Institutes* as a pedagogical text that places the reader in the world as the domain in which to actively pursue the "knowledge of God and ourselves" through participatory uses of divine revelation. Through this lens, she reconceives Calvin's understanding of sovereignty and how it works in relation to the embodied reader. Sanchez also critically examines Calvin's teaching on providence and the incarnation, in conversation with theorists of political theology and modernity who emphasize the importance of those very doctrines.

Michelle Chaplin Sanchez is Associate Professor of Theology at Harvard Divinity School, where she teaches courses on the Protestant Reformations, intersections between Protestant theology and modern philosophy, theories of sovereignty and modernity, and other themes in Christian theology including providence and the existence of God. She has won several teaching awards, and has also published scholarly articles in the *Journal of the American Academy of Religion*, *Journal of Religion*, *Scottish Journal of Theology*, and *Political Theology*.

Calvin and the Resignification of the World

Creation, Incarnation, and the Problem of Political Theology in the 1559 Institutes

MICHELLE CHAPLIN SANCHEZ

Harvard Divinity School

CAMBRIDGE
UNIVERSITY PRESS

CAMBRIDGE
UNIVERSITY PRESS

University Printing House, Cambridge CB2 8BS, United Kingdom

One Liberty Plaza, 20th Floor, New York, NY 10006, USA

477 Williamstown Road, Port Melbourne, VIC 3207, Australia

314–321, 3rd Floor, Plot 3, Splendor Forum, Jasola District Centre,
New Delhi – 110025, India

79 Anson Road, #06–04/06, Singapore 079906

Cambridge University Press is part of the University of Cambridge.

It furthers the University's mission by disseminating knowledge in the pursuit of
education, learning, and research at the highest international levels of excellence.

www.cambridge.org
Information on this title: www.cambridge.org/9781108473040
DOI: 10.1017/9781108631648

© Cambridge University Press 2019

First published 2019

Printed and bound in Great Britain by Clays Ltd, Elcograf S.p.A.

A catalogue record for this publication is available from the British Library.

Library of Congress Cataloging-in-Publication Data
NAMES: Sanchez, Michelle Chaplin, author.
TITLE: Calvin and the resignification of the world : creation, incarnation, and the problem of
political theology in the 1559 "Institutes" / Michelle Sanchez.
DESCRIPTION: Cambridge, United Kingdom ; New York, NY : Cambridge University
Press, 2019. | Includes bibliographical references.
IDENTIFIERS: LCCN 2018034216 | ISBN 9781108473040 (hardback : alk. paper)
SUBJECTS: LCSH: Calvin, Jean, 1509-1564–Political and social views. |
Calvin, Jean, 1509-1564. Institutio Christianae religionis.
CLASSIFICATION: LCC BX9418 .S225 2019 | DDC 230/.42–dc23
LC record available at https://lccn.loc.gov/2018034216

ISBN 978-1-108-47304-0 Hardback

Contents

List of Figures   *page* vii
Acknowledgments   viii

Introduction   1

PART I ITINERANT PEDAGOGY

1   Writing Reform: The Genre of the 1559 *Institutio*
    Christianae Religionis   43
    The Genre of the 1559 *Institutio*   48
    The Enchiridion   54
    The Itinerarium   62
    The Politics of the Itinerary   70
    Conclusion   78

PART II PROVIDENCE

2   The Practice of Writing Providence   83
    Approaching Providence as an Activity   86
    Earlier Greek Writings: Cleanthes and Plato   91
    Later Latin Writings: Stoicism and Boethius   97
    Conclusion   107

3   Providence and World Affirmation   111
    Providence in the Wake of Loss   117
    Calvin's Providence: The Personal and the Political 125
    The Movement of the Divine Will   131
    Hiddenness   138
    Conclusion   146

4 Providence and Governmentality   147
      Agamben's Methodology   151
      Order   156
      Glory   159
      Back to Calvin   161
      Conclusion: Reform, Resistance, and Its Gestures   169

PART III INCARNATION

5 Calvin's "Secularization" of Augustinian Signification   179
      The Paradox of Learning   186
      Calvin's First Difference from Augustine: The *Duplex
      Cognitio*   197
      Calvin's Second Difference from Augustine:
      Creation before Church   201
      Conclusion   208
6 Faith Resignifying Understanding: Atonement and Election   210
      Anselm's *Proslogion*   212
      Book Two: The Legal Fiction of the Faith of Christ   218
      Book Three: Prayer, Election, and the Evidence of Desire   227
      Conclusion   237
7 Calvin against Political Theology   240
      Excursis   240
      Misrecognition   244
      Signifying "Ourselves": The Apparatus of the Visible
      Church   247
      Calvin's Two Bodies and the Question of Political
      Theology   258
      Conclusion   270
Conclusion   274

Bibliography   288
Index   311

Figures

1 *Tabula Peutingeriana* (first–fourth century CE). Fascimile by
Conradi Millieri (1887–8) [Map] At: http://upload.wikimedia
.org/wikipedia/commons/5/50/TabulaPeutingeriana.jpg
(accessed May 9, 2014)   *page 64*

Acknowledgments

If this is the space for thanking everyone who made vital contributions to this book in ways that are difficult to cite in the footnotes, then it is a task that is both impossible and necessary. A project like this may be watered and fertilized by the scholarly exercises of reading, note-taking, testing ideas, writing, and rewriting. But its soil is life: human relationships; political anxieties; ethical dilemmas; decades of Sundays in churches that have caused me both pain and joy; conversations mundane and accidental that somehow set off a spark in my mind or made me realize I'd been wrong.

Over the course of cultivating this manuscript from dissertation to book draft and finally to publication, I have lost three people who were important to me, and those losses are inscribed in the pages that follow.

First, in 2012, I said goodbye to Professor Ronald F. Thiemann, my first doctoral advisor and the person who first cultivated my eagerness to explore the impossibly complicated living impact of Christian doctrinal writing. I remember sitting in his office one day and running out of words to describe what it meant to see the world through the lens of ideas like providence – to read doctrine with a kind of "translucence" that sees the world only more clearly. He told me he didn't know, but that was what he wanted to do, too – to figure out how to say it and write it. When he died of pancreatic cancer, I had only my dissertation prospectus in hand. But I also had the echo of his voice against which to test these readings as they grew: "Never forget to be dialectical."

In 2014, soon after I'd defended my dissertation, I said goodbye to my own father. Norm Chaplin was a building contractor who had an Evangelical conversion in 1980, before I was born, and after that he rarely missed a Sunday in church. My dad was unfailingly kind and unflinch-ingly true to himself. He had no time for things airy and intellectual, but he knew when something didn't sit right. Providence was one of those things that didn't sit right. He believed that God was all the things Christians ordinarily believe God to be, but he also bristled at the sugges-tion that God causes suffering simply for "divine good pleasure." People were too important to my dad, and being faithful to God meant being true to the way Jesus loved people. He taught me that you could be both pious and honest about the things you don't know, and in fact that the two must go together. When I began to ask hard questions about things in college, as one does, my dad felt like the only one who had faith that I would be "just fine" – and he was right, because his faith was always in something bigger than what any one of us can grasp at any one point. And I believe him now about things being "just fine," because watching him suffer and die from dementia taught me that even when things are so far from just fine – so ghastly far – it's possible to love God and the world so much that you'll still be fundamentally at peace with who you are and able to say "let it be" to what has come your way.

Just as I finished the first draft of this book, in late April 2017, my dear friend Lorraine Stanfield was diagnosed with metastatic cancer that took her life less than five months later. She was fifty-six, a physician and a professor known for living and teaching compassionate care; a pastor's wife who stood at some skeptical distance from the faith of the church, but never from its love; a mother who mothered like she sang – like each moment of music was enough to make up for the exhaustion of a full life. On the surface, she didn't have much in common with my dad, but over time I saw the telltale marks: the unfailing kindness, the presence, the unquestioned conviction that people are always more important than ideas and things, the ability to savor life even in pain, to love your own skin because it's what's real and what's sacred.

I've long subscribed to the definition of theology that Marilynne Robinson's character, Lila, puts best in her inner reflection that, "when the Reverend talked about angels ... the notion helped her to think about certain things." I've found Calvin's theology to be worth reading and writing on because it helps me think about certain things. At the same time, these lives have helped me think about Calvin's theology, setting up the relationship that Calvin himself narrates when he cites Augustine at the close of his final preface: "I count myself one of the number of those who write as they learn and learn as they write."

There are, of course, many others who are indelibly woven into this product of writing and learning and writing. I am grateful to Amy Hollywood, first for taking me under her wing and guiding my dissertation to completion, but also for so much more: for years of honest, warm, and good-humored mentorship that always felt fundamentally like care, as well as for always supplying brilliant questions to provoke better thinking. Mark Jordan, perhaps more than anyone else, has taught me through example what it means to read theology for life – in and beyond its traditional disciplinary bounds – and I am deeply grateful to have his voice among those that guide my thinking in and outside of academic settings. And if this book displays any precision of analysis in its reading of Calvin, that would be thanks to David Lamberth's sharp early reading and always-informative conversations. His unwavering interest in this project has given me the courage to continue cultivating it at critical times.

Additionally, as with so many things in life, I am deeply indebted to an array of people who remain nameless and faceless to me, but whose support has enabled my thinking and saved me from many errors and oversights. My gratitude goes out to the two blind readers serving Cambridge University Press whose reports were profoundly helpful; but also to those who peer-reviewed a number of now-published articles related to this project. Thank you all for your generous service to the field. Should you read this book in its final form, I hope you will find your feedback faithfully reflected.

I must also thank Harvard Divinity School (HDS), both for supporting the initial draft of this book with a sabbatical leave and for creating the setting in which I have been able to learn so much with and from others. As any professor will know, teaching and writing are never far removed, and my teaching fellows and students over my first three years at HDS have shaped my thinking in profound ways. I give special thanks to Chandra Plowden, Michael Motia, L. Patrick Burrows, AnnMarie Micikas Bridges, and Michael Putnam. Finally, as I was proceeding on my final revisions, it was my colleague Matthew Potts and student Jeremy Williams who gave me greatest occasion to think more critically about how the doctrine of election either mobilizes or upsets the urge to sovereignly differentiate bodies according to normative rubrics such as friend and enemy or citizen and criminal.

There is another pedagogical space of great importance to me, one without which this book would not have been possible, and that is the community at Fourth Presbyterian Church in South Boston. While no words feel sufficient to describing what it has meant to live life alongside such a variety of humanity in that wild and sacred space, I will just say that being at Fourth has taught me what it looks like to relate scriptural words to real bodies and real bodies to scriptural words in ordinary time. As such, it's persuaded me that when a church invites anyone who walks through the door to take up, challenge, and bear the doctrines being preached, this can in fact upset the violence that hegemony has otherwise exerted over those bodies. I am grateful to routinely bear witness to the steady and generous heart of Reverend Burns Stanfield in particular, who week after week allows his own voice and body to serve as the vessel for that divine love that looks first to the outsider, the refugee, the oppressed – the one in a hundred who have wandered away. His love is never pity but the fullest affection for the vast profundity of creation.

Finally, there remain my two loved ones whose contributions to this work are the most ineffable and most important: my mother and my husband. My mom, Jennifer Chaplin, was my first theological interlocutor. She couldn't talk about theology at church at the depth she desired because she was a woman, so she talked to me instead. My husband, Tim Sanchez, came to the church as an adult, as an outsider, and embraced it, having the audacity to respond to the words being spoken even when his own belonging wasn't quickly recognized by others. Over the years, both of them have graced me with endless conversations that shape my thinking about everything – about pain, politics, and what it means to live a truly responsible life. They make me believe that the experience of goodness here on earth is real and worth praying for. I am grateful to my mom for all of this, but also for the more mundane gift of proofreading this work as dissertation, as first draft, and yet again as final draft. I am grateful to Tim for his care for me as a human being. He is the most stable sign through which I daily perceive divine grace. He was also the first person to occasion my awareness of all the more subtle things this book is about: how admitting what we don't know is not a failure, but the condition for the possibility of love.

This book is dedicated to them, and to anyone who hears the words of the gospel from the margins and has the audacity to think that those words refer to them.

Introduction

Jean Calvin lived life as a refugee. The thinking and writing that produced his most important body of work – the 1559 *Institutio Christianae Religionis* – all occurred at a distance from the institutional bodies of church and state that had cradled and cultivated his own mind and body during his formative years.[1]

In the sixteenth-century, refugees in Europe were unwanted and openly derided – perhaps more overtly than now, when some nations at least present the veneer of hospitality to the displaced.[2] Nicholas Terpstra argues that understanding the early modern European Christian logic of expulsion and migration requires appreciating the ubiquity of the "body" metaphor as a social imaginary or civic religion – or as something akin to what later theorists, such as Carl Schmitt to Ernst Kantorowicz and their interlocutors, would call a "political theology."[3] In *The King's Two Bodies*, Kantorowicz traces how medieval European political theory was shaped by a series of metaphorical exchanges with Christology, sacramental theology, and ecclesiology. These theological debates provided a deep archive of strategies for theorizing the relationship of the body of Christ *as* God-Man to the body of Christ *as* church. Such strategies were deployed and recast by jurists and artists who imagined

---

[1] My estimation of the 1559 *Institutio* as Calvin's most important work follows Calvin's own estimation as well as the longstanding and widespread impact of the work relative to Calvin's other writing – evident, not least, in the fact that the book has recently earned its own biography from Calvin scholar and biographer Bruce Gordon.

[2] Bruce Gordon, *Calvin* (New Haven, CT: Yale University Press, 2009): 198–200.

[3] Nicholas Terpstra, *Religious Refugees in the Early Modern World* (New York: Cambridge University Press, 2015).

the relationships between the natural body of the king and the kingly office, between individual humans and humanity, and later between the citizen and the democratic body politic.[4]

Terpstra argues that by the fifteenth century, the metaphor of the *Corpus Christianum* had been thoroughly internalized at the level of European civic life and that we cannot understand early modern patterns of expulsion and migration without it. The imaginary of the city or nation as *Corpus Christianum* performed several duties. It integrated the lives and activities of lay people with religious and political elites; demarcated the boundary between Christian subjects and their Jewish and Muslim others; and clarified the logic of who should be integrated and who should be expunged. If society was imagined as a body, then a discourse emerges over how to maintain its relative health. To be an exile was to know oneself as that which was deemed "refuse" from the perspective of the institutional center.[5]

By the end of the seventeenth century, following the devastation of the wars of religion, Europe had become a continent replete with exceptional people. In Reformed regions especially, nearly everyone was someone else's refugee. From this vantage, the theological idea of an "exceptional people," chosen by God to wander and establish a promised land, could both borrow from and recast the inherited metaphor of the body politic.[6] The sovereign was no longer identified with the office of the king and sacramental host, whose very substance offered a site of participation capable of adjudicating who was a healthy member and who should be expelled. If there was to be a locus of sovereign power organizing a body politic, that power now had to be identified *with* the exception itself: with a people who knew themselves *as* exceptions chosen to govern a body comprised *of* exceptions. These constraints gave birth to new ways of both imagining and managing collective identity: newly shared religious and cultural practices, ethnic identities, local histories. All of these ways of imagining a corporate entity could strategically resist but also reappropriate the function that had been served by a sacramentally constituted *Corpus Christianum*: to facilitate the determination of which kinds of individual bodies are governable and which are not.

---

[4] Ernst Kantorowicz, *The King's Two Bodies: A Study in Medieval Political Theology* (Princeton, NJ: Princeton University Press, 1985).
[5] Terpstra, 21. The argument spans chapter 1.
[6] Etienne Balibar and Immanuel Wallerstein, *Race, Nation, Class: Ambiguous Identities* (London: Verso, 1991). Wallerstein argues that the modern formation of "peoplehood" argues that state preceded nation. 81–85.

Whether in its overtly sacramental form or its later identarian and purposive forms, this particular and pervasive logic of sovereign power imagines a power that decides whether bodies are identified with the collective body – whether they contribute to presumed criteria of health or not.[7] However, unlike the sovereignty of the *Corpus Christianum*, a sovereignty grounded in the existence of the exception is marked by a kind of puzzle. When sovereignty is imagined as an exceptional people deciding over themselves, this logic perpetuates and organizes – privileges and marginalizes – a multiplicity of exceptional bodies: races, ethnicities, cultures, personality types, genders, pathologies. Yet, in another sense, there is no longer a theoretical "outside." If the site of the collective body is identified with management techniques capable of governing a panoply of exceptions, then what was a sacramental *Corpus Christianum* becomes, simply, *Corpus*. If the refugee *qua* exception could once be expelled and sent outside the body, now the refugee *qua* exception will be reintegrated into the state in a way that preserves the complex identity of the exceptional nation: as slave, migrant, patient, prisoner. How is it possible to get outside the logic of sovereignty when sovereignty operates precisely by producing exceptions and integrating them into the logic of the exceptional nation?

One strategy involves beginning with those bodies and histories that most cut against the grain of the domain in which sovereignty operates.[8] J. Kameron Carter reads Giorgio Agamben's *homo sacer* as one of the few moments in the debate over political theology in which the social body of

---

[7] See, for example, Etienne Balibar's discussion of fictive ethnicity as constitutive of national identity in Balibar and Wallerstein, 96f. Agamben's *homo sacer* project can also be read as an account of how modern sovereignty works not only by deciding the exception, but by creating and managing the exception. Magnus Fiskesjö and J. Kameron Carter have criticized Agamben's relative lack of attention to the embodied production of peoples *as* exceptions in the form of slaves, barbarians, and non-White races. See Magnus Fiskesjö, "Critical reflections on Agamben's *homo sacer*" in *Journal of Ethnographic Theory* 2/1 (2012): 161–180; J. Kamerom Carter, "The Inglorious" in *Political Theology* 14/1 (2013): 77–87.

[8] I take this to be a common concern of poststructuralists – particularly the work of Foucault, but also Derrida, Agamben, and Butler, whose work involves efforts to think of the body as a site of resistance or at least unmanageability. I'll return to that conversation shortly. Another approach to critiquing the fascist structure of a secularized incarnational theology might be to heighten divine transcendence and oppose it to every historical-political structure. This is more or less the approach taken by Löwith, but is also resonant with Walter Benjamin's notion of divine violence.

the sovereign is approached from the perspective of the exclusions it produces.[9] Agamben pulls the notion of *homo sacer* from ancient Roman law as a figure expelled from the city, stripped of legal protections, and thus reduced to "bare life."[10] Agamben proceeds to argue that "production of bare life is the originary act of sovereignty."[11] The modern nation-state makes citizens by first producing the life of the *homo sacer* and then incorporating bare life into dual apparatuses of medical and economic management. In this way, the bodies of citizens are made to participate in the "glory" of sovereignty – or by doxological testaments to success that actually fuels the providential machine. To be a citizen of bureaucratic-economic sovereignty, and to share in its glory, is essentially to participate in the incarnation of the state; to be subject to – and subjectivated by – the bipolar apparatus of modern management that Foucault called "biopower."[12]

Yet, Carter argues that Agamben misses an opportunity in this account when he fails to theorize sovereignty from the perspective of the "inglorious" *homo sacer* – the body of those who remain unincorporated or marginally incorporated into the sovereign body:

*Homo sacer*ization ... now means something quite materially and somatically specific that is lost to view in Agamben's text, but that nevertheless haunts the text. To undergo non-Europeanization, which perhaps is the specific form of *homo sacer*ization in the modern/colonial world, is precisely to be denied governance. That is to say, it is to be denied the position of master within the order of sovereignty. It is to be marginalized or denied the place of the center around which all difference is to be organized and then governed ... Agamben's suggestive

---

[9] Importantly, Carter locates the development of this particular critique of sovereignty much earlier in black studies, beginning at least with W. E. B. DuBois, but notes its near-total absence among white theorists and critics of sovereignty.

[10] Across his work, and particularly the multivolume *homo sacer* project, Agamben distinguishes "bare life" from *zoe* and *bios*, or the form of natural/animal life and the form of political life, respectively.

[11] Agamben, *Homo Sacer: Sovereignty and Bare Life* (Redwood City, CA: Stanford University Press, 1998), 98.

[12] Notably, Agamben charts the emergence of this particular logic of sovereignty much earlier than Foucault, tracing it to early Christian debates over Christology and the trinity. I discuss this in much greater detail in Chapter 4, which is devoted to Agamben's account of glory and glorification as a lens for reading Calvin's doctrine of providence. There, I treat Agamben's relation to Foucault's biopower as well as the way he reads governmentality and glory in relation to theological debates over providence and incarnation, as well as practices of liturgical acclamation. For an important discussion of biopower, see Michel Foucault, *History of Sexuality 1: The Will to Knowledge* (New York: Vintage, 1978), 142f.

claims about glory call for more careful reflections on the glorious and especially the inglorious aspects of corporealization.[13]

In another place, Carter links the corporeality of the inglorious to the metaphor of the abject: a substance which is neither separate from nor central to the body, such as tears, saliva, feces, and urine.[14] "In the field of the political, the abject is neither friend (subject) nor enemy (object)," but "exists in the zone between life (full citizenship) and death (the enemy as one who must be killed)." As in the early modern logic of expulsion, the abject is tied to that which must be marginalized or pushed away to render the body pure. If the early modern *Corpus Christianum* was itself constituted through the institutionalized management of narratives and practices materialized at the level of the body, then the abject of that body would be the refugees who were not executed, but whose position with respect to the health of the collective body was expunged as a peripheral impurity. If such figures might reveal something of the under-side of sovereign glory – or the extent to which that sovereignty is itself constructed and ritually perpetuated *through* the expulsion of the inglorious – then is it possible to harness a critique of modern sovereignty by beginning with the perspective of an early modern refugee?

Calvin lived life as a refugee during a time of tectonic shift. He lived as an exception at a time when the imaginary of the European state as *Corpus Christianum* was most naturalized, yet just before the exception would be reintegrated into the central logic of the nation-state. From the age of twenty-five, Calvin's life and activity took place in liminal cities like Geneva and Strasbourg: at the margins of both the Roman Catholic and French monarchical domains.[15] A number of Calvin scholars have begun to explore what occupying this fraught position might have meant for Calvin as a writer. After all, he did bring the relative privileges of an elite French education. Although Calvin was not high born, he was the

---

[13] Carter, "Inglorious," 81–82; 85.

[14] For more on abjection, see Julia Kristeva, *Powers of Horror: An Essay on Abjection* (New York: Columbia University Press, 1982); and in the context of theorizing the hybridity and marginalization of ethnic identity in the United States, see Rey Chow, *The Protestant Ethnic and the Spirit of Capitalism* (New York: Columbia University Press, 2003).

[15] During the decades in which the papacy was located in Avignon, every single Pope was French, and for many, French identity came to be inscribed with Catholic piety. Christopher Elwood discusses the full extent to which the French monarchy came to represent a privileged locus of the *corpus Christi*, and enjoyed legitimacy according to the same sacramental logic through which the church claimed to hold the monopoly on the sacred. See Elwood, *The Body Broken* (New York: Oxford University Press, 1999).

beneficiary of patronage that led him through some of the most important French universities: Montaigu, Lyon, Bourges, Paris. These privileges did not prevent his exile, but they granted him both a network of other elite exiles and the skills to leave a record of what it meant to write in exile – from the vantage of one rejected by the governing bodies that had formed him. There are some obvious ways that this vantage impacts his writing. For example, it is replete with metaphors of pilgrimage and journey and figures of labyrinths and abysses. In letters and commentaries, there are passages where he depicts himself as the weeping prophet Jeremiah or as the wandering Apostle Paul. He also set to work retheorizing power around the community of the excluded – renaming them as elected.

This underscores the obvious irony attached to the mere suggestion that Calvin be read as an abject figure. Calvin is famous for forwarding a strong version of divine sovereignty. While Herman Selderhuis has suggested that readers of Calvin "who do not connect 'predestination' and 'providence' with the concept of being 'on the road' will never understand any of these ideas," these are also the very theological categories that are most tied to the logic of modern state sovereignty that understands itself as both exceptional and central.[16] Yet it is also true that for Calvin, theorizing these ideas could not have been easy. After all, he had to harness the relative audacity to read scripture and then reframe himself as chosen *for* exile, as a pilgrim whose dangerous journey was not just guided, but willed by hidden providence, a providence that exceeded the body of the *Corpus Christianum*. This places the theorist before a crossroads.[17] The will of one who is excluded might either seek revenge by harnessing a logic of sovereignty around the justification and superiority of the excluded – a move that Nietzsche would call *ressentiment*. Or the will of the excluded might devise the understandably more difficult task of challenging that logic itself – a move that, for Nietzsche, involved the gesture of affirmation.

The image of Calvinism most prevalent in critical and sociological literature opted for the former path. Max Weber, Michael Walzer, Charles Taylor, and Philip Gorski are only some of the most widely read theorists who narrate an affinity between Calvinist theologies and

---

[16] Herman Selderhuis, *John Calvin: A Pilgrim's Life* (Downers Grove, IL: IVP Academic, 2009), 38.

[17] Though my emphases and interlocutors are different, this way of reading Calvin's political thinking – with and against the texture of his writing – is partly informed by Roland Boer's *Political Grace: The Revolutionary Theology of John Calvin* (Louisville, KY: Westminster John Knox Press, 2009).

practices emergent in the seventeenth century to key postures of modern sovereignty.[18] Many are familiar, by now, with the claim that later Calvinists linked signs of election to reason-driven worldly activity rather than ritual practice, thus promoting a vision of market sovereignty to offset and elude that of the *Corpus Christianum*. Or that Calvinists reconstructed their own sovereign body through practices of discipline that could be easily transferred to the logic of the modern state as well as the rationalizing subject. And then, of course, there is the logic of exceptionalism itself, evident in early America from the city on the hill to Manifest Destiny, but visible also in Calvinist-influenced polities including Prussia, the Netherlands, England, South Africa, and even France. Each of these polities integrated or persecuted Calvinism to varying degrees, but in so doing adopted an understanding of their own nation as exceptional that came to underwrite internal discipline alongside external efforts at hegemony.

Yet, the case of Geneva – one of the early cities to welcome refugees, for obvious reasons – presents a little more ambiguity. Geneva seems to have reconstituted itself as a body by drawing on the theological

---

[18] While I do not engage Charles Taylor or Michael Walzer explicitly, this book's argument is in implicit conversation with their urge to link Calvinist reform movements unequivocally with discipline and disenchantment. In *A Secular Age* (Cambridge, MA: Harvard University Press, 2007), Taylor argues that the Calvinist wing of the sixteenth century reform movements served as a particular "engine of disenchantment" (77). Concerning Calvin in particular, Taylor forwards a reading of divine sovereignty as a zero-sum game in which immanent life is evacuated of transcendence: "Calvin's radical simplification could perhaps be put this way: We are depraved; and thus in the work of our salvation God does everything. Man 'cannot, without sacrilege, claim for himself even a crumb of righteousness, for just so much is plucked and taken away from the glory of God's righteousness'" (78). This quotation is from *Inst.* 3.13.3, and for Calvin it sets the stage for a particular kind of relationship between creation and God in which God's righteousness is directly related to all of creation, rather than segmented into parts. This, I will argue, is crucial to ascertaining Calvin's critique of political theology, or of any urge to locate the divine in a single assemblage of person, race, culture, nation, or state. I share certain of Taylor's sympathies in his critique of "modernity." I will argue, however, that close readings of theologies such as Calvin's, with attention to their pedagogical quality, furnishes tools for critiquing and recasting modernity's self-understanding rather than merely diagnosing it. For a range of the class disenchantment arguments similar to Taylor's, see Michael Walzer, *The Revolution of the Saints: A Study in the Origins of Radical Politics* (Cambridge, MA: Harvard University Press, 1965); Max Weber, *The Protestant Ethic and the Spirit of Capitalism*, trans. Baehr and Wells (New York: Penguin, 2002). Philip Gorski's *The Disciplinary Revolution: Calvinism and the Rise of the State in Early Modern Europe* (Chicago: University of Chicago Press, 2003) picks up on these themes, but focuses on sociological evidence to do so. I will engage Gorski's argument at several later points.

imaginary of *creatio ex nihilo*, rather than the body of Christ strictly speaking. For a people living "on the road," like Calvin himself, scripture could facilitate the direct address of divine authority without recourse to royal, noble, or ecclesial mediation. It could act as a map or guide capable of tying present to past and individual people to each other. But scripture alone cannot materialize a body. The Divine Word does not just exist in isolation; it *creates*.[19] Scripture likewise needs a body to address and shape in order to do its work. As early as 1540, Genevans adopted the motto *Post Tenebras Lux* ("After darkness, light"), which alludes both to the primordial act of creation as narrated in Genesis – "Let there be light" – and to Calvin's characteristic claim that divine providence should be understood as ongoing acts of creation. "To make God a momentary Creator, who once for all finished his work, would be cold and barren, and we must differ from profane men especially in that we see the presence of divine power shining as much in the continuing state of the universe as in its inception."[20] Providence is the perpetual act of bringing light out of darkness.

Pamela A. Mason's translation of a 1728 sermon demonstrates the extent to which providential language remained inscribed in Genevan identity two centuries later:

A People made anew, a People created: Our allies & we, we are this People which God has formed, this People which he has pulled, so to speak, out of nothingness, in an amazing manner. Who would have said, a few years before the Reformation, that such a great revolution would occur all over Europe, who would have said that a small number of Persons, pious, striving toward truth & enlightened, [but] powerless, without authority, without credit, would produce such a great change, one would have regarded that prospect as a vision pure and simple, as the least probable thing in the world. Nevertheless, that is what happened. God said once more, Let There Be Light, & there was Light. He revived the dry bones of Ezekiel's vision. He created an entirely new World; a World, consequently, which is obliged to celebrate him, as the Author of its subsistence.[21]

---

[19] The account I'm developing of the relationship between Word and creation comports with the dynamic Randall Zachman advances in *Image and Word in the Theology of John Calvin* (Notre Dame, IN: University of Notre Dame Press, 2009), opposing the idea that Calvin promotes Word over and against material referents. Zachman writes, for example, that "We must always hear the Word in order to be able to see the living images of God; but concomitantly we must always open our eyes to see the living images of God even as we hear the Word of God" (2).

[20] *Institutes* 1.16.1.

[21] This is Mason's translation of a selection from Jean-Alphonse Turrettin, *Sermons ur lejubile de la Reformation établie il y a deux-cens Ans, dans les Eglises de la trés illustre & trés puissante République de Berne. 7. Janvier 1728.* Emphases in original. Mason, 29.

The sermon suggests the formation of a new mode of existence, but not out of existing forms – not out of a move to make the exception into the rule. The claim, here, is not that the *Corpus Christianum* has been reconstituted around the figure of "Our allies & we." It is that creation offers an entirely new world to house a "people." This is the crossroads that depart from the suggestion of a new, shared fictive identity. Will the new world be built around the fictive, imagined body of the exception? Or will the new world offer a setting in which such fictions work to refuse the logic of corporate embodiment? There are at least the seeds here for thinking about different logics of sovereignty and gaining a richer perspective on a present forged out of competing and tangled logics of how the world is organized, what it means, and who decides.

This book pauses at the crossroads and sits with the text that Calvin produced, rewrote, rewrote again, and deemed his most important: the 1559 *Institutio Christainae Religionis*. It was produced before the "Calvinism" of scholars' construction; before the worst of the wars of religion; before the emerging European nation-state; at the very inception of scientific advancements, colonizations, and enslavements that were mostly unbeknownst to Calvin. For all of its style and polemic, its tethers to ancient teachers and present foes, the *Institutio* remains a text produced by a refugee who was exiled for calling the Mass – the ritual of the *Corpus Christi Mysticum* undergirding central imagery of late medieval sovereignty – idolatrous. When Calvin fled his homeland in 1534, it was after reformers had plastered Paris with placards declaring the Mass an abomination.[22] It's significant that this attack was received as not merely heretical, but seditious – as an assault not just on the church, but on the state.[23] Because what was at stake was not an argument over sacramental theology in the abstract, but the more fundamental living question of where and how the power of God materializes on earth. The Placards questioned the social metaphysics that tied the *Corpus Christi Mysticum* to the *Corpus Christianum*. And by refusing the Mass, Calvin counted himself with those deemed inglorious from the vantage of the French *Corpus Christianum*. If Calvin was so deeply opposed to the logic of idolatry that he was willing to risk expulsion, then it might not be unreasonable to expect that his writing opposes the project of *political* theology more generally.

* * *

[22] Gordon, *Calvin*, 40f.
[23] For an account of this logic in its historical context, see Elwood 48–52.

Political theology remains bound up with the modern operation of sovereignty to the extent that sovereignty continues to trade in Christian theological metaphors. We continue to ask how political sovereignty forms a "people" (creation); how it preserves and governs itself in time and place (providence); how it saves the people from threat, often by claiming the legitimate use of sacrificial violence (atonement); and how it might ultimately progress toward some fuller realization of its dominion (judgment and glory). These are at once general questions of the location and operation of power and discourses that resonate with two distinct theological doctrines: that of creation and providence; and that of the incarnation. From the incarnation, we get the claim that divine power reveals and redeems by means of embodiment – through bodies that look and act in a particular way, or bodies who represent sovereignty by organizing themselves properly within time and space. From creation and providence, we get a larger discourse on how divine power makes and governs ordinary time: an imaginary of how God draws, marks, tends, differentiates, and manages. Not surprisingly, both doctrines – providence and incarnation – play key roles in Calvin's *Institutio*.

These doctrines also play key roles in contemporary conversations that continue to circulate around Carl Schmitt's 1922 *Political Theology*. For Schmitt, "political theology" is a critique of the suggestion that liberalism, or a state governed by the rule of law, offers a legitimate alternative to authoritarianism. There are always exceptional cases that reveal the limits of the law, which means that liberal democracy remains structurally dependent on a law *giver* – a person or mechanism that "decides on the exception."[24] Here, Schmitt discerns a permanent theological structure to the logic of sovereignty:

All significant concepts of modern theory of the state are secularized theological concepts not only because of their historical development—in which they were transferred from theology to the theory of state, whereby, for example, the Omnipotent God became the omnipotent lawgivers—but also because of their systematic structure, the recognition of which is necessary for a sociological consideration of these concepts.[25]

For Schmitt, the permanence of political theology does not mean that all political arrangements are tacit theocracies beckoning to and bowing

---

[24] Carl Schmitt, *Political Theology* (Cambridge, MA: MIT Press, 1985), 5.
[25] Schmitt, 36.

before a metaphysical deity. But it does mean that any logic of political sovereignty relies, openly or quietly, on something or someone occupying the position of sovereign who must act as God has long been understood to act: to govern through a will that decides. It also means that the liberal state remains constituted – like Hobbes' *Leviathan* – by contracted participation in the abstract "body politic" whose legal and abstract structure decides and manages the boundaries of that body, mediating between its friends and enemies.

This is, however, only one way of framing the permanence of political theology, and it is significant that many of the disagreements among those who either defend or oppose political theology hinge on certain assumptions about the content and task of theology itself. After all, not all theologies emphasize God as decider. French post-Marxist Claude Lefort defends the permanence of political theology by arguing that religion and politics share an archive of symbols, and he suggests that a democratic structure can make "disincorporated" use of those symbols for political ends. In other words, democratic politics will take up and make use of theological symbols while refusing to reify them as sites of transcendent participation, thereby preserving the body of the individual as that from and to which sovereignty is accountable. Lefort's student, Marcel Gauchet, makes a different argument: that democratic politics do in fact reconstitute a certain kind of corporate body, but not as a site of submission and aesthetic participation. Rather, democracy constructs a new kind of collective body constructed and constrained by rational discourse.

Both Lefort and Gauchet view religion as fundamentally transcendent and, unlike Schmitt, want to defend the possibility that modern politics can be purely immanent. So, in both their accounts, theology effectively makes religious symbols available for strategic and deracinated political use – one through which they can be safely detached from the kind of irrational *mythos* of cosmic participation that funds fascism. For Lefort, democracy resists fascism by refusing to incorporate symbols into bodily formations. For him, symbols generate meaning through repetition and break. As different kinds of bodies take up and reinhabit symbols, sovereign authority cannot be imaginatively (or literally) identified with one material location or body. Gauchet argues that rationalization performs the work of remaking the political apart from the religious. Yet because symbols are used discursively rather than ritually, the body politic will be accountable to rational rather than aesthetic norms. Both, however, see theology as safe and useful to the extent that it is made immanent, neutralized by being separated from the violent, orgiastic tendencies of transcendent participation.[26]

Karl Löwith, a postwar German émigré who studied under Martin Heidegger, approaches the question of theology and politics with more suspicion, understandably wary of Schmitt's brand of political theology

---

[26] See Claude Lefort, "The Permanence of the Theologico-Political?" in *Democracy and Political Theory*, trans. David Macey (Cambridge: Cambridge University Press, 1988): 213–55; Marcel Gauchet, *The Disenchantment of the World: A Political History of Religion* (Princeton, NJ: Princeton University Press, 2007). For a helpful discussion of the two in the French post-Marxist context, see Warren Breckman, *The Adventures of the Symbolic: Post-Marxism and Radical Democracy* (New York: Columbia University Press, 2013). Marcel Gauchet would also go on to influence Charles Taylor's *A Secular Age* (Cambridge, MA: Harvard University Press, 2007), who would ultimately want to defend an openness to transcendence of the kind that Gauchet only gently hinted at in modern uses of art. Gauchet's account differs from Lefort's in several crucial ways. First, where Lefort insists on the emptiness and iconoclasm of democratic power, Gauchet sees the reincorporation of that power precisely in the institutions that facilitate the practices founded upon differentiation and otherness. It is in the continuity of this visible collective "body" that the body is constantly undone and reformed through the exercise of litigation and process. A second difference, however, has to do with the ongoing role of the symbolic, and particularly the place Gauchet gives to writing and literature in relation to modern power. Where Lefort sees the sphere of the fictive as distinct from but constantly figuring and un-figuring the arrangement of democratic power, Gauchet grants to the aesthetic in general a much more oblique, yet provocative place as the one site where the function of "religion" may yet remain. We yet become dispossessed, even momentarily, by "the vertigo of the musical abyss, the poignant heights of poetry, the frantic passion of novelistic intrigue, a dreamlike absorption into the image" as well as "the open-ended attempt to evoke the other deep inside the familiar ... the unfathomable 'hidden world' uncovered in the midst of a landscape seen a hundred times before, the impressionists' magic revelation of the deeply hidden truth of an inhabited landscape" (Gauchet, *Disenchantment*, 198–204). The traces of religion thus remain, but are subsumed under the constitutive intellectual awareness of differentiation – that our subjectivity stands opposed to the unity of which we momentarily experience ourselves as a part. This, of course, supposes that religion – or that participation – entails collapse between sign and signified.

Alternatively, at least three features, largely absent in Gauchet, rise to the fore in Lefort's account of modern political power. First, the assertion of the importance of the aesthetic in and for conceiving the political; second, the sense in which disincorporated power is never fully reincorporated, but is temporarily reincorporated in different collective arrangements (an incorporation Lefort hopes can be disrupted by the symbolic as much as it is constituted by it); and finally, a view of the symbolic as not only aesthetic but also repetitive in quality, and thus as becoming meaningful within a sphere of iterative practices that relate symbols to arrangements of bodies, thus performing the kind of impermanent incorporation of power that he envisions. As I'll show in Chapter 6, Calvin's own view tracks closer to that of Lefort in insisting upon the disincorporation of power and the relative distance between sign and signified. Lefort, however, relied on the work of Ernst Kantorowicz to formulate his view of theologico-political symbolism.

yet proactively worried about whether theological symbols can be made immanent without tacitly transferring the force of transcendent power to sites of immanence. Aware of the fact that a number of Enlightenment thinkers claimed rationality by purporting to reject a theological past beholden to transcendent authority, Löwith worried that this self-stylization only weaponized the transcendent referent of theological discourse by incorporating it into a particular brand of (European) human achievement. If Schmitt argued that modern politics continues to rely on the authority of a sovereign who decides, Löwith agrees. Only, Löwith reads this claim as a particular play of the modern urge to immanentize divinity and relocate divine power in the site of one particular historically located civilization. Löwith's 1949 *Meaning in History* critiques the permanence of political theology by arguing that modern claims to historical progress are founded on a double movement. Such claims found progress on the rejection of a transcendent authority who guarantees the metaphysical shape of time and space. In the same gesture, they also purport to bring about the kind of progress through a particular sociopolitical civilizational arrangement that reinhabits the very structure of a transcendent "guiding hand" that had been naturalized and thereby disavowed.

For Löwith, the doctrines of incarnation and providence are absolutely central to the argument that Western European modernity secularizes, rather than overcomes, its Christian underpinnings. If early articulations of Christendom sought to anchor society in the sacramental presence of the *corpus Christi*, modern rationalism wants to anchor society in the immanent presence of the rational man. Löwith reads this as a Promethean move: It brings theology to earth, naturalizes it, and in so doing, surreptitiously divinizes the privileged site of reason's emergence *as* the guarantor of both political order and historical progress, inevitably over and against colonized and enslaved others. The difference between Löwith and later thinkers like Lefort and Gauchet is that theology is not made dangerous by referring to transcendence. It is made dangerous by *refusing* transcendence and trying instead to confine theological expectation to a strictly immanent conception of historical time and space.

Hans Blumenberg would famously challenge Löwith by advancing an alternate account of modern power as constituted by a decisive break from political theology. That break is rooted in what Blumenberg reads as modernity's adoption of a different linguistic practice – one in which theological language loses the metaphysical "seriousness" it once possessed. Modernity's great achievement is not that it stole fire from heaven, but that it rejected the dream of heavenly fire in order to become genuinely curious about earth.[27] Blumenberg argues that modernity improves upon premodern Christianity by rejecting the presupposition that the world is governed by *any* transcendent authority or *de facto* ontology. Citing Nietzsche, he writes, "[Humanity's] right should consist in imputing the least possible binding force to reality, so as to make room for his own works. 'Not in knowing but in creating lies our health! ... If the universe has no concern for us, then we want the right to scorn it.'"[28] Modern progress does not require a transcendent guarantor because the conditions for progress emerged precisely out of the evident failure of transcendent models to mobilize scientific discovery and technological advancement.[29] In an echo of Lefort's position, a politics and progress reframed as authentically human endeavors will privilege no body apart from the ordinary body that asserts itself in and over the immanent world on its own terms. Theological ideas may still prove useful in a mitigated way, but only if rendered unserious and made artifactual. As a subset of art, theology can supply metaphors to construct human projects that are always fallible and accountable to human needs.

Victoria Kahn ties Blumenberg's defense of modernity back to the question of political theology by arguing that it lifts up an often-forgotten

---

[27] Against the suggestion that modernity retains a Christian temporal structure, Blumenberg argues that historical breaks occur when inherited questions are "reoccupied" by different modes of practical and conceptual activity. Blumenberg's concept of "reoccupation" borrows from the geologic concept of "pseudomorphosis," which occurs when a new crystalline substance fills the hollow left by another crystal, and adapts to this hollow by taking on an alien and potentially misleading crystal form. Applying this to the study of historical periods in effect flips the script on Löwith's accusation: Structural similarities between Christian expectation and immanent progress do not betray an underlying foundation, but rather are mere adaptive vestiges of a past that has ceased due to its own collapse. For Blumenberg's critique of Löwith, see *The Legitimacy of the Modern Age* (Cambridge, MA: MIT Press, 1983), 27f. For his account of reoccupation, see 49, 60–75, 77–79, 353–354. See also Benjamin Lazier, "Overcoming Gnosticism: Hans Jonas, Hans Blumenberg, and the Legitimacy of the Natural World" in *Journal of the History of Ideas* 64/4 (2003): 619–637, 625.

[28] Blumenberg, 141–142. This passage is part of a longer engagement with Nietzsche in which Blumenberg wants to tie Nietzsche's praise for artistic creation to technological mastery. For more on this exchange, and on the way Blumenberg both borrows from and critiques Nietzsche's critique of beholdenness to "reality," see Nathan Widder. "On Abuses in the Uses of History: Blumenberg on Nietzsche; Nietzsche on Genealogy" in *History of Political Thought* 21/2 (2000): 308–326.

[29] Blumenberg, 229–241. See also Zeynep Talay, "A Dialogue with Nietzsche: Blumenberg and Löwith on History and Progress" in *History of European Ideas* 37/3 (2011): 376–381, 379.

"third term" employed by early modern political thinkers to recast the relationship between politics and religion: namely, the use of language as "poiesis," or creative making. According to Kahn, "The modern project is fundamentally poetic in the sense elaborated by Hobbes and Vico that we can know only what we have made or constructed ourselves: *verum et factum convertuntur* (truth and fact – in the sense of that which is done or made – are interchangeable)."[30] This use of language enabled novel renderings of human agency itself as both *defined by* and *accountable to* that which humans have created. Unlike poiesis, Kahn understands theology as a use of language to represent metaphysical realities or to refer to a given ontological order. And that's why she worries that any argument defending the persistence of political theology will end up replicating a logic of sovereignty modeled on a corporate body. Poiesis, however, does not work by referring to metaphysical realities. It works by producing things, by making legal and artistic fictions. These are effectively worded technologies that are not bodies and do not refer to bodies, but enable new and different forms of mobilizing, managing, reading, and relating bodies.

The ability to create art underwrites the distinct "sovereignty of the artist" – a mode of sovereignty that Kahn traces to Ernst Kantorowicz and his reading of Dante.[31] At the conclusion of *The King's Two Bodies*, Kantorowicz locates a moment in the *Divine Comedy* when humanity becomes distinguished from – though not necessarily opposed to – Christianity. That moment occurs precisely when Dante, as poet, becomes invested with a dignity that was once reserved for the sovereign office of the king. According to Kahn, this alternate rendering of sovereignty is distinct because it does not refer to dignity of "the individual" as a metaphysical category, but refers instead to an office that can only be assumed and defined by an individual *as* individual. It is a "notion of representation, whereby the individual comes to stand for the mystical body of mankind."[32] This shift is effected precisely through the production and use of literature. By reframing sovereignty around the site of human artistic production, Kantorowicz gives an account of fictive, representational bodies (like the church, the nation, or the state) that

---

[30] Kahn, Victoria. *The Future of Illusion: Political Theology and Early Modern Texts* (Chicago: University of Chicago Press, 2013), 6.

[31] This is also a reading offered in direct opposition to Schmitt, shifting the relationship of theology and politics from one of a "methodological and existential postulate" to one of a "metaphorology." See Kahn, 66.

[32] Kahn, 76.

expressly *undermines* mystical or fascist claims to transcendent foundations can be approached. After all, fictions are made, which means they can also be unmade. Kahn observes that "whereas fascism and religious fundamentalism attempt to give society a body, the usefulness of the category of fiction is that it complicates any attempt to locate power in one particular body or one particular place."[33] If theology and politics are both approached as a particular kind of fiction, as Kahn suggests they should be, then it is no longer warranted to talk about their perpetuity. Kantorowicz was, after all, an important critic of Schmitt.[34]

Yet, there is a sense in which the elevation of poiesis only heightens the urgency of Löwith's critique. Löwith agrees that if there is going to be an alternative to Christian metaphysics, the alternative must mobilize a creative will tied to the needs and demands of ordinary life. He, too, was an admirer of Nietzsche, and saw Nietzschean affirmation as the nearest modern thinking has come to authentically disrupting the purposive, linear structure of Christian temporality. To disrupt the vengeance of linear time over the past must involve actively *willing* the past eternally, and therefore mobilizing transcendence in service of saying "yes" to immanence. I'll say more about the move to affirmation shortly – and at much greater length in the chapters of this book. But for now, it's important to grasp that both Löwith and Blumenberg were interested in poiesis, or in the ability of language to make and effect things. But Löwith's fundamental concern had to do with *whose body* gets to stand in as the representative of humankind. When Löwith calls for transcendence, it is not to stubbornly reassert the inescapability of Christian foundations of authority. Löwith, after all, demonstrated some preference for what he saw as the legitimately different Greek imaginary of power and time. What he wanted to do was undermine any immanent, particular claim to representatively embody historical consummation at the level of individual, nation, state, culture, or concrete universal.[35]

We find ourselves, then, at another version of the same interpretive crossroads. Does modern sovereignty depart from Christian sovereignty by making an actual break – by emerging, as it were, out of nothing? Or does it depart by reifying the exception (in this case, the European who

---

[33] Kahn, 81.   [34] Kahn, 80.
[35] It's worth noting that Löwith was himself writing as a German exile in the wake of National Socialism. For more on Löwith's relationship to his teacher Martin Heidegger and to the rise of Nazism, see Richard Wolin, *Heidegger's Children: Hannah Arendt, Karl Löwith, Hans Jonas, and Herbert Marcuse* (Princeton, NJ: Princeton University Press, 2001).

purports to reject Christian transcendence) and making it the rule. Part of what is in question, here, is whether and how the poetic "sovereignty of the artist" differs from theology within a field of practice, or in the concrete exercises through which governing arts are made responsible to living and material immanent persons and things. In some ways this is a fundamentally theological question, asking about the kinds of embodied practices and material contexts through which theology generates its meaning. But in exactly the same way it is also a question about the practice of poiesis – about *who* is vested with the power to make things, and about how those things remake a certain kind of world.

The debate over political theology that I've been rehearsing cannot be adjudicated by simply observing the persistence of theological symbols or championing their absence. To gain perspective on political theology in the present political arena means looking at particular *practices* through which doctrines, rituals, legal fictions, national myths, and scientific paradigms are in some way made responsible to the immanence of a world that exceeds and resists their grasp. The world is always already the repository of signs and signatures from which constructions emerge and to which they respond. But those signatures must also be taken up, performed by bodies. What matters is not just how we treat those signs – whether as serious truths or as unserious tools. But also who gets to wield those tools and treat them *as if* truths.

Kathleen Davis draws from Löwith's argument to make this very point in *Periodization and Sovereignty*. She traces how the homogeneous past of "medieval feudalism" was created – as a legal fiction – precisely when sixteenth-century jurists were tasked with theorizing the political basis, and superiority of, "modern sovereignty." On the one hand, the creation of a "feudal past" might be read to support Blumenberg's point that modernity is marked by a turn to human self-assertion that makes use of human-created fictions to organize human life. Yet, because this is a fiction about the past, it performs its work at the expense of the very data it also defers. For Davis, fictions about the past are never just past exclusions. They simultaneously dispose and mobilize power in the present. In this case, the fiction of a "feudal past" legitimized the colonial domination of non-European others in the name of bringing them "from the past" and into the present. The sovereignty of the artist may be responsive to the bodies of those jurists, but it also perpetuates a transcendent logic of sovereignty over those who are marginal or made abject by its operation. As long as poiesis is tied to the logic of incarnation – of a coming to be that disrupts time and space – it will be bound up with political theology, and with the question of how providence manages bodies incarnated at the center and margins of sovereign power.[36] At stake here is not whether theological conceptions of sovereignty continue to haunt secularity or whether there are ways for their power to be excised or neutered. What is at stake is whether, how, and to what extent signatures disposing power and governance can be made responsible to the material conditions and lives they purport to organize. A signature may claim a relation to immanence, but if it disposes immanence by marking it according to some particular relationship to privileged temporality or geography – by representatively privileging a particular kind of body – it will only replicate the kinds of metaphysical theological formations that Schmitt thought were inevitable, and that the critics of Schmitt want to oppose. In different ways, Lefort, Gauchet, Blumenberg, and Kahn deem a politics rooted in transcendence dangerous because it embodies sovereignty in a way that is aesthetic rather than rational. But Löwith and Davis both suggest that any effort to defend modernity *as* a categorical historical improvement over a beholden past furtively reenacts the drama of incarnational emergence of transcendent, unquestioned authority all over again, hiding it under historical conditions that prove tellingly difficult to unmake.

If what is deemed progressive about modernity is modernity's willingness to both make and unmake fictions, then what is entailed in unmaking the fiction of Western modernity's own claims to progress through its

---

[36] Davis finds Löwith's 1949 work helpful precisely on the grounds that it exposes the way the emergence of modern sovereignty was mobilized by a double relationship to history – one that positions itself as superior to a past that is simultaneously a past of its own creation. Here's a helpful quote from Kathleen Davis, *Periodization and Sovereignty* (Philadelphia: University of Pennsylvania Press, 2008):

> Having dismissed the validity of a 'modern' break in the conception of history, Löwith turns, secondly, to the destructive capacity of 'secularized' eschatology, which he sees as having its theoretical basis in the Christian concept of a break with the old law, later materialized through political institutionalization. In this sense, the 'secularization,' as well as the periodization, of time and politics occurs first with Christianity's 'incarnation' of spiritual principles, and breaks with the classical pattern of recurrence (which, following Nietzsche, he favors). Löwith's sense of 'secularization,' then, like Schmitt's, is not a story of Europe's gradual extrication from religion, but rather the sublimation of theology in the 'world': *Heilgeschehen* merged with *Weltgeschichte*—a pattern that, unlike Schmitt, he found disastrous ... Criticism of Löwith based on whether or not his 'secularization' theory is correct entirely misses his point that periodized, telic history is the conceptual basis and the legitimizing tool of world-scale aggression (Davis 84).

particular project of world-making? Davis argues – as have so many others – that unmaking and remaking must involve asking who is speaking. What is problematic in Blumenberg's defense of modernity is precisely that it trades in a claim about "human self-assertion" indexed to a particular locale and then uses that claim to underwrite a universal cut in immanent time. In so doing, Blumenberg "consigns *decision* to history, which periodizes itself."[37] Because modern self-consciousness disavows a transcendent-sovereign agent, the mode of agency that marks its legitimacy and superiority is taken as a natural and inevitable development of "human" consciousness, such that Blumenberg's account never makes room for questions like "whose history?" or "who decides?" According to Davis, "the paradox of a self-constituting modernity is folded into the cut of periodization itself" so that "the 'modern' can emerge as unproblematically sovereign."[38] If theology is so often positioned as the foil against which modernity defines itself, what might theology have to do with the task of unmaking the fiction of political theology?

***

Davis' concern over the function of a "feudal past" in constituting modernity can be recast as a concern over the function of a "theological past." In many regards, the claim that Christian theology is especially bound up with Europe's past may seem self-evident. But a homogeneous conception of a "theological past" is also a product of modernity's self-emerging narrative. Thinkers invested in this narrative had a hand in not only theorizing the advances of the Enlightenment but also disciplining the modes of religion deemed suitable to it. These thinkers were also deeply invested in the ongoing self-stylization of Protestant Christianity as a religious formation more invested in rationality than geographic competitors who remained invested in a superstitious "past" beholden to myths and rituals. More recently, as scholars of religion have become self-critical of the deeply Protestant universalizing and supersessionist underpinnings of our discipline, one strategy has been to distance the study of religion from theology, and to invest theology with the same features that early theorists of religion loaded onto non-Protestant religion – attachment to particularity, beholden to unquestioned beliefs rather than subject to

[37] Davis, 86.   [38] Davis, 86.

objective reason.[39] There are good reasons for critiquing the imbrication of the field of religious studies in Protestant theology. Yet it is also important to avoid once more replicating the sovereign gesture of homogenizing a past to justify a superior present.

One of my concerns, as I reapproach the question of political theology from the vantage of Calvin's 1559 work, is to ask what kind of theology – and what kind of religion – is actually performed in that text. If Calvin himself is interested in unmaking the fiction of a representative sacramental-social body that he takes to be idolatrous – one that elides the Mass with the Crown and in so doing, regulates and defines the nation as a *Corpus Christianum* – then I want to ask the following question: How are the resources of theology (as historical writings on Christian teaching) and religion (as a set of practices of formation) put to that end in Calvin's writing? I take this to be one important way of asking "who is speaking?" at a retrospectively pivotal time in European history – one concurrent with an influx of efforts to remake the world through invention, war, nation-making, colonizing, and enslaving. It is apparent now that Calvin would become an outsized influence on the Protestantism that became so imbricated with European modernity. Yet he was also writing at a time before Protestantism became what it did: a homogeneous category that would critically regulate emerging conceptions of both reason and religion.

In some ways, this project takes a similar posture to that of Brenda Deen Schildgen, who discusses the relationship between history and literature in her 2012 study, *Divine Providence: A History*. Especially in the last several decades, the notion that history operates straightforwardly as an empirical science has been challenged from at least two angles. On the one hand, scholars such as Hayden White have argued that historiography has largely been organized and given legibility in writing by means of the same devices as literature: emplotment, the use of

---

[39] For studies that entertain the question of whether theology belongs in the study of religion, see Robert Orsi, *History and Presence* (Cambridge, MA: Harvard University Press, 2016); Russell McCutcheon, "Words, Words, Words" in *Journal of the American Academy of Religion* 75/4 (2007): 952–987; Jenny Daggers, "Thinking 'Religion': The Christian Past and Interreligious Future of Religious Studies and Theology" in *Journal of the American Academy of Religion* 78/4 (2010): 961–990; Tyler Roberts, *Encountering Religion: Responsibility and Criticism after Secularism* (New York: Columbia University Press, 2013).

metaphors and tropes, irony, synecdoche.[40] On the other hand, Foucault's body of work has drawn attention to the disciplinary power that constructs a sense of reality that becomes reified by uncritical historiography.[41] This has funded interest in so-called hidden histories or methods of historical research that look to narrate historical experiences otherwise excluded from mainstream historical narratives. "Thus, microhistories, the histories of the colonized and exploited, histories of minorities and exiles, or the historical lives of peasants rather than kings and rulers became the subjects of inquiry."[42] While she views this development with favor, she also points out that

One consequence of this approach has been to obscure the fact that canonical works themselves might represent an "insurrection of subjugated knowledge." A canonical work today may have been sidelined when it was composed or even in its reception history. Thus, important as discovering long-ignored facts of human history, and therefore filling in important gaps in our historical understanding has been, we have simultaneously tended to ignore how writers who have been received as canonical or authoritative may themselves have confronted historical lapses or grand presuppositions.[43]

Rereading a complex and influential piece of writing from the past may function similarly to a peoples' history by confronting readers with apparent incongruities – overlooked and forgotten complexities and multiplicities that may themselves subvert mainstream historical assumptions. The refusal to merely summarize the argument of even a "familiar" or "authoritative" text, but instead to read it closely, may, therefore, work as its own kind of critical history.[44]

---

[40] See Hayden White, *Metahistory: The Historical Imagination in Nineteenth-Century Europe* (Baltimore, MD: The Johns Hopkins University Press, 1973).

[41] Foucault's most concise discussion of critical history can be found in his essay, "Nietzsche, Genealogy, History" in *Language, Counter-Memory, Practice: Selected Essays and Interviews by Michel Foucault*, ed. Donald F. Bouchard (Ithaca, NY: Cornell University Press, 1977). This essay is in part a reading of Friedrich Nietzsche, *The Use and Abuse of History* (New York: Cosimo Books, 2010).

[42] Brenda Deen Schildgen, *Divine Providence: A History: The Bible, Virgil, Osorius, Augustine, and Dante* (New York: Bloomsbury Academic, 2012), 7.

[43] Schildgen, 7.

[44] While I agree in general with Schildgen's argument about trends in historiography, it should be noted that Foucault, Jacques Derrida, to some extent Giorgio Agamben, and others have performed close readings of canonical or authoritative texts in the name of critical history and critical theory. In Chapter 1, I discuss Agamben's call to do precisely this kind of work in *The Signature of All Things* (Brooklyn, NY: Zone Books, 2009) and his efforts to do so in *The Kingdom and the Glory* (Stanford, CA: Stanford University Press, 2011). For other important examples, see Foucault's readings of Stoic writings in

If a closer reading of the *Institutio* allows for some "insurrection of subjugated knowledge," one element might be the surprisingly active role that Calvin's pedagogy gives to immanent materiality. For Calvin, material conditions are an intrinsic component of the way revelation teaches. Yet this runs counter to the way Protestantism (and, particularly, Calvinism) is routinely characterized in contrast to other ways of being religious. There is surely ample evidence that major trajectories of Protestant religion came to adopt much of the self-stylization of modernity as uniquely universal and rational, trading in stable propositional claims. There is also evidence that this posture traces back to the sixteenth century, as magisterial reformers attacked both the Catholic sacramental system and radical reformers' claims to new and revolutionary revelations. In this two-fronted war, texts were elevated, and so was reading and thinking, leading to a posture that would later be called "*sola scriptura.*" The use of reason – often in the form of rational tests – was also elevated in order to combat the so-called superstitions perceived by some reformers as operative in both Catholic rituals and Anabaptist prophecies.[45] As these same Protestant traditions developed the category of "religion" and methodologies to study it scientifically, theology has played a dual role in the development of European hegemony itself – both as justification for European rationalism and as its foil.[46]

A generation of scholars including Talal Asad, Robert Orsi, and Catherine Bell have rightly called the study of religion and ritual to become critically aware of its implicit Protestant biases. These critiques,

"About the Beginning of the Hermeneutics of the Self" in *Religion and Culture*, ed. Carrette (New York: Routledge, 1999) and *The Hermeneutics of the Subject*, trans. Graham Burchell (New York: Picador, 2001). The clearest examples, however, may be found in many works by Jacques Derrida, including: "Before the Law," trans. Avital Ronell, in *Acts of Literature*, ed. Derek Attridge (New York: Routledge, 1991); *The Gift of Death*, trans. David Wills (Chicago: University of Chicago Press, 2008); "How to Avoid Speaking: Denials," trans. Ken Frieden, in *Languages of the Unsayable*, eds. Sanford Budick and Wolfgang Iser (New York: Columbia University Press, 1989), 3–70; *On the Name*, ed. Thomas Dutoit (Stanford, CA: Stanford University Press, 1995); *Specters of Marx*, trans. Peggy Kamuf (New York: Routledge, 1994); "Plato's Pharmacy" in *Dissemination*, trans. Barbara Johnson (London: The Athlone Press, 1981), 61–172.

45 The magisterial account of the increasing search for certainty and methods for attaining it across the early modern period is Susan Schreiner's *Are You Alone Wise? The Search for Certainty in the Early Modern Era* (New York: Oxford University Press, 2011).

46 This double gesture is visible in many Enlightenment texts into the nineteenth century. I take key examples to be Schleiermacher's hierarchy of religions in the *Glaubenslehre* and Kant's distinction between enthusiastic religion and rational faith in *Religion within the Boundaries of Reason Alone* (Cambridge: Cambridge University Press, 1998).

while important, must nevertheless avoid ceding a reading of "Protestantism" itself as monolithic and exceptional. Looking at how Calvin rewrites
a body that is not the sociopolitical *Corpus Christianum* reminds us that
before Protestantism became what it did, leading Protestant writers relied
on modes of argumentation that stood at odds with existing magisteria.
My aim here is to return to a text produced at such a moment and ask
whether and how the fault lines of Calvin's external positionality are
visible in his text, and particularly in the way the text conceives and
enacts teaching while remaining at some distance from existing regimes
of pedagogical intelligibility. My aim is to illumine the path of what I take
to be the less appreciated fork in the intellectual crossroads at Geneva: the
one in which the body of writing is more closely tied to the body of the
refugee and responsible to a community whose intelligibility must reside
apart from the *Corpus Christianum*.

One way to begin recovering the fuller role Calvin gives to created
material bodies is to remember the extent of Calvin's debt to Augustine.
Calvin is, of course, a famous Augustinian. He cites Augustine eight times
more than any other non-biblical author, and Calvin's views on salvation
and predestination bear striking resemblances to those expressed in the
later writings of the fifth-century Bishop of Hippo. Often less appreciated
is the full extent to which Calvin reoccupies the Augustinian tradition of
signification, or the general logic of how Augustine thinks human bodies
are taught and oriented by God through the uses of signs in relation to
things. I'll spend a great deal of time in the later chapters of this book
showing how Calvin reoccupies Augustine's pedagogy almost exactly,
except for one crucial difference: the role he gives to the church as an
institutional body. Calvin conceives the body of the church as a body that
exists only in performance. Yet any logic of performance also requires its
own subterranean logic of ritual activity, and that is exactly what is
apparent not only in the way Calvin imagines the use of teachings, but
also the use of texts themselves.

* * *

Across this book, I develop the argument that the 1559 *Institutio* is best
read as a participatory text.[47] This is in part because of its evident

---

[47] I have defended this position in *JAAR*, and that argument is expanded in Chapter 1 of this
book. Before this, arguments about rhetoric and pedagogy have gone up to the threshold
of ritual except for Lee Palmer Wandel, whose article, "Incarnation, Image, and Sign"
captures the pedagogical texture of the *Institutio* in an unparalleled way. See Wandel,

pedagogical debts to not only Augustine but the Stoics who were also partial to participatory texts. This claim also follows from the particular way Calvin presents and sustains the task of the theological project in the *Institutio*: writing is for learning, and theology is participation in divine mediation. Generally speaking, a participatory text locates the force of signification – or the ability to generate meaning – in a dynamic continuum between language and local bodily activities. The artifactual qualities of a participatory text are legible as a kind of poiesis, inasmuch as its written teachings are made or constructed for a certain immanent use. Yet, what stands out in Calvin's approach to writing is that he will refuse to relocate sovereignty in the artist who makes. But it's equally true that Calvin does not abdicate sovereignty to a kind of top–down determinism of God's transcendent will. Instead, for Calvin, the sovereignty governing creation meets human beings through the ongoing materialization of the world through the use of signs.

My argument is informed theoretically not only by Calvin's predecessors, but also by more recent academic debates over the relationship between writing, bodily activity, signification, and the generation of meaning. It will be helpful to briefly recount what I've taken to be crucial in those debates so that I do not have to rehearse them later. Over the last fifty years or so, J. L. Austin, Jacques Derrida, Pierre Bourdieu, and Judith Butler have challenged the assumption – common to positivist philosophies of language – that language generates meaning by representing an external (transcendent or immanent) reality. For Austin, some language is representational, but other language is neither representational nor nonsense. Rather, it generates meaning by *doing* things. It is "performative." The classic examples involve legal or ceremonial resignification: contractual obligations, wedding vows, adoptions, divorces, initiations. In such cases, words perform a different set of relationships in their very utterance, for example with the statement, "I do" or the gesture of a signature.

Austin wanted to maintain a distinction between "felicitous" and failed performatives by referring to external conditions, such as whether the context of a signature is legally binding or whether the speaker's intentions are sincere. This would be Derrida's point of departure. In "Signature Event Context," Derrida argues that context can never be fully contained or determined, and that the intentions are never

"Incarnation, Image, and Sign: John Calvin's *Institutes of the Christian Religion* & Late Medieval Visual Culture" in *Image and Incarnation: The Early Modern Doctrine of the Pictorial Image*, eds. Melion and Wandel (Leiden: Brill, 2015): 187–203.

sufficiently transparent to render the speaker truly sovereign over the meaning of the utterance. Derrida argues that *all* language generates meaning through the structure of the performative, which is internal to the structure of the sign itself. In other words, for language to work, it must be both iterable and contextual. It must *repeat* an existing convention and also mark a *break* from the past context of that convention. Importantly, this means that performative language cannot be easily distinguished from representational language. It is not that there is *no* practical difference between classic performatives (like "I do") and claims about representation (like "the cup is on the table"). But it does mean that the difference between these is itself a performative difference. It relies on a structure of both iteration and context to be meaningful, rather than on the stabilizing force of a sovereign (divine or human) subject.

Derrida's account has been vulnerable to charges of evacuating the body and materiality from an account of signification – a tempting, if cursory reading of his famous and mistranslated claim that "there is nothing outside the text."[48] Butler's account of sex and gender performativity gives a more robust account of the role of the body in signification that draws both from Derrida's account of performativity as a ritual of repetition and differentiation and Pierre Bourdieu's concept of the *habitus*. With Derrida, Butler wants to avoid what she sees as both materialist and constructivist extremes, refusing a non-linguistic "raw matter" capable of adjudicating the meaning of language while also refusing merely linguistic idealism. By arguing that bodies are constantly *materialized* through the ritualized repetition of cited norms, Butler suggests linguistic meaning is always materialized at the level of the body itself. In Derrida's words, "There is no nature, only the effects of nature: denaturalization or naturalization."[49] According to Butler, "materialization is never quite complete ... bodies never quite comply with the norms by which their materialization is impelled. Indeed, it is the instabilities, the possibilities for rematerialization opened up by this process that mark one domain in which the force of the regulatory law can be

---

[48] Jacques Derrida, *Of Grammatology*, trans. Spivak (Baltimore, MD: Johns Hopkins University Press, 1997), 158. The proper translation of *il n'y a pas de horstexte* is "there is no outside-text," which might be more idiomatically rendered as "there is nothing outside of context."

[49] Derrida, *Given Time Counterfeit Money*, trans. Kamuf (Chicago: University of Chicago Press, 1992). This quote serves as an epigram for Butler's *Bodies That Matter* (New York: Routledge), 1.

turned against itself to spawn rearticulations that call into question the hegemonic force of that very regulatory law."[50]

This is where Butler draws from Bourdieu, whose own reading of performativity locates authority in the extra-linguistic site of the *habitus*, a socially formed network of bodily habits that exists, in principle, distinct from language and plays a determining role in how the use of language constitutes the subject. Butler, however, wants to link the extra-linguistic *habitus* not to social practice per se, but to the body itself as that which bears and resists norms. While there is no pure body that can be held up to critique or adjudicate norms, Butler does not think this necessitates the alternative of pure linguistic constructivism; rather, it deconstructs the very binary between signification and matter. Amy Hollywood helpfully elaborates this by returning to the discourse on bodily ritual and arguing that a role for non-linguistic, yet still-signifying "bodily citations," is already implicit in Derrida's theory. Both want to resist positing a thing itself accessible without signification, but they also claim that embodied activities are "subject to the same misfirings and slippages that Austin and Derrida locate in speech acts and signification in general."[51] The way one moves in the world, performs certain tasks, and assumes certain postures generates meaning in the same way that language does: by repetition and contextual deferral. Bodies also *sign*.

To flesh out this point theoretically, Hollywood draws on Talal Asad and Catherine Bell, both of whom are important critics of the undue influence of "Protestantism" on the field of religion and ritual studies. As I've noted, reformation-era polemics did tend to privilege faith and scriptural teaching to critique certain bodily activities and the uses of objects deemed idolatrous or superstitious, and this gesture remains visible in accounts of ritual that want to render bodily activities as a text that can be abstracted and critiqued in terms of pure rational content.[52] It's interesting, then, that a critique of these Protestant biases also helps to illuminate some underexplored dimensions of Protestant pedagogical strategies.

In brief, Bell argues that ritual is better approached as "ritualization," or a way of acting that distinguishes what is being done from other activities. Ritualization, in other words, follows the Derridean structure of signification by citing iterative gestures that nevertheless work in

---

[50] Butler, *Bodies*, 2.   [51] Hollywood, 110.
[52] See, for example, Ulrich Zwingli's "On the Lord's Supper" in *Zwingli and Bullinger*, trans. Bromiley (Philadelphia: Westminster Press, 1953).

context to mark a break from other contexts and other gestures. Hollywood follows this claim to argue that

> for both Bell and Derrida, ritual is like language not because it is a text whose symbolic meanings must be uncovered or deciphered but because rituals are actions that generate meanings in the specific context of other sets of meaningful actions and discourses ... ritual actions are—not surprisingly—more like performative speech acts than like [representational speech]. Meanings are constitutive and generate that to which they refer.[53]

To claim there is no outside text, then, is not necessarily to denigrate or exclude the place of the body, but to assert that even the interpreter is enveloped in a world that is constantly under negotiation, being made and unmade both unconsciously and through deliberate activity. The mind, as well as the body, is always already subject to norms and constraints that comprise the very terms through which the subject can come to know herself – and, possibly, to revise that knowledge.

This is not an account of the subject that mimics the logic of modern sovereignty, requiring a will to decide over the exception. It is one in which exceptionality itself is generated through, and responsive to, iterable norms – and vice versa. According to Butler, "If there is *agency*, it is to be found, paradoxically, in the possibilities opened up in and by that constrained appropriation of the regulatory law, by the materialization of that law, the compulsory appropriation and identification with those normative demands."[54] Hollywood, similarly, remarks that "we cannot freely choose ourselves or our communities," but an account of signification that reads *misfiring* as internal to the sign is also one that generates the possibility for change. Bodily citations and linguistic citations operate on a level playing field, one that assumes the fundamental character of a text *inasmuch as* both rely on iterability and difference to generate meanings.

This approach to signification and ritualization can help us to reread texts, including sacred and theological texts, without preemptively reifying them as representational texts whose value is located in their putative ability to represent metaphysical content and timelessly transfer it from mind to mind. In other words, this approach can help us to appreciate the multiple tactics and strategies through which texts address real, located bodies. Furthermore, if written texts differ from bodily citations primarily because they generate meaning through a *written* iterable gesture – one

---

[53] Hollywood, 113. [54] Butler, *Bodies*, 12.

that can be copied from place to place and reproduced more easily than bodily gestures – then texts have the added ability to persist over centuries and participate in new materializations of life across history and geography.[55] Texts can then be read as a deep well of resources for generating the resignification of persons and worlds, for coming to see

[55] This unpredictable fecundity of books over time is captured in part by Derrida's notion of "hauntology" and, in a different way, by Giorgio Agamben's use of the "signature." I will discuss the latter at greater length in Chapter 4. As for the former, Derrida introduces the "hauntology" in his 1993 book *Specters of Marx* (New York: Routledge, 1994) to mark the inadequacy of an ontology structured by fixed binaries between "life" and "death" or "past" and "present" – indeed, the inadequacy of ontology itself to exhaust the occupation of scholarship. The figure of the ghost functions, in a negative sense, to limit that which the scholar can claim to control as she purports to manage the boundaries of the domain of the real; in a more positive sense, the ghost troubles the scholar's management of temporality by emerging from "time out of joint," or disrupting linear narratives of continuity, to mark the present as a site of excess and unfamiliarity. The event of a spectral emergence is, in one sense, an eruption of novelty; but it is in another sense the return of the dead, of that which *was* past. It is always both "repetition *and* first time" (Derrida, *Specters*, 10–11). If hauntology attempts to mark the limitations of ontology as the sole determination of reality or existence, it does so by linking the nature of existence to the structure of signification. Existence is uncanny because existence itself is structured by the difference and deferral of the signs through which the "stuff" of existence is materialized, experienced, and characterized. Because signs can perform and disrupt meaning across time and place, signs themselves trouble the coherence of the binary between what is living and what is dead. For Derrida, the meaning of a sign is generated not by its identification with an existing thing, but by its difference from and deferral of other signs. This difference and deferral of constellations of signs shuttles the "traces" of material contexts to other contexts, often not in a predictable sequence. See Derrida, *Writing and Difference* (London: Routledge, 1978), 394; Warren Montag, "Spirits Armed and Unarmed: Derrida's *Specters of Marx*" in *Ghostly Demarcations* (New York: Verso, 1999), 74.

These material traces remain, however, and emerge, like ghosts, to upset any methodological presupposition that some privileged correspondence between language and reality is definitive of either the present or the truth. These emergences, then, don't simply unveil a better description of reality itself. Instead, they mark two things: both the inability of language to ever generate the full and timeless presence of the truth; and the capacity of language to carry and relate dimensions of material life that were presumed dead or lost. The texture and arrangement of writing itself, therefore, becomes a site for thinking about what it means to be responsible to a life that can never be fully captured or characterized. Strategies of reading and writing help us to remember – and to gain a fuller grasp on – the complexities of a life that remains inscribed and disposed by relationships to the dead.

For more on hauntology and spectrality, see María del Pilar Blanco and Esther Peeren, eds., *The Spectralities Reader: Ghosts and Haunting in Contemporary Cultural Theory* (London: Bloomsbury, 2013); Peter Buse and Andrew Stott, eds., *Ghosts: Deconstruction, Psychoanalysis, History* (Basingstoke: Palgrave Macmillan, 1999); Jodey Castricano, *Cryptomimesis: The Gothic and Jacques Derrida's Ghost Writing* (Montreal: McGill-Queen's University Press, 2001); Michael Sprinker, ed., *Ghostly Demarcations: A Symposium on Jacques Derrida's Specters of Marx* (New York: Verso, 1999).

and act differently, for placing persons far removed in time in oblique relationship to one another. At the same time, however, texts also must rely on the network of bodily habits that already inhere in the reader, wherever she may be located. This means that the text is always vulnerable to the conditions and concerns of the reader.

To suggest that Calvin's *Institutio* rewards a reading that refuses to neatly separate linguistic and embodied strategies of meaning and materialization does not need to imply that Calvin is somehow a proto-Derridean.[56] Nor does it need to mean that I am haphazardly imposing a postmodern reading onto an early modern text. After all, early modern people were planting in the sunlight before anyone talked about photosynthesis. Reading Calvin with contemporary tools of analysis is a way of simply asking the reader to avoid unduly limiting the text's meaning by imposing a representational theory of signification onto it, and appreciating the extent to which the text itself might be surprisingly responsive to theoretical approaches far removed in time.

At the same time, this very responsiveness underscores the importance of asking *whether* premodern theological writing should be approached as trading in representational claims about metaphysics. This assumption has now been challenged by many scholars, including Peter Candler, Mark D. Jordan, Louis Mackey, Rowan Williams, and Matthew Potts – theorists I will engage at various points across this book as I read for the material and political import of Calvin's arguments on providence and the incarnation. In different ways, each has demonstrated that many ancient, medieval, and early modern texts are constructed as technologies to be used in, or to prepare the reader for, activity within a domain of bodily practice. Classical authors like Plato, Cleanthes, Seneca, and Marcus Aurelius and Christian authors like Boethius, Anselm, and Bonaventure all demonstrate the usefulness of these same doctrines for performing a different rendering of the world and reorienting and empowering a certain kind of embodied subject.

Finally, I also take it as significant that no ancient author has been more readily linked to a kind of Derridean logic than Augustine. For Augustine, teaching is made possible by signs, and all things are also signs (except for God). Learning does not mean receiving and assenting to propositional content; it means coming to know oneself as both thing and sign, oriented within a created complex of signs and things that all point not only to each other but *through* each other to their origin and

---

[56] Zachman, in fact, shows the extent to which Calvin thinks bodily gestures and affections ought to comport with words. See, for example, 351f and 400.

end in God. There are, of course, differences from the Derridean account, not least that Augustine (and Calvin) asserts that *God* anchors the relations between signs and things where Derrida reads only the slippage of *différance*. Yet, for Augustine (and Calvin), God does not secure meaning in a way that promises human beings stable cognitive access to the truth. The human person is, after all, an embodied sign, subject to created constraints and tasked with the *activity* of being a receiver and giver of Christian teaching, thus assuming her place along the chain of signs oriented by a created desire for the divine. Augustine's account thus resonates with Derrida and his interlocutors because it similarly recognizes no fixed binary between bodily citations and linguistic citations. All created things, including language, persons, and material objects, stand ready to serve as signs pointing in love beyond themselves to the divine.

∗ ∗ ∗

The purpose of this book is to recontextualize Calvin's impact on the modern world by focusing on the place of the body – individual, textual, and political – in his most-read pedagogical text.[57] Though few would contest that Calvin has *had* a sizeable impact on the modern world, the nature and scope of that impact are routinely disputed and often flattened. In textbooks of early modern European history, sociology, and even in surveys of Christian thought, summaries of Calvin's contributions

---

[57] One of the most influential accounts of Calvin and the body so far is Margaret Miles' "Theology, Anthropology, and the Human Body in Calvin's *Institutes of the Christian Religion*" in *The Harvard Theological Review* 74/3 (1981): 303–323. Miles indexes the valuation of the body to the glory of God and argues that the aim of Calvin's teaching is for the soul to achieve consciousness of the glory of God. The soul, as the seat of the faculties as well as intellectual understanding, is the primary locus of teaching. Because my reading of divine glory moves through a close analysis of a providential will that affirms the ontological difference and integrity of creation, my conclusions concerning the role of the body are different from Miles'. My account will track more closely to that of Thomas J. Davis in *This Is My Body: The Presence of Christ in Reformation Thought* (Grand Rapids, MI: Baker Academic, 2008), especially pp. 83f. Like Davis, I argue that Calvin's emphasis on the materiality of the sacraments (coupled with and flowing from his emphasis on the all-encompassing, affirming providential will) suggests that Calvin's teaching is deeply invested in the human soul *as embodied*. My position is also fundamentally informed by Randall Zachman's magisterial account of the role of the senses in Calvin's theology in *Image and Word*. For another critique of Miles' position, see Goodloe, James, "The Body in Calvin's Theology" in *Calvin Studies V*. edited by John H. Leith (Davidson, NC: Davidson College, 1990). Lastly, I am grateful for conversations with AnnMarie Micikas Bridges, whose forthcoming work on Calvin's understanding of perception will give valuable and groundbreaking historical-scientific backing to existing accounts – like mine – of how the body operates on a literary–pedagogical level in Calvin's writing.

remain almost exclusively limited to the chapters on predestination and church discipline.[58] Many times, little additional context is given, aside from a Weberian gloss or the assertion that Calvin was a theocrat.[59] To be sure, accounts of the impact of Calvinist societies continue to be written, but many focus on Calvinist social practices rather than theologies.[60] This is no doubt in part because it is difficult to give more than an anecdotal history of reception, especially when the kind of reception I am interested in is so subtle. I am interested in how certain living conundrums give way to certain strategies of teaching and writing, and how these might shape patterns of thinking and living over the *longue durée*.

Calvin's writing emerged from a particular petri dish of intellectual, social, political, and personal conditions that made the body something of a problem for him. In addition to living his adult life as a refugee among refugees, he also suffered an extraordinary array of illnesses, unusual even by

---

[58] See, for example, the following popular anthologies and textbooks: James Bruce Ross and Mary M. McLaughlin, eds., *The Portable Renaissance Reader* (New York: Penguin Books, 1981); Hans J. Hillerbrand, *The Protestant Reformation* (New York: Perennial, 2009); Merry E. Wesner, *Early Modern Europe, 1450–1789* (New York: Cambridge University Press, 2006), 184f; John R. Barber, *Modern European History* (New York: HarperCollins, 2006), 7; Anthony Giddens, *Sociology* (Malden, MA: Polity Press, 2006), 103–104.

[59] For discussions of the structure of Calvin's Geneva and its relation to theocracy, see William G. Naphy, "Calvin's Geneva" in *The Cambridge Companion to John Calvin*, ed. Donald K. McKim (Cambridge: Cambridge University Press, 2004), 25–40; and "Geneva II" in *The Calvin Handbook*, ed. Herman J. Selderhuis (Grand Rapids, MI: Eerdmans, 2009), 44–56; *Calvin and the Consolidation of the Genevan Reformation* (Louisville, KY: Westminster John Knox Press, 2003); and the discussion of Calvin in Ronald Wintrobe and Mario Ferrero, eds., *The Political Economy of Theocracy* (New York: Palgrave Macmillan, 2009), 100–103. Geneva maintained a system of government hierarchically ordered from a General Council (all male citizens over the age of twenty that met annually to elect officers on the smaller councils). The smallest and most powerful of these consisted of twenty-five people who met daily, overseen by four presiding officers. One of these four officers oversaw the Consistory, which was otherwise composed of pastors and church elders. While the consistory was tasked with overseeing the behavior of the city and had the power to mete out a range of lesser punishments (usually admonishments and excommunications) for moral crimes, it was always structurally and legally subservient to the hierarchy of governmental councils. For more, see Robert M. Kingdon, "Adultery and Divorce" in Calvin's *Geneva* (Cambridge, MA: Harvard University Press, 1995) and Robert M. Kingdon, ed., *Registers of the Consistory of Geneva in the Time of Calvin*, Volume 1: 1542–1544 (Grand Rapids, MI: William B. Eerdmans Publishing Company, 1996).

[60] For some particularly interesting approaches to the political–religious legacy of Calvin's Geneva, see John Witte Jr. and Robert M. Kingdon, *Sex, Marriage, and Family in John Calvin's Geneva*, three vols. (Grand Rapids, MI: Eerdmans, 2005); Pamela A. Mason, "The Communion of Citizens: Calvinist Themes in Rousseau's Theory of the State," *Polity* 26 / 1 (Autumn, 1993): 25–49; and Philip S. Gorski, "Calvinism and State-Formation in Early Modern Europe" in *State/Culture: State-Formation after the Cultural Turn*, ed. George Steinmetz (Ithaca, NY: Cornell University Press, 1999), 147–181.

the standards of his time. The preface to the 1559 *Institutio* references the "quartan fever" that almost took him, but he also chronicled kidney stones, parasites, severe hemorrhoids, tuberculosis, ulcers, chronic migraines, and a probable case of what we know today as the chronic irritable colon.[61] It is said that he dictated much of the 1559 *Institutio* from bed. Some take Calvin's physical suffering to explain his perceived overemphasis on all things spiritual, intellectual, and otherworldly.[62] However, attention to the fragility of human life before death cuts across the *Instituio* as much as figurations of journey and exile. Calvin makes frequent reference to our frailty and to the "needs" peculiar to human life in order to specify how God addresses and accommodates *our* weaknesses – not only sin and stupidity, but confusion, grief, physical limitation, and dread. Calvin was certainly not one to recommend or even dwell on the pleasures of the body. But he does not ignore bodily desires or proceed as if human beings were fundamentally constituted as intellect. Indeed, his parallel reputation for effecting a "turn to the worldly activity" would be illegible apart from his enduring interest in writing a theology that is useful for clarifying and guiding humans living *this* life, with all of its realistic constraints

I take it as axiomatic that discussions of political theology cannot be abstracted or cordoned off from living concerns. Not only is politics fundamentally invested in strategies for ordering life, the Christian doctrines that have most consistently supplied analogies for political theology – those of providence and incarnation – are also deeply invested in the material world and the human body. As I read across Calvin's 1559 *Instituio* with questions and insights drawn from a wide swath of both ancient and contemporary theorists who are interested in the political, ethical, and personal dimensions of what might otherwise appear to be abstract theological claims, I will constantly be looking at how the literary and persuasive quality of Calvin's writing addresses and performs a particular choreography of activity – not only toward politics but more fundamentally toward life. In a methodological sense, this is how I seek to overcome the problem of reception. Not only by keeping my focus on the postures through which the text addresses the living body of the reader, but also on the bodily qualities of the text itself as writing with shape, content, and structural force.

---

[61] See Charles L. Cooke, "Calvin's Illnesses," in *John Calvin and the Church: A Prism of Reform*, ed. Timothy George (Louisville, KY: Westminster John Knox Press, 1990).

[62] Cooke 68. See also Margaret Miles, "Theology, Anthropology, and the Human Body in Calvin's *Institutes of the Christian Religion*" in *The Harvard Theological Review* 74/3 (1981): 303–323.

This way of approaching Calvin's writing is not intended to replace other forms of analysis. But I do think it contributes a vital and under-represented piece of the story of Calvin's impact, albeit one that is harder to pinpoint. Calvin is routinely known under many hypostases: theologian, pastor, community leader, controversial figurehead. Here, I want to lift up Calvin the writer – a writer who described his writing as a learning and who presented it to his friends as a teaching, or a guidebook.[63] In that writing, there is no body against which the ambiguities of the text can be adjudicated; there is no mind to serve as final arbiter. There is only text. But in the text, there are traces of inscape, fault lines, and tensions left by a thinking body who struggled to make sense of a world with and for others facing particular, albeit all-too-human circumstances. And because of the nature of texts and of reading, subtle things can be gleaned from exploring that space and looking at its patterns and tensions.

I take this to be an important line of inquiry for at least two additional reasons I haven't yet named. The first has to do with the fact that Calvin remains important to living communities, and those communities have presented – and continue to present – perennial lines of contradiction.[64] For example, Calvinism is routinely accused of undermining the grounds for legible moral action while also generating unprecedented efforts at world-mastery. Calvinists have been known to defend subservience to unjust rulers and to advocate for civil resistance. Calvinist societies are famously linked with free market capitalism, yet they also have a long history of advocating governmental social welfare. In nineteenth century United States, Calvinists were both ardent abolitionists and ardent defenders of slavery. In the twentieth century, Calvinists were for and against the social gospel, for and against civil rights, for and against gender equality. In the twenty-first

---

[63] As I go on to discuss in Chapter 1, Calvin signs the last preface of the final edition of the *Institutio* with an invocation of Augustine, who wrote "I count myself among those who write in order to learn and learn in order to write." See Calvin, 1960, 5.

[64] Calvin remains revered in certain contextual spaces as much as he is suspected in others to bear much blame for certain modern ills. He also enjoys oscillatory resurges. For example, in 2009 *Time Magazine* named the "New Calvinism" one of the "10 Ideas Changing the World Right Now." See David Van Biema, "The New Calvinism," *Time*, March 12, 2009, accessed March 15, 2017. http://content.time.com/time/specials/packages/article/0,28804,1884779_1884782_1884760,00.html. The flip side of this, of course, is that Calvin's name is continually invoked in think pieces trying to account for the reemergence of nationalism particularly in the United States, where the myth of American exceptionalism betrays the distinct marks of election and covenant. See, for example, Damon Linker, "Calvin and American Exceptionalism" *New Republic*, July 9, 2009, accessed April 20, 2017.

century, Calvinists are for and against LGBTQ inclusion, for and against public education. Calvinists have demonstrated both an affirmation of scientific curiosity and suspicion of scientific methodologies.[65]

[65] As I go on to suggest, this book is not a perpetuation of the unproductive and inaccurate "Calvin vs. the Calvinists" argument. My intervention underscores both the diversity and porous boundaries of the domain of Calvin's influence. Because of the wide and complex engagement with Calvinism across and beyond early modern European societies – and the extent to which Calvinism itself claimed a complex lineage – the intellectual impact of Calvinism should not be artificially limited to those groups who most proudly claim the name; it should also be traced, beyond the limits of explicit intentionality, to sites where the signatures are resonant – even to those whose engagement may nevertheless involve their explicit rejection or negotiation of some forms of Calvinism.

With that said, those who most proudly claim the lineage in the present-day United States are often linked to the conservative side of the Princeton Seminary split and the traditions of theology following J. Gresham Machen and Cornelius Van Til; late-twentieth-century Christian Reconstructionism most explicitly indebted to Rousas John Rushdoony; and the complex sphere of influence that both of these intellectual traditions have had on contemporary Evangelicalism, triangulated especially through figures like Carl F. H. Henry and Francis Schaeffer. This discursive formation is often accompanied by a libertarian-intoned suspicion of governmental infrastructures such as welfare and public education, skepticism concerning scientific methodologies, and either veneration or toleration of racialized and hierarchized notions of Christian society traceable to nineteenth-century figures like R. L. Dabney, a theologian and ardent defender of American slavery, and more recent admirers of Dabney such as Douglas Wilson and Steven Wilkins. This latter strand of Calvinism comports with a peculiarly Presbyterian history of opposition to issues such as civil rights and feminism. In addition to the original writings of all the figures mentioned, see Molly Worthen, *Apostles of Reason: The Crisis of Authority in American Evangelicalism* (New York: Oxford University Press, 2013); and "The Chalcedon Problem: Rousas John Rushdoony and the Origins of Christian Reconstructionism" in *Church History* 77/2 (2008): 399–437; see also Mark Noll, *The Scandal of the Evangelical Mind* (Grand Rapids, MI: Eerdmans, 1994) and *The Civil War as a Theological Crisis* (Chapel Hill: University of North Carolina Press, 2006); Barry Hankins, *Francis Schaeffer and the Shaping of Evangelical America* (Grand Rapids, MI: Eerdmans, 2008).

At the same time, the history of Calvinist engagement with all of the issues mentioned is much more complex. For treatments of American abolitionism as a distinctly Calvinist–Puritan movement, see Randolph A. Roth, "The First Radical Abolitionists: The Reverend James Milligan and the Reformed Presbyterians of Vermont" in *Abolitionism and American Religion*, ed. McKivigan (New York: Garland, 1999); David S. Reynolds, *John Brown, Abolitionist: The Man Who Killed Slavery, Sparked the Civil War, and Seeded Civil Rights* (New York: Vintage, 2006). For contemporary engagements with Calvinism from persons occupying diverse materially and critically located perspectives, see Allan A. Boesak, *Black and Reformed: Apartheid, Liberation, and the Calvinist Tradition* (Eugene, OR: Wipf and Stock, 1984); Jones, Serene and Amy Plantinga Pauw, eds., *Feminist and Womanist Essays in Reformed Dogmatics* (Louisville, KY: Westminster John Knox, 2006). James Cone's body of work also engages (while not claiming) the distinct legacy of Barthian Reformed theology. See, for example, *God of the Oppressed* (Maryknoll, NY: Orbis, 1975). For an array of arguments over the humanist and liberal legacies of Calvinism and Puritanism, see Marilynne Robinson's collections of

Surely it is too facile to explain these divergences by differentiating the "nominal" Calvinists from the "genuine" Calvinists. I also find it dubious to reduce these differences to social factors in which the characteristic features of Calvin's own theological teaching are given no consideration. While it is certainly true that only a minuscule percentage of self-described Calvinists have read Calvin in any depth, the *Institutio* has nevertheless been consistently read and taught for centuries at a wide range of institutions.[66] Even if the text is encountered in summary form, its pedagogical texture and interpretive tensions are apparent – particularly, its enduring interest in relating scriptural teachings to the details of a providential world. I am convinced that the oppositions marking five centuries of Calvinist social ethics are indeed suspended in tension within the *Institutio* itself, and right at the site of this question: how to relate the Word to the world. When the text announces this question as its thematic

essays, *The Death of Adam: Essays on Modern Thought* (New York: Picador, 1998) and *The Givenness of Things* (New York: Farrar, Straus and Giroux, 2015). For a sampling of the range of social and ethical positions held by Calvinists, see part two of Worthen's *Apostles of Reason*; Heather White, *Reforming Sodom: Protestants the Rise of Gay Rights* (Chapel Hill: University of North Carolina Press, 2015); Tamara Van Dyken, "Always Reforming? Evangelical Feminism and the Committee for Women in the Christian Reformed Church, 1975–1995" in *Church History and Religious Culture* 95/ 4 (2015): 495–522; Matthew Bowlman, "Sin, Spirituality, and Primitivism: The Theologies of the American Social Gospel, 1885–1917" in *Religion and American Culture: A Journal of Interpretation* 17/1 (2007): 95–126; Ian J. Shaw, *High Calvinists in Action: Calvinism and the City, Manchester and London, 1810–1860* (New York: Oxford University Press, 2002); Robert M. Kingdon's research in general, and particularly "Social Welfare in Calvin's Geneva" in *The American Historical Review* 76/1 (1971): 50–69; Timothy M. Renick, "From Apartheid to Liberation: Calvinism and the Shaping of Ethical Belief in South Africa" in *Sociological Focus* 24/2 (1991): 129–143; and Roland Boer, *Political Grace: The Revolutionary Theology of John Calvin* (Louisville, KY: Westminster John Knox Press, 2009).

For more on Calvinist societies and diverse approaches to emerging science, see Ray Porter and Mikuláš Teich, eds., *The Scientific Revolution in National Context* (New York: Cambridge University Press, 1991), especially on Calvinism in the Low Countries; David S. Sytsma, "Calvin, Daneau, and *Physica Mosaica*: Neglected Continuities at the Origins of an Early Modern Tradition" in *Church History and Religious Culture* 95 (2015): 457–476; Toby E. Huff, *Intellectual Curiosity and the Scientific Revolution: A Global Perspective* (New York: Cambridge University Press, 2011), introduction; Kenneth J. Howell, *God's Two Books: Copernican Cosmology and Biblical Interpretation in Early Modern Science* (Notre Dame, IN: University of Notre Dame Press, 2002); Eric Jorink, *Reading the Book of Nature in the Dutch Golden Age, 1575–1715* (Leiden: Brill, 2010).

[66] Bruce Gordon's most recent book invaluably offers a rich and detailed account of the *Institutio*'s scope of reception. See *John Calvin's Institutes of the Christian Religion: A Biography* (Princeton, NJ: Princeton University Press, 2016).

center, it makes a device for use – but the text itself cannot constrain *how* the reader uses the text. This gap only underscores the importance of locating interpretive "forks in the road" that confront the reader over how signification is to be practiced. In other words, is the tool of the *Institutio* used to articulate a world defined by the Word and to protect it from disruption? – or to do precisely the opposite, combatting idolatrous coincidences of word and thing by fostering attention and responsibility to a world that fallen eyes habitually misrecognize? These questions require certain methodological constraints: my focus, for example, on this one text, as well as a reading that necessarily tracks specific patterns and metaphors of interest to theorists of political theology while necessarily passing over others.[67] But by returning to this textual body with a particular interest in how this text is shaped and how it gives itself to be used in practice, I expect that readers might at least gain interpretive clarity over why this tradition has seen a parting of the ways on many of these issues.

As an object of study, the *Institutio* acts as a synecdoche for many overlapping debates that take place farther afield from people who care about Calvin, Calvinism, and its contemporary lines of impact. All of the questions I pursue here are always also questions about more general sets of relationships: between the idiom of theology and language; theology and politics; politics and living bodies; politics and time; theology and ordinary life; bodies of writing and human bodies; the order of life and the question of suffering. To study how Calvin the refugee writes theology, reinhabiting that privileged office as an exile of the *Corpus Christianum*, is also to study one case where sovereignty is theorized from the site of the inglorious. On a structural level, this is a question of recognition: of how it might be possible to recognize a body that is unrecognizable from within a given regime of intelligibility, and what the historical and literary idiom of doctrinal theology might have to do with the ability to facilitate a recognition of the unrecognizable. A recognition-beyond-misrecognition.

* * *

---

[67] I am aware that important themes like law, covenant, and the life everlasting get less attention in this book simply for reasons of constraint. I hope and expect that the reading I do offer, which turns on creation, incarnation, and sacrament, will set up a fruitful framework for reapproaching these other themes.

This book proceeds in three parts. The first, consisting of only one chapter, introduces the 1559 *Institutio* and argues that its genre is best read as one facilitating embodied mediation. I show that in addition to drawing from the late medieval and early modern genres of *loci communes* and *disputationes*, Calvin's writing shares recognizable features of both the Stoic *enchiridion* and Christian theological *itineraria*, participatory genres with which he would have been familiar. Along the way, this chapter also familiarizes the reader with the structure of the *Institutio*, which guides its reader along a particular pedagogical sequence in search of "the knowledge of God and ourselves" [*cognitio Dei et nostri*]. The first half of Calvin's text moves its reader from the Knowledge of God the Creator, which culminates in providence, to the Knowledge of God the Redeemer in Christ, which culminates in Calvin's account of the atonement. The second half completes the circuit by relating the twofold knowledge of God [*duplex cognitio Dei*] to the ordinary life of the human reader – first as an individual adopted and elected under Christ's name by the Holy Spirit, then in society through differing participations in church and state. This chapter sets up a theoretical template for appreciating the participatory-performative dimensions of theological writing in general and Calvin's text in particular, especially as its structure hinges on the two doctrines most central to debates over secularization and political theology: providence and the incarnation.

The second part focuses on providence and consists of three chapters. Drawing from Stoic and early Christian sources, the first (Chapter 2) argues that providence is best read as a historical discourse designed to reorient its reader in the world and to prepare her for facing immanent inevitabilities of suffering and death. Chapter 3 turns to the *Institutio*, reading Calvin's treatment of providence against that backdrop and alongside later modern anxieties over providence as a morally suspect approach to the meaning of suffering. Drawing from Karl Löwith and Friedrich Nietzsche, I argue that the force of Calvin's providential arguments echo later arguments that advocate the affirmation of life over appeals to divine (or rational) intention. Chapter 4 then returns to Calvin's argument from the vantage of contemporary debates over governmentality in conversation with Michel Foucault and Giorgio Agamben. Because providence is a discourse on the meaning of suffering and an account of divine governance, its argumentative qualities offer both implicit and explicit accounts of how a sovereign will addresses an ordinary body. I argue that the Trinitarian scaffolding underwriting Calvin's providential argument offers resources for more aggressively indexing creative divine activity to the world of nature rather than that of the political economy, therefore recovering a theologically robust possibility of a body that resists (idolatrous) modes of sovereign governance.

The third and final part of the book turns to the doctrine of the incarnation, focusing on the question of *how the incarnation teaches*. The first of its chapters, Chapter 5, presents the Augustinian tradition of signification as one in which Christian teaching occurs through the use of signs that *reorient* the subject in relation to other existing things within a material field of practice. After discussing that tradition in conversation with Mark Jordan, Rowan Williams, and Matthew Potts, I argue that Calvin's particular approach to doctrinal loci participates in that tradition. In Chapter 6, I show how this works – specifically, how books two and three of the *Institutio* are crafted to carry out the resignification and reorientation of the human body through the teaching tool of Christ's own body, and the mediating narratives it supplies. Resignification occurs through the grace of adoption in the Spirit; reorientation occurs through the way Calvin unfolds his doctrine of election. In Chapter 7, I look at Calvin's fourth book, examining how he moves from the individual body of the believer to the collective "body" of the church. I show that Calvin reconceives the church as having a strictly performative existence, which allows him to place primary significance on the real (and ontologically distinct) bodies of Christ and of ordinary people. I pivot, then, to the vital question of whether and how Calvin's teaching allows the state to be theorized as a sovereign body. For Calvin, the real body always exists prior to the fictions that enable mediated relationships between bodies. This relegates the state to the status of a useful tool rather than a sovereign body existing in its own right. It also supplies the fundamental logic of state resistance.

Throughout this last part of the book, I am interested in whether incarnational theology necessarily relies on and perpetuates the logic of a sovereign signified, or a privileged body that locates both sign and signified in one legible arrangement of Word and Flesh. Theorists who both criticize and defend modern Western secularity – Karl Löwith, Victoria Kahn, Kathleen Davis, Gil Anidjar, J. Kameron Carter – have made versions of this argument: namely, that Christian societies have been uniquely vulnerable to fascism and prone to colonial domination because of their implicit adherence to a world-shattering coincidence of incarnation that fundamentally undergirds the sovereign logic of the *Corpus Christianum*.

Across this book, and especially in its conclusion, I argue that this question must hinge once more on how the incarnation is read – which really amounts to the question of how embodied persons understand themselves *as* addressed by the signs that materialize them and grant them both legibility and capability. In Calvin's case, robust attention to the doctrine of providence forestalls the urge to read the incarnation apart from the way it is addressed, in sequence, to the ontologically distinct domain of creation that is affirmed by God – a spatiotemporal context that the incarnation might not shatter, but join. The fictive narratives generated by the real body of Christ act as useful accommodations for both perceiving and following the providential pattern of a creative divine will that first affirms the world in order to also govern and cultivate it. When these narratives are allowed to address the reader as tools for cultivating practices of responsibility to creation and to ourselves, it is possible to read them as setting up the kinds of relationships that also subvert idolatrous urges toward sovereign mastery.

Yet this is never more than a crossroads – one at which the reader is perpetually placed. The question of which way to proceed – I submit – turns on the place of the body.

PART I

ITINERANT PEDAGOGY

I

Writing Reform

The Genre of the 1559 Institutio Christianae Religionis

Tis those whose cause my former booklet pled, Whose zeal to learn has wrought this tome instead.

I count myself one of the number of those who write as they learn and learn as they write.

Jean Calvin, final preface to the Institutio Christianae Religionis¹

These are the two epigraphs that close the final preface of Calvin's final edition of the *Institutio Christianae Religionis*.² If this book proceeds from something like an axiom, it is that Calvin cared about writing, and treated it as a useful practice for learning. Writing, for Calvin, is an important way to respond to the conditions one faces. It is also a useful tool for clarifying existing relationships and performing new ones. He wrote diligently throughout his life. As a university student, he wrote a commentary on Seneca's *De Clementia*.³ It demonstrated the extent to which Calvin had dedicated himself to reading such authors as Aristotle, Cicero, and Pliny the Elder. It also demonstrated how much he enjoyed their writing, weaving their prose into his own prose often with evident humor and appreciation. In conversation with these authors, he developed several fundamental preoccupations that would remain evident

---

¹ Jean Calvin, *Institutes of the Christian Religion*, ed. McNeill, trans. Battles (Louisville, KY: Westminster John Knox Press, 1960), 5. With the exception of prefatory material, all subsequent citations of the *Institutio* will occur in text and follow the standard practice of citing book, chapter, and section: i.e., 1.1.1.

² Hereafter, I refer to this work as the *Institutio*, implying the 1559 (final) edition unless otherwise stated.

³ This summary account of Calvin's Commentary on Seneca's *De Clementia* is indebted to Bruce Gordon's *Calvin* (New Haven, CT: Yale University Press, 2009), 24–29.

across his writing: the value of orderly speech; the usefulness of the law to shape conceptions of personal and public good; that the need for teaching should be carefully accommodated to the needs and conditions of a particular audience; and the conviction that mercy, not punishment, secures the social bond.[4] Many of these classical encounters would remain in the DNA of Calvin's writing, even as he thoroughly ingested the work of his two more fundamental literary loves: scripture and Augustine.[5]

Calvin revised his masterwork, the *Institutio* diligently throughout his adult life. The earliest edition of the *Institutio* was published in 1536, and written during the two years of itinerancy Calvin experienced after fleeing Paris in 1534. He was open about the conditions that elicited his writing, framing that first edition with a prefatory address to King Francis of France on behalf of the endangered reformist community. But the text contains other addressees: the many "barking dogs" that Calvin took as theological enemies of various sorts; the increasingly fragmented reformers themselves, to whom he often wanted to present a "middle way"; and, of course, those fellow exiles whose purported "zeal to learn has brought this tome instead." Calvin revised the *Institutio* diligently throughout his adult life, refining its ability to lead interested readers to and through the text of his highest regard: the Christian scriptures. Latin editions appeared in 1539, 1543, 1550, and finally 1559, with French translations from Calvin's hand in 1541, 1545, 1551, 1553, 1554, and 1560. The first edition was written largely "on the road." The last, from bed. Calvin's physical suffering is well-documented, and it seems that the more his health failed, the more he wrote.

The final edition stands as a kind of emporium of all these concerns, all of these relationships, all of these readings. It is addressed to the "public good," it treats and enacts teaching as an act of accommodation, it engages the uses of the law and theorizes the church as a community performed around a cosmic act of divine mercy.[6] It also cites Augustine

---

[4] The Greek term for the household activity that organizes natural life is *oikonomia*; the Latin is *dispositio*. This is important to notice inasmuch as providence can be read as a discourse on how God governs the "household." I'll look at this closely in Chapter 4.

[5] As will become clear, I do not use "literature" in any reductive sense to foreclose claims to supernatural origin. For many reasons, I do not think Calvin would find it controversial to discuss scripture's meaning by attention to its existence as literature – not least because he was a major proponent of the *sensus literalis*, which locates meaning in the surface of a text.

[6] For references to the quartan fever and the public good, see Calvin, *Inst.*, 3–4.

eight times more than any other non-scriptural author, right down to the final epigraph – a gesture that one might well imagine to be Calvin's final signature, authorizing a text more than two decades in the making under the auspices of a beloved teacher. Augustine's overwhelming influence on Calvin is explicit, and I will explore it at length across these chapters. Like the other relationships giving this text life, it is activated primarily through exercises of reading, writing, and rereading. It is striking that Calvin's final invocation of Augustine has little to do with the familiar Augustinian themes often so visible in Calvin's work – grace, will, predestination. Instead, Calvin closes his work by submitting to participation in an Augustinian *practice* of learning through writing and writing in order to learn.

**

The core of the book focuses on Calvin's 1559 *Institutes,* and particularly on the way that the text is *written* – its structure, its language, and the array of argumentative features through which the writing aims to shape and guide a certain kind of reader toward certain ends. At the same time, it places the text in an array of intertextual relationships that cut across time and place – not only backward, but forward, within and beyond the usually recognized confines of Calvin's influence. Although there is always an impulse to check with the "source" in order to upset certain caricatures that abound concerning such a controversial and influential figure as Calvin, I have no interest in uncovering a pure Calvin or a pure text. As with any text of a certain age, the author is lost and boundaries of the text he left behind are porous. For these reasons, the Calvin I read will be a textual Calvin whose text remains responsively at play with other voices, other ideas, and concerns other than those that a man living from 1509 to 1564 in Francophone Europe could have anticipated. But the text continues to give. As an arrangement of written signs, it remains to interact with the bodies who engage it today and tomorrow, with meanings that are both distinct yet inexhaustible.

To set the stage for the readings that will follow, focusing more aggressively on categories and questions related to contemporary questions of embodiment and political theology, this chapter looks at the intellectual traditions shaping the *Institutio* as a written object of pedagogical use in order to appreciate the forms of embodied relationships that the text both assumes and animates. As I proceed to look at doctrinal loci, it is important to constantly ask what Calvin's doctrinal discussions are supposed to *do* in the context of the *Institutes* as a whole. Is the text designed as a collection of propositions concerning Christian truth, or as a mere summary of what is already in the Bible? Or is there evidence in Calvin's writing of a greater awareness of the role of other aspects of human being in addition to the intellect – such as perception, bodily habit, affection, and desire?

I am far from the first reader of Calvin to emphasize the rhetorical, pedagogical, practical, as well as propositional dimensions of this text, and I've learned to read for them from many others who have drawn out, for example, the way Calvin uses images to cultivate perception, his debt to classical forms of rhetorical persuasion, or the role he maintains for the cultivation of the affections.[7] Still, others have emphasized the participatory and pedagogical dimensions of Calvin's theological project, all of which draw attention to the place Calvin gives to the body as a site of attention and cultivation.[8] And, of course, historical research continues to refine our understanding of the concrete intellectual relationships Calvin cultivated not only personally, but as he developed his doctrinal thinking.[9] All of these approaches aid in articulating one of the interests that motivates my work: how Calvin's writing *itself* can be encountered as a form of a practice geared at equipping a person to actively relate divine revelation to the various spheres of immanent life. This raises the question not only of the style of argumentation Calvin employs, but also the role that argumentation assumes within the larger field of concrete exercises of embodied habituation and a more general interest in the order of immanent life. While Reformed Protestantism and modernity alike often

---

[7] See especially, Barbara Pitkin, *What Pure Eyes Could See: Calvin's Doctrine of Faith in Its Exegetical Context* (Oxford: Oxford University Press, 1999); Randall Zachman, *Image and Word in the Theology of John Calvin* (Indiana: University of Notre Dame Press, 2009); Olivier Millet, *Calvin et la dynamique de la parole: Etude de rhétorique réformée* (Librairie Honoré Champion, 1992); Serene Jones, *Calvin and the Rhetoric of Piety* (Louisville, KY: John Knox Press, 1995).

[8] See especially, Julie Canlis, *Calvin's Ladder* (Grand Rapids, MI: Eerdmans, 2010); J. Todd Billings, *Calvin, Participation, and the Gift* (New York: Oxford University Press, 2007); Matthew Myer Boulton, *Life in God: John Calvin, Practical Formation, and the Future of Protestant Theology* (Grand Rapids, MI: Eerdmans, 2011); Raymond A. Blacketer, *The School of God Pedagogy and Rhetoric in Calvin's Interpretation of Deuteronomy* (Dordrecht: Springer, 2006).

[9] See Richard A. Muller, *The Unaccommodated Calvin: Studies in the Formation of a Theological Tradition* (New York: Oxford University Press, 2001); Susan Schreiner, *The Theater of His Glory: Nature and Natural Order in the Thought of John Calvin* (Durham, NC: The Labyrinth Press, 1991) and *Where Shall Wisdom Be Found? Calvin's Exegesis of Job from Medieval and Modern Perspectives* (Chicago: University of Chicago Press, 1994).

downplay the importance of bodily rituals while opposing them to higher values of rational representation, I want to look at the way that writing and practice are constantly interrelated in and through Calvin's writing.[10] This, of course, points to the guiding thread that orients this work. I want to contextualize Calvin's written arguments in a larger set of questions that are unquestionably related to the present but that also require approaching texts in times out of joint – questions about how the text facilitates a certain kind of reforming posture to collective life and the role that material life plays in such a project. This means, on the one hand, keeping in mind the tensions structuring writings of the fifteenth and sixteenth centuries, the period of "Renaissance and Reformation" situated at the cleavage of the "late medieval" and the "early modern." These writings are materially tied to a tumultuous series of events that precipitated a number of characteristic "modern turns" to the world, the nation-state, the market economy, the individual, and scientific knowledge. But each of these turns also stands at its own interpretive crossroads, and brings its own set of questions as to *how* complex histories and living concerns inform the inhabitation of these postures.

These questions could include what *sources* prove useful for rethinking the present in a way that is radical enough to alter the terms of its intelligibility. For many early modern authors including Calvin, these sources were ancient: Christian authorities like Augustine, but also classical sources like Seneca and Cicero. Reading thousand-year-old texts can furnish fresh ways of imagining how life could be lived and what it could mean. But these questions could also include what *experiences* catalyze the way ideas and exercises are recombined in sources that want to ask radical questions about authority, order, and the location of the sacred. Surely the interpretive crossroads will be navigated differently by someone who wants to maintain a status quo versus someone who has experienced the brunt of its violence, or someone for whom suffering is especially salient. One of my fundamental convictions is that although it is impossible to make Calvin's mind or body present to my analysis,

---

[10] For more on the historical relationship between Protestantism and modern approaches to ritual that rely on a problematic thought vs. practice binary, see especially, Catherine Bell, *Ritual Theory Ritual Practice* (New York: Oxford University Press, 2009); Ann Taves, "The Camp Meeting and Paradoxes of Evangelical Protestant Ritual" in *Teaching Ritual* (AAR Teaching Religious Studies Series), ed. Catherine Bell (Oxford: Oxford University Press, 2007); and Adam B. Seligman, Robert P. Weller, Michael Puett, and Bennett Simon, eds., *Ritual and Its Consequences* (Oxford: Oxford University Press, 2008). See also my fuller discussion in the Introduction.

remembering the surface contours of his location will illumine these interpretive crossroads in his writing in such a way that we later readers might be able to trace the complex and even contradictory cataracts of his influence more ably across some of the different ways that modern Christians, and persons in general, have imagined the fundamental relationship between God and the world or God and the state.

<h2 style="text-align:center">THE GENRE OF THE 1559 *INSTITUTIO*</h2>

What *kind* of a text is the *Institutio*?[11] For what kind of activity is it useful, and what kinds of relationships does it both perform and invite? As this chapter will show, there is no simple answer to the question of the *Institutio*'s genre – which is part of what makes the text interesting and, I think, enduring. Calvin does gesture to several intended features of the text in his final preface. He makes clear that it is not intended as a commentary, but designed to augment his commentaries by removing the need to digress into "long disputations and commonplaces." He also makes clear that it is intended as a guide to scripture for the use of "candidates of sacred theology," specifically so that they might have a better sense of the end to which scripture should be directed.

Calvin's final preface suggests that he personally had a lot at stake in getting the order of the teaching right, in form and content, not only for the sake of his nascent church but also in response to the nexus of relationships surrounding his city and the frailty of his own life:

Although I did not regret the labor spent [on previous editions], I was never satisfied until work had been arranged in the order now set forth. Now I trust that I have provided something that all of you will approve. In any event, I can furnish a very clear testimony of my great zeal and effort to carry out this task for God's church. Last winter when I thought the quartan fever was summoning me to my death, the more the disease pressed upon me the less I spared myself, until I could leave a book behind me that might, in some measure, repay the generous invitation of godly persons [*piorum*, or "the pious"].[12]

To figure out what kind of text this is, one might sensibly begin by looking at the order that Calvin found so satisfying. Although the 1559 is a veritable archive of its previous editions – containing layers of orders of teaching including the Lord's Prayer, the Ten Commandments,

[11] Portions of the following argument also appear in my article, "Ritualized Doctrine: Protestant Ritual, Genre, and the Case of Calvin's *Institutes*" in *Journal of the American Academy of Religion* 85/3 (2017): 746–774.
[12] Calvin, *Institutes*, 3.

and the Pauline *ordo salutis*, the final edition is the only one to appear as four books. They are as follows:

I. Of the Knowledge of God the Creator [*De cognitione Dei creatoris*]

II. Of the Knowledge of God the Redeemer in Christ, first disclosed to the fathers under the law,
    and then to us in the gospel [*De cognitio Dei redemptoris in Christo, quae Patribus sub*
    Lege primúm, deinde & nobis in Euangelio pateacta est]

III. The mode of obtaining the grace of Christ, the benefits it confers, and the effects stemming
    from it [*De modo percipiende Christi gratiae, & qui inde fructus nobis proveniant, & qui*
    effectus consequentur]

IV. Of the external means or helps by which God allures us into fellowship with Christ, and keeps
    us in it [*De externis Mediis vel adminiculis, quibus Deus in Christi societatem nos invitat,*
    & in ea retinet]

From these, one can understand at a glimpse that this is a text interested in knowledge. But it is also interested in how knowledge is related to people, or how it may be used to their benefit. It is interested in accommodation, which is to say that it is consummately pedagogical (rather than, say, classificatory or contractual). This is further underscored by the fact that Calvin first recommends the *Institutio* as a gift for the benefit of "God's Church." In some important way, this text is for the community's formation and its use.

Calvin clarifies that use by invoking the role of "the pious" [*piorum*] as both initiator and recipient of the text's creation. Readers already familiar with Calvin will know that this term emerges early and often. Like a cipher, piety – *pietas* in Latin and *eusebeia* in Greek – effects a relationship between both diverse intellectual traditions and concrete aims. On one level, Calvin's *use* of the term functions similarly to the Augustinian *caritas*. It is the prerequisite for and outcomes of proper learning.[13]

---

[13] This resonates with other traditional patterns of what might be called theological method, including Augustine's use of charity and Anselm's use of faith in his *Proslogion*. For each of these, a certain disposition is required in order for knowledge to be apprehended and put to appropriate use. I will discuss this at greater length in Chapter 6.

He writes in the opening pages of the *Institutio* that God is not known where there is no religion [*religio*] or piety [*pietas*] (*Inst.* 1.2.1). In this context, piety is not its own category of knowledge. It is an operator that refers to the disposition or posture that one must practice in order to be the kind of being who can really know God in the way that God is given to be known.[14] On another level, *pietas* refers to an ethical and civic category central to the classical rhetorical tradition in which Calvin was well trained.[15] It therefore refers not only back to the archive of classical thinking that Calvin so revered, but also the extent to which his own reforming project was invested in the formation of civic life and public good.

A closer look at the way Calvin named the text unwinds these connections even further. Though Calvin settled on the title *Institutio Christianae Religionis* from the first edition onward, that first edition also carried the byline "*Summa Pietatis.*"[16] Though he dropped this in subsequent editions, invocations of *religio* and *pietas* remain very close in Calvin's writing, as they are in the work of classical authors like Cicero, who Calvin reread every year.[17] For Cicero, *pietas* tends to refer to one's disposition in the various immanent spheres of duty, while *religio* speaks more specifically to one's reverence of, and obligations to, the gods. As *religio* was carried over into medieval Christian use, it came almost exclusively to refer to vowed life under a rule. For Thomas Aquinas, however, *religio* is once more a virtue – specifically, the chief moral virtue. Thomas writes that insofar as religion approaches nearer to God than the other virtues, it is not only the chief of the virtues but that which orders and directs all other virtues.[18] Against this classical and medieval

---

[14] This assessment agrees with Muller on the topic of piety: "Calvin continually exhorts his readers to piety and consistently criticizes authorities and teachings that stand in the way of piety or of the teaching of piety (*doctrina, exercitia*, or *stadium pietatis*), but he never describes what he is doing as a form of piety. Piety was to be conjoined with 'teaching' or 'doctrine' (*doctrina*): Calvin did not understand it as an exercise separable from his teaching, preaching, and debating" (107).

[15] See again, Jones, *Calvin and the Rhetoric of Piety* and Millet, *Calvin et la dynamique de la parole*.

[16] Muller speculates that Calvin dropped the subtitle precisely because he did not want to indicate that piety was itself a doctrine or something that could be taught. Muller, *The Unaccommodated Calvin*, 107.

[17] Gordon, *Calvin*, 4. For more on Calvin's relationship to Cicero, see David Steinmetz, *Calvin in Context* (Oxford: Oxford University Press, 2010), 241–244.

[18] See Thomas Aquinas, *Summa Theologica* 2-2.81, particularly article six.

backdrop, Calvin's title addresses the reader at the level of her disposition as it relates to the overlapping spheres of civic, practical, and moral life.[19] What, then, of *institutio*? Of the three, this word may be the most unfamiliar. In contemporary English, "institute" acts as a synonym for "organization" or "establishment" – in other words, as the modern cognate "institution." Ancient and medieval Latin uses of *institutio* convey a much more explicitly pedagogical valence, meaning instruction or arrangement for the purposes of education.[20] In medieval use, the Latin *institutio* referred both to "a method of organizing speech to achieve consensus within a city, an established body of customs and norms (linguistic, literary, and other), and a system for transmitting these customs from one generation to another."[21] Both *institutio* and *religio*, therefore, recall Calvin's interest in the use of order to relate ideas to people, and people to other people, with some eye to cultivating a disposition for the good of church and public.

For a long time, debates over the *Institutio*'s genres were oriented around whether or not the work achieves an expected level of theological systematicity.[22] Arguing that such a focus is anachronistic to the text's

---

[19] For a helpful discussion on the relationship between *pietas* and *religio* for Cicero and Thomas Aquinas, see James D. Garrison, *Pietas from Vergil to Dryden* (University Park: The Pennsylvania State University Press, 1992), 12–13.

[20] See also, Raymond Blacketer, *The School of God*. Chapter 2 contains a helpful discussion of the relationship between Calvin's writing and Quintillian's *Institutio Oratorio*.

[21] Jeffrey T. Schnapp, "Reading Lessons: Augustine, Proba, and the *Détournement* of Antiquity," *Stanford Literature Review* 9 (1992): 99–123, 101.

[22] Interpreters have for centuries been at odds concerning the systematic center or unifying theme of the *Institutes*. Some have simply concluded that the *Institutes* is a disorderly text, structured by no single, discernible logic (Bouwsma). Others, such as Muller, answer these critics by arguing that modern dissatisfaction with the *Institutes* has more to do with modern readers' failure to appreciate Calvin's particular sixteenth-century aim, which was simply to provide doctrinal discussions to accompany his scriptural commentaries. Still others have maintained that a doctrinal theme, such as the twofold knowledge of God, is indeed able to make sense of the text as a whole (Dowey). It has become more common in recent years, however, for interpreters to locate a practical rather than doctrinal center, arguing that the Institutes aims to form affections rather than to build a system (Gerrish, Boulton, and to some extent Jones). I want to argue that reading the text as an *itinerarium* contributes to this discussion by accounting not only for what the text contains, but for ways in which the text gives itself to be read. For the aforementioned books on Calvin, see the following: Matthew Myer Boulton, *Life in God: John Calvin, Practical Formation, and the Future of Protestant Theology* (Grand Rapids, MI: Eerdmans, 2011); William J. Bouwsma, *John Calvin: A Sixteenth Century Portrait* (New York: Oxford University Press, 1988); Edward A. Dowey, Jr., *The Knowledge of God in Calvin's Theology* (New York: Columbia University Press, 1952); Jones, *Calvin and the Rhetoric of Piety*; B. A. Gerrish, *Grace and Gratitude:*

aims, Richard Muller has argued for a more historically constrained approach to the *Institutio* as an example of early modern *loci communes*. The genre of "commonplaces" [Latin *loci communes*] or "topics" [Greek *topoi*] has ancient roots, appearing in the corpora of both Aristotle and Cicero as the arrangement of logical topics designed to structure the memory for dialectic. While it would reemerge as a source of didactic interest among early modern authors like Lorenzo Valla, Erasmus of Rotterdam, Peter Ramus, Philipp Melanchthon, and Peter Martyr Vermigli, the most influential contribution to the renaissance of *loci communes* was arguably to be found in Rudolf Agricola's 1479 *De inventione dialectica* (1479). Agricola's innovation would subordinate logic to rhetoric and accordingly spatialize logical *topoi*.[23] Ancient sources tended to treat the *loci* as *sedes argumentorum*, or nodes to trigger memory and organize the embodied pursuit of knowledge through oral dialectic. Agricola's subordination to rhetoric meant that writing itself could be treated as a receptacle to convey knowledge, or a means through which the presentation of knowledge could be topographically transferred to the mind.[24] This approach would arguably come to typify later Protestant systematics.[25]

Agricola was also an important influence on Philipp Melanchthon, Luther's right-hand successor, whose 1521 *Loci Communes* represents the first attempt to present Reformation theology in an orderly fashion anchored in the *topoi* of scripture itself. There is good evidence that Calvin generally admired Melanchthon's work and that he, too, was influenced by the Agricolan trend that he seems to obliquely reference when he states that the *Institutio* will contain commonplaces [*locos communes*] and disputations [*disputatio*].[26] Yet, these do not exhaust the generic features of Calvin's theological writing. As I've already suggested, Calvin's text betrays an enduring interest in reading and writing itself as a fully embodied and contextual practice of self- and

---

The *Eucharistic Theology of John Calvin* (Minneapolis: Fortress Press, 1973); and Muller's aforementioned *The Unaccommodated Calvin*.

[23] Muller, *The Unaccommodated Calvin*, 109–111; Walter Ong, *Ramus, Method, and the Decay of Dialogue: From the Art of Discourse to the Art of Reason* (Chicago: University of Chicago Press, 2004).

[24] Peter Candler, *Theology, Rhetoric, Manuduction, or Reading Scripture Together on the Path to God* (Grand Rapids, MI: Eerdmans, 2006), 22–26.

[25] Richard Burnett, "John Calvin and the Sensus Literalis" in *Scottish Journal of Theology* 57/1 (2004): 1–13; Ong 2003; Carl R. Trueman and R. Scott Clark, eds., *Protestant Scholasticism: Studies in Reassessment* (Eugene, OR: Wipf and Stock, 2005).

[26] Muller, 103–109.

social-formation. Coupled with his lifelong interest in ancient Christian and classical modes of writing, this means that it should not be surprising to find the evidence of several ancient and medieval participatory genres at play in the structure and content of Calvin's writings.

This chapter makes the case that the features of Calvin's text invite consideration alongside two older participatory genres of moral and theological writing: the *enchiridion* and the *itinerarium*.[27] By participatory genre, I mean a form of writing that wants to reshape its reader's disposition through use in a material field of practice. Such a text asks the reader to refer its signs to things in place and time. It also addresses a wider range of human faculties including sense and affection. Finally, it is ordered to maximize the pedagogical force of that relating activity according to some goal. To develop a way of thinking about the use of texts not only as containers of discursive information but also as tools for a fully embodied practice, I follow Catherine Bell and her interlocutors – Derrida, Butler, Hollywood – who have paved the way for remembering that language can be understood alongside bodily gestures as generating meaning through repetition and deferral – an approach I discussed at some length in the Introduction.[28]

In order to better address Calvin's writing in particular, I also follow theorists who have examined historical uses of participatory genres in the ancient and medieval writings with which Calvin would have been familiar. Pierre Hadot's body of work calls attention to how philosophical writing within the ancient Stoic schools provided "a privileged means by which the philosopher can act upon himself and others ... intended to produce an effect, to create a *habitus* within the soul, or to provoke a transformation of the self" (Hadot 1995: 176). Writing, and philosophical discourse more generally, were subordinate to broader aims – namely, those of crafting a certain kind of embodied subjectivity fit to read and navigate the material field of life. Peter M. Candler's *Theology, Rhetoric, Manuduction* examines the two Christian medieval examples of the *Glossa Ordinaria* and Thomas Aquinas's *Summa Theologiae* to distinguish what he calls a "grammar of participation." Unlike the

---

[27] Because these participatory genres are deployed by many of the traditional authorities that Calvin both read and cited – Epictetus, Seneca, Cicero, Augustine, Thomas Aquinas – such a claim is at least historically plausible. However, given Calvin's robust classical education, rhetorical sophistication, and theological erudition, it would be historically shocking if engagement with participatory genres was in fact *not* a constitutive influence, from out of disjointed time, on Calvin's theological writing.

[28] Bell, *Ritual*, 90–93. See also my longer discussion in the introduction to this book.

"representational" grammar more often presumed by modern readers who treat texts as containers of information or as a tableau or purported truths, the grammar of participation asks readers to relate written signs to their particular spatiotemporal conditions.[29]

By reengaging the question of the genre of the *Institutio*, I hope to challenge some common assumptions that theological writing is fundamentally about cataloging, systematizing, refining, and/or defending revealed dogmatic propositions. Certainly, theology is that. But a text like Calvin's – such a melange of intellectual and practical concerns – asks its reader to imagine more. In what follows, I argue that Calvin's text manifests features that invite an analysis of his arguments as a grammar of participation, and that a closer look at the two genres of the *enchiridion* and the *itinerarium* help to concretize what this means about the content of Calvin's doctrinal arguments.

THE ENCHIRIDION

The Greek word *enchiridion* literally means "that which is held in the hand" (*enkheiridios*, with the diminutive suffix *-idion*). An English translation that captures the bodily and material valences of the Greek might be "handbooklet," or, more idiomatically, "manual." A philosophical manual is not a "book," in the sense of a self-contained written totality.[30] Because it is constructed to guide the living of a life, it is always already a responsible text. Perhaps one could think of the *enchiridion* as the epitome of a "moral" text, to the extent that it is a written tool to be used within a certain field of embodied and intellective practice.[31] It is fundamentally situated within a heterogeneous web of practical relationships: between teacher and student, human and world, tradition and present, reason and sense. Like a conductor, the text is *activated* through these relationships while it, at the same time, *activates* them.

---

[29] Candler, 34.

[30] This attitude toward the nature of books became prominent with the invention of the printing press and the ability to mass produce bound books in the absence of schools of reading or long processes of copying. One can also ascertain why the modern material nature of the book would give way to more fixed notions of authorship. The notion of the autonomous and totalized book defined by its reproducible material boundaries and the subjectivity of the author, however, have come under much recent criticism, more notably by Jacques Derrida in *Of Grammatology* (Baltimore, MD: Johns Hopkins Press, 1967).

[31] That is, the text is moral in the general sense of pedagogically forming human persons to be better disposed toward a good life.

The earliest and best known example of this moral genre is probably the *Enchiridion* of Stoic philosopher Epictetus (55–135 CE). It presents itself as a memory aid that Epictetus gave his students, and its form matches its apparent aim: It is brief, able to be carried in hand, and full of concise exhortations to be repeated in the course of everyday life to trigger better modes of discerning worldly necessity from contingency. By using the handbook, Epictetus' students could train their faculties, practicing various reminders to guide them in "reading" their situations and forming the proper rational and affective reactions to them. Look, for example, at the *Enchiridion*'s opening chapter:

Remember that if you mistake what is naturally inferior for what is sovereign and free … you'll meet with disappointment, grief and worry and be at odds with God and man. But if you have the right idea about what really belongs to you and what does not, you will never be subject to force of hindrance.[32]

Here, the handbook addresses a situation in which a student is likely to misapply a notion of sovereignty to an object that is, in fact, not capable of sovereignty. The handbook guides a more accurate formation of judgments from which more fitting thoughts and emotions will follow.

This exercise, and the writing that facilitates it, presumes a very specific pedagogical framework, one that bears a striking resemblance to the framework Calvin would later articulate in his *Institutio*. Like other Stoic philosophers, Epictetus argued in his *Discourses* that humans are endowed with "preconceptions," or traces of ideas like goodness, justice, and divinity. Yet, because human beings routinely fail to apply those preconceptions to life with clarity and consistency, we are plagued by false opinions and unhappiness.[33] Epictetus' teaching supplies practical tools to "apply [preconceptions] to particular objects and events in a methodical manner."[34] While Calvin's articulation of divine providence leads him to hold a different, more personal understanding of necessity, his theory of knowledge is developed around a similar account of human beings whose inborn *faculties* – specifically, the *sensus divinitis* or sense of the divine – will routinely fail to accurately interpret external experience.

---

[32] Epictetus, *Discourses and Other Writings* (London: Penguin Books, 2008), 221.
[33] Epictetus, *Discourses*, 98.   [34] Epictetus, *Discourses*, 100.

The first six chapters of the 1559 *Institutio* offer an extended account of how the fall into sin distorts what Calvin sees as an original relationship between the human faculties and the creation through which humans ought to be able to not only know, but perceive and love God. The *Institutio* opens with the claim that "the knowledge of God and of ourselves" [*cognitio Dei et nostri*] are "joined by many bonds," and it proceeds to position this cognitive relationship in a fully sensible and emotive context: "No one can look upon himself without immediately turning his thoughts to the contemplation of God, in whom he 'lives and moves' ... indeed, our very being is nothing but subsistence in the one God" (*Inst.* 1.1.1). Ultimately, the proper firing of perception and the cognitions that follow should shape and undergird the natural function of the human desires that drive the will: "The knowledge of ourselves not only arouses us to seek God, but also, as it were, leads us by the hand to find him" (*Inst.* 1.1.1).

Ontically, God is given to be known in one privileged location: the created world itself that bears divine marks and serves as the theater of divine glory (*Inst.* 1.5.8; 1.6.2; 1.14.20). Calvin argues repeatedly that this created world is the deliberately chosen site of primary divine revelation: "the very order of nature" ought to have led to the knowledge of God (*Inst.* 1.2.1), and underscores that this knowledge [*cognitio*] is one made possible through a materialized and embodied relationship. For example, God "daily discloses himself in the whole workmanship of the universe" and "show[s] himself in the visible splendor of his apparel, ever since in the creation of the universe he brought forth those insignia whereby he shows his glory to us, whenever and wherever we cast our gaze" (*Inst.* 1.5.1). Such a perceptive relation thus provides the very basis through which a person could properly cognize the divine: "This skillful ordering of the universe," Calvin writes, "is for us a sort of mirror in which we can contemplate God" (*Inst.* 1.5.1). It also provides the basis for the satisfaction of human desires: "No one gives himself freely and willingly to God's service unless, having tasted his fatherly love, he is drawn to love and worship him in return" (*Inst.* 1.5.4).

Epistemically, this knowledge is generated through the sense of the divine, a special faculty that acts as a receptor for the excessive divine dimensions of concrete experience. Calvin calls it a "natural instinct," "naturally inborn in all and fixed deep within, as it were in the very marrow" (*Inst.* 1.3.1; 1.3.3). It enables God's glory to be seen in the natural world as a kind of peripheral flicker – in and behind the natural world, akin to an experience *of* the divine intertwined with immanent sense data. It is a natural (or created) means by which humans actually behold the world as "divine art"(*Inst.* 1.5.1–3).[35] He even adds that it would not be altogether wrong to say that "nature is God," provided that it "proceeds from a reverent mind" that understands nature properly as "order prescribed by God" (*Inst.* 1.5.5). Calvin's willingness to positively consider the claim that "nature is God" underscores how intimately the sense of the divine intertwines transcendence and immanence when constructing objects of perception.

This is crucial to understanding the structure and phenomenology of sin, as Calvin understands it. Sin involves, but cannot be exhaustively described as the failure to obey God. It is much more holistically the failure to live by God's word, which results in a holistic malfunctioning of all human faculties. The *sensus divinitatis* looks for a divinely mediated relationship in and to other existing things, but because it suffers from depravity – *depravitas*, or crookedness – the signification fails, and the mind generates distorted objects of experience. Fallen human beings "do not ... apprehend God as he offers himself, but imagine him as they have fashioned him in their own presumption. When this gulf opens, in whatever direction they move their feet, they cannot but plunge headlong into ruin" (*Inst.* 1.4.1). Serial misapprehension causes "dread even to the point of loathing" (*Inst.* 1.3.3; 1.4.4) as well as "confused knowledge." Human beings are deeply affected by an idea of God that surrounds them but ultimately overwhelms, exceeds, and escapes them. Rather than responding to an "inescapable power" that "hangs over them" (*Inst.* 1.4.4) with piety and reverence, people tend to opt for pride and a kind of stubbornness that clings to idols for comfort.

Edward Adams is among those who have noticed that the notion of a *sensus divinitatis* is indebted to the Stoic philosophy that Calvin studied so deeply in his youth, writing that it is "established beyond any serious doubt that Calvin draws his theory of the *sensus divinitatis* from the Hellenistic philosophical dogma of the 'preconception' of God."[36] Seneca

---

[35] It should be noted that a close reading of this concept bears little resemblance to contemporary ideas of intelligent design. Calvin is not offering a rational argument for a certain kind of material requiring a certain kind of intelligent cause, but rather the simultaneous experience of nature *as* art. If anything, Calvin's view is much closer to the Stoic view that the difference between nature, chaos, and providence are located in persuasion concerning the whole, and the mind's relation to the world rather than in the raw matter of the world itself.

[36] Edward Adams, "Calvin's View of Natural Knowledge of God" in *International Journal of Systematic Theology* 3/3 (2001): 280–292.

and Cicero, whose writings would occupy Calvin repeatedly over the course of his life, insist that "belief about gods is implanted in everyone," "as if engraved in the mind."[37] These preconceptions enable the proper apprehension of ordinary objects, at the same time allowing human beings to recognize "the source from which (s)he came," or *notitia Dei*.[38] In this sense, the knowledge of God and self are intertwined with the ability to know, in an ordinary sense, objects of experience.

The similarities between Stoic and Calvinian accounts of knowing lead to similarities in pedagogical strategy. Along these lines, Calvin frames scripture in a way that recalls the use of the *enchiridion* as an accommodation to enable a broader practice, or as a mediatory tool to enable and restore the operation of the *sensus divinitatis*:

Just as old or bleary-eyed men and those with weak vision, if you thrust before them a most beautiful volume, even if they recognize it to be some sort of writing, yet can scarcely construe two words, but with the aid of spectacles will begin to read distinctly; so Scripture, gathering up the otherwise confused knowledge of God in our minds, having dispersed our dullness, clearly shows us the true God. This, therefore, is a special gift, where God, to instruct the church, not merely uses mute teachers but also opens his own most hallowed lips ... He has from the beginning maintained this plan for his church, so that besides these common proofs (by way of the sense of the divine) he also put forth his Word, which is a more direct and more certain mark whereby he is to be recognized (*Inst.* 1.6.1).

If divine glory is perceptible in the theater of the world, then scripture is the primary tool to facilitate that perception. Scripture performs this task by relating signs to things in a way that both upsets and also enhances the perception of ordinary objects: by, for example, referring to clouds as divine chariots while allowing that they are also water vapor (*Inst.* 1.5.1). What is crucial for the Stoic *enchiridion*, and what visibly reemerges with Calvin's argument for the use of scripture, is an account of the use of written signs to clarify the faculties within a field of practice.

Of course, there are differences too, not least of which is the fact that Calvin seems to assume an extra layer of mediation. He is assuming the role of teacher and offering a pedagogical text in order to guide the interpretation of the privileged *enchiridion* (teacher) given by the privileged teacher (God). In the final preface, he writes, "For I believe I have so embraced the sum of religion [*religionis summum*] in all its parts, and

---

[37] Seneca, *Epistle* 117.6; Cicero, *On the Nature of the Gods*, 2.12.
[38] Matt Jackson-McCabe, "The Stoic Theory of Implanted Preconceptions" in *Phronesis* 494 (2004): 323–347.

have arranged it in such an order, that if anyone rightly grasps it, it will not be difficult for him to determine what he ought especially to seek [*quaerere*] in Scripture, and to what end [*scopum*] he ought to relate its contents."[39] Why, for Calvin, must Christian pedagogy be layered in this way, and why should the *enchiridion* require the use of another *enchiridion*? This hinges on certain differentiating features of Christianity – specifically, the differences between ignorance and sin, and the accompanying differences between teachers of wisdom and the full import of a redeemer who saves by *incarnating* teaching. To help narrate how these differences affect the evident generic differences between Epictetus's *Enchiridion* and a text like Calvin's *Institutio*, let me briefly turn to Augustine, who also wrote an *Enchiridion*.

In contrast to the practical, everyday tone of Epictetus's handbook, Augustine's presents itself as a compendium of abstract doctrine. Its structures are not built around common experiences but around traditional orders of teaching. Like Calvin's later text, the Apostles' Creed and the Lord's Prayer supply the handbook's order, fleshing out the general categories that follow the theological virtues of "Faith," "Hope," and "Love." At first glance, Augustine's version doesn't look much like an *enchiridion* at all, but more like an anterior echo of later systematics that want to build conceptual tableaus of the contents of Christian belief. But if one considers Augustine's *Enchiridion* alongside his other hermeneutical manual, *De Doctrina Christiana*, it is possible to understand the sense in which doctrine itself can be approached as a mediatory tool. The differences and similarities turn on the role that the incarnation plays in Augustine's own logic of pedagogy.

The incarnation is a divine gesture through which eternal Word took on temporal Flesh. For Augustine, this gesture analogically anchors the reliability of language in assuming a meaningful relationship to being.[40] The incarnation, as an object of faith, supplies the condition for the possibility that a finite being can learn and progress in the truth. It is, in a sense, a claim about a fundamental relationship between Word and Thing that asks to be unpacked. The act of unpacking – which is the whole of the theological task – actively repositions the human person in the world more generally. The incarnation structurally replaces the role of

---

[39] Jean Calvin, *Institutes of the Christian Religion*, ed. McNeill, trans. Battles (Louisville, KY: Westminster John Knox, 1960), 4.
[40] This is related to Calvin's *duplex cognitio*, though in ways that betray some important differences. I'll return to this in Chapters 5 and 6.

the Stoic preconception, to the extent that it gives an account of how learning is possible. According to Augustine, "All teaching is teaching of either things or signs, but things are learned through signs" (*DDC* 1.4). To *learn* the Christian faith means learning to use signs in such a way that one can assume a proper relation to things, and ultimately the one "thing" that does not point beyond itself: God.[41] The incarnation is the end or goal of this teaching, but it also makes the exercise of the teaching possible: "Although [the Word made Flesh] is actually our homeland, it has also made itself the road to our homeland" (*DDC* 1.22–23).

This means that to progress in Christian teaching, it is not enough to simply assent to belief in Christ as Mediator. One must interpret *all* other things according to this central insight, which means relying on revealed signs given in scripture to better discern how things exist in relationship to one another, and ultimately in relationship to God as creator. Augustine therefore suggests that the rudimentary stages of Christian teaching are guided by two rules: the rule of faith, which asks a student to embrace the claims of Christian teaching as guideposts for its exercise; and the rule of love, which underscores the posture the student must take to the things around her – the things *to* and *through* which signs are directed to God (*DDC* 3.5–54). As with Calvin's *pietas*, these two interpretive rules are not doctrinal loci, but objective concepts that frame the dispositional and intellectual parameters *for* the exercises of judgment that form perception and lead to knowledge.

Obvious differences aside, it is possible to locate a common participatory logic of how pedagogy works in both the Stoic and Christian instances of the *enchiridion*. Both supply the reader with teachings that are meant to be used to clarify experience, and formulate better judgments and responses to it. If Epictetus provides simple teachings that facilitate the right use of preconceptions in the world, Augustine elaborates on Christian doctrine to properly situate the student within a field of experience that refers beyond itself. This means referring teaching first to the figure of Christ, who analogically typifies the relationship of immanence to transcendence, and then learning to interpret scripture and ultimately the world by unpacking this central teaching. In the preface to the *Enchiridion*, Augustine presents the handbook in these terms:

[41] To be clear, signs are given both through the causal complex of creation, thus assuming the status of natural signs, and through revelation, thus assuming the status of revealed signs (see *De Doctrina Christiana*, 2.2–9). In Chapter 5, I discuss Augustine's theory of signs in greater detail.

You write that you wish me to make a book for you to keep, what is known as a handbook, never to be let out of your hands, containing an exposition of what you have asked about, namely, what we should seek above all, what we should chiefly seek to avoid because of the various heresies ... When a mind is filled with the beginning of that faith which works through love, it progresses by a good life even toward vision, in which holy and perfect hearts know that unspeakable beauty, the full vision of which is the highest happiness.[42]

By providing a handbook, Augustine is effectively fashioning a kind of conceptual portal through which the endpoint of Christian teaching is glimpsed from the outset, and allowed to perform its work like a preconception that exists in front of and beyond the bounds of the self.[43] Human teachers are a part of the external layering through which a human being learns what is essential: not only conceptual content, but what it means to receive it and relate it.[44]

Calvin evidently had the classic genre of the *enchiridion* in mind as he composed earlier iterations of the *Institutes*. He retrospectively referred to his first 1536 edition as a *"breve enchiridion."*[45] Though the text continued to expand well beyond this neat generic category to the "tome" he refers to in the 1559 inscription, its moral and pedagogical aims remain resonant with those of a handbook. Like Epictetus and Augustine both,

---

[42] Augustine, *The Augustine Catechism: Enchiridion on Faith, Hope, and Charity*, ed. Boniface Ramsey, trans. Bruce Harbert (Hyde Park, NY: New City Press, 2009).

[43] Augustine's *Enchiridion* differs from Epictetus' in other ways. Its mediation is designed to train right belief as prior to right perception, and as such its mnemonic devices are doctrinal rather than apodictic, preparing for a vision that involves but is not strictly tied to the immanent order. Also, as the section on "Hope" makes clear, Augustine's layered and transcendent pedagogical framework maintains a role for a distinct use of language: that of prayer. To learn to re-signify the world, for Augustine, means cultivating a desire to receive gifts and aids from a source not available through repetitive training alone. The consistency of the distinction between the genre of the *enchiridion* and the genre of prayer is also apparent in Erasmus' early sixteenth century *enchiridion*, which frames "learning" (the aim of the handbook) as the companion to prayer, the two chief "weapons" in the Christian's arsenal. See John W. O'Malley, "Introduction" in *Collected Works of Erasmus: Spiritualia* (Toronto: University of Toronto Press, 1988), xliii. See also Erasmus, "Enchiridion" in ibid., 30-ff.

[44] In fact, Augustine writes that submitting to human teachers is not only necessary for one who has heard the call of the divine, it is a key part of learning to assume a proper place in the hierarchy of signification itself (*DDC* Preface 12). I'll be returning to Augustine's theory of teaching through signs in greater depth in Chapter 5.

[45] See Calvin, *Ionnis Calvini opera quae supersunt omni*, eds. Wilhelm Baum, Edward Cunitz, and Edward Reuss, 15 vols., Corpus reformatorum 29–89 (Brunsvigae, Schwetschke, 1863–1900), 31:23. See also Randall C. Zachman's helpful discussion in *John Calvin as Pastor, Teacher, and Theologian* (Grand Rapids, MI: Baker Academic, 2006), 58.

Calvin sets out to provide his students with a text to guide their "deter-minations" and "ends" while navigating a practice of discernment. Traces of Augustine's influence are especially visible in the way that Calvin retains the layered complexity distinctive to the Christian theological use of the handbook. He presents the reading of the "divine Word" as the central task to which scripture itself is directed, and he recommends his own writing as participating in layered traditions of mediation that exist to continue the tradition of drawing ordinary students to scripture as the privileged tool through which to learn the *cognitio Dei et nostri.*

Yet there is one striking respect in which Calvin's approach to mediation actually veers more toward that of his Stoic forebears, and that is located in the emphasis Calvin places on the *sensus divinitatis* as a general human faculty enabling the relationship between God and humanity. The faculty is presented as fit for receiving divine revelation prior to and in excess of the incarnation. But it is also the receptor that enables the incarnation to teach in the way that it does – that which allows Christ the Mediator to *mediate.* And what is mediated is not just transcendent information, but a particular materialization of the world itself. For Calvin, the "contemplation of heaven and earth" is directed to, and through, "the very school of God's children," which is the frame of the universe itself (*Inst.* 1.6.4; 2.6.1). If scripture recommends itself as the primary *enchiridion* given by the divine teacher and substantiated in the immanent reality of the incarnation, scripture thus exists to accommodate that originary perception of creation damaged by the fall into sin (*Inst.* 1.6.4). What this means is that while Christology still plays an important role – and a precise one, which I will explore later – there is a sense in which Calvin actually maintains a much more Stoic emphasis on the use of the text as that which mediates clarified perception of the here and now. For Calvin, as for Augustine, Christian doctrine plays a mediatory and participatory role in cultivating faith. But for Calvin, this faith is directed toward the world that the *sensus divinitatis* presents *as* the theater of divine glory. The this-worldly bent of this peda-gogical text comes into even clearer focus when considering the *Institutio* as an *itinerarium.*

THE ITINERARIUM

The *itinerarium* shares some qualities of the *enchiridion.* It enables a certain kind of living formation by activating memory and desire in the pedagogical context of a teacher and a school. For the *itinerarium,* however, the stages of teaching are explicit. The Latin root, *iter,* means journey. When teaching assumes the form of an *itinerarium*, it takes on the character of a journey with a particular path, particular exercises calibrated to stages of the path, all aimed at a particular goal. The genre of the *itinerarium, therefore,* combines mediation with movement – sequence, order, progress, and usually ascent. I've already noted that Calvin's final preface states that he was "never satisfied until the work had been arranged in the order [*ordo*] now set forth."[46] That order refers to the new arrangement of the *Institutio* into four books, leading the reader through the *duplex cognitio* of God the Creator (book one) and Redeemer (book two), and then back to the life of the believer as an individual (book three) and *in societate* (book four). With this bird's eye view, it is apparent that Calvin wants to move his reader through different domains of participation: from the natural world conceived as providence to the precise way God addresses and redeems human life; and then from the human being considered under the sign of Christ and the adoption of the Spirit, to the question of the substance and role of human institutions. In order to bring this textual movement into more focus, let me say more about the history of the *itinerarium* as a genre.

In the Roman empire, *itineraria* were quite simply maps designed to guide travelers from one place to another, but they also carry flourishes that contemporary readers may find puzzling. There is no real lack of scientific attention to detail. The *Tabula Peutingeriana* (fifth century CE) offers meticulously rendered coastlines, but alongside mythical figures and other aesthetic additions (see Figure 1).[47] To repeat Scott Fitzgerald Johnson's question, "If it is merely a route map, or primarily meant to adorn, what is the virtue of minutely rendered (and often accurate) Mediterranean coastlines?"[48]

Such apparently incongruous features suggest that ancient maps did not set out to "specialize" in one field of knowledge, but aimed to gather and relate layers of knowledge. Scientific, cosmological, astrological, and mythological truths were combined to guide travelers in a multilayered, yet integrated sense, persuading them toward a fuller

---

[46] *Inst.*, 3.
[47] The *Tabula Peutingeriana*, or Peutinger Table (named for the fifteenth- to sixteenth-century German antiquarian Konrad Peutinger) is a guide to Roman imperial roads along the Mediterranean coast, including Constantinople, Persia, North Africa, and Italy.
[48] Scott Fitzgerald Johnson, "Travel, Cartography, and Cosmology" in *Oxford Handbook of Late Antiquity*, ed. Johnson (Oxford: Oxford University Press, 2012), 571.

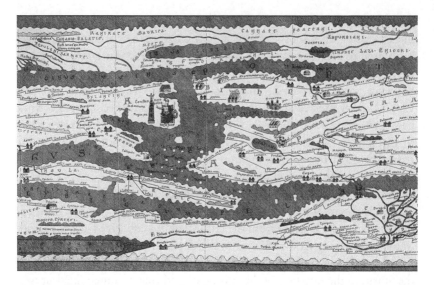

Figure 1 *Tabula Peutingeriana* (first–fourth century CE). Fascimile by Conradi Millieri (1887–8)

aesthetic and vital relation to the land, and contextualizing the larger meanings of the journey itself.[49]

These features were picked up by the medieval Europeans who redeployed *itineraria* as Christian pilgrimage guides. The earliest known example is the *Itinerarium Burdigalense* or *Bourdeaux Pilgrim* (333 CE), which presents similar layers of practical and pastoral guidance. Mileages and way stations guide the body physically to sacred monuments while prayers and meditation sites prepare the body spiritually for arrival at the city of Jerusalem – an event of both physical and spiritual significance.[50] When text of the *Itinerarium Burdigalense* ends, it opens into a fully practical topography of the city that is also structured by biblical sites. This once again blurs any hard distinction between the topographical and the theological.[51] According to Glenn Bowman,

In the *Bourdeaux Pilgrim*'s narrative the order of events is not organized with reference to the moment of observation but in terms either of a spatial contiguity

[49] Johnson, 563; 567–573.   [50] Johnson, 564.
[51] See Glenn Bowman, "A Textual Landscape: The Mapping of a Holy Land in the Fourth-Century *Itinerarium* of the Bourdeaux Pilgrim." In *Unfolding the Orient: Travellers in Egypt and the Near East*, ed. Paul and Janet Starkey (Reading: Ithaca Press, 2001), 7–40.

that collapses temporality, or ... in terms of an eschatological periodicity that render's the narrator's role extraneous ... [The] text, rather than portraying the center of an expanding [Christian] new world order, seems to manifest to its audience a space continuous to, but not continuous with, the secular world. The pilgrim who moves out of his or her native land and into that holy space seems simultaneously to "lose" himself or herself and to "find" a way out of this life and into a world that takes its being from the events and prophecies of the Bible. The *Itinerarium* thus appears to map a passage between two distinct domains: the contemporary and fallen world of the Roman empire; and another world in which time is eschatological and leads toward the eternity of promised redemption.[52]

The map is an artifact that presumes the heterogeneity of orders in order to perform relationships between them. Candler adds that the construction and arrangement of such pilgrimage maps in comparison to modern maps, imply "not only a different ordering of space, but a different orientation of the reader to the 'known' ... a mode of reading which is less comprehension of a tableau than the performance of a sequence of movements."[53]

This idea of a text that effects the layered, physical, and spiritual performance of a sequence of movements ties the traveler's *itinerarium* to the theological *itinerarium*. Indeed, medieval and early modern theological writers drew heavily from its generic form, tactically weaving together material topographies, prayers, liturgies, and scripture with an order of movement driven by desire for God.[54] Contemporary readers of theology are often trained to assume that theological texts should be approached like modern maps – as rational representations of (revealed) information. To help such readers appreciate the participatory function of *itineraria*, Candler isolates four features that strategically facilitate the more holistic participation of the reader. First, the text presents a *ductus*, or route, that is ordered and directed toward the second feature, its stated goal or *scopus*. Third, the text provides *manuductio*, or guidance – the etymology of this term suggests being

[52] Bowman, 14–15.
[53] Peter Candler, *Theology, Rhetoric, Manuduction, or Reading Scripture Together on the Path to God* (Grand Rapids, MI: Eerdmans, 2006), 2. In making this claim and throughout his book, Candler is informed by Michel de Certeau's work in *The Practice of Everyday Life*, trans. Stephen Rendall (Berkeley: University of California Press, 1984).
[54] For example, Candler points to Augustine's *Confessions,* the *Glossa Ordinaria,* Bonaventure's *Itinerarium Mentis in Deum,* and Thomas Aquinas's *Summa Theologiciae* as manifesting the participatory grammar of theological *itineraria*.

led on a "route" by "hand." Finally, the text frames the journey with *traditio,* or manuduction across time.[55]

These same four features are visible in travelers' *itineraria.* For the *Bourdeaux Pilgrim,* the *scopus* is the city of Jerusalem, and the individual movements are the *ductus.* The text itself supplies *manuductio,* while scripture fills out *traditio.* But they also inform many theological texts addressed more explicitly to their readers' souls. Bonaventure's *Itinerarium Mentis in Deum* begins and ends with the revelation of the six-winged seraph superimposed over the Crucified, which supplies both the steps of the sixfold journey (*ductus*) and the end goal (*scopus*) of the journey – the encounter with the Crucified. Bonaventure's authorial voice guides his readers (*manuductio*) by following the paths of those who have gone before (*traditio*): scripture, the teachings of the Trinity, and St. Francis who himself was led along the path by St. Anthony.[56]

Bonaventure was not alone among Latin Christian writers who, following Augustine, wrote theology in the generic structure of a guidebook. Candler argues that a great number of theological texts prior to the use of the printing press are best read as *itineraria* – perhaps especially those influenced by forms of Neoplatonism.[57] Augustine's own *Enchiridion,* despite its name, is best read as an itinerary. So is the *Glossa Ordinaria.* But later examples also abound, from Dante's *Comedia Divina* to John Bunyan's Protestant classic, *The Pilgrim's Progress.* Sometimes *manuductio* is given through the device of a literal figure: Dante's Virgil, for instance. Other times, guidance is furnished by authorial voice of the teacher, as with Augustine's *Enchiridion.* Interestingly, the Protestant *Pilgrim's Progress* most clearly ties the function of *manuductio* to the paper roll that the Pilgrim carries in his cloak – a sign, perhaps, of the early modern turn to a self-authorizing text. Across these examples, *traditio* is supplied in various ways – by references to past authorities (one might think, here, of Thomas Aquinas's *Summa Theologica*) or by reinhabiting traditional pedagogical structures such as the Apostles' Creed or the Lord's Prayer (like Augustine does, and Calvin later would). In many theological *itineraria,* the *scopus* is the divine vision.

---

[55] Candler, 7.

[56] See Bonaventure, *Itinerarium Mentis in Deum,* or *The Soul's Journey into God,* ed. Cousins (Mahwah, NJ: Paulist Press, 1978), 215, 313.

[57] For another helpful reading of theological ascent literature that places more focus on the legacy of Neoplatonism, see Robert McMahon, *Understanding the Medieval Meditation Ascent: Augustine, Anselm, Boethius & Dante* (Washington, DC: Catholic University of America Press, 2006).

Conventionally, the written itinerary will nod to the pilgrimage genre by leading its reader to a metaphorical "Jerusalem" where some form of divine vision is staged.[58] In fact, the trope of concluding with the vision of God in the heavenly city is so common that one might be tempted to treat it as a defining feature.

I've noted already that Calvin favors the language of journey and pilgrimage – a nod, surely, to the place of the wandering exile in his own context. But attention to the genre of theological *itineraria* shows that such language was also common to the Latin theological tradition Calvin assumes.[59] And Calvin's writing acknowledges this in several ways. In the 1559 preface to the *Instutitio*, Calvin describes himself as assuming the "office of teacher [*doctor*] in the church" for the purpose of maintaining the "pure doctrine [*doctrina*] of godliness [*piorum*]."[60] He introduces himself as a guide – a *doctor* of the *doctrina* who wants to "instruct and prepare candidates in sacred theology for the reading of the divine Word" – a phrase rich with Augustinian import. He then proceeds to characterize this Word as navigable by means of a guided "arrangement" and "order," through which a reader might "advance" in it, as if through the "paving" of a "road."[61] The author of the *Institutio* thus marks his own authorial voice as a guide [*manuductio*] to a path [*ductus*] that has been forged, first and foremost, by the divine signification of the Word [*traditio*]. All of these features move toward the text's aim [*scopus*], which Calvin explicitly invokes toward the end of his preface:

> For I believe I have so embraced the sum of religion [*religionis summum*] in all its parts, and have arranged it in such an order, that if anyone rightly grasps it, it will not be difficult for him to determine what he ought especially to seek [*quaerere*] in Scripture, and to what end [*scopum*] he ought to relate its contents (Calvin 1960: 5).

This is striking, on one level, because it underscores the mediatory nature of scripture itself as a tool for directing the engine of desire [*quaero*]. Certainly, Calvin's decision to figure scripture as "spectacles" would support such a reading (*Inst.* 1.6.1). After all, spectacles are not the things themselves. They accommodate the ability to see other things *through* their use. But what, precisely, *is* the end to which the *Institutio* moves?

---

[58] Candler, 44.
[59] Calvin, after all, cites Augustine eight times more than any other author aside from scripture itself.
[60] *Inst.*, 4.   [61] See *Inst.*, 3–5.

Calvin does not say. But given the fact that theological *itineraria* conventionally guide their readers to a vision of God, one might reasonably look for places where Calvin gestures toward the goal of a face-to-face divine encounter. There are indeed many such gestures. The *Institutio* begins with and often reiterates the yearning for self-knowledge that Calvin argues must be pursued along a path that begins with divine knowledge: "Again, it is certain that a human never achieves a clear knowledge of himself unless he has first looked upon God's face, and then descends from contemplating [God] to scrutinize himself" (*Inst.* 1.1.2). Yet, as Calvin makes repeatedly clear, the move-ment here is not one of an ascent – quite the opposite. In Calvin's order of teaching, one must paradoxically *begin* with God's face and then "descend" to scrutinize one's self. Calvin seems aware that beginning where earlier theological manuals end is no simple task, acknowledging that looking upon God's face is itself an exercise that must be exercised according to its own sequence. For Calvin, this micro-sequence is the *duplex cognitio*, or the order of teaching that begins with God as Creator and proceeds to consider God as Redeemer, where the "face" of God comes into clear relief: "First, as much in the fashioning of the universe as in the general teaching of Scripture the Lord shows himself to be simply the Creator. Then in the face of Christ he shows himself the Redeemer" (*Inst.* 1.2.1). This twofold knowledge also takes the form of a descent: The transcendent God who creates *ex nihilo* appears as the incarnate God in whom God's character can be more clearly perceived. The God who "ordered light to shine out of darkness, now has shone in our hearts to give the light of the knowledge of the glory of God in the face of Jesus Christ" (*Inst.* 2.9.1). Calvin remarks that when God appeared in this immanent form, God, "as it were, made himself visible" (*Inst.* 2.9.1).

Yet, for Calvin, divine appearances are always the result of an oper-ation of signification, or a relation through which an object of perception is materialized through the use of signs in a particular material context. The first mode of divine knowledge, that proper to God the Creator, is possible through the use of signs that relate God's existence to features of the created world itself, performing the conditions for the perception of glory in the created world:

Therefore the prophet very aptly exclaims that he is "clad with light as with a garment." It is as if he said: Thereafter the Lord began to show himself in the visible splendor of his apparel, ever since in the creation of the universe he brought forth those insignia whereby he shows his glory to us, whenever and wherever we cast our gaze. Likewise, the same prophet skillfully compares the heavens, as they are stretched out, to his royal tent and says that he has laid the beams of his chambers on the waters, has made the clouds his chariot, rides on the wings of the wind, and that the winds and lightning bolts are his swift messengers (*Inst.* 1.5.1).

God "shows himself" through the use of scriptural signs that collide metaphors with the real contours of immanent objects: light with God's garment, heavens with God's tent, waters with the floor of God's chambers. God the Creator is therefore made visible by means of those signs that reveal God through the surface that also marks God's own hiddenness – the "veil" through which Abraham could simultaneously recognize divine glory under the sign of his own mortal "dust" (*Inst.* 1.1.3). This is the same logic of signification that underwrites the ability for Christ's incarnation to reveal God's face: "[Christ] took the image of a servant, and content with such lowness, allowed his divinity to be hidden by a 'veil of flesh'" (*Inst.* 2.13.2).

Finally, this logic also enables the yet fuller revelation of the divine countenance in the life of a believer:

When first even the least drop of faith is instilled in our minds, we begin to contemplate God's face, peaceful and calm and gracious toward us. We see him afar off, but so clearly as to know we are not at all deceived. Then, the more we advance as we ought continually to advance, with steady progress, as it were, the nearer and thus surer sight of him we obtain; and by the very continuance he is made even more familiar to us. So we see that the mind, illumined by the knowledge of God, is at first wrapped up in much ignorance, which is gradually dispelled. Yet, by being ignorant of certain things, or by rather obscurely discerning what it does discern, the mind is not hindered from enjoying a clear knowledge of the divine will toward itself (*Inst.* 3.2.19).

According to Calvin, the signs of the gospel that lead the pilgrim to the face of Christ – a figure who lives, as it were, on the surface with us – eventually enable us to "with uncovered face and no veil intervening . . . behold God's glory with such effect that we are transformed into his very likeness" (*Inst.* 3.2.20). By book three, the signs that pointed to God the Creator and then to God the Redeemer begin to point back to ordinary human beings: "God's children are pleasing and lovable to him, since he sees in them the marks and features of his own countenance" (*Inst.* 3.17.5). The *sensus divinitatis*, accommodated by scriptural spectacles, comes to perceive the veil as the thing itself, and in so doing, can come to perceive the face of God in the face of the human.[62]

If the *Institutio* begins with the vision of God in order to descend to the contemplation of creation and "ourselves," the effect is to reposition the vision of God not as the literal end of the itinerary, but a *scopus* that inheres at every step, materializing the path as it goes. It is clear that Calvin emphasizes movement. It is also clear that he thinks there are deliberate steps to be taken in a certain order in order to achieve a certain goal of divine vision. But that vision only obtains when signs are related to ourselves and our immanent situation – to peculiar spheres of worldly life. By drawing his reader along a journey that never fully leaves the frame of the universe, Calvin's sequence invites the reader's participation in a constant exercise of resignification that not only reads scripture but asks at every contextual moment *to what end* should it be related. In so doing, its itinerant features actually turn back toward the function of the *enchiridion*. Like the scriptural spectacles it uses, the *Institutio* wants to enable the clarification of life in the present.

THE POLITICS OF THE ITINERARY

Two remaining features of the *Institutio* highlight the distinctively imma-nent orientation of Calvin's itinerary and gesture toward the political implications of Calvin's non-ascent. One is a trope, and the other will return us finally to the text's overall structure. Let me begin with the trope: the image of the "labyrinth," a favorite of Calvin's. The image immediately evokes the kind of scene for which a traveler might really want the help of a map. A labyrinth is a twisted path seemingly *designed* to disorient the senses. While some have linked Calvin's preoccupation with the labyrinth to the peculiarities of his psychology,[63] Muller and

---

[62] Here is the longer passage from *Inst.* 3.17.5: "Whence, also, are these works reckoned good as if they lacked nothing, save that the kindly Father grants pardon for those blemishes and spots which cleave to them? To sum up, by this passage he means nothing else but that God's children are pleasing and lovable to him, since he sees in them the marks and features of his own countenance. For we have elsewhere taught that regeneration is a renewal of the divine image in us. Since, therefore, wherever God contemplates his own face, he both rightly loves it and holds it in honor, it is said with good reason that the lives of believers, framed to holiness and righteousness, are pleasing to him."

[63] Several of Calvin's interpreters have turned to psychologizing in order to account for features of his theology. For one such attempt that focuses particularly on the labyrinth as

others rightly point out that the metaphor alludes to the myth of the founding of Athens.[64] According to that story, the hero Theseus embarks on a dangerous to journey to kill the Minotaur. Theseus is not just a random adventurer. His immediate aim is to stop the monster from devouring Athenian youth who are offered, every year, as tribute to King Minos of Crete. But to defeat the monster, Theseus has to navigate to the place where he lives: Daedalus' Labyrinth. On the way, the hero meets and falls in love with King Minos's daughter, Ariadne, and she gives him a thread to help him navigate the maze. By using the thread, Theseus is able to orient himself and defeat the Minotaur. Ultimately, this series of events leads to the death of Theseus' own father and founding of the free city of Athens.[65]

Calvin uses the image of the labyrinth at several key moments early in the *Institutes* to refer to different things and bring them in relation to one another. The first use ties the figure to the terrain of the fallen mind in its disoriented relation to God:

For each human mind is like a labyrinth, so it is no wonder that individual nations were drawn aside into various falsehoods ... For as rashness and superficiality are joined to ignorance and darkness, scarcely a single person has ever been found who did not fashion for himself an idol or specter in place of God. Surely, just as waters boil up from a vast, full spring, so does an immense crowd of gods flow forth from the human mind, while each one, in wandering about with too much license, wrongly invents this or that about God himself (*Inst.* 1.5.12).

Here, Calvin employs a double image: The labyrinth signals disorientation, and the floodwaters signal the deluge of idols that compound human forgetfulness like a hall of mirrors. The fallen mind is not just crooked [*pravitas*]. It actively erects false objects of comfort and identity that may work in the short-term, but only end up compounding disorientation, pride, and frustration. It's important to notice that Calvin does not limit the tendency toward idolatry to the individual, but also depicts the labyrinth of the soul as the bane of civic life, erecting its idols at the level of the nation.[66]

---

evidence, see William J. Bouwsma, *John Calvin: A Sixteenth Century Portrait* (New York: Oxford University Press, 1988).

[64] See Muller, chapter 4.

[65] For more detail around the myth of Theseus and its relation to the civic life of Athens, see Henry J. Walker, *Theseus and Athens* (New York: Oxford University Press, 1995).

[66] In addition to this civic valence, Calvin also uses the labyrinth to connect to Roman Catholic church teachings and practices which he finds to be extraneous, superstitious, or corrupt. For example, Calvin writes: "What is to be said of the present papacy? What

In another passage that follows shortly after, Calvin redeploys the labyrinth to refer to the "divine countenance" itself – the starting place of the journey to *cognitio Dei et nostri*. Just as the labyrinthine human mind confounds the pursuit of self-knowledge, it also confounds the ability to perceive the divine visage through the *sensus divinitatis*. Even as the student desires the knowledge of God, she is always already caught up in the maze, confused about where she began and where she is going, unable to clearly discern either the operations of her own mind or the signs of divine presence in the world. This use of the labyrinth trope invites the reader to imagine the pursuit of *cognitio Dei et nostri* not only as a journey but as a dangerous and twisted one that requires a guide:

Suppose we ponder how slippery is the fall of the human mind [*mentis lapsis*] into forgetfulness of God [*in Dei oblivionem*], how great the tendency to every kind of error, how great the lust to fashion new and artificial religions. Then we may perceive how necessary was such a written sign [*consignatio*] of the heavenly teaching [*doctrina*], that it should neither perish through forgetfulness [*oblivione*] nor be corrupted by the audacity of humans. It is therefore clear that God has provided the assistance of the Word [*subsidium verbi adhibuisse*] for the sake of all those to whom he has been pleased to give useful instruction [*erudire*] because he foresaw that his likeness [*effigie*] imprinted upon the most beautiful form of the universe [*pulcherrima mundi forma*] would be insufficiently effective. Hence, we must strive onward by this straight path if we seriously aspire to the pure contemplation of God [*syncera Dei contemplationem*]. We must come, I say, to the Word, where God is truly and vividly described to us from his works, while these very works are appraised not by our crooked [*pravitate*] judgment but by the rule of eternal truth. If we turn aside from the Word, as I have just now said, though we may strive with strenuous haste, yet, since we have got off the track, we shall never reach the goal [*ad metam*]. For we should so reason that the splendor of the divine countenance [*vultus*], which even the apostle calls 'unapproachable,' is for us like an inexplicable labyrinth unless we are conducted into it by the thread of the

likeness do they have between them? Here there is no preaching, no care for discipline, no zeal toward the churches, no spiritual activity—in short, nothing but the world. Yet this labyrinth is praised as if nothing better oared and disposed could be found" (4.7.22). Within this metaphor, then, we find a synopsis of the layers of Calvin's project: nature, the self, the church, and ultimately civic life. In Muller's words,

> The labyrinth, the maze of problems, belongs to the troubled life of the church, particularly to the church of Rome—and the term appears in Calvin's diatribe in the second section of his discussion of the 'power of the church' just prior to his discussion of the limitation of churchly power by the Word of God. We have seen the underlying point before: the Word of God is the only sure guide out of the labyrinth of human confusion (Muller, 85).

Word; so that it is better to limp along this path than to dash with all speed outside it (*Inst.* 1.6.3).[67]

Several important themes appear in this passage. First, the double image of the labyrinth and engulfment is reiterated through Calvin's use of the word *oblivio*. Of the multiple words available in Latin for forgetfulness, Calvin's choice is the one that retains the watery connotations still present in its English cognate. Like the labyrinth itself, *oblivio* has mythical connotations that trace back to the Greek word for forgetfulness, *lethe*, which is also the name for the river in Hades that bestows forgetfulness on those who bathe in it.[68] Just as waves wash over sand, the depths of oblivion pose a threat to the divine imprint on creation. This threat is counteracted only by the repeated re-inscription of the written word, which Calvin refers to as a "*consignatio*": a promissory sign and seal that unites two parties in an ongoing contractual relationship.[69] This is an early but clearly recognizable gesture to the terms through which the believer is "renamed" under the sign of Christ in book three when Calvin discusses the "covenant of adoption." Crucially, it also gestures to Calvin's theory of sacramental signification in book four, which provides the theory out of which he rethinks the institutional existence of both church and state.[70]

I'll return to both of these sites in Part III, but here, in nascent form, it is possible to glimpse how Calvin's understanding of the relationship between memory, forgetfulness, the Word, and the many references to the path signals the need for a grammar of participation. Calvin is imagining the Christian life as a journey that takes place at a remove from one's homeland, especially inasmuch as the nation itself is conceived as an idol by which the presence of divinity is represented in one

---

[67] This translation is Battles except in some cases where I have chosen what I take to be better renderings, always providing the Latin.

[68] For more on the relationships between *lethe*, *oblivion*, and the art or practice of forgetfulness in classical and Christian thought, see Marc Augé, *Oblivion*, trans. Marjolijn de Jager (Minneapolis: University of Minnesota Press, 2004); Harold Weinrich, *Lethe: The Art and Critique of Forgetting*, trans. Steven Rendall (Ithaca, NY: Cornell University Press, 2004).

[69] The connection between signs and memory also refers Calvin back to Platonic-influenced Christian thought, not least that of Augustine on whom Calvin so often draws. See Paige E. Hochschild, *Memory in Augustine's Theological Anthropology* (Oxford: Oxford University Press, 2012). The author discusses not only Augustine, but philosophical and theological uses of memory more widely.

[70] This is our first glimpse of a topic which will occupy much of our attention later, especially in Chapter 5.

particular way. In the passage, Calvin employs a number of words and phrases that depict the situation of the reader as a sequence of movements across terrain: "assistance," "strive onward," "straight path," "aspire," "turn aside," "off the track," and "reach the goal." And its conclusion ties the unmistakable mythic valences of the labyrinth and the thread to the end goal of divine contemplation. In order to free the hostages, the traveler has to navigate the labyrinth in such a way that God's true likeness is made visible. And that requires learning *how* to "read" the divine Word – a task that cannot be purely mental but involves relating the Word to the particularities of one's own context. This act requires redirecting the operation of the mind *toward* the senses with the *help* of the thread. The ability to navigate a labyrinth with a thread requires directing the mind to the fingers grasping the thread and the feet that feel their way in the dark one step at a time. Learning does not just involve the body, it is dependent on the body.

One further use of the labyrinth appears in book three, where Calvin is concerned with the means through which a Christian becomes re-signified by the life of Christ. There, he shifts the symbolic referents of the labyrinth and the thread yet again. The labyrinth now comes to refer to the nature of earthly life in general, and the thread refers not just to the Word, but to the actual life of Christ. The metaphor is, in a sense, materialized as the concrete path of embodied life marked by suffering and death, and the thread is materialized as the incarnate God who faces that suffering. Calvin writes:

Therefore, the apostle teaches that God has destined all his children to the end that they be conformed to Christ. Hence also in harsh and difficult conditions, regarded as adverse and evil, a great comfort comes to us: we share Christ's sufferings in order that as he has passed from a labyrinth of all evils into heavenly glory, we may in like manner be led through various tribulations to the same glory (*Inst.* 3.8.1).

With the full materialization of this metaphor, Calvin effectively completes the circuit between text and life. That is, he uses these signs to perform a re-materialization of the way life itself is perceived by the believer. The twisted path that links the fallen human mind with fallen perception of the divine countenance is now embedded firmly within the twists of any ordinary immanent context. Worldly life *is* a labyrinth, marked by opacity and raising the possibility of sudden suffering and death at every turn. In this last instance, however, it is not merely the written itinerary that guides the believer through the labyrinth; it is the human flesh of Christ. The re-signifying and clarifying text, mediating the reader's perception of the world, is understood more fully as a gesture of God incarnate, or a way of life.[71]

With these relationships in view, it is now possible to return to the second feature, which has to do with how the *scopus* of the *Institutio* works on the level of form and structure in relation to scripture and the divine Word. If the divine thread leads the pilgrim step-by-step through the labyrinth toward a vision of the divine countenance – not only in the human flesh of Christ but moreover imprinted on the entire universe – then the *Institutio* can be read as a comprehensive and ordered study of the *many* "ends" [*scopum*] to which the reader "ought to relate [scripture's] contents."[72] In other words, the fact that the *Institutio* relates the divine countenance to multiple domains of life – from creation to incarnation, from individuals to society – means that the "end" of theological training is neither scripture nor a transcendent vision, but the cultivation of a posture toward the material world guided by divine signs, and thereby capable of perceiving the excessive dimensions of its divine significance.

In this regard, the literal end of the text of the *Institutio* could not be more striking, especially considered in contrast to conventional theological *itineraria*. According to Candler,

> The trope of "steps" or "rungs" in a ladder is, of course, a favorite one among medieval theologians (an obvious example is John Climacus' *The Ladder of Divine Ascent*). It captures well the concept of rhetorical *ductus*, but particularly in terms of an ascent from things lower to things higher. Thus reading the account of the soul's itinerary necessarily makes of the reader a co-traveler along that very journey. Thus it is no "mere" metaphor Bonaventure employs when he describes the first six chapters of his work as "like the six steps of the true Solomon's throne, by which we arrive at peace, where the true man of peace rests in a peaceful mind as in the interior Jerusalem."[73]

In the examples I have considered – not only Bonaventure's *Itinerarium* but also Augustine's *Enchiridion* – the shape of the text is explicitly framed as an ascent that not only points to the divine vision but also affects the consummation of "theology," or of *logoi* concerning God. The company of signs enabled the journey, but these signs also conserve the

---

[71] The precise sense in which the Word is "re-signifying" will be discussed across the next two chapters, first in relation to Augustine's theory of signs, and finally in relation to Calvin's sacramental theology.
[72] *Institutes*, 5.   [73] Candler, 46.

alienation between sign and signified, or between the self and God. And so they fall away. The beatific vision at the end of a theological ascent is thus ordinarily signaled by the dissolution of words and arguments. This often appears to the reader as a sudden string of images accompanied by negations. Bonaventure effects this with the shattering image of the Crucified superimposed over the Seraph – an image that cannot be rendered in discursive form.

But one might also think of the end of the Book of Revelation, which closes the Christian Bible itself:

And I heard a loud voice from the throne saying, "See, the home of God is among mortals. He will dwell with them as their God; they will be his peoples, and God himself will be with them; he will wipe every tear from their eyes. Death will be no more; mourning and crying and pain will be no more, for the first things have passed away ... I saw no temple in the city, for its temple is the Lord God the Almighty and the Lamb. And the city has no need of sun or moon to shine on it, for the glory of God is its light, and its lamp is the Lamb. The nations will walk by its light, and the kings of the earth will bring their glory into it" (Revelation 21:4, 22–24, NRSV).

This passage shares some of the typically apophatic features of the Greek negative theological tradition indebted to Plato and Neoplatonism. For example, recall the famous negation of language that occurs with Diotima's "final vision" in Plato's *Symposium*: "First, this beauty always *is*, and doesn't come into being or cease; it doesn't increase or diminish ... when other things come to be or cease, it is not increased or decreased in any way nor does it undergo any change."[74] Or the conclusion of the ascent found in Plato's *Phaedrus*: "Being which really and truly is— without color, without form, intangible, visible to reason alone, the helmsman of the soul, the being to which the category of true knowledge applies—dwells in this place."[75] Another example is found at the close of Pseudo-Dionysius' *Mystical Theology*: "Again, as we climb higher, we say this. [The cause of all things] is not soul or mind, nor does it possess imagination, conviction, speech, or understanding."[76]

I've argued that Calvin gestures throughout the *Institutio* to the vision of the divine as the goal of the journey that is Christian teaching.[77] It is startling, then, to notice the absence of either ascent or negation as

---

[74] Plato, *Symposium*, 211a.   [75] Plato, *Phaedrus*, 246c.
[76] Pseudo-Dionysius, *The Mystical Theology* in *Pseudo-Dionysius: The Complete Works* (New York: Paulist Press, 1987), 141.
[77] See, for example, *Institutes* 1.1.2, 1.6.3., 1.11.3, 1.15.4, 2.7.8., 2.9.1., 3.11.23.

Calvin's text draws to a close.[78] Where a reader familiar with earlier forms of Christian writing might be prepared for Calvin's prose to lead away from the world toward a metaphorical Jerusalem, apophatic negations, or some kind of imagery or poetry pointing to the eternally unnameable – or at *least* replicate the creedal ending of "life everlasting"[79] – Calvin instead leads his reader more legibly in the direction of Epictetus or Cicero, or perhaps even Theseus. The last pages of the *Institutio* are concerned with civic life in any ordinary present. Calvin leads the reader effectively back to where she began: embedded in creation, but living daily life in an ordinary and flawed city – the proper domain, in classical terms, of *institutio, religio,* and *pietas.* For Calvin, the city at the end of the *Institutio* does not represent the consummation of the journey or the proper location of the divine. The journey of the *Institutio* never achieves a linear consummation – or perhaps it achieves it every time the glory of God is perceived in its proper relation to ordinary created things. One thing seems clear: The itinerary that emerges from and is directed toward *cognitio Dei et nostri* offers no particular blueprint for civic life.

To the extent that civic life enables health and wellbeing, Calvin thinks it should be embraced. In fact, he likens it to food and air (*Inst.* 4.20.3). But apart from commanding the embrace of institutional order as useful for sustaining life, the Word of God only collides with civic life in a negative sense:[80]

---

[78] It should be noted that Calvin does have a robust account of the Lord's Supper as an ascent to heaven. A number of scholars have given accounts of this ascent, including Randall Zachman in *Image and Word in the Theology of John Calvin* (Notre Dame, IN: University of Notre Dame Press, 2009), 16–17, 336f; Thomas J. Davis in *This Is My Body: The Presence of Christ in Reformation Thought* (Grand Rapids, MI: Baker Academic, 2008), 65; and Julie Canlis, *Calvin's Ladder* (Grand Rapids, MI: Eerdmans, 2010). This ascent is a crucial part of how the Lord's Supper signifies – by relating material earthly elements to the local body of Christ in heaven in order to perform a spiritual relationship between the believer's body and Christ's body. This, however, is different from an argument that the structure of the text would lead the reader along an ascent as *scopus.* Perhaps the *Institutio* is even more like Plato's *Phaedrus* in this account. It narrates an ascent before "that which is," "without color, without form," etc., before bringing the reader back down: "Beholding the truth, it thrives, it draws sustenance from it, until finally the rotation brings it round in a circle, back to the same place . . . When it gets there, the charioteer stands the horses at their manger. He puts ambrosia before them, and with it nectar to drink" (*Phaedrus,* 246c-ff).

[79] This appears not at the end of the text, but at the end of book three, showing at least that Calvin did not see himself strictly beholden to the creedal pattern.

[80] Scholars as disparate as Sheldon Wolin and Matthew Tuininga agree that for Calvin, government assumes no particular divine-sanctioned form and ought to govern according

If [kings] command anything against [the Lord], let it go unesteemed. And here let us not be concerned about all that dignity which the magistrates possess, for no harm is done to it when it is humbled before that singular and truly supreme power of God ... But since this edict has been proclaimed by the heavenly herald, Peter—"We must obey God rather than men"—let us comfort ourselves with the thought that we are rendering that obedience which the Lord requires when we suffer anything rather than turn aside from piety. And that our courage may not grow faint, Paul pricks us with another goad: That we have been redeemed by Christ at so great a price as our redemption cost him, so that we should not enslave ourselves to the wicked desires of men—much less by subject to their piety. GOD BE PRAISED [*LAUS DEO*].[81]

So concludes the 1559 *Institutio*: not with an image of divinity sur-rounded by negations of words, but with an extension of the logic that Calvin has maintained throughout. The divine Word addresses itself to creation, restoring the ability to perceive the glory of God engraved on every form of created life. The arc of the text suggests that the aim of perceiving the glory of creation is the perpetual *scopus* of a Christian journey – one with which no worldly institution should venture to interfere.

CONCLUSION

As a mediatory text, the *Institutio* leaves the reader in an ordinary city and equips the reader to assume a critical relation to it. It is important that the city is any ordinary city. It is not Geneva, nor is it the city of Jerusalem. It is not a monarchy, not a republic, and its sovereignty is unrecognized. Its task is to maintain order for the purpose of sustaining life. In this way, the language of the *Institutio* does not lift the human being upward, nor does it push itself downward to impose a transcendent order on human life. Rather, the text directs the reader outward into the maze of the world and the obliviated divine visage, enabling it to re-signify and be re-signified with the aid of a signifying thread. If there is a moment of negation, that moment is conserved in the perpetual distance

to the general guidance of prudence to maintain a more robust public good. These are aims that exceed the more particular aims of the church and that assume responsibility not merely to church members. See Wolin, *Politics and Vision* (Princeton, NJ: Princeton University Press, 2004), chapter 6, esp. 162–164, 172; Tuininga, *Calvin's Political Theology and the Public Engagement of the Church: Christ's Two Kingdoms* (New York: Cambridge University Press, 2017), 359.

[81] *Institutes*, 4.20.31.

between signs and things. Calvin refuses any collapse between heaven and earth, including the collapse of the sign with the signified. This very distance conditions the possibility for a relationship between transcendence and immanence, inviting the mediating use of the text: a use in which writing leads to learning and learning leads to writing. Rather than drawing materiality upward, or pressing signification downward, the genre of the *Institutio* suggests that divine signification moves outward, enacting the glory of God expansively by means of exploring the nature of God's active, signifying, and re-signifying relationship with immanence.[82] It remains to examine the particular movements that fill out the content of the *Institutio*: the precise way that the doctrine of providence anchors the field of practice, and the logic of sacramental signification that structures its ongoing negotiation.

---

[82] It is a question, at least at the end of this chapter, whether this enactment *is* the *visio Dei* or whether this is so only insofar as this particular pedagogical text operates within the determined limits of immanent life.

PART II

PROVIDENCE

2

The Practice of Writing Providence

Lars von Trier's 2011 film Melancholia[1] *portrays the final minutes of the earth's existence. As a stray planet barrels toward earth, with no human power capable of halting or diverting its progress, the film takes care to assure us that we cannot find easy meaning in the hope of alien life elsewhere in the universe. The earth is quite singular in that regard, and soon it will be gone.*

Before the final scene fades to black, the viewer is invited to bear the weight of human emotions elicited in the face of such a catastrophe – emotions both rare yet eerily familiar. With the film's characters, we face the fear of uncertainty, the anxiety of the suggestion that the end of our life may be sooner than we hope. When for a brief moment it seems that the imposing planet will not collide with earth after all, we join in the elation of an end deferred – a negative test result, as it were, merely postponing the inevitability of death. In the end, however, that hope proves false. As the planet looms ever larger in the sky, viewers experience a vicarious taste of that most singular of emotions: the fever pitch distention of time before an end that is helplessly inevitable and impending.

Melancholia thus allows its viewers to face the possibility of an end to end all ends: an utter end with no "yet" to follow. And in doing so, it invites us to consider the following question: What meaning may be had in dying a good death which no one will witness and no one will remember? For example, in such a

---

[1] Lars von Trier, *Melancholia*. Film. Directed by Lars von Trier (Denmark: Meta Louise Foldager, Louise Vesth, 2011).

circumstance, could we even retain the appropriate ethical tools to adjudicate whether suicide is prudent or cowardly? Could we test the abiding merit of pleasure over solemnity or of obliviousness over attention? Will it matter, if there is no final accounting?

The film does not purport to answer these questions. It does, however, place before us a curiously under-interpreted display of final activity on the part of the film's remaining characters. As the foreboding planet bears down, they assemble for themselves a small structure – a "cave" of unfastened, neatly balanced whittled[2] sticks – under which they proceed to take communal refuge. Looking into one another's faces and surrounded by the structure marking their boundaries, they keep fear at bay even as death encroaches. Theirs is a ritualized work given singular meaning by its attention to unstoppable necessity – a meaning, like the characters themselves, momentarily contained in one earthen vessel destined to turn to dust.

In this chapter, I begin a reading of Calvin's writing on providence with an eye to the posture toward immanence it generates, or the way it invests the ordinary world with meaning and frames it as a site of active participation. In the chapters that follow this one, I will closely read Calvin alongside more recent interlocutors who are interested in the affective and political ramifications of providence in and after modernity. But this chapter begins by remembering providence as a discourse that far precedes Calvin's writing, and indeed furnishes him with writing strategies and tropes that are crucial to grasping the subtle way he reoccupies the discourse. I want to argue that the extreme case presented in this world-ending scene of *Melancholia* – these emotions, and this activity – have an enormous amount to do with the thematic history of the philosophical and theological discourse around divine providence. That is, I want to argue that providence is a discourse that has often emerged precisely

---

[2] See also the following works of art: Albrecht Dürer *Melancholia I* (1514) copperplate (Städelsches Kunstinstitut und Städtische Galerie, Frankfurt); and three by Lucas Cranach the Elder: *An Allegory of Melancholy* (1528) oil on panel (National Gallery of Scotland); *Die Melancholie* (1532) oil on panel (Musée d'Unterlinden, Colmar, France); and *Melancholie* (1532) oil on panel (Statens Museum for Kunst, Copenhagen, Denmark). All at http://commons.wikimedia.org. These four depictions of melancholy draw out the dimensions of the figurations in this final film scene – apocalypse, stillness, practice, and images of ritualized whittling. In part because they place this conversation in the sixteenth century – the time period of ultimate focus in this larger project – it would be helpful to analyze these connections explicitly in a larger project.

when the figure of the living face the inevitability of death. Additionally, as the term "discourse" has come to suggest, providence has to do with more than abstract philosophical reasoning or argumentation. [3] It is an argument that is taken up in a larger activity of living, relating, and preparing that involves – but is not reducible to – its claims, reasons, and argumentation. In other words, it presents a case *par excellence* where writing has served a performative and strategic function in shaping a life and investing it with meaning.

Here, I begin to develop a framework through which to perceive connections between providential arguments, their written disposition, and the practices through which they purport to holistically shape the feelings, perceptions, and activities of persons. I am interested in cultivating an understanding of how the iterable gestures related to providence dispose and materialize different kinds of meaningful activities across time and context through engagement with particular texts.[4] Surveying some older classical and early Christian writings will help gather features and particular areas of problematization common to the developing and shifting discourse. I will develop the claim that understanding arguments about providence requires attending to the larger frameworks – animated in part through the particularity of the text – through which the meaning

---

[3] See, e.g., Michel Foucault, *Archeology of Knowledge* (Milton Park: Routledge, 2002), 28-ff, 50–51. I use this term advisedly in the wake of Foucault's recasting the term "discourse" to refer to a network of references made stable and altered through performance. However, it is not my intention to give a particularly "Foucauldian" account of providence in any constraining sense (as if such a thing were even possible, given the complexity and range of Foucault's intellectual contributions). The reading I proceed to give of "the discourse on providence" is more strictly in keeping with the theoretical account of the role of arguments in performative practices of materialization and ritualization that I gave in the book's Introduction.

Yet, I retain the term "discourse" here for two reasons. First, because I find that it captures the sense in which specific constellations of terms and ideas continually crop up around certain embodied and social areas of problematization (for example, in this case, suffering and death generate a series of argumentative concerns over nature, order, and exercises of renaming or resignification). Second, and most importantly, the term "discourse" – better than any other of which I am aware – conveys a dynamic relationship between uses of language and located, embodied, and relational practice. I am not primarily interested in the content of ideas or arguments about providence, but in the way the potential uses of ideas and arguments reshapes both the faculties of the subject and her perception of the world. This is what may most distinguish my reading alongside many other erudite readings of Calvin and providence.

[4] This methodological approach is influenced by Giorgio Agamben's *The Signature of All Things* (Brooklyn, NY: Zone Books, 2009). I will discuss Agamben in greater depth in Chapter 4.

of providence has been activated. My analysis of the historic texts, therefore, will seek to establish two things: the contours of general ritualized practices presumed by and intertwined with argumentation on providence;[5] and the kinds of concerns that repeatedly elicit and drive the act of writing on providence. Ultimately, this will yield an approach to providence that emphasizes the inseparability of practice, argument, and the embodied human questions that elicit both, setting up a reading of how Calvin's writing strategies position a reader in the world.

APPROACHING PROVIDENCE AS AN ACTIVITY

Though explicit references to providence have largely disappeared from contemporary speech, the questions they animate remain central to discussions of life – how to govern it, where to direct it, and what it means. Providence, in other words, is deeply invested in arguments about organization and management, temporality and historicity, and how life is constructively situated in relation to other lives, nature, and institutions. Philosopher Genevieve Lloyd's *Providence Lost* offers an intellectual history that privileges the question of precisely what it was that the classical discourse on providence *did* – and whether we still feel its impact, or the impact of its absence, today. Lloyd writes,

> Providence may now be largely "lost" from our secular consciousness; but it continues to exert an influence on our thought and on our lives. My intention is not to argue for a revival of providence—either by reasserting the importance of religion or by attempting to develop an alternative secular version of providence. The guiding conviction informing the book is simply that a better understanding of this largely forgotten strand in the history of Western thought can throw some light on the functioning—and increasingly the malfunctioning—of familiar ideas of free will, autonomy, and responsibility that we now so readily take as defining our modernity.[6]

---

[5] By invoking the terms "ritual" and "practice," I do not have one fixed definition in mind but rather mean to reference several features commonly associated with both. These include: repetition; enacted relation to mythical and otherwise constructed structures of meaning; acts and relationships aimed at refiguring of human subjectivity through the devices of repetition or mythical participation; enactment of varied temporal and spatial frameworks; and finally, writing that performs structured relations through genre and devices including prayer, dialogue, personal practice, and correspondence. To be clear, I do not mean instrumentalized gestures. See my fuller discussion of how I understand ritualization in the Introduction.

[6] Genevieve Lloyd, *Providence Lost* (Cambridge, MA: Harvard University Press, 2008), 1.

As I'll soon explore, providence has indeed been taken up in scholarship modernity, disenchantment, and secularization primarily as a case study in loss – or what it means to live and organize societies in the absence of transcendent grounds and determinate goals. Lloyd's work reminds us that many treatments of providence from ancient Greece to early modern thought never primarily associated providential meaning with transcendent intention to begin with.

The diversity of her investigation – from the dramas of Euripides to Spinoza's *Ethics* – focuses on the connections between providence and practices of self-cultivation that deploy writing to resignify the world and resituate the self in it. "Meaning," here, does not *primarily* rely on a transcendent, intending mind to grant purposes to isolated events, in the way that someone might ask, "What does she mean by that?" Rather, meaning refers to tactics of differentiating the dimensions of material things and asking how they generate meaning in relation to each other, in the way that one might ask, "What does that badge mean?" It is fundamentally important to keep in mind the distinction between meaning-as-intention and meaning-as-significance.[7] If some of the most

---

[7] Contemporary critiques of providence often presume that providence gives an account of the purpose or intention behind events. While I would argue that this is novel against the backdrop of the older discourse, it has become a common way of interpreting providence. It is arguably the primary mode through which providence has been articulated in recent examples of confessional Reformed theology. See, for example, this passage from the recent *Four Views on Divine Providence*, ed. Dennis W. Jowers (Grand Rapids, MI: Zondervan, 2011), where Paul Kjoss Helseth summarizes what he calls "the Reformed view" as follows, citing Princeton Seminary's Benjamin B. Warfield (1851–1921):

> According to those in [the Reformed] wing of [the Augustinian] tradition, "There is nothing that comes to pass that [God] has not first decreed and then brought to pass by His creation or providence." As B. B. Warfield makes clear in his essays on the doctrines of providence and predestination, the God of Reformed believers is no mere "godling" that is subject to forces acting "independently ... and outside of his teleological control" ... Reformed believers conclude that "all things without exception ... are disposed by Him, and His will is the ultimate account of all that occurs. Heaven and earth and all that is in them are the instruments through which He works His ends. Nature, nations, and the fortunes of the individual alike present in all their changes the transcript of His purpose (27, 29; Warfield citations are taken from B. B. Warfield's essays, "Some Thoughts on Predestination," in *Shorter Writings*, ed. John E. Meeter, 2 vols., [Phillipsburg, NJ: P&R, 2001], 9, 45; and "Predestination" in *Biblical Doctrines*, vol. 2 of *The Works of Benjamin B. Warfield* [Grand Rapids, MI: Baker, 1991], 9).

Here, the top-down orientation of providence is striking as a feature which bears consequences on the way human beings know and understand the force of providence. The roots of this are apparent in a number of arguments about providence related to the

ancient and influential works on providence are invested in rendering the world's significance, they are equally invested in furnishing tools through which human persons perceive and respond to that rendering. Here's Lloyd again:

Ideas of providence have strong emotional and imaginative force—whether in their evocation of a loving God or through the wonder elicited by ancient visions of a cosmos structured in accordance with necessary order. The intellectual content of providence has a rich history; but to fully understand it we must take into account its constant interplay with imagination and emotion ... Often, it is not a matter of adjudicating the adequacy of competing theories of providence. For providence changes according to the clusters it forms at different times with other concepts ... As those clusters shift and re-form, the emotional resonances of providence also change. Understanding the history of providence thus involves engaging with the emotions the idea evokes, and the writing strategies that philosophers have used to engage and educate those emotions. It involves taking seriously the literary dimensions of philosophical writing.[8]

Lloyd's approach thus emphasizes the layers of situatedness that permeate such writings. Through their literary artistry, they will often stage a particular dilemma or concern as the point from which argumentative discourse emerges and to which argumentative discourse is directed. In so doing, they assert that providence is always addressed to embodied human subjects: subjects who are materially located in a certain place and time facing certain constraints who interface with their worlds not only rationally, but also physically and emotionally. The variety of factors that render a certain claim about providence as persuasive are inseparable from the import of the claim itself, which means that the materiality of the body that sees, feels, and cognizes is also central to what makes a providential argument persuasive.

When providence is associated merely with a transcendent intending will, it tends to defer the conditions of embodiment, indexing

---

Reformation traditions. For example, the Westminster Confession of Faith (1647) presents providence as an objective account of God's divine power with little reference to how the doctrine is to be received or put into practice on the part of the believer. An earlier Reformed writing which displays this kind of argument can also be found in Ulrich Zwingli's treatise on providence which can be found in *On the Doctrine of Providence and Other Essays* (Durham, NC: Labyrinth Press, 1922). One striking recent *exception* to this approach is found in Richard R. Niebuhr's, *Experiential Religion* (New York: Harper and Row Publishers, 1972), 71–72.

[8] Lloyd, 4.

persuasiveness merely to syllogisms concerning divine omnipotence and asking for the *a priori* rational assent of the believer in the face of countervailing evidence. This, at any rate, is how Calvin's approach to providence is often glossed. But Lloyd locates this version of providence a century later in the work of Rene Descartes, who proposed a notion of free will that Calvin, interestingly, rejects.[9] For Descartes – who was, to be sure, drawing from medieval realist traditions, freedom is possible because the will is moved by a mind that participates in infinitude unconditioned by sensibility or embodiment. Lloyd argues that this fundamentally undermines the classical notion of "natural necessity" in a way that has since proved troubling and disorienting, and looks to Spinoza to recover what she takes to be a view of the will that comports better with the material reality of human life. Spinoza draws on ancient Greek notions of providence that index self-understanding not to the transcendent site of an infinite will, but to the whole of nature itself.[10] This she regards as a modern "road not taken," writing,

We now live out our individual lives against the background of an implicit collective belief—however irrational it may be—that the borders between the controllable and the necessary are indefinitely shiftable . . . [But bereavement often brings] the shock of recognition of the falseness of the general assumption that death can always in principle be averted.[11]

For Lloyd, a robust notion of natural necessity that takes account of limitation offers a more viable framework for reorienting the self in life and before death.[12]

Lloyd largely frames this reorientation as something that happens primarily in the imagination, writing that "to understand providence as it operates in specific texts is to enter into particular ways in which human minds have tried to accommodate themselves to their presence in the world—and to the thought of their absence from it."[13] This means reading different instances of providential discourse not as competing ideas, but as conceptual clusters that shift and realign at different times and facing different situations. This is akin to the way Agamben understands the operation of a signature, or a constellation of signs that exist only in relation to the material context the signature disposes at a given time, but also have the capacity to move across

---

[9] Lloyd, 200, 210.   [10] Lloyd, 207.   [11] Lloyd, 307–308.
[12] See Lloyd, 11–12, 210–211, 307, 317–323.   [13] Lloyd, 3–4.

discursive domains to relate one material site to another. Following Agamben, I will draw out what I take to be implicit in Lloyd's approach to providence: namely, that providence can only address the imagination by also addressing the body, and moreover by becoming practiced and habituated at the level of the body as it learns more holistically to perceive and respond to the relationships that dispose it. Providence, by virtue of addressing the imagination through literary strategies, also operates according to Catherine Bell's logic of ritualization. It acts as a mediating tool through which a subject is performed in concert with a world that is differentiated for a certain kind of activity. Just as providential reading and writing is not *merely* rational, it is also not a *merely* imaginative or emotional exercise but one that assumes and relies upon certain repeated and habituated practices through which one can relate differently both to one's immanent surroundings and to one's own self. Attention to these iterative dimensions of historical renderings of providence will prove crucial to grasping similar dimensions at play in Calvin's arguments.

I'll begin with intimations of the philosophical-doctrinal category of providence in ancient Greece, and move on to look at parallel developments in Stoic and early medieval Christian texts. I will approach each writing by paying close attention to the following four characteristics of each text, in varying orders and to varying extents: (1) the context in which the discourse is elicited and practiced; (2) the spatio-temporal frameworks activated by the discourse on providence; (3) the relation of providential meaning to nature and immanent networks of cause and effect; and (4) the activation of discourse on providence in varying and specific genres, including argument, hymn, prayer, myth, and dialogue. This will begin to clarify what it means to approach the discourse on providence as a theological doctrine that is also a mode of practice involving cognition, affection, and sense.[14]

---

[14] This reading is informed by theory on performativity and bodily citations that I discussed at some length in the Introduction and will not rehearse here. There, I drew from J. L. Austin, Jacques Derrida, Judith Butler, Catherine Bell, and Amy Hollywood to argue that writing and reading both can be fruitfully understood as a form of practice that rematerializes the world and the self through the negotiation of repetition and difference. In this chapter, I argue that these providential writings do precisely this kind of work – they reform the reader's ability to see and engage the world by offering mental and physical gestures that perform a different disposition toward the world.

EARLIER GREEK WRITINGS: CLEANTHES AND PLATO

Unsurprisingly, there is no clear origin for the discourse on providence, though it is functioning as a philosophical category in Stoic literature by the turn of the common era.[15] The purpose of this first section, however, is to look back at the tacit resonances of the doctrine before it was named *as* a doctrine. One place to look is very early in the formation of the Stoic traditions with Cleanthes (331–232 BCE), the first successor to Zeno, founder of the earliest Stoic school. In his "Hymn to Zeus," Cleanthes praises the ordering principle of the cosmos, addressing Zeus as "the Chief of nature (*physeos archege*), who steers with Your Law all things."[16] Zeus is framed as the One whose *logos* [voice, word, reason, argument] human beings must seek to *mimema* [represent, follow, imitate].[17] Cleanthes further names Zeus as the giver of being; the one whose image human beings strive to attain; the universe's guide; and the origin of its ordering Reason. As the hymn progresses, Zeus is praised not just for his position but for his activity: he "directs the common *Logos*," sets straight what is crooked, puts in order what is disorderly, fits good and bad things together, makes things unlovely seem lovely.[18]

The hymn concludes with a prayer of supplication – a prayer for aid in the activity of mimesis:

But Zeus, all giver, shrouded in the dark clouds, ruler of the thunderbolt
You must save men from baneful inexperience
which you, Father, must scatter from the soul [*psyche*]; And give that we become
    to participate
in insight [*gnomes*], by trusting in which You steer all things in justice,
in order that we, being honored, repay You with honor,
singing [*hymnountes*] of Your works, constantly, as befits one, being
a mortal, to do, since there is no greater gift to offer both for mortals and gods
than, in justice, of the universal law [*koinon nomon*] always [*aei*] to sing
    [*hymnein*].[19]

This singer of the hymn performatively desires the capacity to *better* perform the eternal hymning of the wise power of Zeus. There is a repetition between the words and the aim of the hymn itself. Its words

---

[15] As we will see in the next part of this section, Seneca pens a treatise on providence in the first century of the common era. Epictetus' (55–135 CE) *Discourses* also contains several explicit discussions on providence.

[16] Cleanthes, "Hymn to Zeus" in P. A. Meijer, *Stoic Theology* (Delft: Eburon, 2008), 209-ff.

[17] Cleanthes, 210.   [18] Cleanthes, 213–218.   [19] Cleanthes, 223.

acknowledge the distance between the human addresser and the divine addressee, but their very utterance is designed to close that distance by inverting the relationship between the addresser and addressee. Zeus becomes the active origin of the "nature" that also encompasses human life, the one whose image stamps the human image, and the one whose *logoi* human beings strive to mimic, echo, or represent. The hymn is thus constructed to enact its own prayer by turning the orientation of the prayer. In this way, the hymn hopes that the words shaping and guiding the cosmos will also shape and guide the soul [*psyche*] of the human into one that befits the ordering of the cosmos.

There is a ritual structure here. In naming Zeus, the speaker activates a practice through which the speaker's life is submitted to a strategy of iterative resignification that will refashion the order of the speaker's life. Zeus is honored as both origin and active guide, and by saying, praying, and singing the works of Zeus, the singer performs the work of moving from imitation to actually attaining participation in the space and time of Zeus's divinity in relation to the world. The language that will later come to define providence – language of ordering, fitting, steering, guiding the cosmos – permeates the poem. This language serves to enact a venue in which the speaker is able to say Zeus's *logoi* with Zeus, and thus to begin to imitate (*mimema*) and ultimately to participate with Zeus in ordering nature. The closing lines seal this activity as the proper activity of mortals. By singing, by *hymning* the origin and guide, this writing invites mortals to attain what is "fitting" for their mortality – to attain a part in the perpetuity (*aei*) of the divine and universal law enacted by Zeus's care for the world.[20]

Even prior to Cleanthes' hymn, hints of the discourse on providence are visible in several of Plato's dialogues (*approx.* 424–348 BCE). The clearest example of these early echoes may be observed in the *Timaeus,* which Lloyd discusses in *Providence Lost.* The dialogue draws layers of synecdoches between the body, the ideal state and its ideal citizens, and the founding of Athens itself, finally embedding that story in the story of the founding and nature of the universe. Throughout, one can discern recognizable intimations of the discourse on providence. According to Lloyd,

Necessity, chance, and design are interwoven in an intricate dance throughout the *Timaeus* narrative . . . The notion of providence—of the adapting of things to their

---

[20] Even in this early articulation of providential discourse, it's interesting to note that *pronoia* is implicitly opposed to its opposite: *paranoia*.

natures—allows Plato to move between what might otherwise be disparate accounts of the world and of human behavior within that world. Providence is a central concept in the content of the story. It is also methodologically crucial, determining what will and will not be included. It guides the construction of the narrative. As the story proceeds through the generation of the human body and its members, and of the human soul, Timaeus reminds his listeners that the whole narration is a story of how things must have come to be—"for what reason and by what providence [*pronoia*] of the gods; and holding fast to probability, we must pursue our way" (*Timaeus* 44d). Providence is here the other side of the coin to Timaeus's version of "probability." It is what allows the story to carry its own force of necessity: this is how things must have been; this is how "we must pursue our way" (*Timaeus* 48d).[21]

Here, providence is discernable not as an accepted claim, but as an argument that arises to offer a persuasive model of order and shape undergirding the present circumstances of life. The necessity spoken of here is not a mathematical form of necessity as much as a strong sense of what Lloyd calls "fittingness" – a heightening of one's sense of persuasion that, given present experience, things *had to have been* arranged in a certain way.

Furthermore, the dialogue, again and again, connects the question of origins to the matter of ethics. Socrates' opening association between the form of the ideal state and the character of its ideal citizen is repeated as the continuing layers of dialogue on the origins of Athens and the universe continue to relate to the nature of ethical life. While Lloyd does not explicitly name the function of providence in this dialogue as a ritualized activity of moral formation, her language captures the heart of this assertion. She writes,

Timaeus's conclusions can indeed seem arbitrary and bizarre. Yet his reasoning is designed to appeal to intellect, imagination, and emotion all at once. It relies on a sense of fittingness ... which cannot be readily separated out into a level of pure logic and the attendant layers of imagination of emotion that embellish it. It appeals to the soul as a dynamic unity. What we have here is no mere dressing up of something that could—without loss of persuasiveness—be presented as bare logical argument.[22]

This observation offers us the crucial insight that, even in early traces of the discourse on providence, claims about providence were inseparable from the human questions that give birth to the discourse itself.

---

[21] Lloyd, 62, 63–64. [22] Lloyd, 65.

The signatures activated by the speaking or writing on providence – constellating questions of origin, causation, order – function to situate the self such that living activity and meaning become inseparable from, and formed by, the telling itself.

There is another place in Plato's corpus where providence plays a role. This time, however, the resonances emerge – with a slightly different tenor – precisely out of the theme of physical death and the scene of dying. The setting is Socrates' own death, as told in the *Phaedo*. Throughout much of the dialogue, a chorus of companions enact the preparation for this death by gathering around their teacher as time moves to the final inevitability of his passing. The *Phaedo*, like the *Timaeus*, also references the founding of Athens – but this time through the invocation of a layer of mythical time. The time of Socrates' death, we are told, will coincide with the return of the ritual reenactment of the city's founding by the hero Theseus, who had departed to navigate the labyrinth and slay the Minotaur who had been devouring Athenian youth. The execution had been delayed due to the departure of a ship which, upon its return, inaugurates the ritual celebration of Theseus' return. During the interim of the ship's departure and arrival, tradition holds that no executions will take place.[23] The dialogue begins when the ship returns, signifying both the origin of Athens and Socrates' execution at the hands of the city itself.[24]

It is interesting to note the extent to which the activity of the dialogue resonates with certain respects of the final scenes of *Melancholia*. The companions of Socrates gather around him, knowing it will be the last such gathering. The time of the dialogue is heightened and distended by the constant vigilance around an end that is both so final and so near. This activity recalls, or perhaps prefigures, that animated in Cleanthes' "Hymn to Zeus": music, *logoi*, perpetuity. Here, however, the music is not elicited by a prayer but is presented as a response to a sacred "duty" – that of keeping at bay the corrosive fear of death.[25] And the *logoi* are not depicted merely as an object of imitation, as in Cleanthes' hymn. They are actively whittled and assembled for use by those gathered. This practice of argumentation, of assembling *logoi*, performs the community's preparation for death[26] by also performing the structure of eternity.[27] Indeed, the final gathering is quite literally structured by the act of building – picking up, putting down, undoing, and reshaping one argument after another.

---

[23] Plato, *Phaedo*, 58b.   [24] *Phaedo*, 59e.   [25] *Phaedo*, 60e–61b, 77e.
[26] *Phaedo*, 64a.   [27] *Phaedo*, 89b-d.

But as Socrates' death becomes imminent, yet another form of structuring activity emerges: the activity of *mythos*, or storytelling. As the sun begins to set, Socrates' last argument draws to a close. He has made one final case, using the tools of philosophy, for the immortality of the soul. Even as he leaves off, however, he suggests that the task of crafting the *logoi* will outlast his mortal body. The dialogue recounts this as follows:

SOCRATES: Then when death attacks a person, the mortal part, it seems, dies; whereas the immortal part gets out of the way of death, departs, and goes away intact and undestroyed.

CEBES: It appears so.

SOCRATES: Beyond all doubt then, Cebes, soul is immortal and imperishable, and our souls really will exist in Hades.

CEBES: Well, Socrates, for my part I've no further objection, nor can I doubt the arguments [*logoi*] at any point. But if Simmias here or anyone else has anything to say, he'd better not keep silent; as I know of no future occasion to which anyone wanting to speak or hear about such things could put it off.

SIMMIAS: Well no, nor have I any further ground for doubt myself, as far as the arguments [*logoi*] go; though in view of the size of the subject under discussion, and having a low regard for human weakness, I'm bound to retain some doubt in my mind about what's been said.

SOCRATES: Not only that, Simmias, what you say is right, so the initial hypothesis, even if they're acceptable to you, should still be examined more clearly: if you can analyze them adequately, you will, I believe, follow the argument to the furthest point to which a human being can follow it up; and if you get that clear, you'll seek nothing further.[28]

Socrates, acknowledging the need for continued argumentation, nonetheless shifts gears in the final minutes of his time. He puts down the argument and picks up a different kind of discourse: a myth of the nature of the universe. By embedding his arguments for immortality in this larger myth, Socrates functionally embeds the individual's immortal soul in a larger framework or structure that supports it, orders it, or, in Socrates' words, "cares" [*epimeleias*] for it. "But it's fair to keep in mind, friends,"

---

[28] *Phaedo*, 106e–107b.

he instructs, "if a soul is immortal, then it needs care, not only for the sake of this time in which what we call 'life' lasts, but for the whole of time."[29] In a manner different from but resonant with the storytelling of the *Timaeus*, Socrates' myth constructs a picture of the geography of the soul's dwelling in the afterlife so that, according to Socrates, the wise and "well-ordered" soul will not be unfamiliar with what befalls it.[30] This geographical imagery repeats the function of embedding at yet another layer: It situates the earth itself in a cosmos more grand. After finally describing the form of judgment under which the soul is called to account,[31] Socrates concludes as follows:

> Now to insist that those things are just as I've related them would not be fitting for a man of intelligence; but that either that or something like it is true about our souls and their dwellings, given that the soul evidently is immortal, that, I think, is fitting and worth risking, for one who believes that it is so—for a noble risk it is—so one should repeat such things to oneself like a spell; which is just why I've so prolonged the tale [*mythos*].[32]

The seeds of the discourse on providence are legible in the language of "order" and that which is "fitting" as proper aims for the kind of myth-making that can properly care for a soul facing death.

Like the *Timaeus*, the *Phaedo* refuses to draw a firm distinction between practices of making *logoi* and the practices of making *mythos*. Philosophical argumentation and storytelling are bound together, layered to form and guide not only the discursive intellect but also the relation of the intellect to emotions and sense perception. Socrates' final myth encases and protects the soul that has been invigorated by arguments. Together, these function as crafted tools for alleviating fear and forming emotions so that the soul becomes well-ordered to the cosmos, able to face what is inevitable.[33]

Finally, the ritualizing context of the dialogue is explicit. Not only does it unfold in a time layered over the ritual repetition of the founding of Athens, but places providential activity in a related but also tensive relationship to politics. The dialogue also performs a series of ritual repetitions in the midst of a community gathering. Arguments are exchanged and repeated.[34] Myths are crafted with the injunction to "repeat such things like a spell," for the care of the soul requires that

---

[29] *Phaedo*, 107c.   [30] *Phaedo*, 108a.   [31] *Phaedo*, 113d–114c.   [32] *Phaedo*, 114d.
[33] The inevitability of Socrates' death factors in at several occasions: see *Phaedo*, 116d, 117a.
[34] See *Phaedo*, 106e–107b, quoted earlier.

one learns to dwell in a structure befitting that soul.[35] Later Stoics and early Latin Christians would liberally pick up strands from these early instances of the discourse on providence – repeating, innovating, and refiguring them for later uses. In certain ways, these later authors render the doctrine more coherent as a locus of teaching. This enables them to more directly index their use to the generation of certain emotions deemed fit for facing suffering and death. Rarely, however, is the call to put arguments to work in care of the mortal body so central as it is in these earlier writings.

LATER LATIN WRITINGS: STOICISM AND BOETHIUS

Though somewhat staggered in time, it could be argued that Stoic and early Christian writings on providence constitute parallel approaches deriving from the traditions of writing just surveyed. This section can do no justice to the array of writings that emerged in the first five centuries of the common era. But I do want to look at several cases in order to chart some of the most vivid features informing the distinct trajectories of Stoicism and Christianity. This is important because I've already noted the importance of both Stoicism and Latin Christianity on Calvin's education and his mature thinking.[36] In this section, I will pinpoint two trends, existing in tension with one another, that set the stage for Calvin's later appropriation of providential teaching. First, there is the close proximity of the divine to immanent necessity that permeates the Stoic writings of the common era. Second, there is the increasing distance between God's being and God's providence that informs Christian claims to divine transcendence. This discussion will note a number of repetitions with features of providential discourse highlighted in the previous section,

---

[35] Again, *Phaedo*, 114d, quoted earlier.

[36] I've learned much from previous scholarship on Calvin's relation to Stoicism and early Christian thought, and my intention here is not to replace or critique that scholarship, but to further explore the shared attitudes toward argument and embodied practice that cut across these disparate bodies of writing. For a selection of this literature, see Charles Partee, *Calvin and Classical Philosophy* (Louisville, KY: Westminster John Knox Press, 2005); David Steinmetz, *Calvin in Context* (Oxford: Oxford University Press, 2010); Kyle Fedler, "Calvin's Burning Heart: Calvin and the Stoics on the Emotions" in *Journal of the Society of Christian Ethics* 22 (Fall 2002): 133–162; Olivier Millet, *Calvin et la dynamique de la parole: Etude de rhétorique réformée* (Librairie Honoré Champion, 1992); Serene Jones, *Calvin and the Rhetoric of Piety* (Louisville, KY: John Knox Press, 1995).

including the association with ritual practice, the use of the discourse for self-formation before death, and the association of the discourse with genres of writing that include but also reach beyond the conventions of philosophical argument.[37]

In the first century of the common era, Seneca wrote a treatise on providence, *De Providentia*, in response to a petition from his friend Lucilius, the Roman governor of Sicily. Such a title serves to authorize the discourse on providence in a way it had not been authorized in the earlier texts surveyed. Providence, here, is deployed in service of a political governor, but it nevertheless wants to prepare him to lead in the face of the kinds of challenges that traditionally elicit providential arguments. The text begins as follows: "You have inquired of me, Lucilius, why, if the world be ruled by a providence, so many evils befall good men?"[38] Seneca proceeds to echo a theme seen earlier in Cleanthes, namely that to pursue the doctrine of providence is to pursue participation in structuring divine *logoi*. "I will do what is not difficult," Seneca writes. "I will plead the cause of the gods."[39] He expands on this as follows:

I will reconcile you to the gods, who are kindly disposed to the best men. For nature never suffers the good to injure the good. Between good men and the gods exists a friendship—virtue being the bond; friendship do I say? nay rather a relationship and a similarity, since, indeed, a good man differs from a god only in time, being his pupil, follower, and true child, whom that glorious parent—no light exactor of virtues—trains more severely than others, after the manner of strict fathers.[40]

His reiteration of the relationship of imitation between humans and the divine sets the stage for Seneca to address the question of evil: "Let the same thing be clear to you concerning God; He does not spoil a good man by too much tenderness; He proves him, hardens him, and prepares him for Himself."[41] Goodness is immediately dissociated from pleasure or comfort and linked instead to the ordering function that divinity performs in its relation to nature – the function of reason in relation to necessity

---

[37] For more on Stoic philosophy and providence, see Ricardo Salles, *God and Cosmos in Stoicism* (New York: Oxford University Press, 2009); Mark S. M. Scott's also provides a helpful summary connecting Stoic views to early Christian views in *Journey Back to God: Origen on the Problem of Evil* (New York: Oxford University Press, 2012), chapter 2.

[38] Seneca, *De Providentia*, 1. This and all citations of *De Providentia* point to the chapter notation rather than to page numbers.

[39] Seneca, 1.   [40] Seneca, 1.   [41] Seneca, 1.

that will constitute the aforementioned relation of similarity between the human "child" and the divine "parent."[42]

In Seneca's opening words on the character of providence, it becomes apparent that providence is not conceived as a rule or decision made by a mind apart from nature and subsequently imposed on nature. Providence signifies an ordering aspect *within* nature. According to Seneca, to admit the existence of providence means admitting "that it is not without some guiding hand that so great a work [as nature] continues to exist, that this assemblage and running to and fro of the stars are not effected by an accidental impulse . . . and [that] so great a mass of brilliant lights which shine according to the will of their disposer, goes on by the command of an eternal law."[43] Providence, then, is simply a technical term for a certain cultivated posture that enables one to perceive nature according to its law. Lucilius' complaint is not that providence does not exist, but that Lucilius finds himself in discord with the workings of providence. Seneca's writing, therefore, aims to articulate the larger structure of providential ordering active in nature in order to aid Lucilius' participation in this form of divine perception. "But now," Seneca begins in chapter 3, "I will show that what appear to be evils are not so."[44] Lucilius' therapy, therefore, amounts to a form of submission to subjective reformation.

He proceeds to work through a series of analogies – medical, surgical, martial, natural – to shape a conception of good dissociated from pleasure, thus allowing Lucilius to conceive of suffering and death as part of the improvement of natural being.[45] Seneca's aim is not to argue for a mere self-sacrifice to some "greater good," however. On the contrary, he seeks to enact an "I" that can be realized at one with the divine "I." He cites a speech of Demetrius: *"I suffer no constraint, I endure nothing against my will, nor am I a slave to God, but I am in harmony with Him*

---

[42] Seneca explicitly associates the ordering principle not just with the divine parent, but the divine *father* – no doubt drawing an analogy to the order of the Roman family, although the relation of this imagery would be interesting to track into later texts on providence. He writes: "Do you not see how fathers show their love in one way, and mothers in another? The father orders his children to be aroused from sleep in order that they may start early upon their pursuits – even on holidays he does not permit them to be idle, and he draws from them sweat and sometimes tears. But the mother fondles them in her lap, wishes to keep them out of the sun, wishes them never to be unhappy, never to cry, never to toil. Toward good men God has the mind of a father, he cherishes for them a manly love, and he says, 'Let them be harassed by toil, by suffering, by losses, in order that they may gather true strength'" (Seneca, 2).

[43] Seneca, 1.   [44] Seneca, 3.   [45] Seneca, 3–4.

[sic]; *and so much the more because I know that all things move on forever according to a certain and fixed law.*"[46] Just as the human body is part and parcel with nature, the human mind participates in the divine ordering principle of nature. Submission of the body to natural necessity therefore functions to fine-tune the mind to the workings of the law [*nomos*] at the heart of nature's providential operation. Why should one fear the body's natural decay, Seneca asks, when the mind can achieve participation in the eternal through that very submission? Understanding this very truth – that one's time of suffering and dying is inevitably approaching in nature's flux – is a means of aligning one's own self to that of divinity.

Seneca insists furthermore that it is precisely in relation to the perception of nature's necessities that such participation can be achieved. He argues that "those ... whom God proves and loves, He hardens, examines, and exercises: but those whom He seems to indulge and spare, He is keeping because of their weakness for evils yet to come. You are mistaken if you think anyone is exempt."[47] The one who can gird up the strength to face suffering and affirm necessity, however, will rise like the sun over the earth: "I do not say that he does not feel them, but he overcomes them and even quietly and calmly rises superior to their assaults."[48] Such a result is possible and furthermore laudable because, in this recognition, one becomes properly aligned to a reality in which the divine principle, the eternal law, is immanent to the operation of nature itself. "Whatever it is which commanded us thus to live, and thus to die," Seneca continues, "binds the gods also by the same necessity: an unchangeable course carries along human and divine affairs alike."[49] This form of teaching comes with its own affective outcome: that of *ataraxia*, or calmness before things properly cognized as inevitable. Seneca has effectively given a name and cast to Socrates' affective practice of keeping fear at bay.

Seneca's treatise thus develops some of the themes active in both Cleanthes' hymn and Plato's dialogues. The text affirms the association of the divine with the principle of ordering and guiding. It also engages in the activity of writing [*logos*] in order to close that familiar gap between human understanding and divine law. And it develops what it takes to be the affective outcome of this, one that renders a human being calm before events that one would have once misperceived as calamities. But while Cleanthes sought to narrow the gap between the divine and the human

---

[46] Seneca, 5.   [47] Seneca, 4.   [48] Seneca, 2.   [49] Seneca, 5.

through hymn and prayer, and while Socrates spins myths to care for the soul, Seneca prefers the medicine of reason. Rather than approaching the divine *logos* from a posture of devotion, Seneca employs *logoi* in order to "fit," as it were, Lucilius' mind to the working of divine mind in nature. What has become of the role of *mythos*, or of enacting the structure of providence by ritualized storytelling? If providence is immanent to nature, are we to understand that providence is enacted merely by attention to the *logos*, or by giving logical arguments about natural causation? On the contrary, Seneca admits the possibility of representing natural events *as if* they are events generated by chance or fate. This suggests that the discourse on providence presents as a certain kind of crafted argument that simultaneously serves a mythical function. It both constructs a representation of nature *as* ordered and functions to enact that order through the effects of the discourse. Nature becomes providence by virtue of a story that frames its features *as if* ordered as a world of meaning fit to human experience. This narrative is woven into the modes of argumentation that present such purposes persuasively to the mind.

This more subtle function of language – ordering nature through its narrative telling *of* a certain representation of nature itself – is vividly discernible in another classic Stoic text: the *Meditations* written by Roman emperor Marcus Aurelius (121–180, CE). Here, providence is taken up explicitly by a voice who is also tasked with civil governance. The twelve books of the *Meditations* were composed as part of a personal writing practice over the course of a decade through which the emperor reflects on the panoply of themes central to providential discourse: duty, tradition, courage, suffering, and mortality.

In his second meditation, Marcus Aurelius writes, "All that is from the gods is full of Providence. That which is from fortune is not separated from nature or without an interweaving and involution with the things which are ordered by Providence. From thence all things flow; and there is besides necessity, and that which is for the advantage of the whole universe, of which thou art a part."[50] Here, as with Seneca, "providence" is distinguished but not separated from the material content of "fortune" and "necessity." All three – providence, fortune, and necessity – are simultaneously ways of perceiving the working of nature. Their distinctions are not metaphysical, but relational. They are characterizations of nature differentiated by means of the relationship one cultivates *to* nature.

---

[50] Marcus Aurelius, *Meditations*, 2. As with Seneca, citations refer to book denominations rather than page numbers.

One could say that for Marcus Aurelius, providence, fortune, and necessity are different ways of materializing the same reality.

This becomes clearer in a further quotation, which helpfully brings to
bear the concerns that elicit one's particular relation to providence. To
himself, Marcus Aurelius writes,

> Since it is possible that you may depart from life this very moment, regulate every
> act and thought accordingly. But to go away from among men, if there are gods, is
> not a thing to be afraid of, for the gods will not involve thee in evil; but if indeed
> they do not exist, or if they have no concern about human affairs, what is it to me
> to live in a universe devoid of gods or devoid of Providence? But in truth they do
> exist, and they do care for human things, and they have put all the means in man's
> power to enable him not to fall into real evils. This, however, is not only an
> operation of nature, but it is also a thing which conduces to the purposes of
> nature. To observe too how man comes near to the deity, and by what part of him,
> and when this part of man is so disposed.[51]

In a manner reminiscent of Socrates' own encounter with approaching
death, Marcus Aurelius acknowledges the usefulness of the discourse on
providence. Arguments and stories about providence are not to be treated
as matters of brute fact or as representations of a fixed reality. Providence
is a story that must continue to be told, engaged again and again with its
accompanying arguments.

In Marcus Aurelius' case, this telling drove a decade-long habit of
writing: a repetitive practice that once again signals forms of
ritualization associated with the discourse on providence. And perhaps
in this writing practice, we are to understand a repeated effort at *telling
the truth* – one that constantly repositions the whittled sticks of arguments in a structure that makes life habitable by generating calmness and
keeping fear at bay, enabling Marcus Aurelius to say, "But in truth they
do exist, and they do care for human beings." This providence is not
separate from nature but disposes nature through the use of a signature
that ties nature to concepts like purposiveness, fitness, and necessity, thus
resignifying nature in a way that enables better living, suffering, and
dying.

In these several examples from Latin Stoic writings, it is possible to see
a distinct, but not altogether unfamiliar performance of the discourse on
providence. It is novel over and against Plato and Cleanthes insofar as
providential language has become oriented more aggressively around
arguments that render nature itself as a site of necessity. Boethius' early

---

[51] Marcus Aurelius, 2.

Christian reoccupation of Stoicism departs precisely on this point. Like Marcus Aurelius and Seneca, Boethius (480–525 CE) lived adjacent to governmental concerns. He was born of Roman nobility and served as a senator and even briefly as a regional consul before becoming *magister officiorum* over the Roman government. His writing on providence was occasioned by the reversal of that fortune. Accused of participation in a conspiracy, Boethius spent the final days of a shortened life under house arrest where he penned an allegorical dialogue, *De Consolatione Philosophiae*.[52] The dialogue reproduces the setting of the author himself, staging his pedagogical encounter with Philosophy, figured, according to classical convention, as a woman. Like other examples I've surveyed, this text is elicited by the prospect of impending death.[53] Yet, like Socrates and unlike the Stoics, the death is being caused by an unjust fiat of state violence. And unlike all of his classical forebears, Boethius' questions are being posed against the will of a transcendent God.

The text begins with the eponymous character Boethius in a state of melancholy: ill-prepared for death, yet longing for its release:

> Happy is that death which thrusts not itself upon men in their pleasant years, yet comes to them at the oft-repeated cry of their sorrow. Sad is it how death turns away from the unhappy with so deaf an ear, and will not close, cruel, the eyes that weep. Ill is it to trust to Fortune's fickle bounty, and while yet she smiled upon me, the hour of gloom had well-nigh overwhelmed my head. Now has the cloud put off its alluring face, wherefore without scruple my life drags out its wearying delays.[54]

Suddenly, a woman enters his chamber, appearing over his down-turned head and startling him, we are told, with a majestic face and fiery eyes. Her insight and her countenance meet the intellectual and temporal condition of human beings from above, bringing the air of an age or realm *other* than the one in which Boethius suffers.

But the most telling quality of her appearance is found in her costume: "Her clothing was wrought of the finest thread by subtle workmanship brought to an indivisible piece. This had she woven with her own hands,

---

[52] Boethius, *Consolation of Philosophy*, trans. W. V. Cooper (Midlothian, TX: Alacrity Press, 2013).

[53] For an excellent reading of the *Consolation* as literature – with merits well beyond what I encapsulate briefly here – see Stephen Blackwood's *The Consolation of Boethius as Poetic Liturgy* (New York: Oxford University Press, 2015), especially part IV. See also Antonio Donato, *Boethius' Consolation of Philosophy as a Product of Late Antiquity* (London: Bloomsbury Academic, 2013).

[54] Boethius, 1.

as I afterwards did learn by her own showing."[55] The work proper to philosophy is the work of weaving an indivisible covering, a housing. This is the practice that she promises to teach to Boethius. The description of the cloth is also a description of the practice itself: "On the border below was woven the symbol Π, on that above was to be read a Θ. And between the two letters there could be marked degrees, by which, as by the rungs of a ladder, ascent might be made from the lower principle to the higher."[56] The signs on her garment not only recall the spatial situation of the encounter – the woman approaching Boethius from above; they also serve to foreshadow the rearrangement that will be brought about by a teaching that proceeds from the "practical" to the "theoretical," the two hierarchically ordered divisions of Philosophy.[57] When she approaches Boethius, his head is bent to the ground, his mind craving extinction in the earth toward which his body cowers.[58] She declares, however, that her acts of weaving – her whittling of arguments in a certain constructive succession – will treat him according to a "physician's art," grant him the perspective to rise above and return to his situation with renewed clarity.[59]

This art occurs in three stages, each of which is signified and performed by the objective usefulness of the woven robe. First, the robe gives comfort. Boethius recalls that after first addressing him, "She gathered her robe into a fold and dried my swimming eyes."[60] Second, it mediates the activity of providential argumentation as a shared activity. "Surely," Philosophy remarks to Boethius, "Philosophy never allowed herself to let the innocent go upon their journey un-befriended."[61] Following the symbols on the robe, the argumentative weaving that Philosophy teaches Boethius moves him from practice to theory – from imitating her activity to participating in that activity. And, finally, the robe constructs a protective housing for Boethius: a "citadel" that marks his own limits against the exceeding reality of the transcendent God, but that also positions him properly before God.[62]

At each level of construction, the arguments work to reorder Boethius' faculties to the true nature of the world and its occurrences. In providing comfort, the first set of arguments quell his rage, which overcomes Boethius' ability to properly perceive his own situation. The second level is focused on perception. In Stoic fashion, Philosophy moves through a series of dialogical arguments aimed at helping Boethius to practically

[55] Boethius, 1.   [56] Boethius, 1.   [57] Boethius, 3.   [58] Boethius, 3.
[59] Boethius, 3.   [60] Boethius, 3.   [61] Boethius, 3.   [62] Boethius, 4.

distinguish the character of Fortune from the character of Providence in the arc of his own life's experiences. Boethius remarks that such arguments "have a fair form and are clothed with all the sweetness of speech and of song ... but only so long. The wretched have a deeper feeling of their misfortunes. Wherefore when these pleasing sounds fall no longer upon the ear, this deep-rooted misery again weighs down the spirit." And this moves him to the third level of weaving, to those arguments which "penetrate deeply."[63]

The highest arguments do not merely address Boethius' affective and perceptive faculties in piecemeal fashion. They function, in a way that recalls Socrates' use of mythic storytelling, to refigure Boethius' overall situation. They care for his newly ordered soul by placing him in a different kind of world from the one in which he met despair. This last round of argumentation performs its goal by addressing first the nature of the work of providence, and then the nature of providence itself. The nature of providential work resembles, once again, Stoic arguments. Philosophy argues that from the vantage of "divine power, and to that alone, are evil things good, when it uses them suitably so as to draw good results therefrom. For a definite order embraces all things, so that even when some subject leaves the true place assigned to it in the order, it returns to an order."[64] Providential dispensation therefore obtains in the "natural order," but from an origin and to an end that appears from and points beyond the realm of human perception.

But this is not the highest level. Philosophy's argument is pushed beyond familiar arguments over natural necessity by a concern over freedom. If providence is tied to right perception of the order of natural necessity, then how are human beings to render judgments concerning events? In the final argument of the *Consolation*, she argues that providential ordering does not threaten human freedom because freedom is part and parcel of a reasoning nature, and reason requires the freedom to judge based upon the knowledge that comes from perception. Judgment, however, is not equal in human and heavenly beings.[65] In fact, she goes on to argue that God's position vis-à-vis the world allows God a fundamentally different kind of knowledge of the world – a knowledge that does not compete with the human freedom that emerges from limited knowledge of the world, but that embraces the temporality of the world as a whole.[66]

---

[63] Boethius, 16.   [64] Boethius, 66.   [65] Boethius, 71.   [66] See Boethius, 71–73.

This arrangement differs from that of the Stoic desire for participation in the divine *logos* in two crucial respects. First, the relation of the divine to the world is refigured as one of knowledge *and* perception. This does not preclude, but it does *precede* the specifically providential function of ordering and guidance. Providence, in other words, is founded on the relative distance of the knower/known relation rather than on the sheer intimacy of the intellect/body relation that imagines providence as active entirely within the sphere of nature.[67] Nature remains conceived as "unending life," but God's relation to nature is one that resides in a domain that exceeds the conditions of that life. God's domain is capable of containing it as a whole. Ultimately, it is not an encasing myth, but the positing of a real, transcendent gaze. In Philosophy's words, God stands in such a relation to the world that God is able to "grasp" it "simultaneously."[68] God, figured now as a knowing and judging subject in relation to the world, structurally replaces Socrates' myth of the afterlife in the care of Boethius' soul. And the story of the One who sees eternally now couches the soul and prepares it for its departure – not merely by calling for participation in the order of nature, but by calling the subject to become both knowing and submissive before the Eternal knower. In these differences from classical articulations of providence, it is possible to discern the contours of the particular (Christian) notion of providence that would be so central to later arguments – including Calvin's – that read providence as a particular kind of relation between the immanent world and a transcendent being who wills things about the world from space of alterity irreducible to it.[69]

At the close of the *Consolation*, the indivisible cloth of Philosophy is sewn. The acts of weaving reoriented Boethius' perception, and now the finished cloth houses him by resignifying his world and thus forming the proper posture for life within it. But in the text's closing words, the garment serves yet one more function: it becomes a prayer cloth. The weaving – the ritualizing practice of differentiating the world through the repetitive and orderly use of argument – has finally made him the kind of subject who can pray rightly by having a sense of the one to whom he prays. But the form of affect that accompanies this is not *ataraxia*. It is,

---

[67] Boethius, 80–81. I want to make clear that my reading of Boethius does not intend to overplay this distance. There is still a deep intimacy in the relation of the eternal and the temporal. Boethius should not be construed as figuring God "wholly other." There is, however, a qualitative distance added when God relates to the world as a knower *of* the world.

[68] Boethius, 80.   [69] Reference on Blumenberg's critique of Christian providence.

rather, one of the Christian cardinal virtues: hope. Philosophy's last words exhort Boethius as follows: "Hopes are not vainly put in God, nor prayers in vain offered: if these are right, they cannot but be answered."[70] Hope is the affective register most attuned to the peculiar structural relationship assumed by a mortal who engages her surroundings in the putative light of a divine subject who providentially ushers human beings through worldly trials to an eternal home.

CONCLUSION

Boethius' writing demonstrates the extent to which a foundational Christian articulation of providence retains certain key features of its classical forebears, including the repetitive structure of a practice to orient the self before living incongruities. Boethius' text is helpful for recalling the extent to which early Christian thinking located the force of the doctrine within a field of embodied intellective exercise. Of course, this is true for other authors too, and not least Augustine, who productively reoccupies so many of the same classical conventions. Like Boethius, Augustine sees mediation as central to the task of Christian pedagogy and understands mediation as the practiced use of receiving and relating signs within a material field in the aim of not only reshaping but also turning the subject. The practiced interpretation of signs is useful for redirecting the affections before that which physically and cognitively exceeds one's cognitive and perceptive grasp. Augustine theorizes such a turning in the first three books of *De Doctrina Christiana*, but he narrates it more fully in *Confessiones*. Like Boethius, Augustine borrows many conventions of both Platonic and Stoic writing. Augustine's self-narration is, in many ways, a reperceiving of the nature of his own life. His experience is distended before the gaze of eternity and thereby performed through resignification. Even the famous conversion scene, where Augustine finally "puts on Christ" – finally housed in his own version of the robe – is prefigured by his encounter with an allegorical Continence who appears in the form of a woman. Part of what I want to continue to suggest, here, is that Calvin too ought to be read among those Christian authors who do not simply inherit the vestiges of classical ideas, but who understand teaching and learning to be a similarly multifaceted, embodied, invested exercise that involves the full spectrum of human faculties and feelings.

---

[70] Boethius, 83.

But against many lines of continuity, Augustine also evidences a more decisive break from classical thinking about providence than Boethius does. The lines of this break are visible in the basic shape of his thinking on the relation of divinity to materiality and temporality.[71] As I discussed in the last chapter, Augustine frames pedagogical mediation in more linear terms than the Stoic authors, for whom the *enchiridion* mediates the human faculties in an immanent present. For Augustine, the *enchiridion* is redeployed to lead the student along a journey, by means of teaching through the signs of faith, from confusion to hope for transcendent divine vision. Similarly, the two cities contrasted in *The City of God* are distinguished by their differing *telos*. The goal of such teaching is not merely to restore proper perception of, and order to, the worldly city. It is to engage the worldly city with an eye to one's proper destination with a God who abides transcendently. In the words of Brenda Deen Schildgen, Augustine sees the ultimate "purpose" of life as drawn retrospectively by its teleology – a characteristic distinguishing him from both classical and Christian thinkers who maintain a more participatory approach to the good life, "for whom civic action, citizenship, and nobility of soul [are] inevitably aligned."[72] Particularly in passages where Augustine addresses the meaning of suffering, this can have the effect of directing the reader's attention toward the ultimate *purpose* of suffering rather than facing the conditions of suffering in time.[73]

But Augustine's rendering of providence is all the more recast by the extent to which he was a thoroughly incarnational thinker. Christ, famously, never makes an appearance in *The Consolation of Philosophy* – a move that for decades generated suspicion over whether Boethius was an

[71] See also Wendy Raudenbush Olmsted's study of Boethius and Augustine: "Philosophical Inquiry and Religious Transformation in Boethius's 'The Consolation of Philosophy' and Augustine's 'Confessions'" in *The Journal of Religion* 69/1 (1989): 14–35.

[72] Brenda Deen Schildgen, *Divine Providence: A History: The Bible, Virgil, Osorius, Augustine, and Dante* (New York: Bloomsbury Academic, 2012), 73–74.

[73] Lloyd notes, for example, Augustine's willingness to give a purpose to the suffering of children in his relatively early work, *On the Free Choice of the Will*:

Augustine's version of providence is in many ways a stark transformation of the ancient idea of cosmic order. It seems to require acceptance not only of Christian theology but also of the apparent ruthlessness providence exercises in bringing evil into order. The apparent harshness of the providential calculus comes out in Augustine's chilling discussion of the suffering of children in *De Libero Arbitrio Voluntatis* 3.23.229–231. Here he argues that it is right that this suffering should occur, for God works some good by correcting the sinful adults who are tortured by the sickness and death of children dear to them (143).

authentic Christian. It should be noted, though, that such an absence appears far less strange when one notices that Christ is similarly absent in the providential arguments of later authors whose Christian bonafides are unquestioned. Examples include Thomas Aquinas (*Summa Theologica* 1.22); Ulrich Zwingli (*On Divine Providence*); and Calvin himself, for whom divine providence is proper to the knowledge of God the Creator (*Inst.* 1.16–18). The broader absence of Christology should not be surprising. To the extent that providence emerged as a discourse on the nature and order of the cosmos elicited by the embodied experience of incongruity, it entered Christian thinking as a discourse on creation in the most general sense: what creation signifies, and how God governs it.

But while Augustine forwards a capacious doctrine of creation that vests every immanent thing – natural and artifactual – with the capacity to point to God, he understands signification to obtain by means of a fundamental analogy with Christ, the Word made Flesh. In *Confessiones* 7, this claim is central to the reoccupation of the Neoplatonism that lured Augustine from the Manicheans; and in *De Doctrina Christiana*, Augustine moves through a series of arguments that frame the interpretation as a practice anchored in faith that Christ supplies both the "destination and road" of instruction. This claim has the powerful ability to give a robust account of how learning is possible before a God who is transcendent with respect to ordinary temporality and materiality. But it does so at the risk of rendering providence *special* before it can be *general*. If providence is triangulated *temporally* in relation to a fixed purpose, and *materially* in relation to a specific incarnation of the divine, then providence risks becoming a discourse more interested in offering an *explanation for* rather than a *resignification of* ordinary things.

To be clear, framing this as a binary requires a dangerously reductive reading of Augustine – a thinker who was, whatever his flaws may have been, anything but reductive. But the suggestion that providence is best imagined in terms of teleological progress toward a transcendently willed purpose, and best interpreted through the lens of one particular coincidence of Word and Flesh, has cast a fundamental tilt on the way the discourse has been appropriated and resisted in the modern West. Karl Löwith's critique may be the most apropos to cite. As I've noted, Löwith is famous for reasserting the place of transcendence in order to critique what he saw as a surreptitiously "secularized" modern age. In his view, modernity doubles down on the quasi-Augustinian urge to imagine history as linear progress toward a transcendent goal anchored in a privileged incarnation of the transcendent in time.[74] But it also secularizes this imaginary, therefore locating the transcendent goal and the incarnated anchor within immanent time itself. Löwith's reassertion of transcendent divine *hiddenness* functions as a critical tactic for unmasking and disrupting political formations that feed off of transcendent Christian structures. Yet, Löwith did not see the reassertion of transcendent hiddenness as the only recourse against fascism.

Similar to Lloyd, Löwith sees a genuine alternative in the way the Greeks approached natural necessity, embracing immanence through a cyclical (rather than linear) temporal imagination that directs reason and affection toward refining perception of present details and living patterns. And though he thought this view to be irrecoverable in the modern world, he admired what he saw as Nietzsche's bold attempt to overcome Christian thinking about time by directing Christian linearity, in quasi-Greek fashion, *toward* the immanent world. This was neither a return to natural necessity and *ataraxia*, nor was it a mere perpetuation of world-transcending hope. In Löwith's words, "The Greeks felt awe and reverence for fate, Nietzsche makes the super-human effort to love it."[75] Löwith did not find Nietzsche's effort to be successful, but he did think it opened up something of what it might mean to think beyond a modern world shaped paradoxically by its *debt to* and self-conscious *loss of* a *Corpus Christianum*. In returning to Calvin's doctrine of providence, I'll pick up on Löwith's questions, and suggest that the structural underpinnings of Nietzsche's effort reveal a signature of providence. It is one with an older history in vastly different contexts, but one that nevertheless constellates a legible critique of fascism through the gesture of immanent affirmation.

---

[74] To be clear, attributing historical progressivism to Augustine requires the flattening of his thinking, but I do think it's fair to say the imaginative scaffolding of that view is legible in Augustine's thinking.

[75] Löwith 1945, 283. For more on Löwith's readings of Nietzsche's eternal recurrence, see Löwith's longer work on the topic: *Nietzsche's Philosophy of the Eternal Recurrence of the Same*, trans. J. Harvey Lomax (Berkeley: University of California Press, 1997). See also Adrian Del Caro's discussion of Löwith's view in *Grounding the Nietzsche Rhetoric of Earth* (Berlin: Walter de Gruyter, 2004), 30–31, 221–232.

3

Providence and World Affirmation

Modernity invests its trust in the power of the present moment as an origin, but discovers that, in severing itself from the past, it has at the same time severed itself from the present.

−Paul de Man[1]

Belief in the existence of other human beings as such is love. The mind is not forced to believe in the existence of anything. That is why the only organ of contact with existence is acceptance, love. That is why beauty and reality are identical. That is why joy and the sense of reality are identical.

−Simone Weil[2]

When providence became disavowed, it was as an explanatory discourse – one that trades in claims about the purpose of the universe and the purpose of suffering within it. According to sociologist Iain Wilkinson,

A once popular understanding of pain and suffering as components of Divine Providence and as instruments of God's instruction and grace is now held to be both intellectually incredible and morally unacceptable. In modern societies, pain and suffering are generally taken to be morally undesirable and are regarded as elements of human experience that, where possible, should be minimized or eliminated ... Cultural historians observe that by the turn of the eighteenth century popular notions of 'special' Providence came to be widely regarded as intellectually untenable as well as politically dangerous (Wilkinson 2013: 126).

If providence gives transcendent explanations for immanent events, it undermines and even stigmatizes curiosity over why things happen.

[1] Paul De Man, "Literary History and Literary Modernity" in *Daedelus* 99/2 (Spring, 1970): 384–404, 390.
[2] Simone Weil, *Gravity and Grace* (New York: Routledge, 1999), 53, 64.

This, in turn, undermines human efforts to intervene and change conditions that cause pain and injustice. Against this backdrop, the choice to jettison providence can seem obvious, even long overdue. At best, clinging to providential explanations will excuse irresponsibility toward the complexity of our shared natural world. Rejecting providence can clear space for human creativity that might actually do more to ease pain. This is a narrative of an end that is also constitutive of a beginning – because every beginning needs an end, just as every identity needs an other. The end of providence is an end of a dark age beholden to causes and forces beyond our control. It coincides with an *Aufklärung*, a new age of human creativity fertile with immanent possibility.

If this kind of narrative succeeds at constituting the modern – as it has for a number of both proponents and critics – it does so through a double gesture. First, the narrative conceals the complexity of providential writing both before and into early modernity. It forgets the fuller array of strategies at play within ancient providential discourses and the way these discourses performed ways of perceiving and responding to the world quite in excess of rational explanation. It also forgets the life of that inheritance in modern writing itself – in a sixteenth-century work like Calvin's *Institutio*, but later works by authors like Vico and Leibniz for whom providential arguments were generative of modern scientific inquiry.[3] Second, as so often happens when a specific construal of a past is articulated for the purposes of rejection, its outlines continue to inform that which purports to explain it. The self-conscious rejection of purposive, explanatory providence did not quell the urge to think of human activity through the lens of a particular sovereign logic: one that governs by making rationalized decisions over the conditions of worldly life.

Hans Blumenberg's famed characterization of modern self-assertion as a "second overcoming of [world-denying] Gnosticism" carries this tension. For Blumenberg, world affirmation means freeing human beings from the world-denying posture of transcendence so that human beings can govern the world through secular means for secular ends. By making

---

[3] The magisterial account of the relation of providence to the imagination and posture of modern science is found in Amos Funkenstein, *Theology and the Scientific Imagination from the Middle Ages to the Seventeenth Century* (Princeton, NJ: Princeton University Press, 1986). For more on Funkenstein's method and its implications on historical method, see Samuel Moyn, "Amos Funkenstein on the Theological Origins of Historicism" in *Journal of the History of Ideas* 64/4 (2003): 639–657; and Abraham Socher, "Funkenstein on the Theological Origins of Historicism: A Critical Note" in *Journal of the History of Ideas* 67/2 (2006): 401–408.

things – art, fictions, and technologies – modern subjects can foster an authentically secular curiosity over not just what our world is, but what it might come to be in an open future.[4] Human self-assertion marks a break from the past in part by using language differently. Language no longer operates with the seriousness of "old theology," as a vehicle for presenting revealed, metaphysical truth to mortals.[5] Modern language rereads theology as a repository of metaphors useful for developing tools for the fallible, experimental process of both exploring the world and imagining it differently. Metaphors can do this work because they honor and even exploit the perpetual distance between things and the concepts through which we apprehend things.

Language, therefore, places human beings in a position of fallible mastery – knowing ourselves fundamentally as beings of the world, but knowing ourselves also as capable of making fundamental improvements upon it. Citing Nietzsche, Blumenberg writes that "[humanity's] right should consist in imputing the least possible binding force to reality, so as to make room for his own works. 'Not in knowing but in creating lies

---

[4] See Blumenberg, *The Legitimacy of the Modern Age* (Cambridge, MA: MIT Press, 1983), 141–142. Here is the longer version of an important quote:

> One might think that [Nietzsche's] formula defines exactly the self-consciousness of an age that has given itself up to its technical achievements. But Nietzsche ignored this possible interpretation of his basic thought. There is no talk of technique in his writings. Technique retains the posture of self-assertion, with its dependence on theoretical truth about nature. It derives from a teleology that compensates obedience to the laws of nature with mastery over nature. Technique may have seemed to Nietzsche to be the epitome of the surrogates for the lost natural teleology benefiting man ... That technique also could surpass the character of pure self-assertion, that it could not only disguise the element of need but even eliminate it in the immanence of becoming an end in itself, that it could break out of competition with nature's accomplishments and present itself as authentic reality, was still beyond the horizon of experience at the time (Blumenberg, 142).

This is an extraordinarily interesting passage because in it, Blumenberg does two things: He critiques Nietzsche for privileging art over technique on the grounds that technique is beholden to a paradigm linking modernity to Christian teleology and self-assertion to the transcendent subject; but he also reconfigures the goal of self-assertion not as mere technical mastery over the world, but as an end in itself, an authentic reality irreducible and noncompetitive with "nature's accomplishments." Blumenberg wants therefore to keep Nietzsche's critique of being beholden to the perceived norms of "reality" as a rejection of transcendent foundations, while at the same time expanding Nietzsche's definition of "art" to include the techniques of science. For more, see Nathan Widder, "On Abuses in the Uses of History: Blumenberg on Nietzsche; Nietzsche on Genealogy" in *History of Political Thought* 21/2 (2000): 308–326.

[5] For Blumenberg's discussion of serious theology contrasted with modern metaphor, see 99–108.

our health! ... If the universe has no concern for us, then we want the right to scorn it.'"[6] He continues defending the posture that valorizes technique in terms that, for my purposes, are both interesting and revealing: "Technique," he writes, "retains the posture of self-assertion, with its dependence on *theoretical* truth about nature. It derives from a teleology that compensates obedience to the *laws* of nature with mastery over nature."[7] These statements beckon to recognizable features of providential discourse – the universe's "concern for us," "teleology," "law," and "mastery." But Blumenberg redeploys these as signs of providence's failure and modernity's legitimacy. It is *because* the universe has no concern for us, it is *because* we are governed by impersonal laws, that we have the "right" to test our constraints by asserting ourselves creatively and technologically over it.[8]

Several readers of Blumenberg have suggested that this defense of technical mastery perpetuates, rather than reoccupies, the sovereign logic of a transcendent will governing nature. And if this is right, then it also perpetuates the kind of immanent irresponsibility deemed objectionable by modern critics of providence. When Blumenberg links technique to modernity, he follows the lead of Francis Bacon, Vico, Hobbes and other early modern thinkers who defend the coherence of historical progress on the grounds of increasing human knowledge that itself is grounded in human making. This is, of course, a position that follows from the *verum factum* principle that "we can only know what we make ourselves."[9] Nature can be mastered because human beings render nature as – and by

---

[6] Blumenberg, 141–142.   [7] Blumenberg, 142. Emphases mine.
[8] Blumenberg gives an account of this change by positing his "reoccupation thesis," or the claim that history is structured by the periodic reoccupation of old questions under legitimately new terms (see Blumenberg, 49, 60–75, 77–79). The concept borrows from the geologic concept of "pseudomorphosis," which occurs when a new crystalline substance fills the hollow left by another crystal, and adapts to this hollow by taking on an alien and potentially misleading crystal form. Applying this to the study of historical periods in effect flips the script on Löwith's accusation: structural similarities between Christian expectation and immanent progress do not betray an underlying foundation, but rather are mere adaptive vestiges of a past that has ceased due to its own collapse (Blumenberg, 63, 78, 353–354. The reoccupation thesis allows Blumenberg to frame the differences between the modern age and Christian premodernity as decisive, and to underscore what is truly novel in modernity's attitude toward the world. For more, see Widder as well as Benjamin Lazier, "Overcoming Gnosticism: Hans Jonas, Hans Blumenberg, and the Legitimacy of the Natural World" in *Journal of the History of Ideas* 64/4 (2003): 619–637, 625.
[9] As noted in my Introduction, I am indebted to Victoria Kahn for drawing out this connection and remain very much informed by her account of it. See especially her "introduction" to *The Future of Illusion*.

means of – theory and law. Benjamin Lazier observes that a signature linking law, creative making, knowledge, and progress represents more of a break from the Greek valuation of nature [*physis*] than from Christianity:

> Equated with being and qualified as goodness, *physis* was generally thought by the Greeks to provide a natural standard by which [humans] should live. As such, it was often opposed to *nomos*, human convention or law, whenever nomos deviated from its natural model. Whereas the Greeks ordinarily privileged *physis* over *nomos*, Bacon, as a rule, did the reverse. That Bacon the statesman spoke of his scientific program in the language of legalism and rights—the human spirit was thought to "exercise its right with respect to nature"—suggests, however, that he superimposed on the distinction *nomos/physis* the distinction between common and natural law.[10]

In other words, the *verum factum* principle might establish the conditions for a version of secularism – for conceiving society as made by and for humans conceived as immanent and bound to the earth; but only at the expense of retaining a linear will that "exercises its right" over the conditions of nature. Blumenberg's friend and critic Hans Jonas, a renowned environmentalist, makes a similar point in blunter terms: "The *deus absconditus* [hidden God], of whom nothing but will and power can be predicated, leaves behind as his legacy, upon leaving the scene, the *homo absconditus* [hidden man], a concept of man characterized solely by will and power—the will for power, the will to will. For such a will even indifferent nature is more an occasion for its exercise than a true object."[11] Jonas's point is not to defend the theology that increasingly emphasized the hiddenness of the Christian God, and which Jonas agreed tended toward the general posture that modern readers call "Gnosticism." His point was to echo Löwith in locating a continuity between theological conceptions of the will and those embedded in modern theories of sovereignty. Whether or not this morphological similarity constitutes modernity as "illegitimate," the similarity does press the question of whether the secular embrace of technological progress overcomes or remains imbricated in the same ethical quandaries raised by purposive versions of divine providence.

---

[10] Benjamin Lazier, "Overcoming Gnosticism: Hans Jonas, Hans Blumenberg, and the Legitimacy of the Natural World" in *Journal of the History of Ideas* 64/4 (2003): 619–637, 632.

[11] Hans Jonas, "Gnosticism and Modern Nihilism" in *Social Research* 19/4 (1952): 430–452, 432. Quoted in Lazier, 635.

This is the first of two chapters that consider Calvin's providential arguments, zooming into examine their force and effect before scaling back out to look at how Calvin's use of pedagogical resignification is grounded in providence. Calvin's take on providence straddles the threshold of medieval and modern – at least in the way this "threshold" is commonly (and troublingly) periodized.[12] Part of what I want to show, across this book, is how close attention to Calvin's writing upsets simpler versions of that periodization. This is in part because they creatively recombine features of Stoic and Christian discourses to rethink the relationship between divine power, the world, and sociopolitical conceptions of sovereignty tied to a body politic. On the one hand, this relies on a high appraisal of the practiced and repetitive use of revealed divine signs – the focus of Part III. On the other hand, it also performs what I will argue is a radical affirmation of the immanent world as a site of deliberate human activity – the focus of this chapter and the next. Perhaps in part because of Calvin's positionality as a refugee reformer writing theology "for God's church," Calvin's arguments also refuse to identify divine governance with human governance in any way. Instead, he indexes the transcendent divine will to nature itself, positioning creation as the proper domain for Christian teaching and the proper Archimedean point from which to critique institutions.

In this way, Calvin's arguments cannot be easily placed on the side of a "lost" enchanted past of a divinely ordered world – one that refers to supernatural causes to explain natural events or authorize legitimate modes of governmental order; nor can they be placed on the side of a disenchanted present left to fend for itself in wake of divine absence. And because Calvin's providence locates the world's meaning in God's deliberate and affirming relationship to the created world as such – the world of *physis* rather than *nomos* – Calvin's providence suggests an anterior echo to later authors who would similarly mobilize world affirmation as a critical alternative to ideologies that conceive progress and legitimacy in terms of sovereign mastery over nature. Before continuing on to Calvin, let me say more about how I see such an approach fitting into the broader discourse on providence, looking more closely at the case of Nietzsche

---

[12] To be clear, when referring to things such as the "threshold to modernity," I am working with ideas that I also want to undo. If my argument is successful, one of its concrete outcomes would support the restructuring of the periodization through which coursework in theology and philosophy is commonly structured (i.e., ancient, medieval, modern). Yet arguing for the need to rethink such periodization requires critically engaging the scholarly literature that has taken such periodization to be axiomatic.

who is both admired and critiqued by all sides of the secularization debate.

PROVIDENCE IN THE WAKE OF LOSS

Whether or not providence died a natural death (Blumenberg) or was violently repressed (Löwith) by modern self-consciousness, all parties agree that the posture Blumenberg describes as "modern" – the posture of human self-assertion over nature – emerged out of the perceived loss of a providentially ordered world. Löwith and Blumenberg both frame modernity as the time that remains in the wake of such a loss. Their most fundamental disagreement, as I read it, is over how best to grieve and live on in the wake of that traumatic loss. The lines of this disagreement are visible in their diverging assessments of Nietzsche. Pondering why Nietzsche – a famous advocate of human creativity as the final source of the earth's meaning – should have viewed technique with such suspicion, Blumenberg suggests somewhat wistfully that "technique may have seemed to Nietzsche to be the epitome of the surrogates for the lost natural teleology benefiting man."[13] Rather than replacing the lost teleology with a surrogate for it, Nietzschean transvaluation wants to rethink the fundamental conditions for life itself such that the need for natural [ized] teleology no longer arises. Blumenberg sees this move as avoiding the task of giving new answers to existing questions.[14] Löwith, as we've seen, admires Nietzsche precisely on this point, even if he thinks it ultimately falls short. Rather than returning to Greek necessity or secularizing Christian teleology, Nietzsche wants to "make the super-human effort to love" all that is and ever was in the world.[15] The disagreement, here, is not whether there has been a loss. It is over how best to respond to it.

Critics of Blumenberg might wonder if embracing human self-assertion in the wake of divine loss recalls the structure of Freudian melancholia, the "pathological" response to loss that internalizes the lost object and withdraws into the self.[16] But this debate is also fundamentally about

---

[13] Blumenberg, 142.   [14] Blumenberg, 143.
[15] Karl Löwith,"Nietzsche's Doctrine of Eternal Recurrence" in *Journal of the History of Ideas* 6 1/4 (1945): 273-f.
    I discussed Löwith's reading of Nietzsche in the conclusion to Chapter 2.
[16] Sigmund Freud, "Mourning and Melancholia" in *The Standard Edition of the Complete Psychological Works of Sigmund Freud, Volume XIV (1914–1916): On the History of*

history: how we make sense of it, how we tell it, and how we make it. And it's striking to notice the extent to which Michel de Certeau's critical account of distinctly modern historiography mimics exactly the structure through which Blumenberg defends human self-assertion as a legitimate break from the failure of a divinely ordered cosmos. According to de Certeau, modern historiography is methodologically structured as the discourse of separation – a separation that presumes, but also creates and internalizes, distinct breaks between conceptions of present and past, acts of labor and the object of nature, and ultimately discursive creations and the body to which discourse both refers and defers. In the modern West, history is conceptualized as a historical science that drives the older histories away, rather than consciously coexisting with them or reabsorbing them.[17] In this way, modern history remains obsessed with death. But rather than conceiving death as constitutive of a way of living one's life, and the dead as a living presence haunting the present, historiography renders death as data to be mobilized under the banner of scientific progress. Loss becomes a site of production that denies the reality of the loss itself, instead "appropriating to the present the privilege of recapitulating the past as a form of knowledge."[18]

Historiography creates and possesses the lost object as an object of knowledge in order to constitute the subject as master-knower who lives beyond life and death – all while denying the multiple ways in which the present remains constituted by the past, the dead, and the inevitability of death. De Certeau argues that all of this is encapsulated in "a gesture that has at once the value of myth and of ritual." Namely, writing:

> But isn't historiography also an activity that recommences from the point of a *new time*, which is separated from the ancients, and which takes charge of the construction of a rationality within this new time. It appears to me that in the West, for the last four centuries, "the making of history" referred to writing. Little by little it has replaced the myths of yesterday with the practice of meaning. As a practice (and not by virtue of the discourses that are its result) it symbolizes *a society capable of managing the space that it provides for itself*, of replacing the obscurity of the lived body with the expression of a "will to know" or a "will to

the Psycho-Analytic Movement, Papers on Metapsychology and Other Works (London: Hogarth Press and the Institute of Psychoanaysis, 1968): 237–258. See especially 249–250.

[17] Michael de Certeau, *The Writing of History*, trans. Tom Conley (New York: Columbia University Press, 1988), 4.

[18] de Certeau, 5.

dominate" the body, of changing inherited traditions into a textual product, or, in short, of being turned into a blank page that it should itself be able to write.[19]

To the extent that the "modern" is typified by production – by poiesis, artistic creation, technique – it is always already making use of tactics that visibly operate within the discourse on providence itself while also disavowing the extent to which the practice itself is received rather than created *ex nihilo*. The rejection of providence at the threshold to modern self-assertion entails a legible stance on questions concerning life, death, order, creation, knowledge, perception, emotion, and meaning that are themselves addressed through ritualized uses of writing – writings that perform the kinds of relationships they also purport to differentiate and describe. If providential discourse has not been lost, it is worth asking what is lost – a question that will continue to lead back to what it means to live in a body alongside others embodied, to be able to face down the complex history of violence carried out in the name of sovereign order, and to make the "super-human effort to love," rather than resent, such a life.

Reconceiving narratives of modern loss under the auspices of providence allows me to return to an argument I forwarded at the beginning: namely, that narratives *of* modern loss perform a double gesture that conceals the complexity of the past and, by virtue of that concealment, overlooks more complex lines of continuity between the past and the present. This helps to illumine why Nietzsche has played such an important role in the thinking of so many of both modernity's defenders and its critics. As Löwith and Blumenberg both argue, Nietzsche is, in fact, trying to rewrite the terms of the question. Briefly considering the bare outlines of his work in constructive relation to the discourse on providence over the *longue durée* will help illuminate the conditions through which it might be possible to rethink something as basic as a logic of sovereignty that insists on thinking power as a decision exerted by a (transcendent, unitary, human or divine) will over bodies in time. It will also eventually help bring to bear certain underappreciated moves that Calvin makes, and particularly the unexpectedly active role Calvin's rendering of providence gives to material bodies on their own terms.

As Max Weber would later pick up in his writing on rationalization and disenchantment – another important narrative of modern loss – Nietzsche's

---

[19] de Certeau, 5–6. Emphasis mine. See also his discussion of the renaissance gesture on p. 136.

work departs from a question basic to the discourse on providence: how to understand the meaning of our suffering.[20] Nietzsche addresses this question by marshaling a sharp critique of the "ascetic ideal," his descriptive term for a life oriented around the kind of purposive providence that refers the meaning of present suffering to the transcendent field of the afterlife. Although versions of the ascetic ideal might promise to generate calmness or hope and allow their practitioners to better face inevitabilities, Nietzsche reads the ascetic ideal as a proxy mobilizing a more vicious form of affect: *resentment* against the conditions of suffering that enacts *revenge* against life in the present.

Nietzsche is a perceptive reader of the fuller dimensions of providential discourse that I outlined in the last chapter. He acknowledges the sense in which providence realizes teaching within a field of practice by supplying arguments that orient a life in the world and clarify the judgments one forms about the conditions one faces. And while he ultimately reads the

---

[20] Weber picks up on this Nietzschean theme most clearly in his well-known lecture, "Science as Vocation," when he worries that the modern "war on suffering" will ultimately fail to give adequate meaning to an ordinary human life – and, in so doing, undergird conditions for a more profound crisis of meaning. Perhaps a "religious past" that relied on transcendence to address the meaning of life could be construed as too passive before, or too beholden *to*, the conditions that perpetuate worldly suffering. But at least such a regime possessed conceptual tools to signify the meaning of an ordinary, suffering life, rather than viewing it in terms of failure. Here is a memorable passage from the lecture where Weber makes this point:

> Abraham, or some peasant of the past, died "old and satiated with life" because he stood in the organic cycle of life; because his life, in terms of its meaning and on the eve of his days, had given to him what life had to offer; because for him there remained no puzzles he might wish to solve; and therefore he could have had "enough" of life. Whereas [a] civilized [person], placed in the midst of the continuous enrichment of culture by ideas, knowledge, and problems, may become "tired of life" but not "satiated with life." He catches only the most minute part of what life of the spirit brings forth ever anew, and what he seizes is always something provisional and not definitive, and therefore death for him is a meaningless occurrence. And because death is meaningless, civilized life as such is meaningless; by its very "progressiveness" it gives death the imprint of meaninglessness

(Weber, "Science as Vocation" in *Essays in Sociology*. Edited and translated by H. H. Gerth and C. Wright Mills. Oxford: Oxford University Press, 1946, 129–156: 140).

To the extent that death's progressive elimination constitutes the logic of modernity's superiority over the old theology, modernity cedes the possibility of addressing the reality of death – and thus of a mortal life being lived toward death. Weber therefore invokes the continued need for approaching meaning through the lens of significance rather than intention. Rather than seeking a purpose for suffering, this approach would require a discursive practice that can credibly differentiate the real significance of life as it is, as a life marked by suffering and death, and to fashion an appropriate practical and affective response to it.

full range of ascetic deprivations as performances of revenge against the immanent conditions of life that entail suffering, he also acknowledges that even the most severe practices of the ascetic ideal betray a kind of devilish pleasure that emerges from an even more fundamental affirmation of life.[21] In *On the Genealogy of Morals* (1887), Nietzsche describes the ascetic as one whose regimented self-exposure to suffering enacts a yet-deeper strategy for producing greater existential satiation: "The No which he speaks to life brings to light, as if through a magic spell, an abundance of more tender Yeses. Even when he injures himself, this master of destruction and self-destruction, it is the wound itself which later forces him to live on."[22] Ultimately, Nietzsche argues that what is laudable and even fundamental to the ascetic ideal is not its ability to give life meaning through the realization of a teleological aim (of either the transcendent or immanent variety). Rather, it is the way that ascetic tactics *signify* and render affectively *salient* the experience of life itself, drawing attention to the full range of embodied conditions that emerge from "eternal life."

It is furthermore striking to observe that Nietzsche's own writing participates legibly in a version of ascetic practice, yet one aimed deliberately and explicitly at performing the affirmation of life that refuses revenge, overcomes resentment, and generates joy. The most striking example of this may be in *Thus Spoke Zarathustra*, a quasi-scriptural depiction of a teacher whose stated goal is to represent what it means for a human being to overcome resentment by willing a meaning for the earth. He leads and performs a series of embodied intellectual practices that place him down in proximity to human suffering and back up in retreat from it.[23] But each time Zarathustra returns to the valley, he is faced with the "abysmal" thought – that facing suffering without revenge must mean willing the eternal recurrence of all things – willing in linear fashion to give a meaning to the things that happen, but willing as if time itself were a circle in which all the things that happen will recur, even the very worst. To will without resentment means giving up one of the constitutive

---

[21] To be clear, the different modes of the ascetic ideal map almost precisely onto the way providence functions as intention versus significance.

[22] Nietzsche, *On the Genealogy of Morals*, 3.13.

[23] Indeed, Nietzsche's critical diagnosis of the ascetic ideal often occludes his own deployment of a "philosophical" asceticism geared toward the cultivation of the self and the affirmation of life. See Tyler Roberts, *Contesting Spirit: Nietzsche, Affirmation, Religion* (Princeton, NJ: Princeton University Press, 1998) 15–19.

elements of sovereignty, which is the urge to decide: to *decide* suffering as either the sign of a deserving sentence for sin or as a sign of the persecuted's otherworldly superiority. Resisting the temptation to resent means willing to affirm: to chain oneself not only to the future *of the earth* as such, but also its checkered past.

Nietzsche never depicts this as anything other than a task of utmost difficulty, one impossible to conceive in the terms of ordinary rational discourse.[24] It is not easy to articulate, much less to defend, the move to affirm eternal recurrence in normative moral terms (as Nietzsche, a famous critic of conventional morality, knows well). This very difficulty of articulation illumines why Nietzsche emphasizes artistic creation rather than technique, and as such it underscores why both Löwith and Blumenberg ultimately see the Nietzschean project as coming up short. Affirmation of even the worst is not the kind of thing that can be performed through the cool rational methodology underwriting technological advancement designed to improve worldly conditions. Art, however, attains the quality of difficulty, struggle, and memory that provokes meaning in the absence of a clear horizon of progress. For Löwith, Nietzsche was similarly unable to render affirmation in terms that were followable in a programmatic sense. His insight emerges, quite literally, *as* art, making full use of misdirection, irony, implication, signs, and symbols. If it gives a meaning to suffering, it is one that must be enacted through the differentiated embrace of life's complexity in a particular place and time by a particular embodied will. It cannot create meaning by being recorded as an object of knowledge.

When Zarathustra emerges from his trial, he does not summarize the experience. His body performs the signs of its new relationship to immanent life. Here is a lengthy example from the text:

Pain is also a joy, a curse is also a blessing, night is also a sun – go away or else you will learn: a wise man is also a fool. Have you ever said Yes to one joy? Oh my friends, then you also said Yes to all pain. All things are enchained, entwined, enamored –

– if you ever wanted one time two times, if you ever said "I like you, happiness! Whoosh! Moment!" then you wanted everything back!

– Everything anew, everything eternal, everything enchained, entwined, enamored, oh thus you loved the world –

– you eternal ones, love it eternally and for all time; and say to pain also: refrain, but come back! For all joy wants – eternity!

[24] When the dwarf tries, he also fails.

All joy wants the eternity of all things, wants honey, wants resin, wants drunken midnight, wants graves, wants tomb-tears' solace, wants gilded sunset –
–what does joy not want? It is thirstier, heartier, hungrier, more terrible, more mysterious than all pain, it wants itself, it bites into itself, the ring's will wrestles in it – – it wants love, it wants hate, it is super-rich, bestows, throws away, begs for someone to take it, thanks the taker, it would like to be hated –
– so rich is its joy that it thirsts for pain, for hell, for hate, for disgrace, for the cripple, for world – this world, oh you know it well!
You higher men, it longs for you, does joy, the unruly, blissful one – for your pain, your failures! All eternal joy longs for failures.
For all joy wants itself, and therefore wants all misery too! Oh happiness, oh pain! Oh break, my heart! You higher men, learn this, joy wants eternity
– Joy wants the eternity of all things, wants deep, wants deep eternity!
(Nietzsche 2006: 263).

What has been lost, here, is the ability to give the kind of argument that could answer why Zarathustra suffers. But rather than responding to such a loss with a different answer, Nietzsche's character performs a different relationship to the world, and that relationship births different signs of life.

Thus Spoke Zarathustra can be read fruitfully alongside the varieties of writings on providence I charted in the previous chapter. It emerges quite centrally from the scene of incongruity: attempted and failed teachings, persistent sufferings, struggles against melancholy and revenge. In so doing, it depicts arguments as tools to be used in context according to trial and error – to test not only one's surroundings but oneself. Like those examples, it makes use of relational, performative genres of writing to subvert any expectation that answers about the meaning of life can be given as objects of abstract knowledge. At the same time, the mechanics of Nietzsche's providential discourse are different from the Greek and Christian varieties I surveyed. Zarathustra does not learn to remain calm before things that must be endured as necessities. Nor does he learn to hope for some later resolution beyond time. Affirmation of eternal recurrence of the same generates a different kind of affect: a joy that is signified by things that a body does in time: it laughs, sings, and dances.[25]

---

[25] In Nietzsche's more prosaic and aphoristic philosophical writings, the sign of affirmation is also laughter. See, for example, *The Gay Science* §383 and *Beyond Good and Evil* §294.

This approach to providence is distinguished by the activity of the will, both the direction of its movement and the way it relates to the things that exceed it. A will that moves toward the world and submits when it faces necessities will generate calmness. A will that wills over and beyond the world generates hope. But a will that affirms life, not submitting but actively affirming its full reality and complexity, generates joy. What distinguishes this will is not just that it is turned toward the world, but the way it renders the world – not as an object to be characterized, but a domain of engagement. Tyler Roberts characterizes the affirming will as a fully involved practice of responsiveness:

Rather than metaphysical mastery, Nietzsche as writer practices a responsiveness to the mystery and the power of the world—or, as I have put it, a passion for the real, passion in the sense of strong desire, and in the sense of the pain of submission to the real. Only with such passion is the creation of spirit possible: in Nietzsche's ascetic/mystical practice of transfiguration, suffering leads to joy, abysmal thought and bodily pain are transfigured into affirmative spirit (Roberts 1998: 168).

Despite its moral and rational difficulties, this is a philosophically and historically legible response to the problem of suffering. It echoes elements of other writers, chiefly of literature, but also of philosophy: Weil, Camus, Dostoevsky, Kierkegaard, Luther, Duns Scotus, among others. It also echoes biblical themes that tie the peculiar affect of "joy" to scenes where life meets death: the agony of childbirth, an event so often braided with both the deferral and inevitability of death itself (Luke 1–2; Hebrews 12:2); the patient endurance of suffering (Psalm 30:5); a figure whose indictment of his own suffering is quieted by a glimpse of the amoral vastness of creation (Job, especially 38–41). Yet, this articulation of providential discourse has no aspirations to theodicy. It makes no attempt to justify God before creation – or to justify creation before humanity, or humanity before creation.[26] Instead of justification, the aim of affirmation is more squarely located in the deeper good signified by the full import of life – a significance that underwrites all other significances. In this third distinctive articulation of the discourse on providence, one might find the outlines of an alternative to the logic of sovereignty. This, at any rate, is suggested by the tensions and struggles that cut across Calvin's rearticulation of the doctrine.

[26] In fact, Nietzsche writes out of the conditions brought about by what he calls the death of God – the very conditions that authorize the modern rationalization leading to nihilism of which Nietzsche is ultimately critical (even as he remains critical of Christianity).

CALVIN'S PROVIDENCE: THE PERSONAL AND THE POLITICAL

If the 1559 *Institutio* is crafted to return the refugee to the city, it is appropriate that the discourse on providence precedes that journey. Providence is, after all, a discourse on governance – one called upon to give an account of those events that meet one, in the fashion of Boethius, as an undeserved suffering. But as such, it is always already a personal discourse. It addresses pain felt in a body that exists in a time and place, supplying tools for rendering the component parts of the scene of suffering and resignifying them in a way that enables a new posture in the person facing them. In Calvin's text and context, the doctrine carries both of these inflections. It is addressed in time to a refugee community who has experienced persecution. This is signaled in the text itself not just by the overarching structure of the itinerary, but also by the perpetual inclusion of the Prefatory Address to King Francis of France and by Calvin's own self-description as a doctor of the church writing outside the bounds of its traditional, institutional *corpus*. But while these particular concerns generate the need to make providential arguments, those arguments also do their work by making arguments about the divine will that reposition the human person in the domain of creation in general – a creation that exceeds the bounds and operations of institutional bodies, and therefore both constructs and addresses the body as a natural entity that feels, perceives, and knows.

It is in both these respects that providence opens the *Institutio* like a Proscenium Arch, to borrow Susan Schreiner's magisterial image.[27] It both concludes Book One and opens the way to the more aggressively incarnational arguments that follow in Books Two, Three, and Four by addressing the reader in three ways. First, it reframes the theological task as addressing a cognizing being whose self-knowledge is always in some ways given by what it means to be known by another, and whose ability to know hinges radically on responsiveness to other knowers. As I've noted and will note again, the *Institutio* opens by inviting the reader to begin examining not an external object, but the broader network of signs and things (or "many bonds") through which the knowledge of God and ourselves [*cognitio Dei et nostri*] are related. Second, this is a task that immediately involves the affective dimensions of human life, and specifically the cultivation of piety as a prerequisite for and outcome of

---

[27] Susan Schreiner, *The Theater of His Glory: Nature and Natural Order in the Thought of John Calvin* (Durham, NC: The Labyrinth Press, 1991). See especially chapter 1.

knowledge rightly attained (*Inst.* 1.2). Calvin defines piety as "that reverence joined with love of God which the knowledge of his benefits induces," and frames it the affective key to cognitive exercise of resignification that he summarizes in the following way: "For until humans recognize that they owe everything to God, that they are nourished by his fatherly care, that he is Author of their every good, that they should seek nothing beyond [God]—they will never yield [God] willing service" (*Inst.* 1.1). Finally, this cognitive and affective exercise of recognizing how God governs the world relies fundamentally on the exercises of the senses, and particularly the *sensus divinitatis* that, when accommodated, perceives the glory of God in and at the edges of creation (*Inst.* 1.3–5).

Providence, for Calvin as for many authors before him, is a discourse that addresses suffering through holistically embodied exercises. In his particular context, however, these arguments have the effect of rendering a world that is ordered differently than the one from which the "candidate in sacred theology" would know himself as an exile, as a living witness to a world lost. To perform this radical transvaluation of worldly life, Calvin, like later advocates and critics of modernity, relies on the category of creation. But rather than locating the source of creation in "a society capable of managing the space that it provides for itself," to recall de Certeau's phrase, Calvin argues that transvaluation can be spun out from the simple Christian article of faith that begins the Apostles' Creed: "God is Creator." Because God is willfully involved in every detail of immanent life, it is possible to "assign credit." Such an exercise resignifies and thereby transforms one's estimation of what creation is, what it can be, and what one's responsibility might be within it. Calvin puts it this way:

> For even though the minds of the impious too are compelled by merely looking upon earth and heaven to rise up to the Creator, yet faith has its own peculiar way of assigning the whole credit for Creation to God ... For unless we pass on to [God's] providence—however we may seem both to comprehend with the mind and to confess with the tongue—we do not yet properly grasp what it means to say: "God is creator" (*Inst.* 1.16.1).

The method, here, is a fairly recognizable tactic of Augustinian pedagogy that embraces a claim of faith and unwinds its logic toward a fully embodied understanding.[28] To properly grasp what it means to say "God is creator" requires rethinking what it means to ask the right kinds of questions about the world that *is*, how it is the kind of thing that might

---

[28] I will return to this in Part III.

be said to have a meaning at all. And for Calvin, this entails presuming that ordinary things are not merely what they appear to be in isolation, but that they can attain depths of significance by virtue of their relation to other things. Providence, as a discursive exercise, examines the significance of things in relation to a fully involved God who is always already willing everything that exists.

Still, Calvin begins the task of unwinding the claim that "God is Creator" with certain key presuppositions in place. Some, predictably, are fundamentally Augustinian. Calvin imagines God as fully transcendent, free, and ontologically distinct from the creation that God brought into being *ex nihilo*. He also conceives of God's activity as mediated primarily through the will. As such, he imagines "meaning" as the significance of relationships that are brought to bear by relationships of will (rather than, say, by ontological presence).[29] The divine will activates relationships between and among created things, and those relationships point both back and forward to the transcendence that exceeds and underpins them.[30]

[29] Calvin's firm insistence upon an ontological distinction between Creator and creation would prohibit him from adopting a traditional account of participation as participation in divine being. But it opened up the opportunity for him to retheorize participation as sharing in common practices of signification (with debatable success, especially before advocates of participation as a fundamentally ontological concept). Julie Canlis argues, for example, that union with Christ hinges on the gesture and path of the *logos*: "In his doctrine of creation, Calvin refuses to envision a general relationship between the triune God and humanity ... All creation is related to God in the second person of the Trinity, who mediates creation and its *telos*. All things are created by him, and created for perfect union with him. This arrangement is not due to sin, but to the *en Christo* way that God relates to humanity. He has not structured a universe in which life, grace, and 'benefits' can be had apart from [God]" (Canlis 2010, 57). The notion that participation is hinged in a shared performative–creative materialization, rather than a share in divine existence, underscores not only Calvin's interest in writing but also why he historically implemented so many signifying practices: Psalm singing, catechism training, preaching, and frequent observance of the sacraments. For more on the reformers' ontology and implications for participation, see Canlis' *Calvin's Ladder* (Grand Rapids, MI: Eerdman's, 2010), esp. 71–73, 127; J. Todd Billings' *Calvin, Participation, and the Gift* (New York: Oxford University Press, 2007); and, once again, Oberman, "The Pursuit of Happiness," 265-ff. And for more on Calvin's historical pedagogy, see Matthew Myer Boulton, *Life in God: John Calvin, Practical Formation, and the Future of Protestant Theology* (Grand Rapids, MI: Eerdmans, 2011).

[30] For Thomas Aquinas, ontological presence – which carries the most weight among celestial relationships – must still be distinguished from what might be called performative force, or the teaching quality of revealed images operating within the domain of creation. Yet for Calvin, the distance between ontology and revelation is sharper still. For a fascinating comparison of the two on images, see the following two essays: Mark Jordan, "Aquinas the *Aesthetics* of Incarnation" and Lee Palmer Wandel,

But Calvin was also shaped by the Stoic writings he studied in his youth, accounts that do not shy away from identifying "providence" with "nature." For an exile interested in drawing a distinction between an idolatrous *corpus Christianum* and a providentially guided world, the ability to index divinity to a space that exceeds and upsets the stability of the *corpus Christianum* – to submit *nomos* to *physis* – presents a useful argumentative tool. Calvin's account of providence is therefore preceded by several striking claims about creation itself: that creation, for example, should be understood as the "theater of God's glory" and the "very school of God's children." In a way reminiscent of Seneca and Marcus Aurelius, the term "providence" acts as a kind of shorthand for "nature *qua* divine creation," or a way of referring to the world *as if* known in its full relation to the divine will. I've already noted the passage earlier in Book One where Calvin walks right up to the assertion that "nature is God":

I confess, of course, that it can be said reverently, provided it proceeds from a reverent mind, that nature is God; but because it is a harsh and improper saying, since nature is rather the order prescribed by God, it is harmful in such weighty matters, in which special devotion is due, to involve God confusedly in the inferior course of his works (*Inst.* 1.5.5).

This passage underscores the extent to which Calvin wants to assert the closest possible relationship between God and nature *while also maintaining* their fundamental ontological difference. On the part of the student-reader, this sets up a providential posture that is trained to look for order, meaning, and glory in creation itself and not in the corporate institutions that govern the world.[31] This again recalls the Stoic writers for whom ethics and wisdom emerge from nature properly perceived according to its necessity.[32]

Both of those elements are crucial to structuring the position through which the reformer-refugee becomes the position of the theologian, the

---

"Incarnation, Image, and Sign: John Calvin's. *Institutes of the Christian Religion* & Late Medieval Visual Culture" in Walter S. Melion and Lee Palmer Wandel, eds., *Image and Incarnation: The Early Modern Doctrine of the Pictorial Image* (Leiden: Brill, 2015): 161–172; 187–203.

[31] See Heiko Oberman, *"Europa Afflicta"* in *John Calvin and the Reformation of the Refugees* (Geneva: Librairie Droz S. A., 2009), 193.

[32] At the risk of drawing too sharp a distinction between the Augustinian and Stoic strains in Calvin's thinking, I'll note that Calvin extends and emphasizes an important yet often underemphasized feature of Augustine's thinking: namely, that every created thing stands ready to be apprehended as a sign of divine love. I'll discuss this further in Part III.

doctor of the church. And it will mean, like Nietzsche, attempting to fashion arguments that creatively combine a transcendent linear will with the affirmation of temporal material life as such. Key, here, is that this move *locates a valid referent for "transcendence" in immanent life itself.* If, as Heiko Oberman has argued, the "true religion had now become the concern only of the *pauci* [remnant]," then providence does not just mean being able to face suffering with calmness, hope, and even joy – although Calvin's arguments engage all three emotions, as we'll see.[33] But for Calvin, providence also entails looking for the signature of transcendence pointing toward and emerging from the bodies of the refuse gathering furtively beyond bounds of the *corpus politicum* and its claims over time and space.[34]

At the same time, Calvin's recombination of a linear will that is actively involved in every detail of creation emerges from claims he makes about God, and this has earned him a reputation for forwarding a version of divine sovereignty so disturbing that it shocked and troubled many even in his own time. Calvin is unflinching when it comes to asserting the priority of divine will at every turn, even when it implicates God in evil. And because Calvin, unlike the Stoics, conceives the divine relation to the world as mediated by a transcendent will, he seems to be depicting a world in which suffering, pain, and injustice are deliberately willed by a hidden sovereign for reasons that remain stubbornly undisclosed. This reading is not without some textual evidence. For example, Calvin claims that "all events are governed by God's secret plan [*occulto Dei consilio gubernari*]," (*Inst.* 1.16.2) and that nothing "exercise[s] its own power except in so far as it is directed [*dirigutur*] by God's ever-present hand" (*Inst.* 1.16.2). Later, he writes: "There is no erratic power, or action, or motion in creatures, but … they are governed by God's secret plan [*arcano Dei consilio sic regi*] in such a way that nothing happens except what is knowingly and willingly decreed [*sciente et volente decretum*] by him" (*Inst.* 1.16.3). And, finally: "We must prove God so attends to the regulation of individual events, and they all so proceed from his set plan [*definito eius consilio*], that nothing takes place [*contingat*] by chance [*fortui*]" (*Inst.* 1.16.4).[35] Statements like these, taken in isolation, might suggest that Calvin is articulating a view of providence on par with occasionalism.[36]

---

[33] Oberman, 189. [34] Oberman, 188

[35] My thanks to Mark Jordan for pointing out that Battles' rendering of *consilium* as "plan" may be misleading. In Scholastic terminology, *consilium* is the intellectual act that

Yet, Calvin also describes divine governance using a deep pool of verbs that challenge any urge to read him as asserting an imaginary of machine-like, controlling determinism.[37] In the chapters where he introduces his discussion of the doctrine, Calvin describes divine governance as "shining," "creating," "preserving and governing activity," "energy," "sustaining," "nourishing," "caring," and "quickening." He also claims that a person's awareness of the work of divine providence in the world should generate "inspiration," "contemplation," "feeling of grace," "taste of special care," and "the knowledge of fatherly favor" (*Inst.* 1.16.1–2). One way of moving past the apparent incongruity between Calvin's apparently deterministic claims and the way he actually describes providence is by noticing that he consistently frames providence as a divine *activity*, rather than an abstract plan. Here's one passage:

When Abraham said to his son, "God will provide," he meant not only to assert God's foreknowledge of a future event, but to cast the care of a matter unknown to him upon the will of him who is wont to *give a way* out of things perplexed and confused. Whence it follows that providence is lodged in the *act*; for many babble too ignorantly of bare foreknowledge. Not so crass is the error of those who attribute a governance to God, but of a confused and mixed sort, as I have said, namely, one that by a general motion revolves and drives the system of the universe, with its several parts, but which does not specifically direct the action of individual creatures (*Inst.* 1.16.4).[38]

In another passage, Calvin makes clear that providential power should not be seen to quell or compete with human activity, but rather to offer the necessary cognitive, affective, and perceptive conditions for the very possibility of deliberate human activity:

precedes choice or *electio*. It is concerned with means, not ends: It is a form of "backwards" reasoning from a desired end to the available means. See e.g., Thomas, *Summa Theologica* 1–2.14. Also, in Scholastic terminology, *gubernatio* is regularly contrasted with physical determination. Against this backdrop, the apparent evidence for more rigid determinism is further discredited.

[36] Such would be the obvious reading of someone relying on a timeless and spaceless "grammar of representation" that reads propositions apart from considerations of pedagogical accommodation and/or a material field of interpretive reference. See Candler 2006 and my discussion of his argument in Chapter 2.

[37] For a treatment that distinguishes Calvin from what is commonly understood by "determinism," see Charles Partee, "Calvin and Determinism" in *Christian Scholar's Review* 5/2 (1975): 123–128.

[38] Emphases mine. McNeill notes that Calvin is here criticizing Cicero's *De natura Deorum*. See *Institutes*, ed. McNeill, 202.

And truly God claims, and would have us grant, omnipotence—not the empty, idle, and almost unconscious sort that the Sophists imagine, but a watchful, effective, active sort, engaged in ceaseless activity ... For when, in The Psalms, it is said that "he does whatever he wills," a certain and deliberate will is meant. For it would be senseless to interpret the words of the prophet after the manner of philosophers, that God is the first agent because he is the beginning and cause of all motion; for in times of adversity believers comfort themselves with the solace that they suffer nothing except by God's ordinance and command, for they are under his hand. But if God's governance is so extended to all his works, it is a childish cavil to enclose it within the stream of nature. Indeed, those as much defraud God of his glory as themselves of a most profitable doctrine who confine God's providence to such narrow limits as though he allowed all things by a free course to be borne along according to a universal law of nature (*Inst.* 1.16.3).

Here, he distinguishes his account of God from that of an Aristotelian unmoved mover or Stoic natural necessity – in short, from accounts of providence that link divinity to a general principle rather than special, deliberate action. And he argues, strikingly and perhaps counterintuitively, that the special rendering of providence should provide comfort, not terror.

In one more passage, Calvin also makes the explicit case that only this kind of special, deliberate providence can set up conditions for special, deliberate action on the part of human beings:

"Man's heart plans his way, but the Lord will direct his steps." This means that we are not at all hindered by God's eternal decrees either from looking ahead for ourselves or from putting all our affairs in order, but always in submission to his will. The reason is obvious. For he who has set the limits to our life has at the same time entrusted to us its care; he has provided means and helps to preserve it; he has also made us able to foresee dangers; that they may not overwhelm us unaware, he has offered precautions and remedies. Now it is very clear what our duty is: thus, if the Lord has committed to us the protection of our life, our duty is to protect it; if he offers helps, to use them; if he forewarns us of dangers, not to plunge headlong; if he makes remedies available, not to neglect them (*Inst.* 1.17.4).

The logic here is that you can't really act deliberately if you don't have confidence that action can accomplish something meaningful, and that one effect of the providential argument is to give believers that kind of confidence – and, as such, grant both comfort and motivation.

THE MOVEMENT OF THE DIVINE WILL

It's fair to say, at this point, that Calvin's arguments about providence present puzzles. The *Institutio* clearly advances the case that the world is governed by an active, deliberate omnipotent will that operates with radical freedom over worldly events and answers to no one – a seemingly straightforward account of sovereign absolutism. But it also claims, at the same time, that accepting this account of the world's order is the condition not just for affective happiness, but for learning to render more precisely deliberations on the granular level of an ordinary life. Can this account hang together on its face value – without either softening Calvin's claims about the providential will or his claims about how he thinks this claim might offer both comfort and motivation to worldly action?

To get some traction on this puzzle, I'll begin by looking more closely at how Calvin develops the choreography of the providential will. For Calvin, and from the perspective of the human being who requires levels of divine accommodation, the providential will is neither unitary nor should it be construed as assuming a zero-sum relation to other wills and causes. In fact, Calvin routinely refers to at least three distinct modes of *divine* activity at play in any occurrence: that of efficient causality on a strictly material level; the signification enacted by multiple wills at play in any given event; and the overarching providential activity that Calvin understands as "the divine decree." In addition, Calvin unwaveringly asserts the reality of created "intermediaries," or efficient causes that play a role in creating and perpetuating causal chains within the domain of the created universe. Because he maintains a strict distinction between God's being and the world's created being, it is possible for Calvin to conceive of a divine will that is always active, and indeed always operating from a vantage of greater control at the boundaries of worldly events, but is all of these things because it first actively affirms the reality of the world it governs.[39] Calvin writes that "God's providence does not always meet us in its naked form, but God in a sense clothes it with the means employed" (*Inst.* 1.17.4). For Calvin, too, the vantage supplied by providential argument meets his readers like clothing. But unlike Boethius, Calvin's providential cloth rests on created things. And this makes a difference when it comes to what Calvin's providential arguments might allow a reader to see, feel, and do.

[39] Note that this is the topic of Calvin's debate with Osiander which takes place across the *Institutes*. See *Inst.* 1.15.3–5, 2.12, and 3.10.4–3.11.11. For more on the relational reorientation of ontology characteristic to the Reformers, see Heiko Oberman, "The Pursuit of Happiness" in *Humanity and Divinity in Renaissance and Reformation: Essays in Honor of Charles Trinkaus.* (Leiden: Brill 1993) 265-ff.

First, Calvin's arguments make distinct use of two verbs that flesh out the nature of divine activity in different ways. First, there is "will" [*voluntas*], which carries a range of meanings in Latin, including will, desire, disposition, favor, affection, goal, purpose, and signification. Second, Calvin maintains that the divine will is a causal factor with respect to events. For example, "We must so cherish moderation that we do not try to make God render account to us, but so reverence his secret judgments as to consider his will [*voluntas*] the truly just cause [*iustissima causa*] of all things" (*Inst.* 1.17.1). On one level, God wills things about the world and that will functions as a cause of all things in the world. Knowing this should generate reverence. But Calvin also insists that God's will works through intermediaries: "*instrumentum*" or "*causas inferiores*" that are part and parcel of the world's real, quasi-independent existence, and which should also generate a degree of reverence. According to Calvin,

> Yet I do not wholly repudiate what is said concerning universal providence, provided they in turn grant me that the universe is ruled by God, not only because he watches over the order of nature set by himself, but because he exercises especial care over each of his works. It is, indeed, true that the several kinds of things are moved by a secret impulse of nature, as if they obeyed God's eternal command, and what God has once determined flows on by itself (*Inst.* 1.16.4).

If God's will is the *just* cause of all things, that does not mean God's will is the *sole* cause of all things, or that all things, read in isolation, are *ipso facto* just. The force of the claim is that God's will is actively involved in every event – even, as we will see, events deemed sinful or evil (*Inst.* 1.18.1).[40]

As Calvin's argument unfolds, he continues to describe the divine will using verbs that underscore the way it causally works in concert with – or, sometimes, against – really existing efficient causes. For example, "God out of the pure light of his justice and wisdom tempers and directs [worldly disturbances] in the best-conceived order to a right end" (*Inst.* 1.17.1). The language of "tempering" and "directing" asserts a distinction between multiple efficient causes, which may or may not be immanently legible, and the active causality effected by the transcendent divine will. This can also mean bridling, which Susan Schreiner has described as the tactic of "curb[ing] the wicked and the devil lest they completely

---

[40] For a helpful discussion of this problematic, see Kathryn Tanner, *God and Creation in Christian Theology* (Oxford: Blackwell, 1988).

overturn all order and make life unlivable."[41] *Voluntas* thus refers to several distinct dimensions of causal activity. Because the divine will creates *ex nihilo* and its power "shin[es] as much in the continuing state of the universe as in its inception," it is accurate to attribute *first* causality to God (*Inst.* 1.16.1). And because that will actively joins with the internal (material and efficient) causes internal to creation, it takes on the character of a *just* or benevolent cause – a good will that brings about good outcomes. This is something akin to the Aristotelian "final cause," although it's worth flagging the fact that Calvin avoids appealing to a unified *telos*, which has to do with his emphasis on special providence over, or as constitutive of, general providence – I'll say much more on that later. For now, "just cause" seems to suggest that God is committed to directing or tempering the significance of the ordinary over the long-term for the good.[42] And Calvin, of course, does not preclude that some events are directly and primarily caused by the divine will.

But things get more complicated when it comes to the *character* of the divine will – the question, even in the face of Calvin's warnings against speculation, of both how and why the divine will acts as it does. Calvin's doctrine of providence is often regarded as infamous and troubling because of the extent to which Calvin is willing to implicate God in events that, from an ordinary vantage, are conventionally deemed evil. And Calvin is willing to go quite far in this regard, writing, "I have already shown plainly enough that God is called the Author of all the things that these faultfinders would have happen only by his indolent permission. He declares that he creates light and darkness, that he forms good and bad; that nothing evil happens that he himself has not done" (*Inst.* 1.18.3). This is a remarkable passage, in part because it shows Calvin's sheer commitment to two things: to rendering providence as God's willing and creating activity in all things without exception; and his commitment to the reality of evil itself. He would rather implicate God in evil than deny either God's active presence or the full and experiential force of evil and suffering.

Calling God the sole Author of evil might seem the opposite of comfort – indeed, the very definition of the kind of horror-art that

---

[41] Schreiner 1991, 30. See also Schreiner's study specifically on Calvin's sermons on Job, *Where Shall Wisdom Be Found? Calvin's Exegesis of Job from Medieval and Modern Perspectives* (Chicago: University of Chicago Press, 1994), 143.

[42] That is, because God is always working toward good ends from beyond and alongside creation, the justice of a cause is never fully apparent in time.

explores *paranoid* rather than *pronoid* psychology. It would have been easy from Anselm's and Thomas's distinction between God's antecedent and God's consequent will, or even Duns Scotus's *duplex justitia*. The former approach would have enabled him to argue that God wills differently in relation to the world's actual existence than God wills merely in the abstract.[43] The latter analogously refers to God's justice *ad intra* versus God's justice as it relates to creation – a complex that, for both, preserves realistic conditions for human responsibility and therefore for punishment. But Calvin will have nothing of this language:

> [L]et our law of soberness and moderation be to assent to his supreme authority, that his will may be for us the sole rule of righteousness, and the truly just cause of all things. Not, indeed, that absolute will of which the Sophists babble, by an impious and profane distinction separating his justice from his power—but providence, that determinative principle of all things, from which flows nothing but right, although the reasons have been hidden from us (*Inst.* 1.17.2).

Conceptually, it may be possible to reconcile the spirit of Calvin's position with these "Sophists," but the rhetorical differences are not merely ornamental. Calvin seems to have something deeply at stake in holding together the fundamental unity of the divine will *as a matter of discourse*.[44]

Referring to Calvin's similar struggle with the prospect of a "hidden divine justice" in his Job sermons, Schreiner observes the following:

> In his Job sermons, Calvin seeks to find this self-limitation of God in the heart of the divine essence and hence tries to place God's self-limitation not only in the *potentia ordinata* [ordained power, contrasted to absolute power] but also to God's rule *etiam extra legem* [beyond the law]. God's rule of history may be inscrutable but is reliable because God's power cannot act contrary to God's goodness, justice, and reason.[45]

Schreiner continues that this reflects Calvin's "search for a God who is both completely sovereign and totally reliable" – a tall order, no doubt, if one is also unwilling to shrink from the full weight of what evil represents in the world of ordinary experience.[46] Oberman, from whom Schreiner

---

[43] Thomas Aquinas, *Summa Theologica, Prima Pars* Q. 19 A. 6.

[44] McNeill notes that Calvin's targets here are William of Ockham, Gabriel Biel, and John Duns Scotus – through who, in various ways, upheld the distinction between the *potenta absoluta* and *potentia ordinata*.

[45] Susan E. Schreiner, "Exegesis and Double Justice in Calvin's Sermons on Job" in *Church History* 58/3 (1989): 322–338, 337–338.

[46] Schreiner, 338.

draws, argues that Calvin's consistent emphasis on tying God's reliability to God's absolute power flows from what he calls Calvin's "modern vision of God's rule thrusting beyond the heart of the justified sinner and beyond the boundaries of the Church to encompass the State, Society, and the whole created order" – a feature he ties to Calvin's refugee positionality.[47] Putting aside what it might mean to call this a "modern" view, I want to argue that there is a distinct articulation of providential choreography here, drawing from but irreducible to the Stoic and Christian versions I've surveyed. It has precisely to do with Calvin's interest in tying the divine will to creation in the most general sense without mitigating the full and special content of the divine will. In other words, like the Stoics, Calvin wants providence to be concerned with life in nature, with how human beings learn to perceive the world, feel about the world, render judgments about it, and learn to act better within it. But like advocates of transcendent Christian teleology, Calvin wants God to have a specific will *concerning* the world, to will a meaning for it that is irreducible to its component parts. In this respect, Calvin wants reflection on the divine will to be anchored in, though not transparent to, worldly experience – a claim that he thinks will in fact yield comfort and even joy. But he's willing to walk up to the prospect that God wills evil.

There's one passage where this argument hits its highest tension, which is worth parsing at some length.

When we do not grasp how God wills to take place what he forbids to be done, let us recall our mental incapacity, and at the same time consider that the light in which God dwells is not without reason called unapproachable, because it is overspread with darkness. Therefore all godly and modest folk readily agree with this saying of Augustine: "Sometimes with a good will a person wills something which God does not will ... For example, a good son wills that his father live, whom God wills to die. Again, it can happen that the same man wills with a bad will what God wills with a good will. For example, a bad son wills that his father die; God also wills this. That is, the former wills what God does not will; but the later wills what God also wills. And yet the filial piety of the former, even though he wills something other than God wills, is more consonant with God's good will than the impiety of the latter, who wills the same thing as God does. There is a great difference between what is fitting for a human to will and what is fitting for God, and to what end the will of each is directed, so that it be either approved or disapproved. For through the bad wills of evil humans God fulfills what he justly wills." (*Inst.* 1.18.13, ellipses in text).[48]

---

[47] Oberman, "The Dawn," 257.

[48] Calvin's commitment to the distinction between will and cause is further evident in a passage from Book Two. Discussing God's salvific work in the context of the *cognitio Dei*

So far, this passage underscores the causal point I just made, only on the level of the will. Multiple wills are at play in any one event, and one of them is God's just will. He is also making the common Calvin move of drawing from Scholastic debates while leaping over them to directly engage Augustine's more rhetorically inflected language on the matter.[49] At any rate, Calvin demonstrates what I take to be a telling level of comfort with conceptual tension in the conclusion of the passage, which reads as follows:

All the wicked, from their point of view, had done what God did not will, but from the point of view of God's omnipotence they could in no way have done this, because while they act against God's will, his will is done upon them. Whence [Augustine] exclaims: "Great are God's works, sought out in all his wills." In a wonderful and ineffable manner *nothing is done without God's will, not even that which is against his will*. For it would not be done if he did not permit it; yet he does not unwillingly permit it, but willingly; nor would he, being good, allow evil to be done, unless being also almighty he could make good even out of evil" (*Inst.* 1.18.13, emphasis mine).

---

redemptoris, Calvin concludes: "Therefore we see no inconsistency in assigning the same deed to God, Satan, and a human; but the distinction in purpose and manner causes God's justice to shine forth blameless there, while the wickedness of Satan and of a human betrays itself by its own disgrace" (*Inst.* 2.4.2).

[49] This passage also brings out the extent to which Calvin's understanding of the will follows Augustine by operating within a broader logic of desire. Like Augustine and Anselm (and Plato before them), Calvin is assuming that God's will is legible as the active pursuit of that which God desires, and that the human will similarly is moved by what *it* desires – either in conformity to that which God desires or sinfully desiring its own contrary ends. In Chapter 5, I discuss continuities between Augustine's and Anselm's understandings of signification. For here, it's worth noting the extent to which this similarity connects resonant views of the will. Augustine is notoriously harder to pin down on the will, with debatable changes occurring over the course of the bishop's career from *De Libero Arbitrio* to his later writings on grace, free will, and predestination. By way of summary, I'll suffice it to say that the mature Augustine agrees with Anselm that the will is moved by desire and that, for a free will, that desire is rectitude (rightness, justice as in the *affectio iustitiae*, or God's will), for its own sake. What this means is that a human will, subject to sin, cannot be free without the aid of divine grace. (This can be contrasted, in a small but significant degree, with the later view of Duns Scotus, for whom freedom is tied to the power of the will itself rather than to rectitude.) Calvin stands in this tradition, one in which the will is moved by desire, and goodness means alignment with God's will. However, as I'll argue in this chapter and Chapter 6, Calvin's understanding of the will runs through the resignified perception of creation in a way that is more expansive than Augustine and Anselm. For more on these views of the will, see Augustine's *De Libero Arbitrio*; Anselm's *On the Free Choice of the Will, On Truth,* and *On the Fall of the Devil*; and Douglas C. Langston's helpful article, "Did Scotus Embrace Anselm's Notion of Freedom?" in *Medieval Philosophy and Theology* 5 (1996): 145–159.

"Nothing is done without God's will, not even that which is against his will" – a remarkable claim, a moment of apparent rupture where the argument turns in on itself. If one refuses the obvious but deceptively simple urge to read this claim as a bald contradiction, it raises a whole host of considerations around how Calvin is using language – not, apparently, to present clear truths; but to orient and frame the experience of the reader.

In this passage, as in his providence locus as a whole, Calvin often avoids available technical terminology. His goal is not conceptual clarity, but affective reorientation, and the means is an argument that consistently forwards three successive claims about the will of God in the world: (1) God is actively willing everything that happens in the world; (2) God is involved in these events through diverse tactics that can involve bridling and direct causality, but primarily work through threading themselves in and among creation's "clothing"; and finally, (3) God is so dedicated to creation that God wills its existence, even if this means willing what God – strictly speaking – might not "like." For God to will evil, then, is for God to will life. And for God to will life – created life – is ultimately crucial to what it means for God to will justice. Providence is, for Calvin, not a set of arguments designed to represent conceptually transparent truths, but a set of tools through which the reader can profitably reinterpret her world. In this way, it is akin to a cloth woven by argument. Yet Calvin's cloth is not to be worn like a citadel as much as it is one that asks the Christian to perceive the whole world as if adorned by a cloth, a veil that both renders the world *as if willed by God* and covers the transcendence hidden within it. I'll have more to say about the political implications of this view, but for now, let me conclude with some reflections on the role of hiddenness in Calvin's thought.

HIDDENNESS

Calvin wants God's will to be conceived as a unity that is not only all powerful but also good, with its goodness actively intertwined goodness that is actively intertwined with every worldly event. As I've noted, this places him in an odd relation to evil – one that necessitates his own appeals to divine "hiddenness" that obtains at the site where human limitation meets divine accommodation – the site, in other words, where immanence is materialized as an object of experience. See, for example, the following passage:

Yet since the sluggishness of our mind lies far beneath the height of God's providence, we must employ a distinction to lift it up. Therefore I shall put it this way: however all things may be ordained by God's plan, according to a sure dispensation, for us they are fortuitous. Not that we think that fortune rules the world and men, tumbling all things at random up and down, for it is fitting that this folly be absent from the Christian's breast! But since the order, reason, end, and necessity of those things which happen for the most part lie hidden in God's purpose, and are not apprehended by human opinion, those things, which it is certain take place by God's will, are in a sense fortuitous (*Inst.* 1.16.9).

This is, again a Stoic moment – one in which Calvin is contrasting the perception of nature *qua* fortune with the perception of nature *qua* providence. Unlike his Stoic forbears, however, Calvin does not refer primarily to the reasoned honing of the preconceptions, although something like this is also operating in the background in the form of the *sensus divinitatis* Calvin introduced at the outset as a faculty-receptor for perceiving divine glory in the world (*Inst.* 1.3–6). But in that vein, the training on offer here is oriented around exercises of signification that train the believer to assume the right kind of posture before the sense in which the world itself signifies. Calvin repeatedly refers to providence as an act of ascription: of properly ascribing to God the role of Creator. But this means learning to see nature *as if* creation, as if it is a thing that also signifies – and therefore as a thing that exceeds the grasp of the sign, much like the body exceeds (but also informs) the clothing that covers it. This is what it means, for Calvin, to perceive the divine glory in the world. In this vein, the language of hiddenness does not split God's will, it rather repositions the human in a different posture related to it. That posture is one of "reverence," though not abstract reverence for God as a spectral force (*Inst.* 1.17.1). Rather, I want to suggest here in conclusion that reverence, or the impulse to worship, is tied to the ability to perceive nature *as if* divine clothing – *as if* a veil – rather than as a naked surface for which no further explanation than "fortune" is needed.[50]

---

[50] Schreiner's reading of Calvin's Job sermons demonstrates that perception was principally aided by faith in the resurrection, or the ability to read nature and history from the vantage of immortality (Schreiner, *Where Shall Wisdom Be Found?*, 125, 133–135). Though Schreiner does not explore the mechanics of Calvin's latent theory of perception, I read her analysis as largely consistent with and supportive of my argument here, with the salient differences having to do with the distinct genre of the sermon versus the pedagogical manual.

In the 1559 *Institutio*, Calvin is constructing a deliberate order of pedagogy, whereas the sermons on Job are an active exegetical exercise in putting that pedagogy to use. In both cases, however, clearer perception is enabled through the interplay of scriptural

It may be helpful, at this point, to contrast Calvin to his reforming forbear Martin Luther, whose recourse to divine hiddenness was itself both tantalizing and frustrating. Brian Gerrish argues that two distinct conceptions of hiddenness can be discerned in Luther's thought – one that refers to a God hidden *in* revelation, the other referring to divine aims that are *other* than God's revelation and absolutely removed from human view. Luther's doctrine of the *sub contrario* represents the first. In his 1524 *De Servio Arbitro* – his boisterous counter to Erasmus of Rotterdam's defense of free choice – Luther makes the following claim about the relationship between the hidden and the revealed:

Faith's object is in things not seen. That there may be room for faith, therefore, all that is believed must be hidden. Yet it is not hidden more deeply than under a contrary appearance of sight, sense and experience. Thus, when God quickens, God does so by killing; when God justifies, God does so by pronouncing guilty; when God carries up to heaven, God does so by bringing down to hell. As Scripture says in 1 Kings, 'the Lord kills and makes alive; He brings down to the grave and brings up.' Thus God conceals His eternal mercy and loving kindness beneath eternal wrath, His righteousness beneath unrighteousness.[51]

This can be read as a providential claim to the extent that Luther is interested in how God actively governs the faculties of the human person in the world. Rather than positively identifying revelation with ordinary worldly signs for divinity – monarchical regalia, for example – God engages with the visible world in a way that is designed to frustrate the fallen pretension of human reason and, in so doing, to reorient human expectation. What can be known and said of God is thus hidden "in, with, and under" ordinary and seemingly unfit things, including scripture and the incarnation. What Luther's *sub contrario* does *not* do is divide

---

teaching and material life, or through a process that I find to be most aptly described as performative materialization. Taken in isolation and approached from the vantage of the fallen perceiver, Christian doctrine (promise) and nature (material creation) each yield a dialectic of hiddenness and revelation. Taken together and put into deliberate practice, however, doctrine and nature enable a set of interpretive activities through which God graciously grants the kinds of affective and practical results Calvin anticipates: clarity, comfort, forbearance, confidence, reverence, and gratitude.

On my reading, the "eyes of faith" that Calvin so emphasizes – eyes enabled by divine promises as if by spectacles – must be understood in active rather than static terms, or as a way of participating in signification that is actively materializing the world (just as Calvin thinks divine providence itself must be understood as constant and deliberate divine activity of such materialization).

[51] Luther, *On the Bondage of the Will*, 138. I have changed masculine pronouns to "God" where appropriate.

God's will from the aims of salvation. Elsewhere in *Bondage*, however, Luther does seem to suggest exactly this other form of hiddenness by suggesting that there is a side to God with which human beings have nothing to do.[52] These passages suggest a more frightening and destabilizing God – a God whose utterly transcendent will could theoretically be pursuing aims that are radically contrary to fundamental conceptions of love, goodness, and comfort. This is one way of responding to evil phenomena, but it comes at a high cost, the very cost that Calvin refuses to pay when he wants to insist that God is somehow willing against God's will *for good reason*.[53]

Calvin's claim that God's providence is clothed in the means employed does approach something like the first form of hiddenness, the hiddenness of the *sub contrario*.[54] Yet rather than indexing divine providence merely to the sign of things contrary, Calvin indexes divine providence to a material world as a whole, investing the natural world itself with a kind of revelatory status.[55] Randall Zachman describes this move in the following way:

---

[52] *Bondage*, 200f.

[53] In addition to Gerrish's essay, my reading has benefitted from Ronald F. Thiemann's *The Humble Sublime* (London: IB Taurus, 2013), chapter 1.

[54] Calvin, for example, will use the word "under" [*sub*] at various points to describe God's relation to visible things, which is referentially suggestive of Luther's doctrine of the *sub contrario*. For Luther, *sub* also appears in his discussions of the sacramental presence as being hidden "in, with, and under" ordinary things. See the *Formula of Concord*, Article VII, The Holy Supper of Christ. See Martin Luther, The Large Catechism (1529), "It is the true body and blood of the Lord Christ in and under the bread and wine, which we Christians are commanded by Christ's word to eat and drink."

Calvin's theology of sacramental signification differs from Luther's, and the traces of that difference are perhaps visible in the different way he uses these propositions to signal how God may be known in relation to the world. For example, Calvin writes that the knowledge of God the Redeemer was "first disclosed to the fathers under the law, and then to us in the gospel" (2.1.1). First, it is notable that neither knowledge of Christ (nor knowledge of God) is synonymous to the content of the law, but that it is related to it in a paradoxical sense. I would argue that there is something about the way the law disposes a person toward the world that is revelatory of the final end of God's will. Later, when Calvin discusses his own theory of the sacraments, he writes that "the sacraments ... are exercises which make us more certain of the trustworthiness of God's Word. And because we are of the flesh, they are shown us under [*sub*] things of flesh, to instruct us according to our dull capacity, and to lead us by the hand as tutors lead children" (4.14.6). Here, once more, sacramental signification entails an affirmation and then a disposition of material things. It is not that God is merely present under all material things, rather God is active with respect to material things to direct them in specially oriented ways. I'll discuss Calvin's sacramental signification in Chapter 7.

[55] See also Schreiner, *Where Shall Wisdom Be Found?*, 135–136, 145, 153. Schreiner rightly notes that creation serves both a positive and negative function, yet the negative function

Calvin ... is more willing than Luther to link the transcendent will of God to visible creation, or to God's works, in a positive sense. This accounts for Calvin's much more positive use of visible glory, which for Luther is almost always pejorative, pointing only to human self-exaltation in visible things and thus deferring the encounter with the things of God hidden *sub contrario*.[56] For Calvin, God "clothes" God's self in the intermediaries that mediate providential activity— a clothing that simultaneously hides God's being, but also renders that being to be engaged in and with the immanent contours of creation. Unlike Luther, Calvin interprets the clothing of God in terms of the universe as the living image of God, in which the invisible God appears in a manner visible to us. "In respect of his essence, God undoubtedly dwells in light that is inaccessible; but as he irradiates the whole world by his splendor, this is the garment in which he, who is hidden in himself, appears in a manner visible to us." Calvin contrasts the hiddenness of God with the beautiful clothing of the world that we see and accentuates the beauty of that clothing: "That we may enjoy the sight of him, he must come forth to view in his clothing; that is to say, we must cast our eyes upon the very beautiful fabric of the world in which he wishes to be seen by us, and not be too curious and rash in search in his secret essence" (Zachman 2006: 179–180).[57]

Calvin's willingness to treat creation as a mode for positive divine revelation is also evident, as I've argued, in the order of the 1559 *Institutio*'s itinerant structure, where the form and content alike present the frame of the universe as the proper domain in and through which the knowledge of God and ourselves – the *cognitio Dei et notri*

---

has to do with its diminution of human power and perceptual capacity. The revelation of nature, then, is a positive revelation of God's power – or, as Schreiner puts it, "a God whose goodness is inseparable from his power" (146).

[56] In Luther's *Heidelberg Disputations*, he famously pits a theology of glory against a theology of the cross. See, for example, theses 19–21:

> 19. That person does not deserve to be called a theologian who looks upon the "invisible" things of God as though they were clearly "perceptible in those things which have actually happened,"
>
> 20. he deserves to be called a theologian, however, who comprehends the visible and manifest things of God seen through suffering and the cross.
>
> 21. A theology of glory calls evil good and good evil. A theology of the cross calls the thing what it actually is.

When Luther glosses these theses, he critiques the tendency to associate human conceptions of glory with divine glory, underscoring the paradoxical nature of God being revealed *sub contrario* or under God's opposite (for more, see the previous note as well as my subsequent discussion in this chapter). Calvin, on the other hand, seems to want to bring human perception into a more positive alignment with knowledge of the divine. This tendency is apparent, for one, in Calvin's view of the *sensus divinitatis*, which is damaged by the fall but partially accommodated by the spectacles of scripture (see Chapter 4). Similarly, Calvin's positive use of the law (which will also be discussed in this chapter) suggests that sanctification leads ideally to a situation in which human appraisals of earthly life align positively (though never perfectly) with divine appraisals.

[57] Quotes from Calvin's commentary on Psalm 104 are from CO 32:85A.

of the *Institutio*'s first chapter – is first constituted and ultimately reconstituted.[58]

But what of the other form of hiddenness? This is the thornier and in many ways the more interesting question. The claim that God has a "dark side," unillumined through revelation and entirely inaccessible to human reason, is a possibility conjured by any strong claim about divine providence, inasmuch as those strong claims want to grant God full control as creator, governor, judge, *and* redeemer. This possibility becomes actual when such claims are read as representational accounts of metaphysical realities – the *reality* that God created us, willed us to sin, willed to punish us, then willed to save us precisely from that punishment. If such a God has a unified will, then it seems that this is precisely the kind of God Calvin wants to resist: the God who "mak[es] sport of men by throwing them about like balls" (*Inst.* 1.17.1). This kind of hidden God yields very much the kind of tension that Blumenberg saw inherent in a Christian theology marked by a prevailing "Gnostic" temptation not unlike Nietzsche's ascetic ideal. To trade in this account means distrusting the human ability to perceive, know, and act with clarity within our own world and guided by our own judgments.[59]

For Calvin, the specter of the second form of hiddenness emerges most prevalently when he talks about God's secret *decree* – a decree that, later in the *Institutio*, predestines some for salvation and others for damnation. But it emerges also with providence, when Calvin insists, as he does, that God providentially *wills* evils according to that same decree, rather than merely withdrawing his will to permit them to occur solely by other causal means.[60] If such claims were taken in isolation from everything else Calvin says about providence, and indeed from his whole pedagogical

---

[58] Another factor that distinguishes Calvin from Luther has to do with Calvin's view of the law and its effect on his view of faith. I will return briefly to Calvin's view of the law in Chapter 6.

[59] For an analysis of Blumenberg's argument, see Benjamin Lazier, "Overcoming Gnosticism: Hans Jonas, Hans Blumenberg, and the Legitimacy of the Natural World" in *Journal of the History of Ideas* 64/4 (2003): 619–637. For a theologically oriented discussion of this tendency with respect to atonement theory, see S. Mark Heim, *Saved From Sacrifice: A Theology of the Cross* (Grand Rapids, MI: Eerdman's, 2006), 201-ff.

[60] Although predestination and providence are distinct for Calvin, this is largely due to their respective locations in the pedagogical itinerary. In other respects, these doctrinal discussions are repetitions of the same basic problemata. Predestination, which appears in Book Three on how the grace of Christ is rightly received, is uniquely fit to follow the full discussion of the *cognitio Dei redemptoris* just as providence emerges earlier with the *cognitio Dei creatoris*. For Calvin's discussion of predestination and election, see *Institutes* 3.21–24.

project, it would be entirely fair to accuse Calvin of indulging the "Gnostic" temptation and risking both the theological and practical problems that ensue. But this stands in contrast to the other features of Calvin's argument that I've been detailing: namely, that God's providential will works primarily through the distinct intermediaries of the causal complex of creation; that God wills all things for "just ends"; and, of course, that God's will is in fact unified as it *affirms* and then *acts within* the causal complex of creation toward ends that are revealed in Christ.[61]

Read against these claims, it behooves a devoted reader to continue to try and understand why and how it is that Calvin thinks his view hangs together. This is where the tilt of the reader's head, when looking at words that very clearly seem to claim something in black and white, might change everything about how that claim is interpreted. By a tilt of the head, I mean that the reader reads while taking into account the fuller, practical, and performative framework that providential discourses long assumed, and that Calvin has taken great pains to set out. Recall two features of Calvin's framework. One is the overtly pedagogical arrangement of Calvin's writing that I examined in Chapter 1, designed to mediate – and thus remain accountable to – the concrete realities and needs of human life. The second is something I've spent less time discussing until now, but which will occupy much of the remainder of this book: namely, the emphasis Calvin gives to *fictive language* – the language of poiesis, in that it is made for strategic, imaginative (and thereby practical) use. I've already shown how Calvin explicitly envisions the signs of scripture and of the incarnation to direct a "reader" toward the world materialized as a domain of glory fit for life. But going forward Calvin's use of fictive language – images, narratives, devices – are crucial to understanding not just *that* God affirms the world as its Creator, but how that will, in turn, renders the world *as* creation, or as an object of love.

---

[61] For Calvin, the knowledge of God the Redeemer in Christ supplies the second part of the twofold knowledge of God, allowing the knowledge of the power of God as creator to be known as good in "the face of Christ" (*Inst.* 1.2.1; see also 2.6.1). As I will soon argue in greater depth, both here and in the next part of the book, Christological revelation functions as a special mode of embodied signification – one that works, in part, by differentiating the will of God with respect to material life through both through the affirmation of life itself and through a deliberate choreography of action within creation. On my reading, this is crucial to Calvin's strategy for taking up and advancing his providential argument that God's power is both indexed to nature and part and parcel of divine goodness.

Calvin's nod to the function of narratives in reframing attention to the world and enabling different forms of behavior is sometimes granular. For example, he has a penchant to use "as if" in both positive and negative ways to refer to the practical effects of the use of different kinds of signs. In the locus on providence, Calvin uses "as if" to refer to wrong ways of framing the world's order, such as to see the world *as if* God is making sport of humans (*Inst.* 1.17.1) or by living "as if" a sword hung over their head (*Inst.* 1.17.10). However, when speaking of justification in Book Three, he uses the "as if" more positively to construct a kind of legal fiction concerning the state of the believer: a Christian lives "as if their innocence were confirmed" (*Inst.* 3.11.3). And, in Book Four, he gestures in a similar way to this kind of fiction mediating the operation of Eucharistic signification: "Now, that sacred partaking of his flesh and blood, by which Christ pours his life into us, *as if* it penetrated into our bones and marrow, he also testifies and seals in the Supper – not by presenting a vain and empty sign, but by manifesting there the effectiveness of his Spirit to fulfill what he promises" (*Inst.* 4.17.10, emphasis in original). In other respects, Calvin relies on the fictive use of language more holistically. The doctrines of accommodation and adoption rely almost entirely on the ability of the fictive to perform a new materialization of life through resignifying it. By insisting that God accommodates revelation to human capacity, or that God declares human beings as God's adopted "children" through Christ's representative work, language is used to differentiate and perform relationships between material conditions where previously there were none.

But perhaps the most interesting case is found in Calvin's treatment of the law, which is assumed by many to occupy the category of "revealed will." Calvin understands the law to have a positive function, especially when compared to Luther who saw the law primarily as a tool for the conviction of sin and the restraint of evildoers. Calvin's positive "third use" of the law follows the fictive logic I've been tracing: It fashions an imaginative mode of life that does not yet exist, but that he thinks can perform more useful and beneficial ways of living. Calvin writes that the law contains a "promise," namely that humans may "learn more thoroughly each day the nature of the Lord's will to which they aspire, and to confirm them in the understanding of it" (*Inst.* 2.7.12). The law, as a kind of object, reiterates the function of spectacles by clarifying features of material existence and enabling new forms of participation within creation. The physical incarnation of Christ – whose bodily actions "fulfill the law" – will further repeat and secure the relationship between the fictive nature of the revealed will and its concretization on earth. When Christ embodies the signification of the law in the real context of *instrumentum* and *causas inferiores*, Christ's gestures furnish a narrative that further enables "mediation" through a choreographed participation of one living into the name "child." I'll say more about all of this later, but it's important to begin seeing how the thread of signification effects a resignification of various domains of life as the books of the *Institutio* proceed, ultimately facing the city.

So, if the revealed will of God is fictive, and its power is the power of the signifying Word, it is performative – it makes things. This means that it is *not the kind of thing* that can stand in contradiction to any "given" immanent reality. It adds to and is useful for engaging what is treated as given. In this sense, its basic structure is one of *poiesis*, in the sense that it projects an arrangement of signs creatively, apart from the concreteness of present conditions. The difference, of course, is that for Calvin these stories are not thought to originate in the human mind, but to address the human mind from a site of originary hiddenness.

CONCLUSION

With this, the reader is returned – even five hundred years later – to the crossroads. Do these theological narratives, as received but addressed to a refugee community, upset the logic of sovereignty or merely reorient and perpetuate it? After all, if the God who "creates light and darkness" and "forms good and bad" and "does" all of the evil that happens is also the one who gives the narrative through which it can be perceived, then those who receive the narrative might well see themselves as those of the light and the good with the decoder ring for then deciding the status of others. But when Calvin tethers the specter of utter divine hiddenness to underscore the transcendent qualities of the world – to the way it wears clothes and signs divine glory quite beyond and against the glory of kings – it can have the effect of redirecting the desire for transcendence *to* a posture of reverence for the natural world as that to which God is saying "yes" at every turn, even the suffering.

4

Providence and Governmentality

But in thinking of the mechanisms of power, I am thinking rather of its capillary form of existence, the point where power reaches into the very grain of individuals, touches their bodies and inserts itself into their actions and attitudes, their discourses, learning processes and everyday lives. The eighteenth century invented, so to speak, a synaptic regime of power, a regime of its exercise within the social body, rather than from above it.

–Michel Foucault[1]

Calvin's providential discourse is fit for the experience of readers who begin by knowing themselves under the sign of exile. By insisting that God is actively present in every event, prior to and perhaps even against the evidence at hand, Calvin sets up the structure of a cognitive practice that facilitates a new materialization of the world that disrupts the conditions through which exile is a recognizable social location. If providential arguments render the created world *as if* the bearer of "divine insignia" at every turn, this elicits a posture that places the reader more fundamentally in the world rather than defining her in relation to a corporate institution. The doctrine aids the reader by training her "to seek every good from God, and having received it, to credit it to God's account" (*Inst.* 1.5.1; 1.2.2), and thus to approach creation itself as "a sort of mirror in which we can contemplate God who is otherwise invisible" (*Inst.* 1.5.1). Among other things, this creates conditions for the possibility of surprise and revaluation:

---

[1] Michel Foucault, *Power/Knowledge: Selected Interviews and Other Writings 1972–1977* (New York: Pantheon Books, 1980), 39.

In their desperate straits God suddenly and wonderfully and beyond all hope succors the poor and almost lost; those wandering through the desert he protects from wild beasts and at last guides them back to the way; to the needy and hungry he supplies food; the prisoners he frees from loathsome dungeons and iron bands; the shipwrecked he leads back to port unharmed; the half dead he cures of disease; he burns the earth with heat and dryness, or makes it fertile with the secret watering of grace; he raises up the humblest from the crowd, or casts down the lofty from the high level of their dignity. By setting forth examples of this sort, the prophet shows that what are thought to be chance occurrences are just so many proofs of heavenly providence, especially of fatherly kindness (*Inst.* 1.5.8).

Calvin thinks the exercise of seeing the world as if affirmed and then engaged by God will generate forbearance, reverence, expectation, and even love – all staging for pursuing the knowledge of God and ourselves (1.2.1–2).

This exercise also creates conditions for the possibility of a disciplinary state in which sovereignty is reimagined as a tactic of producing and organizing a population of exceptions. In *Security, Territory, and Population*, Foucault argues that the seventeenth century marks a shift from sovereignty as a top-down act of legal enforcement to a strategy of management that works by disposing persons into a multifaceted organizational apparatus. In *The Disciplinary Revolution*, Philip Gorski ties this argument to the impact of Calvinism. Calvinist disciplinary practices facilitated "the bottom-up creation of new strategies and mechanisms of discipline and governance and their gradual instrumentalization and absorption by political elites."[2] Gorski's argument draws primarily from

---

[2] Philip Gorski, *The Disciplinary Revolution* (Chicago: University of Chicago Press, 2003), 19. Unlike Weber, who tied Calvinist pastoral practices to the conditions of the emergence of modern capitalism and instrumental rationality, Gorski locates the bottom-up effect of Calvinist disciplinary practices in modern statecraft – in other words, in the impulse to rethink the operation of state power (and, later, corporate power) in managerial terms. Gorski explicitly links his understanding of the state to the economy in several places, but perhaps most succinctly in his conclusion on page 164f. He also notes the interconnection of bureaucratic management in both state and corporate logic on page 167: "It suggests that the efficacy of government, the development of the economy, the stability of democracy, and various other collective goods are strongly and positively linked to the existence of dense networks of associational life that facilitate cooperation, enforce norms and sustain trust within everyday interaction ... Or take the voluminous literature on corporatism. Theorists of corporatism emphasize the role of organized interests (for example, unions and employers associations) in governing the economy and increasing productivity and argue that organized capitalism yields better outcomes than laissez-faire capitalism or state dirigisme. To put it into the terms of the present analysis, they contend that the most effective system of economic governance involves a high degree of organizational entwining."

case studies of the Dutch Republic and Prussia – studies that would draw us far afield from the 1559 *Institutio*. But along the way, Gorski highlights two salient features of Calvinist practice that are legible against the doctrine of providence as I've presented it so far, and useful to bring to bear on a close reading of the text.

One is that Calvinists, who were so opposed to the perceived idolatry of a church constituted around the Mass, uniquely rethought the outward form of the church as a *disciplina*. To be sure, like other reformers, Calvin places a strong emphasis on the ultimate reality of the "invisible" church comprised of the elect. But Calvin was also interested in maintaining a visible church that "required institutions, laws, and governing officials," and in this sense, Sheldon Wolin argues that "it belonged to the realm of human art." As a product of creative making, the church "challenged the ecclesiastical legislator to make of it *une église bien ordonnée et reglée* [a well ordered and regulated church]."[3] For in the critical absence of the quasi-genetic imaginary of a *Corpus Christianum* visibly grounded in transcendent origins and ends, Calvin and his colleagues developed fully immanent structures through which believers could join each other in exercises like "Bible reading, daily journals, moral log books, and rigid control over time."[4] Through such practices, believers could repeatedly exercise naming themselves and other events under the sign of God's care, which – according to the logic laid out in Book One of the 1559 *Institutio* – enables the materialization of the world *as* the theater of divine glory. If such exercises were performed in concert – as a form of public art – the Calvinist church could then enjoy a different kind of unity as a collective entity who share the quality of (at the very least) a posture toward the world. In this sense, the church's existence was grounded not in claims to divine substance, but "a constant exercise of power."[5]

Second, Gorski emphasizes the social character of Calvinism – that "the Calvinists ... were not content with a disciplined church; they wanted a disciplined society as well."[6] In the preface to the 1559 *Institutio*, Calvin makes clear that his aim is to "spread [God's] Kingdom and further the public good," and I've been emphasizing ways that his

---

[3] Sheldon Wolin, *Politics and Vision* (Princeton, NJ: Princeton University Press, 2004), 152.

[4] Gorski, 20.   [5] Wolin, 153.

[6] Gorski, 27. He notes that this point is made by Weber in *The Protestant Ethic*, though overshadowed by the larger emphasis on the human reaction to strong predestination. While this cannot be strictly associated with Calvinist societies – new efforts of poor relief, for example, appeared across early modern Europe – Gorski argues that Calvinist societies "went farther, faster" (177n. 73).

doctrine of providence carries an activist bent. By seeing the world as the site of divine affirmation and activity, Calvin is establishing what he takes to be the conditions for the possibility of robust and self-directed worldly activity. In Geneva as well as other later Calvinist civic polities, this impulse was concretely manifest in organized projects of poor relief and social welfare as well as the expectation that magistrates would protect religious practice and reinforce Christian discipline more generally. Wolin argues that, for Calvin, "the ends of political society were not exhausted by its Christian mission."[7] Nevertheless, the seventeenth-century confessionalization of Calvinist churches would facilitate new structural cleavages between a cross-section of citizens and political structures, thus expanding the cleavages between the state and the population.[8] In both direct and roundabout ways, then, Calvinism can be persuasively linked to a logic of sovereignty that manifests as modern governmentality. It is fair, and perhaps obvious, to say that elements of Calvin's teaching fund an imaginary of power that works by differentiating social actors and redefining them in concert with new methods of management that would continue to involve, and even rely more strongly, on evolving state–economic apparatuses.

This returns us to the Calvinist crossroads: the question of whether and to what extent this theology mobilizes a critique of the urge to imagine society as a body governed by appeals to transcendent sovereignty. Does Calvin's positionality facilitate a fundamental critique of the urge to picture society as a quasi-incarnate *Corpus Christianum*, or does it simply refine and reorient that body around the positionality of the exile who becomes the new norm? This chapter will not fully consider this question. Much of that work is still to come in the next part as I look at the role of the incarnation in Calvin's thinking across the remaining books of the *Institutio*. But this chapter will pause to consider whether Calvin's articulation of providence, in particular, accords with or challenges the logic of a disciplinary state, conceived in the broadly Foucauldian sense. Since at least the appearance of Max Weber's *Protestant Ethic* and Schmitt's *Political Theology* in the first decades of the twentieth century, it has not been unusual for theorists of political sovereignty to consider the dogmatic theology an oblique but fundamental force shaping the modern imaginaries of power. (By dogmatic theology, I mean theological writing that is directly engaged with traditional creedal loci rather than social ethics.) Yet, arguments involving Calvinism tend to remain focused on

---

[7] Wolin, 163.   [8] Gorski, 170–171.

either Calvin's explicitly political remarks or on the historical, social, and legal record of Calvinist polities.

In my view, the *Institutio* has a strong enough record of influence, intellectual heft, and evident pedagogical texture to recommend itself for analysis alongside theories of political theology that focus on the slow rhetorical effects of theology in shaping imaginaries of power. I'll begin that effort in this chapter by considering Calvin's providence alongside one of the more interesting recent readings of the Christian theological archive around questions of governmentality: Giorgio Agamben's 2011 *The Kingdom and the Glory*. Drawing on an array of dogmatic sources from Tertullian to Thomas Aquinas, and theoretical interlocutors including Schmitt, Peterson, and Foucault, Agamben argues that the bipolar apparatus of modern governmentality is legible well before the early modern era, which is when Foucault marks its emergence. The argument makes its case by analyzing tensions cutting across central doctrinal loci, focusing especially on the trinity and providence. Both of these are central to Calvin's thinking, yet Agamben's genealogy makes no mention of Calvin and little mention of Reformation-era or Protestant theology at all.[9] Reading them alongside each other will help to focus an analysis of what particular points in the argument might lead one to read Calvin's *Institutio* as either a blueprint for governmentality or as a source for more radically rethinking how sovereignty reaches the body.

AGAMBEN'S METHODOLOGY

Agamben reoccupies the conversation around Schmitt's political theology by arguing that divine providence is a more fundamental than divine sovereignty for grasping the operation of modern governmentality.[10]

---

[9] Giorgio Agamben, *The Kingdom and the Glory: For a Theological Genealogy of Economy and Government* (Redwood City, CA: Stanford University Press, 2011). In the opening paragraphs, he forwards a limited reading of the contributions of Protestantism to the question of governmentality, writing: "In modern Protestant theology, the problem of *oikonomia* reappeared, but only as an obscure and indeterminate precursor of the theme of *Heilsgeschichte*, while the opposite is true: The theology of the "history of salvation" is a partial and, all in all reductive resumption of a much broader paradigm (*KG*, 2). Apart from a brief mention of the "Lutheran error" (*KG*, 137) and a longer engagement with Karl Barth (*KG*, 211f), Protestantism is left largely unengaged.

[10] Erik Peterson argues that the Christian doctrine of the trinity fundamentally disrupts the Aristotelian legacy that draws an analogy between God and monarchy. The argument Agamben engages is found in Erik Peterson, "Monotheism as a Political Problem" in

According to Schmitt, the sovereign is the one who decides over the exception, and we've seen that debates continue to be had over whether or not the theological structure of this claim continues to inform liberal democracy. But for Agamben, the more pertinent question has to do with how sovereignty meets the body in modern democratic societies, and this means extending Schmitt's observation not just to the legal state, but also "to the fundamental concepts of the economy and the very idea of the reproductive life of human societies."[11] To mark the difference between how life was managed by premodern modes of sovereignty versus the modern disciplinary state, Agamben follows Foucault by borrowing conceptual terms from Aristotle, who distinguished between *zoe* (biological-animal life) and *bios* (political life). *Zoe* is the form of life proper to the *oikonomia*, or the "law of the home" governing natural life. *Bios* is the form of life proper to *politika*, or the "law of the state" mediating the "good life" available to the citizen.[12] Foucault's term "biopower" refers to the novel tactic of power that *integrates* these two forms of life into one complex disciplinary paradigm. Biological, medical, and psychological techniques of knowledge produce naturalized identities (*zoe*) that in turn yield – and fuel – complex apparatuses of social capabilities and expectations (*bios*) that are mobilized toward productive ends.

Premodern societies tended to treat natural life as invested in natural or divine necessity. In its classical sense, the *oikonomia* referred to a practical set of tasks to maintain a home or household while full human flourishing was reserved for (elite male) civic participants. Biopower, in contrast, functions by "making immanent" and then mobilizing what had once been seen as the transcendent dimensions of material, natural life. The difference between these two tactics of power can be seen especially in the figure of the refugee. According to an older logic of sovereignty, those deemed a threat to civic flourishing were either executed or expelled from the body of the state. Modern governmentality exercises sovereignty by

Theological Tractates, trans. M. Hollerich (Stanford, CA: Stanford University Press, 2011: 68–105). For more, see György Geréby, "Political Theology versus Theological Politics: Erik Peterson and Carl Schmitt" in *New German Critique* 105 (Fall, 2008): 7–33; and Daniel McLoughlin, "On Political and Economic Theology" in *Angelaki* 20/4 (2015): 53–69.

[11] Agamben, *KG*, 3.

[12] This distinction is found in Book I of the *Economics* – a work attributed to Aristotle but widely believed to be authored by one of Aristotle's students, possibly Theophrastus. See Aristotle, *Economics*, 1.1343a.

rendering unruly bodies manageable by first identifying their naturalized pathology (*zoe*) and then, by means of that knowledge, integrating them into an ever-more-refined disciplinary regime (*bios*) that constantly reproduces and reorganizes itself around implicit norms that are themselves naturalized through appeals to knowledge.[13] According to Foucault,

> For the first time in history, no doubt, biological existence [*zoe*] was reflected in political existence [*bios*]; the fact of living was no longer an *inaccessible substrate* that only emerged from time to time, amid the randomness of death and its fatality; part of it passed into knowledge's field of control and power's sphere of intervention. Power would no longer be dealing simply with legal subjects over whom the ultimate dominion was death, but with living beings, and the mastery it would be able to exercise over them would have to be applied at the level of life itself; it was the taking charge of life, more than the threat of death, that gave power its access even to the body.[14]

Foucault can be read as obliquely recognizing but also critiquing Blumenberg's characterization of modernity as a "turn to immanence" that works through efforts at human making that masters nature itself. But where Blumenberg is sanguine about the progressive nature of this turn, Foucault's accounts tend to underscore the fundamental violence of a governmentality that invades the body at the micro-level, deploying claims of knowledge that take charge over the soul itself by reproducing a disciplinary subject.

Foucault remained interested in how the body itself acts as a site of resistance to discipline, and Agamben follows this lead by contributing several terms to the analysis, including "bare life" and "eternal life." "Bare life" refers to the fundamental residue of a life that cannot be captured by governmental machinery but is produced as abjection by the full force of the biopower. His primary empirical example is drawn from accounts of the "*Muselmänner*" – those confined to the power of concentration camps who were neither alive nor dead and whose "lives" bore witness both to the brutality and the limits of disciplinary power.

---

[13] As noted, abnormality does not lead to expulsion. Rather, abnormality is integrated into the governmental apparatus to fuel normativity. Modern governmentality therefore generates ever-more identities that each reinforce the knowledge/power of the episteme itself. Among various works, this is treated in Foucault's 1974–1975 lectures at the Collège de France, subsequently titled *Abnormal*. See Michel Foucault, *Abnormal*, trans. Graham Burchell (New York, Picador, 2003).

[14] Foucault, *History of Sexuality 1: The Will to Knowledge* (New York: Vintage, 1978), 142–143. Emphasis mine.

"Eternal life," or *zoe aionios*, refers more positively to an inoperative form of life that cannot be harnessed for productivity, but only contemplation.[15]

These ways of distinguishing materializations of life are deeply inscribed in the different tactics of providential discourse, and attention to providential discourse enables him to mark the emergence of the bipolar apparatus of governmentality much earlier than Foucault: namely, in Christian antiquity, when patristic authors – themselves positioned at the margins of an empire – struggled to give an account of how transcendent divine ordering (sovereignty) is realized in the world (providence). At the same time, Agamben argues that this cannot be read as a linear tale. The point is not that some purely theological concepts became secularized as political concepts. The imbrication of theological and political conceptions of power happened through a disjointed series of encounters that become legible when one looks not for continuous concepts, but "signatures" that refer one archive to another. In this chapter, I'm interested in the way Agamben addresses three of those signatures: order, glory, and secularization itself.

To gain some clarity on Agamben's methodology and what he means by signatures, let me begin with secularization. Agamben suggests that debates over secularization and political theology have been so frustrating and intractable in part because they presume a notion of causality – in other words, of how change happens with respect to space and time – that is not fit for the question under investigation. By looking for a linear progression of knowledge tied to certain geographic centers, the secularization debate is frontloaded as an investigation of whether politics and theology are conceptually identical or not. Agamben argues that "secularization" is better read as a signature, which means as a constellation of signs that "mark political concepts in order to make them refer to their theological origins."[16] He uses a number of examples to cite how a

---

[15] Agamben routinely employs the Aristotelian distinction between *zoe* and *bios* not only to largely agree with Foucault concerning their modern confluence, but also to distinguish both from his own category of "bare life." For Agamben, bare life is a residue of material life that *resists* governmentality, that *resists* signification, and as such points to something like the transcendent materiality at which I have been gesturing. For Agamben, bare life also represents a kind of mirror-image to the logic of the sovereign exception. If sovereignty operates by deciding over exceptions to the rule, bare life is what exceeds the rules of identification and, as such, cannot be governed. Bare life is therefore both an outcome *of* sovereignty (which creates excess) and a perpetual threat *to* sovereignty (by challenging its capacity to identify excess).

[16] Agamben, *The Signature of All Things* (Brooklyn, NY: Zone Books, 2009), 76–77.

signature works as a strategic operator: The visage on a coin is a signature that relates its historical-artifactual quality to its potential power as currency; certain cuts and colors of fashion refer contemporary social class to past settings.[17] "Secularization, then, is a signature that marks or exceeds a sign or concept in order to refer it to a specific interpretation or to a specific sphere without, however, leaving it in order to constitute a new concept or new meaning."[18] Signatures perform relationships between separate discursive domains as an encounter between a particular and a particular, refusing the urge to create an abstract universal to perform the work of comparison. Secularization is therefore not a concept the content of which must be contested, but an invitation for scholars to examine one domain by paying closer attention to the other domain to which the signature refers. The question is not what secularization is; it is how the political question of secularization invites a deeper and closer reading of theology, and vice versa.

It's crucial that this account avoids the subjective confines of either bounded space or sequential time. Agamben demonstrates this point by locating the methodological use of signatures in authors who are otherwise far removed from one another in both time and aim: Proclus, Augustine, Thomas Aquinas, Paracelsus, Jakob Boehme, Nietzsche, Benjamin, Melandre, Foucault, and Derrida.[19] But whether the pursuit is sacramental theology, natural magic, or deconstruction, all of these sources perform their respective investigations by relating recognizable shapes or constellations of signs across domains to "make the world, mute and without reason itself, intelligible."[20] The goal here is not an ontology in the sense of disclosing the general contours of existence, but encountering existence through its "passions," or by what is left behind "by virtue of the very fact of existing." This kind of archaeology proceeds by noticing resonant ways that the struggle of existence has been articulated, and using that to discern the material traces attached to

[17] Agamben, *ST*, 38, 73.   [18] Agamben, *ST*, 76–77; See also Agamben, *KG*, 4.
[19] Agamben, *ST*, 33–49, 57–64. See also Agamben 2011, 4. For Augustine, the signature informs a theory of the sacraments as excessive symbols that place God and humanity in relation to one another and enables the activity of worship; for Proclus and later Paracelsus, signatures move between domains of nature and enable theurgic manipulation; and within Foucault's theory of discourse, the "statement" is a "function of existence ... that cuts across domains of structures and possible unities, and which reveals them, with concrete contents, in time and space." See Foucault, *The Archaeology of Knowledge*, trans. Smith (New York: Pantheon Books, 1970), 86–87. Quoted in Agamben, *ST*, 63.
[20] Agamben, *ST*, 40–41.

argumentative differences, much like a photograph reveals contours of things merely by capturing scattered light.[21] This methodology disrupts linear temporality, not only by emphasizing the particular encounters from times out of joint but by continually calling into question our normative assumptions about the limitations of the past. After all, if a signature pointing to some past archive can enable some new and transformative understanding of the present, this simultaneously revises our conceptions about the past itself.[22]

ORDER

In *The Kingdom and the Glory*, Agamben argues that "order" [*taxis, ordo*] and "glory" [*doxa, gloria*] are key signatures underwriting questions about secularizations because they move across theological and political domains. By tracing them in theological archives, he claims to locate the legible outlines of biopower – the bipolar apparatus of modern governmentality that takes *zoe* up into *bios* – in early Christian debates over how the transcendent God governs the immanent creation.[23]

Agamben's argument goes deep into a series of places where early Christian authors both generated and then tried to restitch a fracture between divine *being* and *praxis*. This, of course, is one way of describing the work of providential discourse itself, inasmuch as providence is invoked to persuade a reader how ordinary activity attains significance in relation to the "truth" of being. Stoics tended to opt for praxis, defining the world in largely economic terms *as* the domain of immanent divine activity. To learn to live in the world means learning to live in imitation of the gods.[24] Aristotle, in contrast, would suggest that the world is put into general motion by an unmoved mover. Human activity, therefore, occurs against the backdrop of fate, but the *oikonomia* is not grounded in the nature of the divine being. Christians, however, would struggle to articulate a position between these extremes, wanting both to posit a monotheistic divinity who is also fundamentally concerned with and involved in the worldly *oikonomia*. According to Agamben, Christian theology needed to continually weave arguments to stitch together this perpetual fracture.[25]

---

[21] Agamben, *ST*, 65–66.   [22] Agamben, *ST*, 106; see also 94–95, 103–105.
[23] Agamben, *KG*, 87–89.   [24] For more, see my discussion in Chapter 2.
[25] Agamben traces the shift from the Pauline "economy of the mystery" to the Patristic "mystery of the economy" as follows. When Paul refers to the "*oikonomia* of God"

Agamben points to many locations in the Christian archive where debates over order reveal a fracture between being and praxis, but I will focus on two of the most important. One is the struggle to articulate the doctrine of the trinity – an orthodoxy forged out of resistance, again to two extremes: to Gnostics, who proliferated divine hypostases; and Arius, who posited the Son's begottenness in the name of preserving monotheism.[26] By trying to hold together both the unity of the transcendent God and the full significance of the Son's worldly activity *as* divine activity, early figures like Irenaeus and Hippolytus began to reframe the *oikonomia* – the activity proper to *zoe*, or ordinary natural life – as a manifestation or working-out of mysterious divine activity. This generated the terminology of order through which the trinity itself would be theorized as an economy or mysterious activity of divine being itself. Later, that same terminology informed Christian efforts to articulate divine providence.

In order to maintain the divine unity while also refuting the claim that the Son was begotten by (and therefore inferior to) the Father, the Nicene thesis maintains that the Son is the *logos* that "exists absolutely" and "does not have an *arche*," but "reigns together with the Father absolutely, anarchically, and infinitely."[27] *Arche*, of course, refers both to a beginning and a principle. Agamben interprets the language of *anarchos* to mean that Christians were willing to posit a paradigm of praxis that is not only without a beginning in time but actually unfounded in being.[28] By marking a break between the paradigm of sovereignty (the being of the Father, who rules) and the paradigm of economy (the economy of the Son, who governs), trinitarian theology offers an early articulation of Foucauldian governmentality: a mode of disciplining activity that articulates sovereignty by articulating existence. If the Son, who is the revelation of the Father and who dispenses the earthly work of the Father, is

(1 Cor 1:24–25) and later (in what is probably a pseudo epistle) to a calling to "make all men see what is the *oikonomia* of the mystery hidden for ages in God" (Eph 3:9), Agamben argues that he is merely borrowing the Aristotelian term for "household administration" to characterize his divinely given task. Later readers would reverse the terms in order to invest the flesh – and therefore the claim of Christ's incarnation – with divine authority. Irenaeus, for example, argues that in denying the flesh, Gnostics "overturn [...] the entire economy of God" (*KG* 33). Later, Hippolytus would fully reverse the order of the Pauline statement to "mystery of the economy" and effectively invest the general administration of worldly affairs with the significance of the working-out of a divine plan, therefore investing the *oikonomia* with fully divine significance. (*KG* 38–39).

[26] Agamben, *KG*, 33,   [27] Agamben *KG*, 58.   [28] Agamben, *KG*, 59.

ungrounded with respect to the Father, this sets up a paradigm in which claims to being function merely to legitimize and fuel activity.

Agamben locates a similar fracture and reversal much later when Thomas Aquinas takes up the question of how God, as a unified being, also providentially governs the multiplicity of the world. The argument relies, once again, on the *oikonomia* in order to articulate sovereignty. Thomas writes that, "In an ordered household or family different ranks of members are found ... And just as the order of the family is imposed by the law and precent of the head of the family ... in a similar fashion, the nature of physical things is the principle by which each of them carries out the activity proper to it in the order of the universe."[29] Here is how Agamben glosses that passage:

> The aporia [between being and praxis] that marks like a thin crack the wonderful order of the medieval cosmos now begins to become more visible. Things are ordered insofar as they have a specific relation among themselves, but this relation is nothing other than the expression of their relation to the divine end. And, vice versa, things are ordered insofar as they have a certain relation to God, but this relation expresses itself only by means of the reciprocal relation of things. The only content of the transcendent order is the immanent order, but the meaning of the immanent order is nothing other than the relation to the transcendent end. *"Order ad finem"* and *"ordo ad invicem"* refer back to one another and found themselves on one another.[30]

This recalls another earlier rendering of providence in Augustine's *De genisi ad litteram*, where he argues that worldly existence is constantly generated by incessant divine activity that engages in *dispositio* – the Latin word for *oikonomia*.[31] Agamben argues that providence is "the name of the '*oikonomia*,' insofar as the latter presents itself as the government of the world."[32]

Agamben's argument finds further clarity in the gradual move to prioritize special providence over general providence – a move that, I've argued, is foregrounded in Calvin's articulation. According to Agamben,

---

[29] Thomas Aquinas, *Commentary on the Metaphysics of Aristotle*, Book XII, Lesson Xll, 2633–2634. Quoted in Agamben, *KG*, 87.

[30] Agamben, *KG*, 87. Emphasis in original.

[31] Agamben, *KG*, 89. *Dispositio* also suggests a possible relation to the French term *dispositif* that appears so often across Foucault's writings to denote the system of heterogeneous relations that both articulate and manifest the effects of knowledge on, in, and around the body. See Foucault's 1977 essay, "Confessions of the Flesh."

[32] Agamben *ST*, 111.

The history of the concept of providence coincides with the long and fierce debate between those who claimed that God provides for the world only by means of general or universal principles and those who argued that the divine providence extends to particular things—according to the image in Matthew 10:29, down to the lowliest sparrow ... If the Kingdom and the Government are separated in God by a clear opposition, then no government of the world is actually possible: we would have, on the one hand, an impotent sovereignty and, on the other, the infinite and chaotic series of particular (and violent) acts of providence. The government is possible only if the Kingdom and the Government are correlated in a bipolar machine.[33]

If the Kingdom and the Government are not to be thought of as existing in opposition to one another, then providence cannot work by establishing universal laws and then suspending them for special purposes. Instead, general laws must be thought of as constituted by the special activity of the divine manager. They appear general inasmuch as that work is increasingly refined, but the stability – for example, of the external church – is always the product of ever-refined techniques of discipline. This activity, in effect, *constitutes* the sovereignty of God – a sovereignty that "exists" only insofar as providential activity is transcendentally referred to it.[34] The signature of order therefore refers diverse examples of tactics for sewing together being and praxis. Theologically, providence refers back to sovereignty, but only by recommending itself as the realization of sovereignty. Politically, governmental-economic management refers back to legitimate rule, but only by meting out that rule at the level of bodies managed by bureaucratic apparatuses. Providence, in this construal, is a theological prototype for biopower.

GLORY

Like the other writings and readings of providence I've looked at, Agamben locates an affective response produced by providential discourse. Interestingly, it is one that is also strongly emphasized (though not exclusively) by Calvin: namely, reverence, or the impulse to worship. Theologically, glory or *doxa* – praise and acclamation – are crucial to the work of providence. They generate a posture that reads worldly activity in a semiotic connection to divine governance, and they respond to the world that is performed as a result. Liturgy, prayer, and sacraments all function to facilitate and exercise this posture. But Agamben argues that glory itself

[33] Agamben, *KG*, 13, 14.   [34] Agamben, *KG*, 24.

is not a concept with a content, but a signature that relates concepts and also refers theology to politics where a similar dynamic occurs. Political "liturgies" and doxological spectacles of power provide the related function of fueling governmentality – of cultivating both the posture and the response that enables society to reproduce itself. The relation, here, is not arbitrary. The signature of glory moves between ecclesiology and politics because it performs a more fundamental task: It weaves a garment that conceals the *emptiness* of sovereignty at the center of the providential machine. Agamben writes,

> In a passage from *Joseph and His Brothers*, a novel that caused such labor among scholars of myth, Thomas Mann observes that—in a phrase that is [Jan] Assmann's starting point—religion and politics are not two fundamentally distinct things but that, on the contrary, they "exchange clothes." It is possible, however, that this exchange can take place only because underneath the garments there are no body and no substance. Theology and politics are, in this sense, what results from the exchange and from the movement of something like an absolute garment that, as such, has decisive juridical-political implications.[35]

The garment woven by providence, on this account, is the multifarious social body that exists to, and by, the reproduction of sovereignty through a discipline that enacts decisions over bodies constantly at the micro-level.

It's true, of course, that Christian theology often invokes glory at the discursive limits of what an argument can accomplish. Glory is the answer to questions of infinite regress, such as why God allows incongruous things, why creation exists as it does, or why God created in the first place.[36] (Answer: "For God's own glory.") As such, the gesture to glory is structurally linked to the transcendent "seat" of divine power that is never itself disclosed. According to Agamben, glory covers the power that is, in

---

[35] Agamben, *KG*, 194.

[36] While Agamben tracks many places in the earlier archive where glory marks discursive limits, it is interesting that it doesn't emerge as an abstract license for (or signal of) sovereign power until later. For example, the 1647 *Westminster Confession of Faith*, which represents a codified reworking of Reformed theology, treats glory as a sovereign manifestation that simultaneously functions as a legitimation of sovereign activity. God "manifests" glory in God's sovereign decrees which are justified by reference to God's glory (see especially chapters I.V, II–VI, XXIII). Later, in Jonathan Edwards' *A Dissertation Concerning the End for Which God Created the World* (1765), divine glory represents the chief end of all things: their origination, their justification, their goal. Contrast this with Thomas Aquinas, for whom glory appears most prominently as the medium through which the intellect can "see" God – an account that, on my reading, tracks much closer to what Calvin is doing with the *sensus divinitatis*. See *Summa Theologiae* Ia.12.2, 5–7.

fact, void and inoperative apart from the activity that refers to it. It therefore constellates an array of dazzling yet amorphous concepts: light, majesty, ineffability, and spectacle. Like the curtain before a stage, it is that before which a production with a hidden *telos* will emerge. But this only sutures a fracture that Agamben reads as fundamental to how power has been theorized in the West, one that constantly promises but never discloses the power of redemption:

> Praise and adoration directed toward the immanent trinity presuppose the economy of salvation, just as in John, the Father glorifies the Son and the Son glorifies the Father. *The economy glorifies being, as being glorifies the economy.* And only in the mirror of glory do the two trinities appear to reflect into one another; only in its splendor do being and economy, Kingdom and Government appear to coincide for an instant. Hence the Council of Nicaea, in order to avoid all risk of separating the Son from the Father, the economy from the substance, felt the need to insert into the symbol of faith the formula *phos ek photos*, "light of light." For this reason, Augustine, while seeking obsessively to eliminate all risk of subordination by the trinity, takes up an image of light and glory.[37]

Light appears, again and again, to cover the gap between being and praxis, working on an aesthetic level to "cover and dignify what is in itself pure force and domination."[38] But like the being it veils, glory itself has no substance beyond repeated exercises of glorification – gesticulations, songs, ceremonies, media spectacles, advertisements promising some flourishing but merely invading life at the level of *zoe* to put it to *bios*-production.[39] Like Foucault, Agamben is cagey on how to resist a power that works in this bipolar and multifaceted way, and for good reason. How can resistance be theorized as an activity within a system that is fueled by spectacle, that reproduces itself by integrating diverse activities into apparatus? But also like Foucault, when Agamben does gesture to resistance, he gestures to the body that exceeds the grasp of discipline. I'll return to this, but first, let me turn back to Calvin and consider how his approach to the trinity interfaces with his doctrine of providence with Agamben's account in mind.

BACK TO CALVIN

Elements of Calvin's providence suggest an astonishing resonance with Agamben's account. For Calvin, of course, providence is a discourse

---

[37] Agamben, *KG*, 209.   [38] Agamben, *KG*, 212.   [39] Agamben, *KG*, 253–256.

through which sovereignty is thematized as constant activity. Calvin also insists that this activity should be conceived as *primarily* special rather than general. It works in and through intermediaries at the granular level through a complex array of micro-negotiations. This could legitimately be read as a mode of governance that works by invading creation at the site of the body in order to dispose that body productively toward the hidden ends of sovereignty. Yet, there are some key places in Calvin's accounts of both the trinity and providence where he departs from Agamben in interesting ways. Paying some attention to these departures might help readers become attuned to a different set of possible relationships between theological thinking and the body, or between transcendent theorization and postures of and toward worldly activity.

The ability to notice these kinds of possible divergences of theological interpretation – divergences that have to do precisely with how theological writing is being received – more generally underscores the kind of fundamental interpretive choices that face any reader or practitioner of dogmatics. She must always ask: Are the arguments given as a conceptual tableau suggesting cognitive access to a transcendent order for the visible world? Or are the arguments addressed to a reader on a more holistic level in order to induce a set of relational postures – a kind of attention – to the things around her, such that she is in principle open to grace, teaching, and transformation? With Calvin, as with any (theological) author, it is crucial to ask not only how theological categories are indexed to material life, but also whether and how the text addresses itself to readers *as* embodied intellects located in particular places.

One of Agamben's greatest contributions to conversations around modern sovereignty is his recovery of the figure of the *homo sacer* as a theoretical basis for the individual in general. Modern sovereignty, he argues, begins by treating every person *as homo sacer* – as in principle an exception to the law, or as an ungovernable, and is then rendered governable through the tactics of biopower. I've noted that Agamben has been critiqued for too quickly making this a general category without asking what it might mean to theorize sovereignty from the perspective of those who are actually rendered ungovernable, or abject, within modern societies: For example, those incarcerated, undocumented migrants, and refugees who do still in fact exist as stateless persons.[40] Don't these figures

---

[40] To give only a few examples of persons who are not easily reintegrated into the "providential machine," or whose reintegration involves overt forms of violence. As I noted in the Introduction, I am indebted to J. Kameron Carter's articulation of this

mark some difference from the citizen as *homo sacer*? And how might we begin to theorize that difference?

If the basic conceptual apparatus of governmentality was already well in place by the early modern period, as Agamben argues, this makes it all the more important to ask how Calvin writes providence as a refugee – as someone whose experience bears obvious differences from modern refugees and those otherwise ungovernable, but whose intellectual production can be expected to register some critique of the way sovereignty organized bodies in his own time. I've already shown the extent to which Calvin's providence reframes *material creation* as a domain of divine affirmation, as the proper site of divine hiddenness, and, as such, as the proper location of transcendent divine glory – rather than, say, the church, and certainly rather than the state. These all suggest some dissonance from Agamben's account, which assumes that the signature of order ties providence inexorably to *political* governance. To gain some critical perspective on Agamben's account and its differences from Calvin's providence, let me back up to where Agamben locates the originary fracture between being and praxis in Christian thinking: the doctrine of the trinity. I'll argue that Calvin's treatment of the trinity similarly relates divine activity holistically to the human person conceived as a natural, knowing, and perceiving being, prior to and irrespective of her status as a citizen.

The trinity holds an odd place in Calvin's thinking. On the one hand, he treats it as absolutely fundamental. As the ordering principle of the Apostles' Creed, the trinity supplies the legible structure for Calvin's 1559 and final edition of the *Institutio*. The logic through which Calvin understands the trinity similarly structures many of his doctrinal loci, giving Calvin a conceptual rubric through which to persuade the reader how to encounter a teaching and relate it to her own life. But there is also a doctrinal locus dedicated to the doctrine of the trinity embedded in Book One, and when Calvin addresses the trinity, he evidences some discomfort with the doctrine. After all, the term never appears in scripture, which for Calvin is the proper lens and thread through which a human person comes to behold the true God.

Because Calvin is an unwavering Trinitarian, this problem pushes him all the more to foreground the pedagogical usefulness of the doctrine in

critique of Agamben. See J. Kameron Carter, "The Inglorious" in *Political Theology* 14/1 (2013): 77–87.

order to make sense of its place in Christian teaching.[41] So rather than emphasizing the technological terminology or conceptual debates over the relationships between the Trinitarian persons, he addresses traditional Trinitarian distinctions between Creator/Father, Word/Son, and Spirit as useful images given to aid a believer in differentiating and integrating teaching into her own life. The trinity is, therefore, an artifice that helps distinguish the salient *modes of activity* through which God addresses and relates to human persons. Calvin essentially bypasses the scriptural reticence of the doctrine by arguing that human learning allows and even requires us to put things "into our own words," as it were:

We ought to seek from Scripture a sure rule for both thinking and speaking, to which both the thoughts of our minds and the words of our mouths should be conformed. But what prevents us from explaining in clearer words those matters in Scripture which perplex and hinder our understanding, yet which conscientiously and faithfully serve the truth of Scripture itself, and are made use of sparingly and modestly and on due occasion? (*Inst.* 1.13.3).

Scripture may not refer to any "trinity," and much less to the "layers of verbiage" that have been employed to "explain" it, such as "hypostases," "person," "subsistence," and "*homoousios*" (*Inst.* 1.13.4–5). But scripture does "utterly compel" readers to rely on such a conceptual apparatus in order to faithfully and adequately characterize the God who *is* proclaimed in scripture.

This is very much in keeping with the way Oberman describes Calvin's approach to doctrinal writing more generally:

Calvin tries in the *Institutes* to order "the data of revelation," constantly warning that he does so only "for the purposes of teaching" (*docendi causa*)—a self-limitation constantly ignored by his later interpreters. He cannot and does not claim to smooth all corners or present a complete system. God reveals what is necessary to know, live, and survive without granting insight into the "ultimate" metaphysical cohesion of these "glimpses."[42]

Along these lines, Calvin writes that Arius's flaw was not that he failed to confess that Jesus is God and the Son of God; but that his insistence that the Son had a beginning means that Arius was focused on the wrong things. He lacked the "wholeheartedness" and "sincerity" that would

---

[41] It's worth noting that Calvin sanctioned Servetus' execution in part because Servetus denied the trinity.

[42] Heiko Oberman, "The Pursuit of Happiness: Calvin between Humanism and Reformation" in O'Malley, ed., *Humanity and Divinity in Renaissance and Reformation: Essays in Honor of Charles Trinkaus* (Leiden: Brill, 1993), 258.

have quelled the urge to make claims about the inner workings of God's essence (*Inst.* 1.13.4). The unfortunate result of this was that the pious were lured into a speculative debate, one in which terms are generated more as "secret poison" than edification. For this reason, Calvin claims to find it "more expedient to challenge them deliberately than to speak more obscurely to please them" (*Inst.* 1.13.5). It's interesting to piece together what this challenge looks like.

When Calvin begins his locus on the trinity, he gestures in characteristic fashion to God's experiential enormity from the vantage of the reader, approvingly quoting Seneca: "Whatever we see, and whatever we do not see, is God" (*Inst.* 1.13.1). Then he immediately refers to the usefulness of the "special mark" by which God "designates" Godself in distinction to idols: namely, by giving Godself to be "grasped" as three persons. So while God the Father is generally associated with a deity who is "simple and indefinite," the Son is demarcated as the Word, who performs the divine activity of intelligibility. The Word is the "wisdom of God" and the "wellspring of all oracles." God-as-Word is the condition for the possibility not only of scriptural revelation and saving mediation but also of the basic structure through which the Word's activity can be understood as performed in space and time (*Inst.* 1.13.7, 1.13.13). If the teaching particular to God the Creator is that divine power exceeds and upholds creation, the teaching particular to God the Word is that there is existential power in words.

In line with the orthodox creeds, Calvin admits that the Word is begotten. This acknowledges the fact that the power of words is secondary to the power of existence itself rather than vice versa. But he also insists that the Word has no beginning [*nullu exordium*, not *anarchos*], a claim that takes its force from the ontic locatedness of the reader being addressed. The biblical account that ties creative activity to the Word ("Let there be light") also suggests the very conditions for conceiving a beginning at all. There is no beginning apart from a divine power that performs a beginning in and through the Word (*Inst.* 1.13.8).

Following this logic, Calvin brushes off the suggestion that the Word assumes activity as a task or command distinct from the divine being, or even from the work proper to God the Creator. According to Calvin, "It would be easy or censorious babblers to . . . [say] that the Word is to be understood as bidding and command. But the apostles are better interpreters, who teach that the world was made through the power of the Son, and that he upholds all things by the power of his word" (*Inst.* 1.13.7). Scriptural accounts of Jesus' salvific activities similarly resist the urge to draw any distinction between the trinitarian persons on the grounds of distinguishing power versus administration. Scripture, in fact, constantly elides the two:

[T]o govern the universe with providence and power, and to regulate all things by the command of his own power, deeds that the apostle ascribes to Christ, is the function of the Creator alone. And he not only participates in the task of governing the world with the Father; but he carries out also other individual offices, which cannot be communicated to the creatures. The Lord proclaims through the prophet, "I, even I, am the one who blots out your transgressions for my own sake." According to this saying, when the Jews thought that wrong was done to God in that Christ was remitting sins, Christ not only asserted in words, but also proved by miracle, that this power belonged to him. We therefore perceive that he possesses not the administration merely but the actual power of remission of sins, which the Lord says will never pass from him to another. What? Does not the searching and penetrating of the silent thoughts of hearts belong to God alone? Yet Christ also had this power (*Inst.* 1.13.12).

Here, Calvin insists that power and administration are proper to both Father and Son. In another place, he writes that "we are taught not only that by the Son's intercession do those things which the Heavenly Father bestows come to us but that by mutual participation in power the Son himself is the author of them" (*Inst.* 1.13.13). While the distinction between Creator and Word helps to underscore the precise way that God the Son teaches – by making God's being and activity intelligible – this only works if the Son participates fully in both the being and (providential) activity proper to the Father.

Along these lines, Calvin characterizes the Spirit as assuming the distinct activity of enabling creation to participate, according to its proper measure, in this divine power and activity.

For it is the Spirit who, everywhere diffused, sustains all things, causes them to grow, and quickens them in heaven and in earth. Because he is circumscribed by no limits, he is excepted from the category of creatures; but in transfusing into all things his energy, and breathing into them essence, life, and movement, he is indeed plainly divine" (*Inst.* 1.13.14).[43]

---

[43] As might be expected, the pedagogical use of the trinity crops up in other doctrinal loci. Take, for example, the role the trinity plays in Institutio 1.7–9 where Calvin stages a series of disputations to defend the authenticity and usefulness of scripture. On one level, this is a pragmatic argument. Calvin defends scripture's authenticity by arguing that it is able to meet the deepest needs of the believer because it is fit to provide what human beings desire in a way that they are able to recognize. So, for example, he writes that scripture cultivates piety by enticing the senses with majesty (*Inst.* 1.7.4); it effects conviction by inciting feeling in the heart and flesh (*Inst.* 1.7.5, 1.8.2, 1.8.4); it supplies

The Spirit is life itself. It is divine power, performed through the Word, that actively upholds the existence that the Word generates, and facilitates participation in the signification through which the Word redeems. The Spirit, then, is the name for the power of God that actually affirms and moves a person at the site of the body.

According to Calvin's thinking, trinitarian distinctions do not track along a fracture between being and administration. They supply a rubric for distinguishing between different kinds of power – in fact, the very kind of multifaceted power that Calvin's doctrine of providence delineates. God the Father is the power that creates being and actively affirms it; God the Word is the power that performs the intelligibility of created being, differentiating and acting within its causal complex; God the Spirit effects the ability for created life to live into relationship with divine power. The trinity, as a conceptual apparatus, enables the reader of scripture to grasp the multifaceted gesture of a divine being who activates a relationship with created being. I'm going to return to this trinitarian pedagogical logic, which pervades the *Institutio*, in greater detail later. But for now, it's worth noting that Calvin tracks with Agamben's account at least this far, to the extent that he suggests an analogy between the logic of trinitarian power-administration and providential power-administration.

But Calvin crucially departs from Agamben's account when he is willing to cede theoretical clarity in order to refuse any form of distinction

---

"useful aids" (*Inst.* 1.8.2), such as presenting God the Creator as if by means of a mirror (*Inst.* 1.8.8); and its teaching effects widespread human "concord" and "peace of mind" (*Inst.* 1.8.12–13). But when Calvin unpacks the precise mechanics through which all these effects obtain, he does so by invoking the participatory structure of a thoroughly trinitarian pedagogical framework:

> For by a kind of mutual bond the Lord has joined together the certainty of his Word and of his Spirit so that the perfect religion of the Word may abide in our minds when the Spirit, who causes us to contemplate God's face, shines; and that we in turn may embrace the Spirit with no fear of being deceived when we recognize him in his own image, namely, in the Word. So indeed it is. God did not bring forth his Word among men for the sake of a momentary display, intending at the coming of his Spirit to abolish it. Rather, he sent down the same Spirit by whose power he had dispensed the Word, to complete his work by the efficacious confirmation of the Word (*Inst.* 1.9.3).

In order to give a robust account of scripture's usefulness, Calvin invokes the activities proper to God the Creator who gives the world the being proper to it; the Word (to whose work scripture is analogous) who occupies the "teaching office" (*Inst.* 1.9.1); and the Spirit who dispenses and confirms the Word in particular locations. The argument then relates all of these particular ways of being and acting to the existence of the world and the reader who acts within it.

between being and activity, and instead to invest the Word with a real, if performative, relation to being. The tasks particular to God the Word share in divine power. They convey that power, however, by demonstrating what that power looks like in a way that can be more clearly grasped by fallen creatures. Calvin writes, "For why does [Genesis] expressly tell us that God in his individual acts of creation spoke, Let this or that be done, unless so that the unsearchable glory of God may shine forth in his image?" (*Inst.* 1.13.7). He goes on to argue that "this *practical* knowledge is doubtless more certain and firmer than any idle speculation," and to reiterate the affective prerequisite that he thinks Arius lacked: "There, indeed, does the pious mind perceive the very presence of God, and almost touches him, when it feels itself quickened, illumined, preserved, justified, and sanctified" (*Inst.* 1.13.13). The proper use of the trinity is a practical use that flows from the "wholehearted" and "sincere" embrace of Christian teaching rooted in the experience of life.

Along these lines, he constantly exhorts his readers to avoid speculation – to "dearly love soberness" and "be content with the measure of faith, [to] receive in brief form what is useful to know" (*Inst.* 1.13.20). He even reiterates the labyrinth metaphor to amplify the warnings over what can happen if one gives up the thread to pursue the lure of useless knowledge: "But if some distinction does exist in the one divinity of Father, Son, and Spirit—something hard to grasp—and occasions to certain minds more difficulty and trouble than is expedient, let it be remembered that the human mind, when it indulges curiosity, enters into a labyrinth" (*Inst.* 1.13.21). The very nature of the guiding thread is that it is addressed to a reader who is located in a dark and frightening place and whose cognition must, in effect, be guided by what her hands feel. For Calvin, trinitarian terminology is not fit for such use. "I felt that I would be better advised to not touch upon many things that would profit but little, and would burden my readers with useless trouble. For what is the point in disputing whether the Father always begets?" (*Inst.* 1.13.29). That's how Calvin concludes his chapter devoted to the trinity: with a warning against thinking too strictly about the relationship of the Father to the Son apart from the needs of a living context.

If Agamben's account is taken as persuasive, this is inasmuch as it demonstrates how the stress of trying to make conceptual sense of the trinity perpetuated a fracture in thinking about being and activity. This ends up funding the conceptual priority of the Son's *oikonomia*, and of providential administration more generally, to cover the absence of any ability to connect the Father's power to worldly life. Calvin, in contrast, ties the Father's power to worldly life by making it an affirming power and thereby indexing the sign of divine transcendence to the power of life itself. This is crucial because it means that when God acts in relation to the world – as Calvin is very clear that God does, in deliberate and strong ways – this activity is, in effect, begotten of divine affirmation. It is effected not by invading or overriding material conditions, but by assuming an intimate and active relationship to them. This difference fundamentally informs the one final difference between his theoretical account and Calvin's writing: namely, the place and function of glory.

CONCLUSION: REFORM, RESISTANCE, AND ITS GESTURES

In Calvin's account, the Father is not at rest, but at work, and that work is the constant affirmation and care of creation: "To make God a momentary Creator, who once for all finished his work, would be cold and barren, and we must differ from profane men especially in that we see the presence of divine power shining as much in the continuing state of the universe as in its inception" (*Inst.* 1.16.1). This recasts the location and operation of divine glory. Even for fallen faculties, Calvin insists that "wherever you cast your eyes, there is no spot in the universe wherein you cannot discern at least some sparks of God's glory" (*Inst.* 1.5.1). He argues that it is a tragedy of sin that "most people, immersed in their own errors, are struck blind in such a dazzling theater … and certainly however much the glory of God shines forth, scarcely one person in a hundred is a true spectator of it!" (*Inst.* 1.5.8). In a way that is reminiscent of the way Calvin locates divine hiddenness in and under creation itself, he also argues that the glory of God is proper to places that are dislocated and excessive of governmental power and its pageantries:

David, when he has briefly praised the admirable name and glory of God, which shines *everywhere*, immediately exclaims: "What are human beings that thou art mindful of them?" Likewise, "Out of the mouths of babes and sucklings thou hast established strength." Indeed, he not only declares that a clear mirror of God's works is in humankind, but that infants, while they nurse at their mother's breasts, have tongues so eloquent to preach his glory that there is no need at all of other orators (*Inst.* 1.5.3, emphasis mine).

Glory and its related imagery – splendor, shining, light, dazzling, brightness – is used by Calvin with astonishing consistency to refer to the relationship that God assumes *to* the realm of creation. Calvin locates the signature of glory, in other words, in material sites that precisely exceed governmental ordering. The ability to perceive that glory comes from receiving the name of God and then directing God's name to every detail of creation, treating creation as if every detail signifies the name of God. This materializes created things as glorious by virtue of the relationship that God affirmingly assumes to each thing.

This differs from Agamben's account of glory as generated by the inoperative language of acclamation. For Calvin, glorification does not fuel governmental apparatuses. In fact, as I'll show later, it challenges them and even signals the grounds for refusing their legitimacy. If glory emerges when the inborn *sensus divinitatis* is enabled by scriptural lenses to once more perceive God's providential relationship to every detail of life, then government exists to enable this operation and becomes illegitimate to the extent that it disrupts it – not least by idolatrously claiming to be the central representative of divine glory. But this suggests that, for Calvin, resistance to an idolatrous mode of governance is grounded in the providential posture that takes affirmation of life as a fundamental prerequisite for subsequent acts of ordering, bridling, intervening, or directing activity.

There is nothing like a blueprint for reform in *The Kingdom and the Glory*, but there are gestures toward what resistance might entail. On the one hand, the clear argument of the book is that "Christian theology is, from its beginning, economic-managerial, and not politico-statal," and that Christian thinking evolved to achieve the elusive goal of transcendent sovereignty by integrating life into an ever-more-efficient economic-managerial paradigm.[44] This means that any appeal to being will always already be implicated within an apparatus that has already rendered every person *homo sacer* in order to rename and integrate them into the governmental machine. However, Agamben does suggest that it may yet be possible "to think an Ungovernable, that is, something that could never assume the form of an *oikonomia*."[45] This brings us back, finally, to whether and how he thinks some dimension of "life" might itself resist governmentality.

Agamben describes "eternal life," *zoe aionios*, as a form of life irreducible to Aristotelian *zoe* and *bios*. It is the form of life proper to the non-activity of contemplation and rest. If the Father rests, and if the Son's praxis functions to cover the embarrassment of a resting sovereign, then the governed might resist governance by contemplating participation in that very rest. The Sabbath is, of course, another concept central to the

[44] Agamben, *KG*, 66.   [45] Agamben, *KG*, 65.

archive of Christian theology. In a move that is not unlike Foucault's late interest in Greek practices of self-care, Agamben redeploys the Sabbath tradition to frame *zoe aionios* as the possibility for assuming a relation to one's own life that is not mediated by the logic of the providential machine. It is, instead, a pure potentiality that paradoxically "exists" before and outside of bureaucratic management. At one point, he characterizes it as a "participation in Christ," but under the negative auspices of Messianism that addresses the form of worldly life "*as if* not" [*hos me*], thereby raising the question of what, then, remains.

Glossing a passage from the second letter to the Corinthians where Paul discusses the messianic community in these terms, Agamben writes,

Under the "as not," life cannot coincide with itself and is divided into a life that we live (the set of facts and events that define our biography) and a life for which and in which we live (what renders life livable and gives it a meaning and a form). To live in the Messiah means precisely to revoke and render inoperative at each instant every aspect of the life that we live, and to make the life for which we live, which Paul calls the "life of Jesus" (*zoe tou Iesou*—*zoe* not *bios*!) appear within it: "For we which live are always delivered unto death for Jesus's sake, that the life also of Jesus might be made manifest in our mortal flesh" (2 Corinthians 4:11). The messianic life is the impossibility that life might coincide with a predetermined form, the revoking of every *bios* in order to open it to the *zoe tou Iesou*. And the inoperativity that takes place here is not mere inertia or rest; on the contrary, it is the messianic operation par excellence.[46]

The natural life of Jesus [*zoe tou Iesou*] is shaped out of the denial of every sociopolitical form of life [*bios*] and disjointed in time from every active natural life. It refers to the contemplation of a subjectivity proper to *zoe* that exceeds governance, that "opens itself as a central inoperativity in every operation." The mode of subjectivity proper to the natural life [*zoe*] of Jesus is contemplated as the negative (or missing) power that glorification defers by covering it.

Eternal life [*zoe aionios*] therefore refers to the very inoperativity that the providential machine, as biopower, seeks to capture within itself. At the very same time, it refers to a pure potentiality that refuses to be captured. It can become degraded as "bare life" – the ungovernable remainder or remnant, the abject exile that even the disciplinary state cannot manage. But if that same inoperative rest can become the object of contemplation, this may mean contemplating not just the emptiness of a subjectivity ungovernable by biopower, but also an incarnate body that

---

[46] Agamben, *KG*, 248–249.

lives into its rest and evades the bipolar tactic of management that wants to conflate *bios* and *zoe* toward productive-progressive ends. Agamben isn't clear on the extent to which his gestures toward Messianism and the *zoe aionios* refer to and run through the materiality of the body, although the use of *zoe* and the references to Jesus (rather than the Son or the Word) suggest that this is a valid interpretation, and that the body itself might be contemplated as a site of transcendence that yields a different posture toward immanence. But these gestures do direct attention toward the body of Jesus as resisting the praxis of "the Son" to represent the site of the ungovernable and offer it as an object of contemplation.

When Calvin's providential thinking addresses the conditions of suffering, it also emphasizes the contemplation of the body of Christ. This happens much later in Calvin's itinerary – in Book Three, where he is focusing attention on "how we receive the grace of God" and eventually "participate" through the Spirit in the signification proper to the life of Christ. Yet while his discussion of suffering does not belong to the locus in Book One, it does visibly recall and flesh out the structure of providence found there. These later passages also serve to remind peripatetic readers that providence was always concerned with the meaning of suffering and how to equip oneself to face it when it comes.

The ordinary experience of suffering is only spectral to Agamben's account, but it's worth remembering that his account does, in fact, emerge as a response to the violence of a modern governmental apparatus that treats bodies as fuel for productivity, or as raw material to be identified as an object of human knowledge (*verum factum*) and then mastered toward productive ends. Getting outside of this dynamic, for Agamben, means contemplating inoperativity, subjectivity, and the raw potential of a body at rest. That is how you deal with what you realize is happening to you as a product of modern governance both isolated from and integrated in a multifarious social body.

Calvin also gives an account of how to face suffering that hinges on contemplating the subjectivity proper to the humanity of Jesus. But Calvin's account invests Jesus with much more positive content. Jesus's life is visible as a particular mode of *activity* through which the subject is performed as one who wills a certain set of both immanent and transcendent relationships. What distinguishes this life of Jesus is not its inoperativity, but the nature of its movements and the kinds of relationships through which they create meaning, or *signify* the troubles and incongruences that an ordinary person faces. Calvin recommends contemplating that movement – both the movement of a body that suffers and the movement of a will that wills in and through that suffering, making the superhuman effort to love it. Or, in the Augustinian terms Calvin uses, it is a movement that wills God's will against God's will, creating emergent conditions for animating a different kind of perspective to the things that claim the sovereign power to define a life (*Inst.* 1.18.3).

When Calvin explicitly address how a reader should concretely face worldly suffering, he starts by denouncing the Stoic move that imagines providence entirely as praxis and recommends acclimation and *ataraxia*, or calmness, as the proper human response. Here is the passage:

> It is not as the Stoics of old foolishly described "the great-souled man": one who, having cast off all human qualities, was affected equally by adversity and prosperity, by sad times and happy ones—nay, who like a stone was not affected at all ... We have nothing to do with this iron philosophy which our Lord and Master has condemned not only by his word, but also by his example. For he groaned and wept both over his own and others' misfortunes. And he taught his disciples in the same way: "The world," he says, "will rejoice; but you will be sorrowful and will weep." And that no one might turn it into a vice, he openly proclaimed, "Blessed are those who mourn." No wonder! For if all weeping is condemned, what shall we judge concerning the Lord himself, from whose body tears of blood trickled down? (*Inst.* 3.7.8).

This passage places Jesus very much in the concrete space of immanence, a world in which suffering is both inevitable and also real, and positively ties Jesus – the Lord and Master, the image of the divine sovereign – to the full range of emotions commonly deemed inglorious. The Word does not initially respond to its suffering by furnishing an explanation or solution, but by sitting with it and willfully acknowledging both the full reality of the experiences and the way human beings respond to them. Calvin continues:

> If all fear is branded as unbelief, how shall we account for that dread with which, we read, [Christ] was heavily stricken? If all sadness displeases us, how will it please us that he confesses his soul "sorrowful even to death"? ... This, therefore, we must try to do if we would be disciples of Christ, in order that our minds may be steeped in such reverence and obedience toward God as to be able to tame and subjugate to his command all contrary affections. Thus it will come to pass that, by whatever kind of cross we may be troubled, even in the greatest tribulations of mind, we shall firmly keep our patience. For the adversities themselves will have their own bitterness to gnaw at us; thus afflicted by disease, we shall both groan and be uneasy and pant after health ... thus at the funerals of our dear ones we shall weep the tears that are owed to our nature ... But the conclusion will always be: the Lord so willed, therefore let us follow his will. Indeed, amid the very pricks of pain, amid groaning and tears, this thought must intervene: to incline our heart to bear cheerfully those things which have so moved it (*Inst.* 3.7.8; 3.8.10).

The movement of the linear will begins to emerge here under the sign of "patience" and then of "following." In so doing, it begins to vividly recall the theoretical steps of providential choreography that Calvin first laid out in Book One: first, the divine affirmation of the created conditions for life, even those that cause suffering; and second, a divine engagement that wills in and through those causes. The difference here is that these two steps are revealed to ordinary believers through the very medium of the body of Christ. Believers are asked to observe and learn from how Christ's body responds to the things it encounters.

Finally, Calvin promises that following these providential movements will generate a particular form of emotion. But it is not Stoic *ataraxia*, nor is it even Boethius's transcendent hope. Instead, like Nietzsche and other earlier and alter examples of authors who foreground the affirmation of reality as the proper response to suffering, Calvin links the movement of the transcendent will *toward* the world to the experience of joy:

Therefore, in patiently suffering these tribulations, we do not yield to necessity but we consent for our own good. These thoughts, I say, bring it to pass that, however much in bearing the cross our minds are constrained by the natural feeling of bitterness, they are as much diffused with spiritual joy. From this, thanksgiving also follows, which cannot exist without joy; but if the praise of the Lord and thanksgiving can come forth only from a cheerful and happy heart—and there is nothing that ought to interrupt this in us—it thus is clear how necessary it is that the bitterness of the cross be tempered with spiritual joy (*Inst.* 3.8.11).

Providence teaches one to conceive providence in terms of an active transcendent will: the will, so to speak, of the one who rules. But it's striking that in this passage, that will is indexed not only to a fully human person but to a person who is suffering under constraints and expressing the full range of emotions that, under ordinary terms, would be deemed inglorious. This is all the more striking in light of Calvin's Trinitarian thinking that frames Christ as the *image* of active sovereign power – as the proper lens to perceive how divine rule acts in time and place. Where the locus on providence merely theorized a divine will that affirms the world in all of its troubling detail as the domain of a more fundamental good – of life itself – this passage concretizes that claim by depicting a person who affirms the world in all of its troubling detail.

Whatever Calvin's providence may offer – in intended and unintended ways – it is not a discourse designed to give a rational explanation to suffering or to distract from attention to it. The *Institutio* doesn't deny or reify the losses that mark life. At the risk of losing rational mastery and even moral coherence, it ties the presence of God to the experience of loss and indexes divine revelation to that site. Calvin could not make this point more literally than by depicting an incarnate Word that cannot speak, only weep – for a time. But this account does suggest that whatever the highest and most active account of divine sovereignty looks like, it must involve active attention to creation as a whole with no exceptions and no mere permission. This is not a blueprint for governmental power, but a more primary set of relationships to which governmental power must be held to account. To live in the present, to continue to will as God wills, means constantly being torn apart by competing wills and willing to be restitched around those losses. If the concept of a people – of "ourselves" – is to reemerge against a *Corpus Christianum*, Calvin's text suggests it will have something to do with learning to signify our natural life the way that divine providence does.

PART III

INCARNATION

5

Calvin's "Secularization" of Augustinian Signification

The secularized religion of which [Edward] Said writes, for example, which was the privileged agent of Orientalism, is after all not just any religion. Nor was it just any theology or culture. It was Christianity, and more precisely, Western Christendom.

–Gil Anidjar[1]

By this machinery (so to speak) such an edifice of faith, hope, and love has been built in them that they do not seek what is imperfect, for they hold what is perfect—perfect, that is, as far as anything can be in this life.

–Augustine[2]

A number of theorists link Christianity's distinguishing claim – the incarnation – to the originary gesture of the Western "secular." As dogma, the incarnation asserts that God was once born into the immanent world and historical time to live and die as a human and that this event is the means by which the world is both justified and reordered. If secularization is the transference of transcendent things into the domain of ordinary time and space, then it is not hard to follow the suggestion that Christianity is a distinctly self-secularizing tradition. Gianni Vattimo reads the incarnation as a kenotic move – as God's turning everything over to human beings.[3] Marcel Gauchet marks the incarnation as a crucial development in a millenniums-long process through which human beings came to embrace their own aptitude for rational discursivity over and against "primitive"

[1] Gil Anidjar, "Secularism" in *Critical Inquiry* 33 (2006): 55–77, 58.
[2] Augustine, *De Doctrina Christiana*, 1.94.
[3] Gianni Vattimo, *Belief* (Stanford, CA: Stanford University Press, 1996).

participation in the cosmic order.[4] John Milbank and Slavoj Zizek have contended over whether the incarnation entails the radical freedom of a world either *detached from* transcendence or *opened to* transcendence, nevertheless agreeing that the incarnation structurally secures worldly freedom.[5]

When it comes to the incarnation's world-shattering logic, Gil Anidjar remains less sanguine than these theorists, attending to the world that is in fact shattered *by* the political and economic operation of the Modern Christian West. For Anidjar, Christianity is secular because an incarnational logic was renamed to consolidate a hegemonic claim to a specific assemblage of power in the world – one by which other "religions" are renamed as "religions" and distinguished from the "secular" by the use of familiar binaries like reason/superstition, spirit/body, and of course, free/authoritarian[6]. Anidjar can be placed alongside a diverse array of theorists who link the incarnation not only to the secular but to the particular tactics of sovereignty that would emerge from the sixteenth- and seventeenth-century, from a European continent, simultaneously shattered by religiously intoned wars and embarking on colonial projects. I've noted that Karl Löwith's critique of modern historical progress hinges on the claim that the logic of sovereignty guaranteeing progress remains founded on disavowed transcendent authority. Under the new regime of sovereignty, revelation is no longer dialectically related to divine hiddenness and addressed by faith, but unfolds from the purported accomplishments of Western reason and is addressed by knowledge. In Kathleen Davis's estimation, Löwith's secularization is "not a story of Europe's gradual extrication from religion, but rather the sublimation of theology in the 'world': *Heilgeschehen* merged with *Weltgeschichte*—a pattern that, unlike [Carl] Schmitt, he found disastrous" because it served as "the conceptual basis and the legitimizing tool of world-scale aggression."[7]

[4] Marcel Gauchet, *The Disenchantment of the World: A Political History of Religion* (Princeton, NJ: Princeton University Press, 2007).
[5] John Milbank and Slavoj Zizek, *The Monstrosity of Christ* (Cambridge, MA: MIT Press, 2011).
[6] I leave aside the question of Anidjar's (and these other theorists') methodology—whether and how such passive-voice or diffused agential claims about "Christianity" or "the incarnation" can be satisfactorily substantiated. By anchoring my own argument in a close reading of a pivotal text, I am methodologically responding to what I see as the both the importance and the danger of theorizing the relationship between theological conceptual structures and a broader social imaginary.
[7] Kathleen Davis, *Periodization and Sovereignty* (Philadelphia: University of Pennsylvania Press, 2008), 84.

Political theorist Wendy Brown agrees that the paradoxes of modern sovereignty refer back to frustrated theological expectations – expectations that, for example, a secular state could better achieve the goal of stability and unity shared by the premodern *Corpus Christianum.* The nation-state that reoccupies the fractured site of the *Corpus Christianum* with an immanent theory of social contract actually retains all of the tensions inherent to the previous form of sovereignty: for example, the need to figure the inherent multiplicity of the people [*demos*] under a sign of unity; or the need to impose rigorous social order in the name of procuring freedom.[8] As *Corpus Christianum*, the state can openly defer to a transcendent source to secure unity and freedom. Yet even when someone like Thomas Hobbes theorizes the social commonwealth as a product of human-made art – something we can know because we have made it ourselves [*verum factum*] – he still identifies its sovereignty with the "soul" of the commonwealth, which gives "life and motion to the whole body."[9] The term "soul," of course, refers back to a theological account of the divine animating element of the human body, and Brown suggests that this is no accident:

The borrowing from God here is complex. By analogizing sovereignty to the soul of the "Artificial Man" generated by human artifice, Hobbes reveals a fundamental trick of sovereignty: We generate and authorize what then overawes us and is unaccountable to us because of its divine status. Man generates political sovereignty through the conferral of his own power, but since sovereignty is the divine element within the commonwealth, this process of generation or fabrication is disavowed and covered over.[10]

Here, the logic of modern sovereignty betrays its need for something like an incarnational theology to operate.[11] If there can be "no 'sort of' sovereignty, any more than there can be a 'sort of' God," then secular accounts of sovereignty need to give some kind of account for how that unity is activated within the ordinary domain of immanent life.[12]

Brown, therefore, argues that sovereignty retains an "imagined dimension" – a kind of theological register through which "sovereign power, supreme on earth, at once imitates God and becomes something like a mediator for God."[13] Modern sovereignty has no power apart from its ability to effect order and circulation, meaning that sovereignty has to be

---

[8] Wendy Brown, *Walled States, Waning Sovereignty* (Brooklyn, NY: Zone Books, 2010), 51.

[9] Thomas Hobbes, *Leviathan* (New York: Oxford University Press, 1998).

[10] Brown, 60.   [11] Brown, 47.   [12] Brown, 51.   [13] Brown, 47, 61.

pictured as a power that reliably manages order and circulation. Theology supplies an archive of discursive tools for shaping that imagination, literally making society "work."[14] But when theology is hidden under the sign of the secular, the imagined dimension of power is reconfigured in secular terms – for example, in a particular national identity or a specific kind of body. J. Kameron Carter makes a similar argument, arguing along with Etienne Balibar that the figure of the "citizen" – a figure co-created with social-contractual sovereignty – is also forged in an incarnational imagination. If sovereignty imitates and mediates divinity to secure the unity and order of the political, the citizen mediates the operation of sovereignty at the point of contact with the ordinary. The citizen who stands in for the body politic must also in some way constitute and protect the unity of sovereignty.[15]

This relationship between the incarnational imagination and modern sovereignty is deeply involved with dynamics of representation. The question of how "the state" represents "the people" hinges on the question of how "the people" themselves represent (or seemingly fail to represent) the imagined (racial, affective, cultured) ideal. If the state is the representative mediator of sovereignty akin to the *corpus Christi*, the citizen is the Christian. Balibar, in fact, argues that the process of becoming a citizen under the regime of modern sovereignty must be viewed precisely as analogous to the process of becoming a Christian disciple: learning, once more, to imitate and then come to participate in the person of Christ as God-Man.[16] To the extent that this operation is renamed "secular," as such claiming universality, it effectively continues to mark and exclude those whose particularity exceeds the embodied and historical markers of the ideal citizen. Carter writes that "the image operating as the ideal — in other words, as the Beautiful and thus as the master of the grotesque, is tied to the making of the slave."[17] And to the extent that this operation is performed by the mimetic repetition of the ideal, the stability of the ideal relies on the *misrecognition* of the actual human bodies organized by sovereignty.[18]

---

[14] Brown, 59.
[15] J. Kameron Carter, "An Unlikely Convergence: W. E. B. Du Bois, Karl Barth, and the Problem of the Imperial God-Man" in *The New Centennial Review* 11/3 (2011): 167–224, 175, 200.
[16] Carter, 176.   [17] Carter, 200.
[18] Carter's essay gives a compelling account of this dynamic in a reading of W. E. B. DuBois's *Darkwater*. The argument is analogous to Davis's critique of Blumenberg, discussed in the Introduction: that the sovereign claim to modern legitimacy through a break in historical time brushes over the complexity of the actual historical archive. See Davis, 86.

This continues to foreground the role of art, artifactuality, and embodied practice in how worlds are materialized for life. Art itself is both creation and representation. It makes something new out of, and in reference to, received gestures and marks. Its power thus comes in part from its ability to challenge patterns of recognition and to generate responsibility to that deemed unfamiliar. Victoria Kahn argues that remembering the artifactuality of secular politics under the logic of poiesis is crucial to theorizing a politics that does not rely on the mystifications of theology. A politics theorized as creative making is a politics self-consciously fashioned by human beings for the purpose of constructing a world order that can be known in a human way, critiqued, and improved. Such a politics distinguishes itself from transcendent sovereignty by openly trading in fictions, recognizing that what is made can also be unmade, thereby constantly challenging citizens to revise their conceptions of the truth.[19] Yet, Foucault, Agamben, Brown, and Carter all suggest in different ways that what is objectionable about modernity is precisely the call to conceive society as the project of making persons – making biologized identities – fit for modern strategies of knowing and producing. This, after all, is the definition of biopower.[20]

The question of how to escape the paradoxes of sovereignty is a pernicious one. Kahn suggests that poiesis challenges a theological imagination because it asks us to mind the gap between symbolic and real power, or between representations of bodies and those bodies themselves. This obfuscates the fascistic and fundamentalist (and, I might add, generally nationalistic) urge to "give society a body."[21] But this claim invites further analysis of what happens when artistic representation constructs bodies *as if* real, approaching them in the undecidable space between excessive materiality and performative enactment, or materialization. This, I think, is what Brown calls a theological imagination that reads ordinary things as privileged mediators of sovereignty. And it is precisely the phenomenon Carter critiques when he argues that bodies are routinely *misrecognized* through a racialized "way of seeing" shaped by the imaginative dimensions of the institutional order.[22] Much as the early modern conception of the state as *Corpus Christianum* put a

---

[19] Victoria Kahn, *The Future of Illusion: Political Theology and Early Modern Texts* (Chicago: University of Chicago Press, 2013), 6.
[20] See my discussion in the previous chapter.   [21] Kahn, 81.
[22] For a lucid account of this phenomenon aimed at a more general audience, see the *New York Times'* 2015 interview with Judith Butler on the emergence of Black Lives Matter. https://opinionator.blogs.nytimes.com/2015/01/12/whats-wrong-with-all-lives-matter/.

bodily logic of exclusion and inclusion into motion when managing ordinary bodies, nation-state social-contractual sovereignty performs the same gesture when it indexes the unity of the collective body of "the sovereign people" to the imagined body of the ideal citizen.

If the doctrine of the incarnation enables these operations of sovereignty, it is because the doctrine carries its own representational and imaginative force. As dogma, the incarnation may be a metaphysical claim. But the incarnation can effectively be "secularized" because it does not exist merely as a proposition but as an operation of poiesis – an imaginative technology aimed at enabling a certain unified approach to the organization and interpretation of life on earth. Theologically, the claim of the incarnation is addressed to creation by means of representational tactics and practices. That is, the incarnation is given to be "known" through textual narrative (scripture) and embodied rituals (Eucharist), each of which generates meaning through gestural repetition and differentiation.[23] And at least in the Latin traditions following Augustine, the incarnation is foregrounded for its capacity to *teach* – specifically, to teach us how to interpret and act in the world as a network of signs and things – *signa* and *res* – that refer, ultimately, to God.

Calvin picks up on and extends the centrality of signs and things in his account of how teaching happens, and the similarities and differences in this debt to Augustinian pedagogy carry important implications for whether and how his rendering of the incarnation slips from its theological-pedagogical register to shape an imaginative lens for secular politics. Certainly, the doctrine lends itself as an analogy for any strategy that wants to render invisible power visible. But analogies are also disjunctive. And it is precisely because of the mimetic and artistic dimensions of the incarnation that it might also subvert existing materializations and challenge the ability to imagine an institutional structure as a soul, or as the body of a God-Man – depending on how it is deployed, in language, to confront the learner. If it is possible to become critical of the operation of incarnational logic, attention must be paid not just to the propositional claim of the incarnation, but to how the doctrine is taught and practiced.

In Part II, I argued that the discourse on providence is best approached with attention to the embodied practices it stages, or the repetitive strategies through which it invites a reader to both discern the world and resignify the relationships that obtain within and beyond it. Calvin's particular arguments about providence effectively index

---

[23] See my discussion in the Introduction.

divine power to the material dimensions of creation conceived pre- and extra-institutionally, inviting the reader to read the world as if affirmed by God in order to begin to resignify her own self-understanding and her assessments of the meaning of worldly things. Here, I turn to the second part of Calvin's "twofold knowledge of God" [*duplex cognitio*] where he addresses how God the Redeemer in Christ, the Mediator, teaches human beings about God and themselves [*cognitio Dei et nostri*] within the frame of the universe (*Inst.* 2.6.1). For Calvin, it is crucial that the incarnate Christ teaches through his incarnation – through representing what it means to be a human bearing the fullness of divine signification while living, moving, and dying as a creation in a particular created field. This anchors the teaching that follows in the remainder of the *Institutio*: it furnishes Calvin with a distinctive account of how the fuller resignification of the self is enabled through a particular use of revealed language within a particular kind of material field.

I've suggested throughout that each of these argumentative moves carry theological as well as political import, addressed as they are not only to the political situation of Calvin's immediate audience but also to the political-religious figure of King Francis of France. Given this initial address, it is perhaps inevitable, and certainly not surprising, that Calvin's order of teaching ultimately leads to the question of how a reader should understand the corporate institutions of church and state. How, in other words, should we should know ourselves "*in societate*"?[24] But while Calvin gives a robust and interesting account of the church as a kind of performatively activated collective body, it is significant that he does not allow the body-analogy to extend to the power of civil government.

I will argue that the logic underwriting this omission is deeply rooted in Calvin's development of, and divergence from, Augustinian pedagogy. When combined with Calvin's account of providence, his view of how the incarnation *teaches* sets the terms for a more forceful critique of state sovereignty (though not the state *per se*) than is often appreciated. Calvin will, of course, maintain a view of divine power that is unquestioningly omnipotent and should rightly be termed "sovereign." But Calvin's logic of signification also builds in mechanisms that refuse the urge to allow the incarnation of divine sovereignty in Christ to furnish an analogy for the political body or the nation-form. For Calvin, sovereignty is incarnated, and rendered imaginable, as a specific and active gesture of human flesh

---

[24] This is part of the title of Book Four of the 1559 *Institutio*, and I take it as significant that Calvin uses the ablative case, referring to "associations" [*societas*] as an instrument or tool to be used by another.

that gives specific content to the providential gesture of affirmative ordering. I'll suggest that rather than an ordering principle or imaginary, the incarnation can be thought of as a "technology of selves" – a claim taking the form of narrative art that is useful for gaining a new vantage on the meaning and activity of ourselves, thereby facilitating the knowledge of God and ourselves [*cognitio Dei et nostri*]. Put another way, the incarnation facilitates a way of assuming a new relation of the embodied self to the context of embodiment, not only to perceive but to live in the world *as if* it is indeed the proper school of piety and we, as humans, are signs of glory. Institutional entities are useful, but for Calvin their proper analogy is to air or water – elements necessary for the cultivation of life – not the actual body of the God-Man.

This is an argument that I will necessarily build one piece at a time in this chapter and the one that follows. To begin with the best footing, however, I pause again to look at Calvin's most-invoked teacher, Augustine – a fellow aficionado of the relationship between writing and learning as well as the pedagogical force of the doctrine of the incarnation. I've argued that Calvin's 1559 *Institutio* is best read as a mediatory guidebook designed to enable readers to both clarify and navigate their world through the use of divine signification. On a more granular level, the individual loci that constitute the itinerary of the *Institutio* are structured to echo and teach the performance of Augustine's interpretive pedagogy. Understanding the extent of Calvin's debt to Augustine on matters of pedagogy helps to clarify the placement, meaning, and function of many of Calvin's most distinctive doctrines, including that of election, as part of a larger choreography aimed at pursuing *cognitio Dei et nostri*. In what follows, I'll look at the role of the incarnation in Augustine's teaching and examine Calvin's relationship to it. I'll also draw out Calvin's most obvious departure from Augustine: namely, that whereas Augustine places the practice of interpretation within the corporal bounds of the church, Calvin places it in the world.

THE PARADOX OF LEARNING

Like Calvin's 1559 *Institutio*, Augustine's pedagogical writings take a hermeneutical circle as their point of departure. Calvin asserts that self-knowledge is only possible with God-knowledge, and asks where and how it is possible to start (*Inst.* 1.1–2). Augustine's manual on Christian education, *De Doctrina Christiana*, begins similarly by asking how to progress in learning if the student lacks knowledge of the thing to be learned.[25] This calls back to a classical eristic paradox, or the paradox of how learning is possible when one isn't already in possession of the thing being sought.[26] Plato addresses the problem with his theory of recollection, arguing that effective teaching will coax the student's soul to remember what it once learned among ideal forms.[27] The Stoics respond to the same problem by positing the theory of preconceptions, alleging that traces of ideas such as truth and goodness secure the ability to differentiate necessity from contingency and thereby form better judgments. Augustine appeals to the incarnation – a revealed claim concerning the meeting of divine Word and human Flesh – to secure the possibility for framing Christian education as an interpretive practice that learns to actively "read" self and world as a vast network of signifying things that refer back to their Creator.[28] Rather than emphasizing a particular faculty or idea imprinted in the human mind, Augustine frames human learning as being taken up by divine activity that exceeds yet involves the self.[29] On a practical level, Christian teaching occurs through the use of a kind of technology or "machinery" – the rules of faith and love – that

---

[25] Augustine's response to the eristic paradox – and his theory of signs in general – is more sophisticated than the summary I offer here. For more, see *De Doctrina Christiana* and Mark Jordan's discussion of the eristic paradox in "Words and Word," 183–184.

[26] For more on the eristic paradox, see Gail Fine, *The Possibility of Inquiry: Meno's Paradox from Socrates to Sextus* (Oxford: Oxford University Press, 2014).

[27] The classic example is found in the *Meno*, when Socrates demonstrates that an uneducated and enslaved boy – aided by the proper guidance – can derive the Pythagorean Theorem.

[28] Charles Partee's work remains what I take to be the best account of Calvin's relation to Plato and Platonisms, which is to say that while Calvin necessarily was influenced by the Platonism running through Augustine and the medieval Christian traditions, he took care to distance himself from its metaphysical and ontological commitments in order to rely on scriptural revelation. This is a position I take care to maintain here and in my subsequent discussions of the relationship between Calvin and Augustine. In addition to Partee, *Calvin and Classical Philosophy* (Louisville, KY: Westminster John Knox Press, 2005), especially chapters 4 and 8, see Partee, "The Soul in Plato, Platonism, and Calvin" in *The Scottish Journal of Theology* 22 (1969): 278–295. However, this also does not mean that Calvin did not draw positively from the narrative arc of Platonism. For more on that, see Zachman, *Imagine and Word in the Theology of John Calvin* (Notre Dame, IN: University of Notre Dame Press, 2009), 14–16.

[29] Augustine, too, forwarded a robust theory of spiritual senses. Yet, they do not play a foregrounding role in Augustine's treatments of Christian teaching. See Matthew R. Lootens, "Augustine" in *The Spiritual Senses: Perceiving God in Western Christianity*, eds. Paul L. Gavrilyuk and Sarah Coakley (Cambridge: Cambridge University Press, 2011), 56–70.

direct the person to engage in scripture reading and church practice toward productive ends.[30]

Augustine's fuller account unfolds through several layers. First, at the broadest level, he argues that creation consists of "things" (isolated objects) and "signs" (that mean only by referring to something else), and things that are also signs. God, however, is the only "thing" that does not also refer beyond itself, and this means that created things always also point beyond themselves to other things in a chain of significations that refer ultimately back to God the Creator. Created existence, therefore, entails more than isolated presence or thing-ness. To exist more fully means participating in the network of relationships that orients things in relation to other things, granting each fuller significance that is ultimately rooted in the relation of creation to Creator.[31] Learning, therefore, means honing the ability to interpret things in the context of their relationships. And this entails also asking questions about intentionality – about the wills and desires that put things into motion and seek some sort of satisfaction. For Augustine, then, asking about the relationship between signs and things means also asking which things are to be used [*uti*] and which are to be enjoyed [*frui*]. Strictly speaking, the only "thing" to be enjoyed is the only "thing" that is not also a sign: God.[32]

The use of language is crucial to this interpretive and affective pursuit. Augustine writes that "all teaching is teaching of either things or signs,

---

[30] I would like to once again underscore the holistic nature of this "machinery" in contrast to a contemporary like Ignatius of Loyola for whom particular exercises had particular ends. I take Calvin to be following Augustine (and to a degree the Stoics) in refusing particular exercises in favor of a holistic approach to the use of revelation as an exercise to be done in relation to worldly life. For a discussion of Calvin's refusal of particular exercises, see Margaret Miles, "Theology, Anthropology, and the Human Body in Calvin's *Institutes of the Christian Religion*" in *The Harvard Theological Review* 74/3 (1981): 303–323, 317–318.

[31] Rowan Williams, "Language, Reality, and Desire in Augustine's *De Doctrina*" in *Journal of Literature & Theology* 3/2 (1989): 138–150, 141.

[32] DDC 1.7. This theme also suffuses the *Confessions*, which were written directly after Augustine jettisoned DDC (to which he returned and completed later in his life). For example, in Book V, he contrasts mere knowledge of nature with the more dynamic and integrated knowledge of piety: "When I hear of a Christian brother, ignorant of these things, or in error concerning them, I can tolerate his uninformed opinion; and I do not see that any lack of knowledge as to the form or nature of this material creation can do him much harm, as long as he does not hold a belief in anything which is unworthy of thee, O Lord, the Creator of all. But if he thinks that his secular knowledge pertains to the essence of the doctrine of piety, or ventures to assert dogmatic opinions in matters in which he is ignorant—there lies the injury" (5:5).

but things are learned through signs."[33] Language enables learning precisely because language is a system of open-ended signs – written and verbal marks that are reproducible and thus useful for performing contextual differentiations and deferrals that clarify and enable relationships between things.[34] But signs are incapable of fully presenting that to which they purport to refer.[35] Some things refer naturally to other things – Augustine, for example, distinguishes between natural signs and conventional signs, with the example of natural signs being the organic relationship between smoke (a created thing) and fire (also a created thing). But conventional signs – those that operate within the realm of intention – refer in part to a will that can never be fully transparent to the knower.

See, for example, this passage from *De Doctrina* where Augustine narrates the dynamics surrounding the conventional sign for "God":

> Have I spoken something, have I uttered something, worthy of God? No, I feel that all I have done is wish to speak; if I did say something, it is not what I wanted to say. How do I know this? Simply because God is unspeakable. But what I have spoken would not have been spoken if it were unspeakable. For this reason, God should not even be called unspeakable, because even when this word is spoken, something is spoken. There is a kind of conflict between words here: if what cannot be spoken is unspeakable, then it is not unspeakable, because it can actually be said to be unspeakable. It is better to evade this verbal conflict silently than to quell it disputatiously. Yet although nothing can be spoken in a way worthy of God, he has sanctioned the homage of the human voice and chosen that we should derive pleasure from our words in praise of him. Hence the fact that he is called God: he himself is not truly known by the sound of these two syllables, yet when the sound strikes the ear it leads all users of the Latin language to think of a supreme excellent and immortal being.[36]

---

[33] *DDC* 1.4; *De Mag.* X.31.   [34] See *DDC* 2.1.2 and Jordan, 181.

[35] Here, Augustine is similar to Derrida even as Augustine posits the possibility of an "eternal and self-sufficient *res*" in God. For Derrida, of course, language is marked by endless deferral and difference by which it generates meaning but also eludes it. For Augustine, however, this is also the structure of the use of language by human beings: "The Christian reader of scripture is inconsolable and unsatiated in her work of interpretation and praying. Interpreting scripture, in other words, is as much about learning how not to give oneself over to a parody of love as it is about how to love." See Jeffrey McCurry, "Towards a Poetics of Theological Creativity: Rowan Williams Reads Augustine's *De Doctrina* after Derrida" in *Modern Theology* 23/3 (2007): 415–433, 427. See also Luke Ferretter, "The Trace and the Trinity: Christ and Difference in Augustine's Theory of Language" in *Literature & Theology* 12/3 (1998): 256–267.

[36] *DDC*, 1.13.

This recalls the structure of the eristic paradox, or the problem of how you can come to know that which isn't already somehow present. For Augustine, the sign is formed through desire for the thing – for some object – which means that the existence of the object is considered prior to the sign even though it is not yet grasped by the speaker.

This is where Augustine's theory of learning relies centrally on the doctrine of the incarnation. The incarnation furnishes a fundamental analogy for how God works precisely to enable the intelligible use of words in the world. If signs only generate meaning in relation to a referent, then the eristic paradox emerges because the referent must somehow already be given in order for the sign to mean. The incarnation forwards the claim not only that God is the ultimate thing to which signs point, but also that God makes Godself present in language in order to enable a series of intentional relationships among created things.[37] It teaches, in other words, that the universe is put into motion by a God who inhabits Flesh as Word, therefore furnishing the world with a kind of intelligibility within and beyond the infinite manifold of material things.

For Augustine, the incarnation secures the usefulness of words. But at the very same time it emphasizes the even more fundamental importance of things. For example, in the passage quoted previously where Augustine discusses the word "God," it is significant that the conventional sign can – and indeed must – involve both words ("God") and natural things (the voice that utters the word). When signs teach, they must involve both word and flesh in order to teach, because what they're teaching is not a fact as much as it is a posture or a relation. That passage continues like this:

> Our minds must be purified so that they are able to perceive that light and hold fast to it. Let us consider this process of cleansing as a trek, or a voyage, to our homeland; though progress towards the one who is ever present is not made through space, but through integrity of purpose and character. This we would be unable to do, if wisdom itself had not deigned to adapt itself to our great weakness and offered us a pattern for living; and it has actually done so in human form because we too are human ... So although [the becoming-flesh of God] is actually our homeland, it has also made itself the road to our homeland.[38]

Although conventional signs are incapable of fully presenting the thing to which they refer, this does not mean they are meaningless. Signs are useful, in fact, precisely because their incapacity acknowledges, and

---

[37] As I'll show later in greater detail, Augustine (like Calvin) frames teaching around divine accommodation to human weakness. See, e.g., *DDC*, 1.22–23.

[38] *DDC*, 1.22–23, 25–26.

makes the self receptive to, the end that both precedes and exceeds the sign. According to Williams,

all that can be said or understood of [divine] fruition is through the image of the moment of mutual transparency that can issue from the intense exchange of words: where the fluidity of utterance itself, a play of words that is also the modification and re-forming of a relationship between material persons, so indicates or rather embodies its own unfinishable nature that it expresses or introduces the irreducible 'difference' of God.[39]

The incarnation teaches not only by forwarding the claim *that* the word is present in flesh, but also by presenting to the student a "pattern" of receiving and giving signs, and thereby physically acknowledging that Christian teaching is an embodied exercise that is possible by faith while implicitly acknowledging the inherent limits of signs and things. This exercise is effective because it concretely *places* the learner not at the head, but in the middle of a chain of signs pointing back to God, the proper referent of every sign.

This is a process that Augustine emphasizes can take place according to rules – rules that are not objects of knowledge but that act as a tool for enabling the pursuit of knowledge.[40] The first is the rule of faith, or the

---

[39] Williams, 145.

[40] Here are two key passages where Augustine expounds on the rules of love and faith. First, love:

So a person who loves his neighbor properly should, in concert with him, aim to love God with all his heart, all his soul, and all his mind. In this way, loving him as he would himself, he relates his love of himself and his neighbor entirely to the love of God, which allows not the slightest trickle to flow away from it and thereby diminish it ... But because the divine substance is altogether transcendent and far above our own nature, the commandment to love God was kept distinct from the commandment to love our neighbor. God shows compassion to us because of his own kindness, and we in turn show it to one another because of his kindness: in other words, he pities us so that we may enjoy him, and we in our turn pity one another so that we may enjoy him (*DDC*, 1.43, 72).

Second, faith:

For 'we walk by faith not by sight,' and faith will falter if the authority of holy scripture is shaken; and if faith falters, love itself decays. For if someone lapses in his faith, he inevitably lapses in his love as well, since he cannot love what he does not believe to be true. If on the other hand he both believes and loves, then by good conduct and by following the rules of good behavior he gives himself reason to hope that he will attain what he loves. So there are these three things which all knowledge and prophecy serve: faith, hope, and love. But faith will be replaced by the sight of visible reality, and hope by the real happiness which we shall attain, whereas love will actually increase when these things pass away ... The eternal ... is loved more passionately when obtained than when desired (*DDC*, 1.89–92).

rule by which one embraces the claim of the incarnation and its pattern of learning and teaching. The second is the rule of love, which emphasizes the embodied and affective context in which learning can happen. In order to learn, you've got to do what the incarnation does: you've got to make yourself present in a concrete community that itself teaches you what it means to signify others as if loved by God.[41] Mark Jordan describes this whole pattern in the following way:

> To become redemptively manifest in human life, the Word takes flesh. Just so, thought takes on word-sounds in order to be spoken and heard. In the same way, again, the continuity of knowledge about God requires a 'fleshly' community within which it can become active. To put the proportion perhaps too naively: What the assumed human person is to the Son, that the spoken word is to the inner word of thought, and that the believing community is to the context of revelation.[42]

Learning, therefore, requires not merely reading but a more fundamentally embodied practice. *De Doctrina* is a hermeneutical manual, but it is significant that it begins by calling its reader into the church.

At this point, it may be helpful to pause and consider some possible implications of the way Augustine has set up this theory of pedagogy, in particular, the implications on the valuation of materiality. There is a way of reading Augustine's theory as locating the force of the sign in the inner or hidden transcendent referent – the Word hidden in flesh, or the thought hidden behind vocal utterance or written gesture. In some ways, this is a fairly straightforward reading, and it resonates with the posture of many Protestant theologians who would later claim the mantle of Augustine to critique the "deceptive" qualities of external, material things. During the sixteenth century and after, Protestants were critical of rituals, images, and bodily experiences in favor of appeals to sincerity and rationalized inner certainty. This posture has a long afterlife – both among Enlightenment authors who would more openly subject religious rituals or *Vorstellung* to critique according to strictly rational criteria and among practitioners who prefer to defend the objective truth of Christianity in terms of strict biblicism.[43]

---

[41] *DDC* 1.94.   [42] Jordan, 179.

[43] The complexity of the concern over certainty across the sixteenth century – and attempts to locate it in various places – is wonderfully outlined in Susan Schreiner's *Are You Alone Wise? The Search for Certainty in the Early Modern Era* (New York: Oxford University Press, 2011). While she does not carry the topic forward, I think it is fair to link works like Kant's *Reason within the Bounds of Reason Alone* and Hegel's *Lectures on the Philosophy of Religion* to the afterlife of these concerns, and to read their turn to reason as a reoccupation of the question in Blumenberg's sense.

Both moves echo one another and reflect the typically Protestant Christian attitude toward materiality that Asad, Bell, Anidjar, and others have linked to the fraught rational regime of Western "secularity." Broadly speaking, secularity remains tolerant of religion to the extent that religion can be explained in either rational terms or defended as inner, and thus private, conviction. On the flip side, it is still common for Protestants to define their own sacraments, in a paraphrase of August-inian language, as an "outward sign of inner grace."[44] If Augustine is understood to be locating the "true" meaning of both words and material things in the invisible facticity of an inner state – in the transcendent Word who becomes flesh not to teach, but merely to save – then this would reinforce an incarnational imaginary that locates the "true" meaning of matter in the production of discursive thought.

There are features of Augustine's writing, however, that complicate this reading. Matthew Potts argues that a closer reading of Augustine's sacramental theory shows that Augustine locates meaning not in the invis-ible referent of the Word, but in the "behavior of the communicant" gener-ated by her relation to the Word. Signification obtains, in other words, because like the Word who is active in flesh, the use of revealed signs performs the communicant as a body signified by God. Augustine himself describes the whole sacramental scene as a "visible word" – that is, a sign with movement and extension that performs what it signifies. Potts writes,

The notion of visibility, in this case, is somehow caught up in Augustine's semiotics, as well as his theological hermeneutics of the words and deeds of Christ. Thus for Augustine "those things, both the words and deeds, that our Lord Jesus Christ did should produce astonishment and wonder: the deeds because they were things done, the words because they were signs." The syntax here is labored and the translation slippery, but I read Augustine as asserting that the words of Christ are deeds too; or rather, that the words are deeds and the deeds are signs: that Christ's signs are enacted and that his acts function as signs. Or in Augustine's more straightforward paraphrase, "Christ himself is the Word of God; [so] even a deed of the Word is a word for us." Acts carry meaning, and the acts of the Word can be understood visibly to manifest what that Word means. These acts at once signify and realize the meaning they present.[45]

The incarnation enables signification not just because it gives an account of how the signified precedes the sign in a Word who becomes flesh; it

---

[44] Zachman gives a helpful account of Calvin's departure from this Augustinian dictum. See *Image and Word in the Theology of John Calvin* (Notre Dame, IN: University of Notre Dame Press, 2009), 309.

[45] Matthew Potts, "Preaching in the Subjunctive" in *Practical Matters* 7 (2014): 27–45, 33.

enables signification because it ties the referent of the sign *to* its concrete materialization in flesh as a sign of God for the believer. If Christ's words and deeds perform that which they also signify, the incarnation enables an understanding of learning as performed through the faithful encounter with the sign that is also materialized in community through acts of love.

Potts, drawing on Williams and Ronald Thiemann's late work, goes on to argue that Martin Luther's sacramental theology picks up on precisely this rendering of Augustinian signification. While Luther was embroiled with his contemporaries in technical debates over sacramental metaphysics that would have been foreign to Augustine's thinking, his doctrine of the *communucatio idiomatum* is intelligible through the logic of Augustine's incarnational analogy. For Luther, "What is true in regard to Christ is also true in regard to the sacrament. It is not necessary for human nature to be transubstantiated before it can be the corporeal habitude of the divine ... Both natures are present there entirely, and one can appropriately say: 'This man is God,' or 'This God is man.'"[46] Potts elaborates this claim by suggesting the language of the subjunctive to capture the way Augustine and Luther imagine signs to operate as neither brutally factual nor fictitious:

> There is not a deeper reality behind the bread and wine that the elements mask, any more than the man Jesus was just a docetic cloak for the Christ. Both are present in full. The bread and wine are simply holy. Or ... in behaving *as if* the bread and wine and the gathered community are all holy, the Christian finds them, in fact, to be holy. Luther would likely not embrace this subjunctive idiom, of course, but whatever language one chooses, the crucial concern for much Reformation sacramental theology is that we will not 'encounter God in the *displacement* of the world we live in, [in] the suspension of our bodily and historical nature.'[47]

For Luther as for Augustine, the incarnation teaches by becoming real in a way that underscores the reality of the created sign itself – by assuming, rather than evacuating, its material visibility as a deed or a gesture.

If the incarnation fundamentally teaches by acting, Williams emphasizes that this acting is not best read as a disruption or evacuation of ordinary matter and time:

---

[46] Martin Luther, "The Babylonian Captivity of the Church" in *LW* Vol. 36: *Word and Sacrament II, eds.* Helmut T. Lehmann and Abdel Ross Wentz, trans. Frederick C. Ahrens (Minneapolis: Fortress Press, 1959), 35.

[47] Potts, 35. Quotation is from Ronald F. Thiemann, *The Humble Sublime* (New York: I. B. Tauris, 2013), 29.

The Word's taking of flesh is not a dissolving of history as eternal truth takes over some portion of the world: it is not, says Augustine, that God comes to a place where he was not before. Rather the incarnation manifests the essential quality of the world itself as 'sign' or trace of its maker. It instructs us once and for all that we have our identity within the shifting, mobile realm of representation, non-finality, growing and learning, because it reveals what the spiritual eye ought to perceive generally—that the whole creation is uttered and 'meant' by God, and therefore has no meaning in itself. If we do not understand this, we seek for or invent finalities within the created order, ways of blocking off the processes of learning and desiring. Only when, by the grace of Christ, we know that we live entirely in a world of signs are we set free for the restlessness that is our destiny as rational creatures.[48]

On this reading of Augustine, the incarnation secures meaning by not only enabling an exercise of relating words to things in concrete community, but by also actively refusing to collapse meaning in any other way, thereby leaving open the endless re-materialization of life made possible in relation to a divine end.[49]

Calvin, of course, departs from Luther on the matter of the *communicatio idiomatum*, insisting as he does that divinity and humanity are ontologically joined only in the incarnation and that there should be no other mingling of heaven and earth.[50] This raises questions of Calvin's relationship to Augustine – questions that will not be fully addressed until I discuss Calvin's theory of sacraments, but which I will begin to consider in the remainder of this chapter. Like Augustine, Calvin thinks that teaching happens through the mediation of signs, and more precisely through the kinds of relationships effected through the use of signs and the world that these relationships materialize. Like Augustine, Calvin describes this process by indexing the pursuit of knowledge to the use and benefit of Christian doctrine. Calvin also argues that learning requires the prerequisite of piety, which for him functions as posture combining elements of faith and love (*Inst.* 1.2.1).

---

[48] Rowan Williams, "Language, Reality and Desire in Augustine's *De Doctrina*" in *Journal of Theology and Literature*, 3/2 (1989): 138–150, 141. Augustine reference is from *DDC*, 1.12.

[49] See again Jeffrey McCurry, "Towards a Poetics of Theological Creativity."

[50] The ontological and soteriological implications of Luther's *communication idiomatum* are still debated. For a helpful discussion, see the compiled volume *Creator est Creatura: Luthers Christologie als Lehre von der Idiomenkommunikation*, edited by Osward Bayer and Benjamin Gleede (Berlin: Walter de Gruyter, 2007), especially the essay by Jörg Baur that emphasizes the ontological weight of Luther's ubiquity.

Yet, Calvin makes a notable departure from Augustine's more neoplatonic gestures by insisting on an ontological difference between Creator and the creation. Though he resolutely refuses to frame Christian teaching as a materialization of *divine* being in the world, he does gesture to the legitimacy of interpreting the world as if divine, suggesting that he wants to retain the pedagogical usefulness of such a claim. Recall, for example, this provocative statement from Book One of the *Institutio*:

> I confess, of course, that it can be said reverently, provided that it proceeds from a reverent mind, that nature is God; but because it is a harsh and improper saying, since nature is rather the order prescribed by God, it is harmful in such weighty matters, in which special devotion is due, to involve God confusedly in the inferior course of his works (*Inst.* 1.5.5).

Here, Calvin characteristically refuses the impulse to "involve God confusedly in the inferior course of his works." But he also admits a powerful example of a subjunctive use of language – one that is not, strictly speaking, factually true, but that enables a new relation between the reader and the world *as* a domain of radical divine involvement, thus disrupting the totalizing effect of merely factual definitions.[51]

But what, then, becomes of the incarnation in Calvin's approach to teaching? If Calvin wants to avoid the claim that learning is possible because the divine makes itself the object of learning in the world, then how does Calvin avoid the eristic paradox? In the remainder of this chapter, I will be spinning out and defending the following claim: that for Calvin, the incarnation teaches by addressing believers as a work of divine poiesis addressed, specifically, to the fallen faculties and their function within a fully realistic immanent world. The incarnation teaches by presenting human persons with a unique object: a human life that also purports to fully represent divine activity. This life, or more precisely its literary rendering in scripture [*sensus literalis*] – becomes a sensuous-cognitive object of faith that facilitates the resignification of the world more generally through the modes of human activity it enables. Not unlike a technology or even a useful fiction, the claim of the incarnation tangibly performs a precise choreography that enables the believer to assume a new vantage on the meaning of life in the world, one that can

---

[51] To be clear, my aim here is not to undermine the status of facts, but to suggest that these theological approaches to signification aim in part to place facts in their proper place and not allow evidentiary accounts of existence to limit the possibilities projected by new kinds of relationships between things.

ultimately become a site of participation. In this way, it effects knowledge of what it means to be really human *as if* God [*cognitio Dei et nostri*].

CALVIN'S FIRST DIFFERENCE FROM AUGUSTINE:
THE *DUPLEX COGNITIO*

While Calvin borrows much from Augustine's theory of signs and Christian education, he makes two notable divergences from Augustine. They stand out precisely because Calvin follows Augustine to such a great degree. First, when it comes to the question of how teaching is possible, Calvin (perhaps predictably by now) demonstrates the influence of both Stoic and Augustinian impulses. I've already argued that these dual impulses undergird the way he constructs the theological genre of the 1559 *Institutio*. But the same pattern obtains on the question of how the text persuades a student that she can, in fact, grasp the teaching and make progress.[52] To give such an account, Calvin relies on the relationship that obtains *between* the inborn human faculty of the *sensus divinitatis* and the clarifying gift of the mediating Word. On the one hand, teaching is possible because, in Stoic fashion, human beings are understood to

---

[52] The proper Calvin term for this is, of course, sanctification. For Calvin, sanctification is joined to justification performed by Christ on a human's behalf, yet not by ontologically collapsing Christ and humanity. According to Calvin,

> [A]s Christ cannot be torn into parts, so these two which we perceive in him together and conjointly are inseparable—namely, righteousness and sanctification. Whomever, therefore, God receives into grace, on them he at the same time bestows the spirit of adoption, by whose power he remakes them to his own image. But if the brightness of the sun cannot be separated from its heat, shall we therefore say that the earth is warmed by its light, or lighted by its heat? Is there anything more applicable to the present matter than this comparison? The sun, by its heat, quickens and fructifies the earth, by its beams brightens and illumines it. Here is a mutual and indivisible connection. Yet reason itself forbids us to transfer the peculiar qualities of the one to the other (*Inst.* 3.11.6).

This underscores the role of gracious mediation in effecting the possibility of a moral progress that nevertheless meets the individual at the level of her own created and fallen condition. For some different accounts of sanctification in Calvin's thinking, see J. Todd Billings, "United to God through Christ: Assessing Calvin on the Question of Deification" in *The Harvard Theological Review* 98/3 (2005): 315–334; John Fesko, *Beyond Calvin: Union with Christ and Justification in Early Modern Reformed Theology (1517–1700)* (Gottingen: Vandenhoeck & Ruprecht, 2012), chapter 1; and an interesting take on Calvin's sanctification in conversation with contemporary theories of child development: Angela Carpenter, "Sanctification as a Human Process: Reading Calvin Alongside Child Development Theory" in *Journal of the Society of Christian Ethics* 35/1 (2015): 103–119.

possess an inborn receptor for perceiving divine glory along the edges of worldly life – one that is damaged, but not destroyed, and one that is furthermore accommodated by the lenses of scripture. On the other hand, it is also clear that Calvin wants to follow Augustine by triangulating an account of coming to knowledge that runs through the incarnate Christ as Mediator.[53] In fact, many familiar with Calvin's theology would probably view saving grace not merely as necessary, but as sufficient as an answer to this very question. Why, then, does he posit the *sensus divinitatis*?[54]

One way to begin to unwind the pedagogical relationship between the *sensus divinitatis* and the incarnation is to look more closely at the *duplex cognitio*, or the twofold knowledge of God, which is one of Calvin's few theological innovations. He introduces the *duplex cognitio* at the beginning of Book One, writing that an investigation of *cognitio Dei et nostri* must unfold according to a deliberate order: by examining the knowledge proper to God as Creator, and only then turning to Christ the Redeemer (*Inst.* 1.2.1).[55] In this way, the *duplex cognitio* is therefore offered as the teaching device structuring the entire first half of the 1559 *Institutio*. Furthermore, when Calvin differentiates the two modes of teaching proper to Creator and Redeemer, he also differentiates two modes of

[53] It is interesting and significant that Calvin reserves the title of "Inner Teacher" not for Christ, but for the Spirit. I'll return to this in the next chapter.

[54] Some scholars develop a Calvinian doctrine of natural law from the *sensus divinitatis* – for example, C. Scott Pryor, "God's Bridle: John Calvin's Application of Natural Law" in *Journal of Law and Religion* 22/1 (2006/2007): 225–254. I take it as worth noting that Calvin does not refer to the *sensus divinitatis* in these terms, and reserves the terminology of "natural law" for discussions involving the knowledge of God the Redeemer (*Inst.* 2.2.22, 2.8.1). The analogy to the *sensus divinitatis* is apt to the extent that Calvin treats natural law as a kind of receptor for the use of revealed law. Revealed law, as mediation, refers to what is already engraved on the mind and sharpens the "conscience," without which human beings could not be held to account for their actions (*Inst.* 3.15). Interestingly, when Calvin returns briefly to "natural law" in Book Four, its force is to underscore the equity of the law – the fact that the law should not privilege one kind of being over another. This logic refers back to the implied equity of God's all-involved divine providence, which humans should imitate and pray to come to participation. See *Inst.* 4.20.16. For more on natural law and conscience, see Susan Schreiner, *The Theater of His Glory* (Durham, NC: The Labyrinth Press, 1991), chapter 4 (and page 79 in particular); Edward A. Dowey, Jr., "Law in Luther and Calvin" in *Theology Today* 41/2 (1984): 146–153; David Bosco, "Conscience as Court and Worm: Calvin and the Three Elements of Conscience" in *Journal of Religious Ethics* 14 (1986): 331–355.

[55] For more on this, see Dowey 1951: chapter 2, and Muller, 2001: 134–138. On the "originality of the *duplex cognitio*, see Richard A. Muller, "'*Duplex cognitio dei*' in the Theology of Early Reformed Orthodoxy" in *The Sixteenth Century Journal* 10.2 (Summer 1979): 51–62.

learning – one in which God the Creator is understood to enable a distinct kind of teaching that is distinct from and also prerequisite for that teaching of God the Redeemer. The first mode addresses the inborn sense of the divine with scriptural teachings that clarify its operation; the second mode refers to the more concrete, enfleshed, and active mediation furnished by Jesus Christ as God-Man as a choreography of, and for, faith.[56]

Calvin glosses the first mode of teaching by describing it as "the primal and simple knowledge to which the very order of nature would have led us if Adam had remained upright," one that would have allowed human beings to "experience" God "as Father or as Author of salvation" – to "feel that God as our Maker supports us by his power, governs us by his providence, nourishes us by his goodness, and attends us with all sorts of blessings" (*Inst.* 1.2.1). The terms he uses here suggest that the knowledge of God the Creator is a kind of knowledge fit for embodied faculties that receive sense and emotive input. In contrast, Calvin frames the second mode of teaching as a kind of persuasion by which humans "embrace the grace of reconciliation offered to us in Christ" (*Inst.* 1.2.1) – a gift that, among other things, enables the first mode of teaching more fully.

This becomes more clear when Calvin returns to the *duplex cognitio* early in Book Two. Here is the first part of a key passage:

> The natural order was that the frame of the universe should be the school in which we were to learn piety, and from it pass over to eternal life and perfect felicity. But after humankind's rebellion, our eyes—wherever they turn—encounter God's curse. This curse, while it seizes and envelops innocent creatures through our fault, must overwhelm our souls with despair. For even if God wills to manifest his fatherly favor to us in many ways, yet we cannot by contemplating the universe infer that he is Father. Rather, conscience presses us within and shows in our sin just cause for his disowning us and not regarding or recognizing us as his sons. Dullness and ingratitude follow, for our minds, as they have been blinded, do not perceive what is true. And as all our senses have become perverted, we wickedly defraud God of his glory (*Inst.* 2.6.1).

Two things stand out here. First, Calvin underscores that the doctrine of creation – not the incarnation – is, in fact, the proper place to begin Christian teaching. The "frame of the universe should be the school in which we were to learn piety." The incarnation enters the scene because, after the fall, creation can no longer be apprehended with clarity – but not

---

[56] To be clear, these are not hierarchically arranged nor are they mutually exclusive in any way. But the distinction does affect the way that that Christian teaching is directed in ways that I'll explore presently.

because itself has become inferior or irrelevant. Creation cannot be apprehended because *our faculties* are now incapable of performing their created function. They no longer allow human beings to perceive, feel, and know the love of God by experiencing the order of the world, or to live as if *pronoia* [providence] was a given. Instead, our faculties receive sensory input as *paranoia*, or as a constant stream of evidence for divine wrath (see *Inst.* 1.1–5; 1.17.1; 1.18.3).[57]

This is the second thing to notice. Calvin clearly asserts that paranoid interpretations of sensory data are performed *at the subjective level*. It is not an objective fact that God curses humanity, or refuses to regard humanity as God's own children. Instead, that which we take as worldly signs of divine displeasure are the products of "our eyes," "our conscience," "our minds," "our senses." This suggests that the twofold remedy given by the grace of divine teaching must address the human faculties at *both* the natural *and* the interpretive or intentional level. The teaching culminating in providence [*cognitio Dei creatoris*] performs a kind of therapy on the *sensus divinitatis* by furnishing lenses by which a believer can learn to perceive the world as if actively affirmed and engaged by God. This teaching performs the work of constructing the world as the proper domain for further resignification to occur on the subjective level, but it alone is not sufficient. For humans to learn, they must first be confronted with a contrary, counterfactual account of the nature of the world. But they also require something more. For teaching to actually obtain – for signs to move toward their object – human beings also need a positive tool for actively and persuasively reinterpreting the world.

This is where the knowledge of Christ the Redeemer [*cognitio Dei redemptoris*] enters the scene. The passage continues:

We must, for this reason, come to Paul's statement: "Since in the wisdom of God the world did not know God through wisdom, it pleased God through the folly of

---

[57] Though Calvin does not use the language of *paranoia*, its logic is implied in the rhetorical force of his argument *for pronoia* (or more accurately, the Latin *providentia*). In a very interesting article, Derek S. Jeffreys argues that Calvin's muted-though-distinct valuation of civil government is read through the lens of providential resistance to paranoia-inducing disorder. See Jeffreys, "'It's a Miracle of God That There Is Any Common Weal among Us': Unfaithfulness and Disorder in John Calvin's Political Thought" in *The Review of Politics* 62/1 (2000): 107–129.

In addition, though the present study lacks the space, it would be worthwhile to read Calvin alongside later treatments of paranoia. See, for example, John Stachiewski, *The Persecutory Imagination: English Puritanism and the Literature of Religious Despair* (Oxford: Clarendon Press, 1991); John Farrell, *Paranoia and Modernity: Cervantes to Rousseau* (Ithaca, NY: Cornell University Press, 2006).

preaching to save those who believe." This magnificent theater of heaven and earth, crammed with innumerable miracles, Paul calls the "wisdom of God." Contemplating it, we ought in wisdom to have known God. But because we have profited so little by it, he calls us to the faith of Christ, which, because it appears foolish, the unbelievers despise. Therefore, although the preaching of the cross does not agree with our human inclination, if we desire to return to God our Author and Maker, from whom we have been estranged, in order that he may again begin to be our Father, we ought nevertheless to embrace it humbly (*Inst.* 2.6.1).

The faith of Christ is given not by a doctrine addressed to the mind and senses. It is given, more precisely, through preaching – through a sacramental act that presents God through linguistic and moreover artistic devices, not merely as a claim, but in the idiom of the subjunctive. Preaching is a persuasive account, addressed to a worldly audience, of how precisely God acts in the world that God also affirms. It is not, however, that Christ is known as the object of teaching, fully present in, with, and under the material world, as Augustine's sacramental thinking might suggest and Luther's *ubiquitas* suggests more overtly. Rather, the act of preaching addresses human beings themselves – as creations – in their ordinary context. Worldly life is the object of learning, already affirmed by divine providence, already embedded in a providentially signified world.

CALVIN'S SECOND DIFFERENCE FROM AUGUSTINE: CREATION BEFORE CHURCH

This leads to Calvin's second significant departure from Augustine's thinking – namely, that he begins his order of teaching by calling the reader into the world, not the church. To bring this difference into more precise relief, however, let me return briefly to Augustine. We've seen that, for Augustine, words are incapable of signifying on their own. They cannot move from sign to signified without an action on the part of the signified. As Williams reads Augustine, "God has 'placed himself in the order of signs'" and thus "brought to light the nature of all signs in respect of [God's] own nature as uniquely *res* [thing]."[58] On their own, signs always retain an air of ambiguity and slippage. What generates meaning is not the hardening of the sign into a non-signifying thing – the

[58] Williams, 148.

general definition of an idol for Calvin.[59] Meaning is instead generated by the relationship among signs and things such that created things are read as objects of, and thereby mediators of, divine love. Love is "the goal that lies in and beyond the skill of 'continuing with' the shifts of discourse."[60] Love, understood by analogy to the incarnation, strives in faith to actually perceive what cannot be said.[61]

It is precisely for this reason that Augustine presents learning, first and foremost, as a fully embodied and practical exercise governed by the rule of love. He argues that learning can only begin with submitting to a human teacher from whom one receives that to which the rule of faith adheres. For Augustine this submission means joining the church and thus entering the "body of Christ" as the proper object to which one learns to direct the use of signs. According to Augustine,

> It has been said "For God's temple is holy, and that temple you are": how could that be true if God did not make divine utterances from his human temple but broadcast direct from heaven or through angels the learning he wished to be passed on to humankind? Moreover, there would be no way for love, which ties people together in the bonds of unity, to make souls overflow and as it were intermingle with each other, if human beings learned nothing from other humans (*DDC* P.13–14).

Because divine love addresses every created thing, assuming one's place before God must also involve the physical act of hearing and responding to the Word alongside others, and most importantly interpreting *other people themselves* according to the rule of love. Other people then become the incarnate "things" to which – and through which – signs point on their way to their end in God.

Mark Jordan helpfully explains why a manual concerned, on its face, with scriptural exegesis, requires its user to enter a material context for bodily habituation among others:

> Scriptural exegesis is thoroughly subordinated to the way-of-life found in the faithful community because the way-of-life embodies the intention behind the Scriptural signs. Such subordination prevents Augustine's remarks about histor-ical and literary contexts from becoming merely a logician's doctrine of

---

[59] See *Inst.* 1.11 for Calvin's discussion of idolatry. He generally defines an idol as the attribution of any worldly form to God, which I take to mean in Augustinian terms, the attempt to locate the *res* of the signified in what is properly a created *signa* or sign.

[60] Williams, 148.

[61] Here, I refer both to the end of divine vision and the mediate end of loving others joined in the church.

interpretation by consistency. Because he is relying on a lived grounding of all interpretations in the community, he says that rules are always less valuable than a keen memory.

If memory in the form of recollection gave Plato a solution to the eristic paradox, memory is collective and subjective. It is forged through a community that shares signs and relates them to each other and through each other to God. In this sense, memory is of that which shared life under the guidance of scripture continually performs:

> The memory is not only of what was said elsewhere in the text; it is memory of the community's continuity back to the time of the Scriptures. It is, more importantly, the *memoria Dei*; students of the Scriptures must pray most seriously (3.37.56). It is the life of the community and the prayerful meeting with God which give assurance that the Scriptures are everywhere meaningful.[62]

When a student answers the call to faith by entering the body of the church, the student becomes physically embedded in an incarnational context that, in theory, is already busy enacting what faith looks like, and thereby furnishing a kind of apparatus or material substrate that continues to enable a Christian education.

There is little question that Augustine's account does, in fact, rely on a sovereign, transcendent will to secure the "true" meaning of worldly life. As Williams has argued, this will should not lend itself to description as "dissolving of history as eternal truth takes over some portion of the world."[63] The divine will created the world. And when it becomes indexed to the body of the church, it is not by portraying the church as the privileged holder of the truth, but as the privileged site in which to practice a relation to the truth. Within the church, the divine will is incarnate through liturgical and sacramental uses of signs that bear in mind their incapacity along with their ability. From an individual's perspective, signs should not offer cognitive access but should set up different relationships useful for clarifying and directing the call to love God and neighbor. If the church is the visible body mediating divine sovereignty, it is because an organized embodied network is crucial to learning what the incarnation teaches about how divine sovereignty addresses worldly life.

Paul Connerton's *How Societies Remember* offers a helpful lens for appreciating why Augustine foregrounds a domain of bodily habituation in his account of Christian teaching. Like other theorists I've discussed, Connerton is critical of a "hermeneutical approach" to ritual activity.

---

[62] Jordan, "*Words and Word*", 185–186.   [63] Williams, 141. Also quoted earlier.

He argues that earlier analyses of social ceremonies often began by reinterpreting ceremonies as "inscriptions," thus rendering them into the kind of thing that can be grasped as and studied as discursive information. Against this, he argues that the study of ceremonies is better conceived as the study of the medium of social memory and approached by means of a notion of performativity that studies how bodily patterns are enacted through the repetitive exercises of habituation.[64] The body's capacity to form habits is itself part and parcel of its ability to perceive and feel, meaning that discourses on perception are also discourses on habituation. By creating and maintaining an underlying network of patterned movements, modes of rendering, and capacities for action, bodily practices physically house memories.[65]

Habits, therefore, furnish a seat for memory that functions alongside the mind. According to Connerton, "the habit-memory—more precisely, the social habit-memory—of the subject is not identical with that subject's cognitive memory of rules and codes; nor is it simply an additional or supplementary aspect; it is an essential ingredient in the successful and convincing performance of codes and rules."[66] This form of habituation is crucial to the possibility of sharing life with others:

The kind of association that makes possible retention in the memory is not so much one of resemblance or contiguity but rather a community of interests or thoughts. It is not because thoughts are similar that we can evoke them; it is rather because the same group is interested in those memories, and is able to evoke them, that they are assembled together in our minds. Groups provide individuals with frameworks within which their memories are localized and memories are localized

---

[64] Paul Connerton, *How Societies Remember* (Cambridge: Cambridge University Press, 1999), 4–5.

[65] Connerton, 25f. He further argues that habits not only undergird, but also many times materially enact or display the very moral or social good that is being performed through repetitive, ritualized, ceremonial action (e.g., Connerton, 29). Patterns of creating and wearing socially legible clothing at a certain time and place, for example, coincides performatively with the normative embrace of values expected of the clothed individual. For example, the wearing of a corset by a wealthy woman in late nineteenth-century Europe should not merely be taken as a conscious message on her part to the larger society that she understands and conforms to its values and expectations; it is more important that the corset actually performs those values in and through her body at the level of its basic disposition by forming habits of posture, movement, and affect (Connerton, 33–34). For Augustine and Calvin, however, this way of approaching habituation is holistically oriented around the sacramental exercises that relate faith and love rather than located instrumentally in more particularized actions.

[66] Connerton, 36.

by a kind of mapping. We situate what we recollect within the mental spaces provided by the group. But these mental spaces ... always refer back to the material spaces that particular social groups occupy.[67]

By drawing attention to the importance of habit-memory in forming group relationships, Connerton's argument sheds some theoretical light on why Augustine might prioritize entry in the church as the necessary prerequisite toward advancing in Christian teaching. If Augustine argues that learning is possible through postures that affect relationships of signification enabled by and referring to, the incarnate object of divine love – then this also involves the cultivation of collective bodily patterns that both display and enable relationships between signs.

This is significant because it suggests that a Christian novice does not perform the liturgy or works of love because she already knows the full purpose of the liturgy or the works of love; rather, she enters a collective performance of liturgy and love in order to become the kind of body who can participate in realizing their purpose. We've seen that Augustine, like Calvin, frames this not as a fixed presence, but as a journey – a "trek, or a voyage, to our homeland," one the incarnation enables through "integrity of purpose and character," "adapt[ing] itself to our great weakness and offer[ing] us a pattern for living."[68] The sovereignty of the divine will is realized through a way of life available to practitioners in community with one another under the rule of faith. And "faith," Augustine writes, "will be replaced by the sight of visible reality, and hope by the real happiness which we shall attain, whereas love will actually increase when these things pass away."[69]

I think it is fair to say that a close reading of Augustine's incarnational thinking avoids uncritically reinforcing a generalized conception of the nation or other collective as a sovereign entity. Ernst Kantorowicz narrates a genealogy through which the sacramental body of the church as *corpus Christi mysticum* became the worldly *corpus Christianum*, and I'll return to that account in the next chapter. But there is the potential for a slippage in Augustine's account, even if it is one that he would never have anticipated, that links the pattern given by the Christian incarnation to the pattern of life enacted in a particular and localized corporate body. It is one that makes it at least theoretically possible to look at one particular instance of a collective body, with its shared historical narrative and shared set of rituals, and say "this man is God" or "this God is man."[70]

---

[67] Connerton, 37.   [68] *DDC*, 1.22–23, 25–26.   [69] *DDC*, 1.90.   [70] Luther, 35.

The metaphor of a group that shares in collective life as defined holistically by the memory rooted in the pattern of a sovereign body is legible as a
metaphor for any putatively sovereign collective, including that of the
nation.

This is where Calvin's departure from Augustine raises some interesting
questions, not only for a theory of Christian teaching but for debates over
the relationship of Calvin's thinking to political theology. Like Augustine,
Calvin signals the importance of a context in which to perform exercises of
divine resignification. We've seen that "the frame of the universe should be
the school in which we were to learn piety," an almost word-for-word
echo of Augustine's call to the church in which to learn to relate signs to
things with the rules of faith and love (*Inst.* 2.6.1). For Calvin, learning to
relate signs to things is an exercise that must happen somewhere. But that
place is not the church, at least not principally. It is the world – the world
as materialized, first and foremost, by divine providence. The world is
"before" the church in both senses of the word: Its existence is *prior* to the
church, the existence of which is grounded in exercises related to
the second part of the *duplex cognitio*; and the world remains *in front of*
the activity of the church as that activity's proper referent.[71]

This particular shift from the church to the world as the site of
habituation in signification is evident in many other features of the
1559 *Institutio*, not only in the overall structure of its itinerary that begins
with the world and then moves through the church back to the world in
general; but also in Calvin's theory of sacramental signification, which I'll
discuss in the next chapter, and which emphasizes the ability for ordinary
worldly things (water, bread, wine) to stand as the legitimate referent of
sacramental signs. There are, of course, good historical and contextual
reasons why Calvin's writing would make such a shift. One is fairly
obvious and accounts for Calvin's shift away from the church in a
negative sense. Calvin's career was, after all, defined by his willing exclusion from the collective body of the church and his subsequent, less
willing exclusion from the collective body of the state. Even as Calvin
admires Augustine and authorizes his own teaching by claiming continuity with the church father, he cannot exhort his reader to uncritically
submit to the church, because he is already writing from a position

---

[71] In 1.7, Calvin asserts the priority of scripture over the traditional teachings of the
church – over and against what he claims are poor readings of Augustine. This carries
the traces of the polemic against the contemporary church that threads Calvin's writing,
becoming explicit in Book Four.

outside of it. To the extent that he follows Augustine on matters of writing and learning, this leaves him with a kind of vacuum around the question of what context ought to fill the role of material habituation in signification.[72]

This also leaves Calvin with the burden of giving a persuasive account of why and how the church could have gone so wrong in the first place. If the church is all that Augustine saw it as being – the body of Christ, inhabited by God through and for the ongoing habituation of believers – then Calvin has to be able to give some compelling argument for how it could have ever become susceptible to the extent of radical corruption that he alleges – the kind of corruption that would warrant such drastic and large-scale efforts at reform. The traces of these material conditions illumine some of the more positive reasons why Calvin departs from Augustine by placing the world before the church.

Recall, for example, precisely how the *sensus divinitatis* informs Calvin's distinct account of the nature and phenomenology of sin. Because sin entails a holistic distortion of all human faculties in totality, Calvin's phenomenology of its effects involves more than Augustine's privation of being. For Calvin, the distortion of the *sensus divinitatis* prompts a wide range of compulsive reactions that lead human beings to positively construct idols as false objects of comfort. Remember, it is *our eyes* that construct God's curse, and our conscience that presses within us. The fear and dread that attach to misfiring perceptions and cognitions prompt a person to construct false narratives and treat them as if they are real in order to supply the floundering self with a kind of explanatory security (*Inst.* 1.4–5).

This account establishes a more general framework for how the church – even the church – could begin to manifest corrupting effects within its borders. Augustine himself would easily agree that the church is not immune to sin.[73] But if one of sin's primary effects is the positive

---

[72] It is noteworthy, of course, that Calvin does *not* fill this vacuum with the body of the state.

[73] This was the dispute around which the Donatist controversy turned. For more, see Maureen A. Tilley, "Redefining Donatism: Moving Forward" in *Augustinian Studies* 42/1 (2011): 21–32. Robin Layne Fox, *Augustine* 25–28; Peter Brown, *Authority and the Sacred: Aspects of the Christianisation of the Roman World* (Cambridge: Cambridge University Press, 1995), 17–26; 43–45; Brown, *Augustine: A Biography*, 2nd edition (Berkeley: University of California Press, 2000), esp. 207–221; Bret D. Shaw, "African Christianity: Disputes, Definitions, and Donatists" in *Orthodxy and Heresy in Religious Movements: Discipline and Dissent* eds. M. R. Greenshields and T. R. Robinsons (Lampeter: The Edwin Mellen Press, 1992), 5–34.

creation of idols, along with the full range of arguments and practices to
furnish them with quasi-sovereign power, then a Christian teaching fit for
reform must involve more than simply joining the church and affirming its
traditional authority. What is needed is an external perspective from
which to adjudicate the critique of idolatry. If in fact Christian teaching
is to be practiced in the world – and if Christian signs are to be related to
the realistic contours of worldly things as objects of divine affirmation
and signs of divine glory – then Calvin's providence suggests just such an
Archimedean point.

CONCLUSION

The implication of this move is that the visible church should be interpreted in the same terms as the wider sphere of creation. In fact, this is
precisely what Calvin suggests when he presents the world as the school
of God's children. If the aim is to habituate students for ultimate participation in a reformed church, then habituation must be extra-ecclesial. It
must occur before and outside of the institutional structure of the church.
It is not surprising, then, that when Calvin finally arrives at his teaching
on the church in Book Four, he defines its authenticity, not in terms of its
arche – for example, its genetic apostolic origin or its institutional continuity – but by the performative quality of the peculiar practices that
mark its authenticity: preaching and sacraments. Both of these practices,
for Calvin, receive divine signs and use them to refer to, and even to
rematerialize, worldly things. Calvin even describes the church in positive
terms as a providential accommodation for learning (*Inst.* 4.1.1, 4.1.5).

If the church is an accommodation to enable a way of living in the
world more broadly, then it's not surprising that the problem of the
church is only a more particular version of the problem of the world.
The question, "How could God's church have gone so wrong?" is really
only a more focused iteration of the question that perpetually haunts and
also elicits the discourse on divine providence: "How could God's creation have gone so wrong?" The question that challenges the prospect of
church reform is not a wrong question, but rather *the* question of life in
general. For Calvin, that question refers back to the particular way that
sin distorts *our* eyes, *our* conscience, *our* minds, and *our* senses such that
we construct a world ordered by and related to false divinities. Answering
it thus requires a Christian teaching that addresses and accommodates
those very faculties. If the doctrine of the incarnation enables the

possibility for that kind of teaching, it does so not by radically disrupting the world, but by somehow enabling the student to pay closer and more reverent attention to its details. In the next chapter, I'll trace how Calvin's incarnational logic enables a resignification of the self, setting up the church as a community that facilitates that resignification more generally, and ultimately disrupts the urge to imagine the object of teaching as a political body.

6

Faith Resignifying Understanding

Atonement and Election

The "decision" that enacts sovereignty by declaring exception and defining friend and enemy expresses resentment or fear, not commitment; produces violence or tyranny, not nobility; and enacts closure, not faith.

–George Shulman[1]

You would not seek me if you did not already possess me. Therefore, be not anxious.

–Pascal[2]

To say that teaching is possible is to say that it is possible to move from faith to understanding – that even if the mind cannot objectively grasp ultimate and unmediated truth, it is possible to assume a better relation to what is real through certain pedagogical exercises. It is to insist that although human beings cannot transcend the surface of materiality that defers and forbids the disclosure of what is opaque or hidden from view, this need not imply that we index our existence merely to the most forceful awe. If the pursuit of understanding has to do with the kinds of relationships we assume to the surface of things and the effects of those relationships on our faculties, then the pursuit of understanding need not take place according to the binary logic of mastery and submission. Learning is more akin to belonging, or the feeling of knowing oneself as more integrated with and responsible to what is real. Faith is the originary response to the suggestion that this kind of belonging might, in fact, be possible.

---

[1] George Shulman, "White Supremacy and Black Insurgency as Political Theology" in *Race and Secularism in America*, eds. Jonathan S. Kahn and Vincent W. Lloyd (New York: Columbia University Press, 2016): 23–42, 29.

[2] Pascal, Blaise, *Pensées*, 554.

Louis Mackey uses the analogy of a portrait to figure Augustine's incarnational dialectic between faith and understanding:

Belief is useful because it enables us to move from sign to reality without understanding ... Understanding moves from reality to sign. For example, if I know a man, then I will also know his portrait. I will recognize it as a portrait of him, and I will (because I know him) be able to judge the adequacy of the picture as a representation (sign) of the man (reality). But if I have just the portrait and do not know the person, then I can only *believe* that it is a portrait and that it fairly represents the man.[3]

According to this account, the problem that human beings face is that the full reality of things is not immediately accessible to the faculties. Understanding is not given. For Augustine and Calvin, this is due to the effects of fallenness. Experience is never unmediated but always constructed, and it's constructed with untrustworthy tools. This means that persons have the quality of living portraits. They are presented through mediation, and therefore never quite fully present. What the incarnation supplies is the suggestion that the portrait of Jesus Christ, as narrated by revelation, also presents a claim about reality, or how reality is encountered by the activity of God. Faith in the incarnation grounds "the possibility of belief itself," giving adequate "reason to suppose that truth is attainable and the pursuit of it worthwhile."[4] Yet, this does not mean it presents understanding, or reality in unmediated terms. For Augustine, the incarnation enables the pursuit of truth as an exercise of love for reality as encountered by the activity of God. I might rephrase this as a concrete choreography for navigating the perpetual gap that is conserved and not refused or collapsed when faith pursues understanding.[5]

Mark Jordan similarly reads this approach to signification as a significant refusal of both unmediated claims to reality and the arbitrary power of pure aesthetics: "By insisting on the dialectical analogy between word and Word, Augustine has performed the valuable *philosophic* service of preserving the two-sided character of the sign," one that "shows that there is a deep connection between the structure of any one sign and that larger movement between the creator and the Creator."[6] Important to note, here, is that according to this tradition of signification, theology is

[3] Louis Mackey, *Peregrinations of the Word* (Ann Arbor: University of Michigan Press, 1997), 62.

[4] Mackey, 75.   [5] Mackey, 74–77.

[6] Mark D. Jordan, "Words and Word: Incarnation and Signification in Augustine's *De Doctrina Christiana*" in *Augustinian Studies* 11 (1980): 177–196, 196.

just as invested with understanding real things in general as it is with the pursuit of the understanding of God in particular. The analogy between words and Word implies an analogy between being and Flesh, and therefore a connection between our relation to divine transcendence and what I've suggested might be called the transcendence of materiality – the elusive and excessive "reality" of ordinary things to which language reaches. I've argued already that Calvin reoccupies this dimension of Augustinian thinking when he frames the world as the domain for exercises of signification grounded in providential discourse.[7] But Jordan also suggests Anselm of Canterbury as another standard-bearer of this Augustinian tradition, arguing that the grammatical method undergirding the *Proslogion*'s argument proceeds according to this same analogy.

It's worth taking a brief look at how Anselm reoccupies this tradition, because it's helpful for drawing out certain key moments in Calvin's itinerary – in particular, the way the doctrines of atonement and election work in the overall arc of the *duplex cognitio* that guides the reader on to *cognitio Dei et nostri*. Along these lines, however, it is not just that Anselm is interested in the ability of the incarnate Word to teach by generating a certain active posture of the self toward language, although that is part of it. The *Proslogion*, after all, brackets out revealed content. What is interesting is that, by virtue of this bracketing, the *Proslogion* provides a focused demonstration of how faith approaches language in general as it pursues a more fully embodied understanding. The purpose of this chapter is ultimately to trace some of what I take to be the key intermediary steps through which Calvin leads his reader to reimagine the collective bodies of church and state. To clarify the role of what I take to be a fundamental Augustinian logic of practice at play in carrying this out, I begin by looking more closely at Anselm's argument and its relevance before turning to books two and three of the *Institutio*.

ANSELM'S *PROSLOGION*

The *Proslogion* is commonly read as the source for the classic deductive argument for God's existence, the "ontological proof." It is noteworthy that the argument itself is not deduced from axioms but from grammar.

---

[7] I've noted already that Calvin departs from Augustine to the extent that Augustine remains committed to Neoplatonic ontology. However, Augustine himself reoccupies Neoplatonic ontology through the doctrine of *creatio ex nihilo* and the subsequent doctrine of the incarnation, by which God the *logos* becomes flesh. For Augustine's own narration of the significance of this departure from Neoplatonism, see *Confessiones* 7.

It is further noteworthy that the brief text does not set out to offer a proof for God's existence, but an account of the meditation through which Anselm's "faith" pursued – and received – an "understanding" of his own relation to being.[8] When Anselm offers the argument itself in books two to three of the *Proslogion*, he does so by unfolding the grammatical meaning of the claim that God is "that than which a greater cannot be conceived." This is a divine name borrowed, not incidentally, from *De Doctrina Christiana.*[9] Like the claim that Christ is "Word made Flesh," the linguistic character of the claim that "God is *that than which a greater cannot be conceived*" addresses the human knower with a particular force: not only as a knowing being but more precisely as a thinking and speaking being who is, by virtue of thinking and speaker, embedded alongside and among other signs and signifying things. In this case, the negative formulation of the statement refers language to some superlative existence that surrounds and exceeds the sign, paradoxically referencing that very excess.

The ontological argument has often been criticized for making an illegitimate jump from the reality of the concept to the reality of the object.[10] To borrow from Kant's famous example, one hundred dollars (or "thalers") exist perfectly coherently in concept, but this does not mean that one hundred dollars also exists in my bank account.[11] This, however, misses the force of Anselm's argument. For Anselm, what is special about the argument is its generality: It is the fact that in this one instance, the grammatical formulation of the concept itself ("that than which a greater cannot be conceived") refers to a materially exiting reality (the largest of existence).[12] Mackey is once again helpful on this point:

---

[8] Here is the way Anselm narrates the *Proslogion* as a text produced in relation to an experience:

> Then one day, when my violent struggle against its hounding had worn me down, the thing I had despaired of finding presented itself in the very clash of my thoughts, so that I eagerly embraced the thought I had been taking such pains to drive away. Therefore, thinking that what I had rejoined to discover would please a reader if it were written down, I wrote about it and about a number of other things in the work that follows, adopting the role of someone trying to raise his mind to the contemplation of God and seeking to understand what he believes (Anselm, Proslogion prologue).

[9] Anselm, *Proslogion* 2; *DDC*, 1.7.7; Jordan, 196.

[10] This is Kant's classic "refutation" of the ontological argument as found in the *Critique of Pure Reason* (Cambridge: Cambridge University Press, 1998), beginning at A592/B620.

[11] Kant, *CPR*, A599/B627.

[12] It would be a much longer task to relate the reading of Anselm's argument that I'm forwarding to the details of the Kantian system. I will suffice it to say that this defense of Anselm's version of the argument pushes on the strictly propositional/formal way language operates in the Kantian project. A Schleiermacherian adaptation of the

The (misleadingly) so-called ontological proof of God's existence is more aptly described as a proof of the ontological reliability of language. It presumes to locate the moment of linguistic soundness, the plenitude of presence from which other language may deviate but to which (so long as it continues to say "be") it is always bound. The phrase "that than which a greater cannot be conceived" expresses the created innocence of language underlying its original guilt and identifies the point of contact for a redemption of derelict discourse.[13]

Understanding, here, means comprehending a thing's real existence. As I've shown, if teaching happens by signs, it can only do so if there is some relation to those things to which signs refer. A sign's intelligibility is therefore tied to the reality it signifies. The revelation of this argument involves not only the possibility but the necessity of the connectedness of language to being.

Whatever understanding Anselm receives, however, comes at the cost of his conceptual mastery over "God" (or any other thing). As with Augustine, Anselm's understanding materializes by placing him in relation to other things – in the middle, as it were of a chain of signs. The effect is that the initiate becomes a conduit for a divine activity of signing. The genius of the ontological proof is also its undoing as a proof per se. The "innocence of language" is language's naïve interest in representing the truth about things – the fact that, according to Anselm, believers and unbelievers alike can "understand" the content of the claim that God is "that than which a greater cannot be conceived." But the possibility for the proof's obtaining is bound up with the perpetual possibility of its failure: the practical manner in which the language of the proof is used by and in relation to the human subject. The proof works when and if the subject becomes reoriented by the use of language whose referent exceeds the subject. It fails when and if the subject, wanting to maintain sovereignty over the use of language, drives a wedge between language and that to which it (negatively) refers, wanting to keep the possible referent of "that than which a greater cannot be conceived" safely within grasp.[14] This is why it matters that the fuller text of the *Proslogion* places the character of Anselm in a specific posture, one that is exemplary of a faith

Kantian two-stemmed account of subjective experience would be a better conversation partner for Anselm.
[13] Mackey, 81.
[14] Anselm insisted that Gaunilo's reply "on behalf of the fool" and his own reply to Gaunilo be included in the published text. For Mackey's reading of what this accomplishes, see pages 99–100.

that grasps and affirms the claim that God is "that than which a greater cannot be conceived."

Surrounding the argument concerning God's existence, the *Proslogion* is a literary rendering of a practice – a practice that takes the form of a prayer. The prayer, moreover, is one that begins in the manner of Augustine (and Calvin): with the problem of the eristic paradox. Anselm prays,

> When will you show yourself to us again? ... For I cannot seek you unless you teach me how, and I cannot find you unless you show yourself to me. Let me seek you in desiring you; let me desire you in seeking you. Let me find you in loving you; let me love you in finding you. I acknowledge, Lord, and I thank you, that you have created in me this image of you so that I may remember you, think of you, and love you. Yet this image is so eroded by my vices, so clouded by the smoke of my sins, that it cannot do what it was created to do unless you renew and refashion it.[15]

Notice, as Anselm proceeds, how the paradox is addressed: not by the desire to be disrupted or occupied by divine intellect, but with the petition that divine grace "renew and refashion" his own modicum of created understanding. The prayer continues: "I am not trying to scale your heights, Lord; my understanding is in no way equal to that. But I do long to understand your truth in some way, your truth which my heart believes and loves. For I do not seek to understand in order to believe; I believe in order to understand."[16] Mackey writes that this prayer becomes "like language itself (itself language) ... never yet at the limit but always only straining toward it."[17] Anselm's prayer positions him as the kind of subject that can hope to understand in the way a created thing understands: by entering into a relationship to that which it does not understand.

Similar to Calvin's text, the artifactual construction of Anselm's meditative illumination addresses the reader to a mediatory argumentative tool while guiding the reader along an itinerary from faith toward at least a glimpse of understanding. On one level, the argument places the reader before the world and recommends a strategy for effecting the world's clarification – here, approaching the grammatical structure of language *as if* inflected with a passion for being.[18] This is a posture of faith that language is in fact invested in being, and one that thus enables procession of the argument toward some understanding of that being to which

---

[15] *Proslogion*, 1.   [16] *Proslogion*, 1.   [17] Mackey, 95.
[18] I mean, here, to invoke Agamben's discussions of signatures. See Chapter 3.

language refers. On another level, the *Proslogion* draws its reader along a sequence of moves that could be summarized as *quaerens*, or seeking. These moves, or moments, are the record of an illumination unfolding through Anselm's posture toward language that concerns God.

Yet, the boundary of the text is also addressed and disrupted by Gaunilo's "reply on behalf of the fool," which Anselm directed to be included perpetually with the *Proslogion* alongside Anselm's own reply. With the inclusion of Gaunilo's reply, the text is haunted by its own failure, or by the possibility of that wedge between language and being that hinges, in some decisive way, on the practical posture assumed by the thinking/speaking/writing subject before language.[19] This is another way of articulating the very interpretive crossroads that I've been considering along the way. Anselm's text can help us – as readers of this tradition of pedagogy – to get a better sense of what that crossroads entails in a structural sense, or the mechanism by which one would go down one road or the other.

For Gaunilo, Anselm's argument fails when the language of "that than which a greater cannot be conceived" is approached as a concept unrelated to the subject, or objectively external to the subject's own constitution. From such a standpoint, the concept is a mere thing among other abstract things that does not refer without a contextual act of force. As mere language, it has only a conventional claim on being, and as long as the being-of-God-in-particular cannot be objectively disclosed and related to the language, the argument fails. The argument's very success thus turns on the perpetuity of the gap between sign and signified. This is a gap that Anselm thinks can only be closed performatively: when the subject is turned in her relationship to words and things more generally, coming to know herself fundamentally as related to everything else by virtue of a language invested in being. Mackey thus characterizes the outcome of the *Proslogion* as "faith no longer, not yet understanding, the argument as a 'seeking,' remains an unfulfilled signification, a discourse in the hiatus between signifier and signified."[20] As the inclusion of Gaunilo's reply alongside Anselm's account attests, the argument is not meant to disclose a transcendent signifier, but to facilitate "a perpetual pilgrimage through the differences of language that sunder sign from being and delay until eternity the advent of presence," while also gesturing toward the worthiness of the pilgrimage itself.[21]

---

[19] Mackey, 101–102.   [20] Mackey, 107.   [21] Mackey, 107.

This approach to language-in-general as structured by faith seeking understanding offers a crucial intellectual link between the approaches to signification taken by Augustine and Calvin. I would argue that it is also an apt description of the way Calvin characteristically approaches the propriety and usefulness of theological discourses for effecting a project that involves institutional reform. Recall that the 1559 *Institutio* is recommended to its reader as both a record of, and a blueprint for, the claim that he has "embraced the sum of religion [*religionis summum*] in all its parts, and have arranged it in such an order, that if anyone rightly grasps it, it will not be difficult for him to determine what he ought especially to seek [*quaerere*] in Scripture, and to what end [*scopum*] he ought to relate its contents." His writing is an ongoing exercise of seeking and relating that he also characterizes as the "paving" of a "road."[22]

This all sounds much in line with Augustine's and Anselm's projects. For Calvin, however, there is a difference, and that difference is one I've already discussed in several places – that, for Calvin, there is an ontological difference between heaven and earth. This means that for language to refer, language has to be inherently relational. Like Agamben's account of the signature, language has to act as an operator relating two separate domains to one another. Like Anselm, Calvin wants language about God to be understood as a claim invested in questions about language and being in general. That's why he begins the *duplex cognitio* with the radical claim that God is actively signifying – affirming and turning – every aspect of the complex of created life, such that one could even say "Nature is God" (*Inst.* 1.5.1). But the second part of the *duplex cognitio* triangulates divine choreography around one figure of the human, the contextually enacted signs of the "faith of Christ" operating from within the domain of creation. These two aspects need to remain distinct in order to be related to one another. And this complex divine relationship between signs and created things sets up a pattern through which the self is turned through the artifactual address of language in relation to ordinary existing being – in this case, that of her own person.

In the course of this chapter, I want to argue that for Calvin the illuminative moment around which signs and things coincide to reorient the subject occurs in his infamous doctrine of election. In a way that calls back to the Augustinian tradition I've been discussing, election comes at a

[22] Calvin, "John Calvin to the Reader," 4–5.

decisive time in Calvin's itinerary. It not only follows the articulation of "the knowledge of God the Creator" and "the knowledge of God the Redeemer in Christ" as deliberately ordered objects of a seeking faith. It also follows Calvin's discussion of prayer – the structural apex of Book Three's discussion of "The mode of obtaining the grace of Christ" and the longest chapter in the 1559 *Institutio*. Prayer is the move to ask that the signification of creation and redemption be materially realized in the life and person of the one who prays. Election, which follows immediately after prayer and closes Book Three, is the precise moment when the believer receives such particular and personal assurance.

BOOK TWO: THE LEGAL FICTION OF THE FAITH OF CHRIST

I've argued that for Calvin, it is the believer's fallen faculties that present God as an enemy, and this misperception is what scripture is given to address and treat. The first step of the *duplex cognitio*, the knowledge of God the Creator, culminates in divine providence. When this particular dimension of revelation is accommodated to the peculiarities of the fallen condition, it refigures creation as the domain of constant divine care so that God "may again begin to be our Father."[23] The practical payoff is

---

[23] Father-language is obviously a striking and pervasive feature of Calvin's theology, contributing a range of indications to Calvin's mixed record on matters of gender and family. On the one hand, Calvin's reliance upon the analogy between God and fatherhood consistently constructs a loving, caring, attentive and generous father – one who insists upon a familiar title and adopts strangers into his family. Furthermore, in his commentaries, Calvin did not show any discomfort in analogizing God's love equally to a mother's love (CO 37:204C). On the other hand, one is well advised to critically consider the larger effects not only of overwhelmingly associating God with a sexed and gendered office, but also the relationship between this theological imagery and the early modern turn (especially in Reformed circles) to vesting the patriarchal family with a certain religious authority. The affirmation of family life was a common feature of reformers' critique of the medieval religious life, and the repercussions of this are still apparent in contemporary politics of religion and family. To what extent does Calvin link the father's love with the father's rule? And what kind of rule is exemplified in the actions of the economic Trinity with reference to the world and human life? These are important questions to keep in mind, even as one appreciates the rhetorical effects of Calvin's father language. Additionally, for more on Calvin's relationship to women theologically and historically, see Charmarie Jenkins Blaisdell, "Calvin's Letters to Women: The Courting of Ladies in High Places" in *The Sixteenth Century Journal* 13/3 (1982): 67–84; and John Lee Thompson, *John Calvin and the Daughters of Sarah: Women in Regular and Exceptional Roles in the Exegesis of Calvin, His Predecessors, and His Contemporaries* (Geneva: Librairie Droz, 1992).

that, when attending to the complexities of one's own situation, one will "not doubt that it is the Lord's blessing alone by which all things prosper" (*Inst.* 1.17.7); "will not continue to be ungrateful" (*Inst.* 1.17.8); and will maintain hope amidst adversity, knowing that the "Heavenly Father so holds all things in his power, so rules by his authority and will, so governs by his wisdom, that nothing can befall except he determine it" (*Inst.* 1.17.11). Calvin thinks that this enables "patience and peaceful moderation of mind," in other words shifting one's general posture from *paranoia* (that God conspires against me) to *pronoia* (that God's active will affirms me in order to guide me to good ends) (*Inst.* 1.17.8). As a first step, providence treats the reactionary impulses that confound the journey to self-knowledge.

In Book Two, the second part of the *duplex cognitio* begins again with the matter of self-knowledge. The work of providence positions the reader in creation and asks the reader to read creation itself as divinely affirmed. But this, on its own, is not sufficient. Without the particular form of teaching proper to God the Redeemer in Christ, providence might be misconstrued as self-flattery. According to Calvin, "Nothing pleases man more than the sort of alluring talk that tickles the pride that itches in his very marrow. Therefore, in nearly every age, when anyone publicly extolled human nature in most favorable terms, he was listened to with applause" (*Inst.* 2.1.2). Calvin writes that while we should not forget "our original nobility," the pull to pride will position the human as an idol in a providential world – as a special, self-reliant touchstone for the divine (*Inst.* 2.1.3). What we ought instead to learn is obedience, and this is what Christ the Redeemer teaches. Obedience, for Calvin, entails embracing the use of divine revelation as the appropriate source – the appropriate tool, as it were – from which one attains self-knowledge (*Inst.* 2.1.4).

Across Book Two, the "faith of Christ" teaches by both representing and demonstrating what it means to live in connection to God. The Mediator's life teaches by *writing a life* that performs human life as if lived under the sign of divinity – a life that speaks, acts, interprets, and responds to people and things in a particular and persuasive way. On a more abstract level, this is what Calvin thinks the law was given to accomplish according to the old covenant. He departs from Luther in not merely reading the law as useful for maintaining order and revealing sin, but also for more positively revealing a more useful way of life deemed beneficial for worldly flourishing (*Inst.* 2.7.12). But the law is not the best-suited form of teaching. Christ fulfills the law not only by demonstration of its function, but by doing so through the superior medium of actually being human.[24]

So, on one level, Calvin will present Christological life-writing as persuasive due to its continuity with scriptural inscriptions of collective memory. For example, he spends a good deal of time outlining continuities between Christ the Redeemer and the signatures of certain Hebrew scriptural types. The activity peculiar to God in Christ is not primarily that of a sudden event that disrupts the order of ordinary space and time. Christ's activity is legible because it is also continuous: It reiterates existing patterns for presenting life in the world as navigable in a living way (see *Inst.* 2.7–11).[25] But on another level, what is truly unique about Christological life-writing – what signifies a break – is the fact that reiteration occurs from the site of a human body in whom divine patterns are "naturally" operating inseparably in the patterns of his humanity. Calvin makes clear that Christ the Mediator is able to teach because the character of his really human life makes the character of divine obedience legible and followable.

Here is a long quote where Calvin discusses these two dimensions of the *cognitio Dei redemptoris*:

In undertaking to describe the Mediator, Paul then, with good reason, distinctly reminds us that He is human: "One mediator between God and humanity, the human Jesus Christ." He could have said "God"; or he could at least have omitted the word "human" just as he did the word "God." But because the Spirit speaking through his mouth knew our weakness, at the right moment he used a most appropriate remedy to meet it: he set the Son of God familiarly among us as one of ourselves. Therefore, lest anyone be troubled about where to seek the Mediator, or by what path we must come to him, the Spirit calls him "human," thus teaching us that he is near us, indeed touches us, since he is our flesh. Here he surely means the same thing that is explained elsewhere at greater length: "We have not a high priest who is unable to sympathize with our weaknesses, but one who in every respect has been tempted as we are, yet without sinning" (*Inst.* 2.12.1).

---

[24] Thomas J. Davis gives a wonderful account of the importance of Christ's human body in *This Is My Body: The Presence of Christ in Reformation Thought* (Grand Rapids, MI: Baker Academic, 2008), chapter 4.

[25] Calvin, in other words, will link both wills of God (see discussion in chapter 4) to the incarnation itself. Christ simultaneously carries and fulfills the signification of the law, which Calvin treats as an accommodation that is useful and beneficial to the life of a believer (see 2.7.12) and lives, concretely, with the limitations, sufferings, and ordinary cares of a human being (2.12). The sense in which Christ himself is a given as an accommodation involves Christ's particular incorporation of these two wills and its capacity to similarly teach and orient the lives of Christians.

Here, the Mediator is able to teach because the narrative through which that teaching occurs is realistic to the kinds of beings we are and the kinds of conditions we face. But precisely because of this, Christ's life also supplants and challenges whatever self-generated strategies were in place for facing life.[26] It is here that Christ's activity can be characterized not just as mediating, but as redeeming – as making a new relation to God possible out of the old. Calvin continues:

This will become even clearer if we call to mind that what the Mediator was to accomplish was no common thing. His task was so to restore us to God's grace as to make of the children of men, children of God; of the heirs of Gehenna, heirs of the Heavenly Kingdom. Who could have done this had not the selfsame Son of God become the Son of man, and had not so taken what was ours as to impart what was his to us, and to make what was his by nature ours by grace? Therefore, relying on this pledge, we trust that we are sons of God, for God's natural Son fashioned for himself a body from our body, flesh from our flesh, bones from our bones, that he might be one with us. Ungrudgingly he took our nature upon himself to impart to us what was his, and to become both Son of God and Son of man in common with us. Hence that holy brotherhood which he commends with his own lips when he says: "I am ascending to my Father and your Father, to my God and your God." In this way we are assured of the inheritance of the Heavenly Kingdom; for the only Son of God, to whom it wholly belongs, has adopted us as his brothers" (*Inst.* 2.12.2).

By embracing flesh, special Christological mediation effects a kind of machinery for reorienting the significance of human life in more specific terms, directed to human beings as such.[27]

---

[26] For more fluency in how Calvin reads the narratives themselves, it's best to direct readers to the commentaries which consistently privilege the *sensus literalis* – a phrase that suggests, above all, the realistic literary quality of scripture. For an excellent treatment of how Calvin interprets, see Richard Burnett, "John Calvin and the *Sensus Literalis*" in *Scottish Journal of Theology* 57/1 (2004): 1–13. Also, though he focuses on the Epistles, see R. Ward Holder, *Calvin and the Grounding of Interpretation* (Leiden: Brill, 2006). Finally, it's worth noting Calvin's influence on the twentieth-century Yale School, also known as narrative theology. See, for example, Hans Frei, *Eclipse of Biblical Narrative: A Study in Eighteenth and Nineteenth Century Hermeneutics* (New Haven, CT: Yale University Press, 1974).

[27] In this moment, the resignification of self and ourselves in Books Three and Four is foregrounded. At this point, in Book Two, this account is received as merely an article of "trust." Later, in Book Three, the narrated actions of Christ will function as a kind of legal fiction to enable the adoption – and full participation – of others into the "family" of God. There, the "adoption" of ordinary persons through the Spirit facilitates the resignification of the self: "Justified by faith is one who, excluded from the righteousness of works, grasps the justice of Christ through faith, and clothed in it, appears in God's sight not as a sinner but as a just person" (*Inst.* 3.11.2). Then, in

The doctrine of the atonement capstones Book Two, much as providence capstones Book One.[28] Claims about justification and modes of mediation comprise the content of Book Two – relationships between old and new laws and covenants, the two natures of Christ, the offices held by Christ. In the closing locus on atonement, the content of who Christ is and what Christ does is directed to the situation of the reader. Just as providence wants to persuade the reader to relate doctrines about God to every facet of worldly life, the discourse on atonement wants to relate every aspect of Christ's life to the ordinary domain of the reader's own existence before God. It wants to convince the reader not only of what justification provides, but how. Calvin writes that "we must earnestly ponder how [Christ] accomplishes salvation for us. This we must do not only to be persuaded that he is its author but to gain a sufficient and stable support for our faith, rejecting whatever could draw us away in one direction or another" (*Inst.* 2.16.1). If Christ teaches by presenting a life that is both familiar and different from our own, the atonement gives an account of how that life specifically addresses us.

The argument begins by echoing 2.6.1's claim that "our eyes" and "our conscience" perceive ourselves as cursed by God, suggesting that "no one can descend into himself and seriously consider what he is without feeling God's wrath and hostility toward him" (*Inst.* 2.16.1). At a rudimentary stage of learning, to ponder salvation is already to render salvation impossible. For what could a fallen person ever do to change God's judgments? And how can a person be saved without God's judgments changing? At this point, Calvin names the paradox at which he'd only hinted earlier, which is a soteriological reworking of the eristic paradox: "How could he have given in his only-begotten Son a singular

---

Book Four, the sacramental practices of the church resignify the collective who lives in and by means of the world more generally: "God has received us, once for all, into his family, to hold us not only as servants but as sons. Thereafter, to fulfill the duties of a most excellent Father concerned for his offspring, he under-takes also to nourish us throughout the course of our life ... To this end, therefore, he has, through the hand of his only-begotten Son, given to his church another sacrament, that is, a spiritual banquet, wherein Christ attests himself to be the life-giving bread, upon which our souls feed unto true and blessed immortality" (*Inst.* 4.17.1).

[28] In these chapters, the stated topic is in line with the dialectical pedagogical pattern Calvin has established. They do not merely offer arguments about the human condition (2.1–6), prior mediations (2.7–11), or the nature of Christ himself (2.12–15). Just as providence concluded Book One by integrating creation and providence, Book Two integrates the Mediator's work with human lives. It effectively materializes the signification of Christ in the living context of the reader.

pledge of his love to us if he had not already embraced us with his free favor?" Calvin sets out to dispel this apparent contradiction by framing Christian teaching once again as a device accommodated to the peculiar "needs" of fallen human subjectivity. Scriptural expressions that seem to portray God changing God's mind about humanity in the moment of Christ's atoning death are actually "accommodated to our capacity that we may better understand how miserable and ruinous our condition is apart from Christ."[29] Had we not been given a "clearly stated" narrative that involved a turn from wrath to salvation, "we would scarcely have recognized how miserable we would have been without God's mercy" and "we would have underestimated the benefit of liberation" (*Inst.* 2.16.2).

Calvin foregrounds the divine use of a crafted, fictive narrative by comparing two possible stories. The first is brief:

For example, suppose someone is told: "If God hated you while you were still a sinner, and cast you off, as you deserved, a terrible destruction would have awaited you. But because he kept you in grace voluntarily, and of his own free favor, and did not allow you to be estranged from him, he thus delivered you from that peril." This man then will surely experience and feel something of what he owes to God's mercy (*Inst.* 2.16.2).

This first story is not false. In fact, perhaps in some strict sense, Calvin would see it as a more accurate summary of things. But this first story fails to pinpoint and differentiate the affective complexity of the realistic human experience, as it is experienced, in a living temporal sequence. This failure makes it less realistic.

The second story contains more drama and detail:

On the other hand, suppose he learns, as Scripture teaches, that he was estranged from God through sin, is an heir of wrath, subject to the curse of eternal death, excluded from all hope of salvation, beyond every blessing of God, the slave of Satan, captive under the yoke of sin, destined finally for a dreadful destruction and already involved in it; and that at this point Christ interceded as his advocate, took upon himself and suffered the punishment that, from God's righteous judgment, threatened all sinners; that he purged with his blood those evils which had rendered sinners hateful to God; that by this expiation he made satisfaction and sacrifice duly to God the Father; that as intercessor he has appeased God's wrath; that on this foundation rests the peace of God with men; that by this bond his benevolence is maintained toward them. Will the man not then be even more

---

[29] Interestingly, Calvin seems to treat the needs of fallen persons as on par with Augustine's rule of love as a hermeneutical principle. In other words, the needs of fallen faculties guide interpretation of scripture much like, and in accord with, the demands of love.

moved by all these things which so vividly portray the greatness of the calamity from which he has been rescued? (*Inst.* 2.16.2).

The three most interesting words of this interesting passage might come in the first line: "as Scripture teaches." *Scripture*, which Calvin holds in the highest estimation and treats as the written Word of God, *teaches* through the deliberate use of a story as a crafted tool. This story is apparently less interested in representing putatively transcendent objective facts, as if such facts could be transparently represented. Instead, the scriptural story is responsible to the needs of a humanity that cannot otherwise name the unspeakable depths of its own complexity in relation to a God who exists beyond its ontological-epistemological grasp.

It is important that this second mode of teaching cultivates knowledge by focusing primarily on affect. This is apparent in the conclusion Calvin draws:

To sum up: since our hearts cannot, in God's mercy, either seize upon life ardently enough or accept it with the gratefulness we owe, unless our minds are first struck and overwhelmed by fear of God's wrath and by dread of eternal death, we are taught by Scripture to perceive that apart from Christ, God is, so to speak, hostile to us, and his hand is armed for our destruction; to embrace his benevolence and fatherly love in Christ alone (*Inst.* 2.16.2).

The proper result of teaching, here, aims holistically at affirming, addressing, and reforming affect, perception, and cognition together. All facets are mentioned in Calvin's summary. This requires a certain approach to language, however, that reads its relative metaphysical seriousness right alongside the necessary qualifiers to which Calvin resorts frequently: "so to speak," and "as if."[30]

When Calvin goes on to discuss the doctrine of the atonement directly, according to its mechanics, he reads the atonement as kind of legal drama that operates on two levels. A spiritual trial is superimposed over the historical trial of Jesus by Pontius Pilate. The man Jesus Christ stands before Pilate accused of claiming to be God, and is found guilty and condemned to death. At the same time, Christ stands before God as a representative of humanity, accused of human guilt. In this trial, however, the evidence of his "whole life" and "the whole course of his obedience"

---

[30] See e.g., *Inst.* 1.1.2; 1.5.1, 11–12; 1.7.1; 1.11.8; 1.13.5; 2.15.5; 3.17.10; 4.16.2; 4.17.33. For more on the importance of the subjunctive in ritual, see Adam B. Seligman, Robert P. Weller, Michael Puett, and Bennett Simon, *Ritual and Its Consequences* (Oxford: Oxford University Press, 2008).

leads to a verdict of innocence and eternal life – not only for Christ, but also for the class of human beings who Christ represents (*Inst.* 2.16.5).

This account of the atonement depends on the function of a legal fiction or an assertion that is accepted as if true for legal purposes even though it may be factually untrue or unproven. The assertion is that Christ, in fact, stands as a representative of all humanity. Before Pilate, his condemnation (untruthfully) renders Christ's person *as* "the person of a sinner and evildoer" (*Inst.* 2.16.5). Yet, this untruth enables what happens before God: As a representative of humanity – a figure of the sinning person – Christ functions as a class action *defendant* who enables all to be judged by the evidence of his own particular circumstances. Observing the play of these two trials side by side, Calvin writes that "from his shining innocence it will at the same time be obvious that he was burdened with another's sin rather than his own," meaning that God's judgment is just (*Inst.* 2.16.5). Yet, in the spectacle of the unjust punishment rendered by Pilate, Christ actually bears "all the signs of a wrathful and avenging God," and this allows Christ's own innocence to count for others under the sign of guilt (*Inst.* 2.16.11).

The divine use of the fiction of Christ's guilt makes justification legible because it enables a misfiring human interpretation (that Christ is guilty because Christ is God) to bear the causal weight of the perception of divine wrath. Through taking up this misfiring into the narrative itself, it then stages an account through which this very misperception enables a divine verdict of innocence that justifies many. According to Calvin, this narrative "teach[es] us that the penalty to which we were subject had been imposed upon this righteous man" (*Inst.* 2.16.5).[31] If, alternatively, humanity were to try to defend itself based on its own relative merit – based on the brute facts of our case before God – this would demand a righteous judgment from God based on these facts, which would indeed be a "curse caused by our guilt." To the extent that human beings try to justify ourselves according to isolated merits, we perpetuate the perception of a divine curse.

But according to Calvin's account, the death of Christ is given not for God, but "for us," to fictively "transfer our condemnation to himself." The power of the story – its tragedy as well as its legal ingenuity – is the very mode of its persuasion: "We must not understand that he fell under a curse that overwhelmed him; rather—in taking the curse upon

---

[31] Calvin writes, a little later, that "man, so long as he remains a sinner, must *consider* [God] an enemy and a judge" (*Inst.* 2.17.2, emphasis mine).

himself—he crushed, broke, and scattered its whole force" – the force by which sin distorts the human faculties of judgment and perception. Where "our eyes" once saw a "curse," Calvin writes that "faith apprehends an acquittal in the condemnation of Christ" (*Inst.* 2.16.5). The legal fiction, here, is treated as the highest truth because its rendering of the human condition enables what is more fundamentally true: that despite what humanity actually deserves, God loves us.

To be clear, it is crucial that Christ's life and death are thoroughly grounded in the reality of ordinary material conditions, not only for the persuasive structure of the story but for the sense in which that persuasive structure enables a more fundamental truth. For example, Calvin writes that believers ought not to be scandalized by accounts of Jesus' fear and sorrow. In facing unjust accusations and impending death, he "was troubled in spirit," "stricken with grief," "feared death," "groaned to his Father in secret," prayed from an "unbelievable bitterness of heart," and even "[felt] himself, as it were, forsaken by God" (*Inst.* 2.16.12). These signs of human nature are the very signs that make the life-writing of Christ rise above "mere" fiction by more accurately presenting real human beings with a picture of our own humanity. We are subject to the same embodied fears and weaknesses but "without moderation" (*Inst.* 2.16.7, 12). By submitting to these trials, Christ takes on the phantasmic effects of the "curse of God" as a phenomenon of human life, but in order to demonstrate the greater reality of God's love for us: "[he] was induced purely by his love for us and by his mercy to submit to it" (*Inst.* 2.16.12).

Calvin's reading of the atonement is layered over the structure of providence, with the characteristic movements of affirmation, endurance, and resignification of creation all in play. But the figure of the Redeemer articulates what before was only "ineffable": namely, that manner in which God's providence wills against its own will (see *Inst.* 1.18.3; chapter 4). The divine call to will against one's own will for the existence of another is fleshed out in the concrete life of one who "loved us even when he hated us" (*Inst.* 2.16.5) – whose loving action affirms even the reality of one deemed enemy. And that narrative generates persuasion because it enables the performance of materialized relationships that shatter the phantasm of human guilt while making new and different claims about human reality. Christ's story incorporates artifice as evidence of "his incomparable love toward us" – evidence that he was willing "to wrestle with terrible fear, and amid those cruel torments to cast off all concern for himself that he might provide for us" (*Inst.* 2.16.5). Providential governance becomes embodied in this double movement of Christ, who, "disregarding his own feelings, subjected and yielded himself wholly to his Father's will" – Christ, who, in turn, "wills not to lose what is his in us, out of his own kindness he still finds something to love" (2.16.5, 3). In Book Three, the signs of Christ's life enable not only justification but fuller participation in sanctification.

BOOK THREE: PRAYER, ELECTION, AND THE EVIDENCE OF DESIRE

Any thoughtful reader of Calvin's 1559 *Institutio* might wonder why Calvin posits a *duplex cognitio* and not a *triplex cognitio*. He was, after all, an ardent Trinitarian.[32] Why the absence of *cognitio Dei spiritus*?[33] Calvin never addresses this, meaning that any theory must rely on conjecture. But I do think insight can be gleaned from the pedagogical patterning that I've been tracing. Let me walk through some of the logic.

The obvious impulse would be to expect the Spirit in the title of Book Three like the Creator and Redeemer headlined in Books One and Two. Yet, Book Three is titled, "The mode of obtaining the grace of Christ, the benefits it confers, and the effects stemming from it." And Book Four's title seems to merely extend this from the internal to the external, or from the individual to the social: "Of the external means or helps by which God allures us into fellowship with Christ, and keeps us in it." Both of these titles signal a turn, at the structural midpoint of the 1559 *Institutio*, toward modes for using and enjoying the teachings already given according to the *duplex cognitio*. But while the "knowledge of God the Spirit" is never given its own distinct pedagogy, the Spirit is central to the task of Book Three. Here is how Calvin presents that task in the opening section:

We must now examine this question. How do we receive those benefits which the Father bestowed on his only-begotten Son—not for Christ's own private use, but that he might enrich poor and needy humans? First, we must understand that as long as Christ remains outside of us, and we are separated from him, all that he has suffered and done for the salvation of the human race remains useless and of no value for us. Therefore, to share with us what he has received from the Father, he had to become ours and to dwell within us. For this reason, he is called "our Head," and "the first-born among many brethren." We also, in turn, are said to

---

[32] If this weren't amply apparent in his writings, it is attested forcefully by his involvement in the execution of Servetus for denying the trinity.

[33] My thinking on this question is indebted to conversations with L. Patrick Burrows.

be "engrafted into him," and to "put on Christ"; for, as I have said, all that he possesses is nothing to us until we grow into one body with him. It is true that we obtain this by faith. Yet since we see that not all indiscriminately embrace that communion with Christ which is offered through the gospel, reason itself teaches us to climb higher and to examine into the secret energy of the Spirit, by which we come to enjoy Christ and all his benefits (*Inst.* 3.1.1).

This paragraph contains two important themes that will come to define the latter two books of the 1559 *Institutio*: (1) that the stated goal of Christian pedagogy is not just the *duplex cognitio*, but the fuller realization of those teachings in human bodies and communities and (2) that the Spirit is the "energy" that effects this mutual "possession." Across Book Three, the Spirit is not an object of knowledge, but the proper name for a distinct mode of divine activity that is graciously active in and around the created faculties of the human being. If God the Creator's proper activity involves the affirmation and governance of creation; and if the Redeemer's activity is the privileged and persuasive inscription of faithful death and life before God in the world; then the Spirit's activity is primarily directed to facilitating the fuller *cognitio Dei et nostri*. The Spirit actively restitches the "many bonds" by which the *duplex cognitio* is related to *cognitio nostri* (see *Inst.* 1.1.1). The pattern of Calvin's pedagogical thinking suggests that the spectral *cognitio Dei spiritus* can be read as coterminous with the *cognitio Dei et nostri*.

This is striking because it underscores Calvin's commitment to the practicality of knowledge, or the need to realize divine teaching in relationship to ordinary, created, distinct things. The knowledge of the *duplex cognitio* is not knowledge *of*, but knowledge that sets up the terms for a kind of participation that is not grounded in ontology but rather in signification.[34] Much as providence "wills against its own will" to preserve the integrity of creation and the Word "loves even when he hates," the Spirit is devoted to performing a kind of divine-human relation in which the distinct reality of creation is not only preserved but plays an active role.

---

[34] On my reading, the ontological difference here does not imply or invite a thick ontology of either divinity or creation. Its force is twofold: to assert that the divine relationship to the human occurs through a range of strategies that presuppose different kinds of existences, rather than on a shared ontological foundation; and to assert that the divine will affirms that creation in a general way *as creation*, rather than privileging certain modes of created existence more than others. (This follows also from Calvin's critique of merit; see *Inst.* 3.13–15.)

This is also striking in the larger context of Augustinian pedagogy. For both Augustine and Anselm, there are crucial moments where a self-referential sign enables learning by displacing and turning the subject in her relation to signs and things. For Augustine, the incarnation as "Word made Flesh" draws a student to the church where the object of knowledge is given in other people. For Anselm, the grammar of God as "that than which nothing greater can be conceived" places him in a new relation both to the being that surrounds his existence and the language that is primordially invested in it. Calvin's pedagogy also makes use of a self-referential, reorienting sign that relates the human to the divine and enables learning. But because this happens across ontological difference, the sign is not mediated by being, but by affect.

This turning happens in the closing chapters of Book Three as Calvin moves through the couplet of prayer and election.[35] The chapter on prayer (3.20) is the longest in the *Institutes*, longer even than the combined four chapters on election that follow (3.21–24). Read together, they describe the reception of a fleeting illumination that reorients the self. For Calvin, illumination occurs when the self comes to know itself as specially elected, specially called not only to mimic Christ but fully to participate in Christ's status before God – and in the attending activities that involve realizing and enjoying God's relationship to the existing world. As with Anselm, the moment of illumination emerges in a response received in the act of praying – yearning – for a self that knows itself as resignified. Election is the certainty that one has been resignified.[36] The sign that self-certifies *cognitio Dei et nostri* is not a word or a statement, but a desire that is self-referential. It refers not beyond itself, but to the prior existence of the thing being sought in the self, yet excessive of the self's

---

[35] Unlike the other chapters that cap Calvin's books, Book Three closes with a chapter on the life everlasting. It flows from the logic of prayer and election in that it treats the kind of life that an elect person is given, one that is moreover raised to the transcendent mode of enfleshed existence occupied by Christ himself. But it is also interesting because it marks the end of the creedal structure guiding the *Institutio* before Book Four has even begun. This, to me, is in keeping with Calvin's constant insistence on relating teaching *back to* concrete immanent life. In spite of the creed, the life everlasting is not the conclusion of the teaching Calvin offers. It is, once again, a sign (in the form of a promise) that further situates an individual life. For the reader, however, that life's formation is not complete with the promise of the afterlife, but has yet to engage both church and civic life.

[36] An expanded version of this argument appears in my article, "Reading Tradition as Pedagogy in Calvin and Augustine: The Case of Election," forthcoming in *The Scottish Journal of Theology*.

conscious subjectivity. It refers, in short, to the relational existence of *cognitio Dei et nostri.*

According to Calvin, the crucial components of a prayer involve the *duplex cognitio.* One who prays invokes the signs of providence and faith not in the abstract, but from a position rooted in the singular embodied context of the person who prays:

> After we have been instructed by faith to recognize that whatever we need and whatever we lack is in God, and in our Lord Jesus Christ, in whom the Father willed all the fullness of his bounty to abide so that we may all draw from it as from an overflowing spring, it remains for us to seek in him, and in prayers to ask of him, what we have learned to be in him. Otherwise, to know God as the master and bestower of all good things, who invites us to request them of him, and still not go to him and not ask of him—this would be of as little profit as for a man to neglect a treasure, buried and hidden in the earth, after it had been pointed out to him (*Inst.* 3.20.1).

Prayer is the scene, in concrete time and space, when faith and providence are concretely embraced and directed to material life. It is also the moment when the one who prays expresses a desire not only to receive the goodness of God, but to actively participate in that goodness; not only to assent to faith *that* God is Father, but to actually *experience* God as Father.[37]

Prayer is, therefore, a bold and deliberate practice. In phenomenological terms, it is a mode of activity that begins with a desire that is then informed and directed to sets of promises previously received. Calvin describes prayer as a "training of the heart," and depicts it as the activity that seeks to combine the received language of the *enchiridion* with a regime of bodily practices that are responsive to one's own circumstances (*Inst.* 3.20.1). See, for example, the way the familiar language of providence is invoked, not just in the abstract, but to concretely order the life of the one who prays:

---

[37] One can note the thread of references, not least in Calvin's discussion of providence, to the light emanating from the divine Word that exists temporally and ontologically prior to created light. See, for example, *Inst.* 1.6.1 and 1.13.13. It's worth noting, also, that this represents an important distinction between Calvin and more Platonically and Neo-Platonically influenced writers before him. As my colleague Dr. Michael Motia puts it, for those following Plato and Plotinus, participation suggests that one is "held in being by that which created and sustains you." For Calvin, who maintains ontological distinction between God and the world and a robust use for both human faculties and practices of signification, participation suggests something like being a part of what's going on – participating in a game or a performance. I'm indebted to Dr. Motia for many conversations on this topic.

Words fail to explain how necessary prayer is, and in how many ways the exercise of prayer is profitable. Surely, with good reason the Heavenly Father affirms that the only stronghold of safety is in calling upon his name. By doing so we invoke the presence both of his providence, through which he watches over [*advigilet*] and guards [*curandis*] our affairs, and of his power, through which he sustains us, weak as we are and well-nigh overcome, and of his goodness, through which he receives us, miserably burdened with sins, unto grace; and, in short, it is by prayer that we call him to reveal himself as wholly present to us (*Inst.* 3.20.2).

Prayer, here, is legible within the structure of faith seeking understanding. The person praying has grasped the claims of faith and is willing to submit to them as a kind of technology useful for differentiating and ordering life and experience. But the person praying also actively seeks a deeper understanding. She wants to see, feel, and know the world *as* ordered by providence.

Desire animates every dimension of this account. When praying, Calvin writes that we ought to "earnestly ponder how we need all that we seek, [and] join this prayer with an earnest—nay burning—desire to attain it" (*Inst.* 3.20.6). Desire is also explicitly connected to the ordinary qualities of the body:

For even though the best prayers are sometimes unspoken, it often happens in practice that, when feelings of mind are aroused, unostentatiously the tongue breaks forth into speech, and the other members gesture. From this obviously arose that uncertain murmur of Hannah's, something similar to which all the saints continually experience when they burst forth into broken and fragmentary speech. As for the bodily gestures customarily observed in praying, such as kneeling and uncovering the head, they are exercises whereby we try to rise to a greater reverence for God (*Inst.* 3.20.33).

Within the structure of a prayer, real need gives birth to desire, which gives birth to words. Those words are, in turn, regulated by disciplined bodily movements that in turn discipline and recast desire itself.[38]

Prayer is, therefore, an exercise that presses faith to its limit, hoping to touch the reality of the things signified by faith. This means that prayer is also a prayer about the self – that one will become the kind of self that can touch the reality of things signified by faith by becoming ecstatically turned and reoriented by the reality for which faith seeks. Calvin writes that "the use and experience [of prayer] may, according to the measure of

---

[38] At another point, Calvin calls for a certain form of detachment in order to assume the posture of one in conversation with God. Even there, however, he writes that the "great anxiety" tied to carnal concerns ought not to be suppressed, but ought rather "to kindle in us the desire to pray" (*Inst.* 3.20.4).

our feebleness, confirm his providence," for it is an "exercise of faith by which human minds are cleansed of indolence" (*Inst.* 3.20.3). In the act of calling upon God, consciousness strains to bring about that which is, strictly speaking, not one's own power. These gestures actively mimic the activity of God's providence to the best of ordinary ability. Much like Calvin's providence denies any perceived "indolence" on the part of God (*Inst.* 1.18.3), the faithful invocation of providence evacuates indolence on the part of the believer. Prayer is the desire to not only receive benefits but to *be* useful.

If the exercise of prayer comprises the threshold of the shift from passivity to activity, it also represents the moment when the activity proper to God the Spirit actually animates the immanent activity of the human who prays:

> These things are not said in order that we, favoring our own slothfulness, may give over the function of prayer to the Spirit of God, and vegetate in that carelessness to which we are all too prone. In this strain we hear the impious voices of certain persons, saying that we should drowsily wait until he overtakes our preoccupied minds. But rather our intention is that, loathing our inertia and dullness, we should seek such aid of the Spirit ... The prompting of the Spirit empowers us so to compose prayers as by no means to hinder or hold back our own effort, since in this matter God's will is to test how effectually faith moves our hearts (*Inst.* 3.20.5).

This ability to act is enabled by the fundamental resignification of the self to which the *Institutio* has been driving, and which emerges under the rubric of the "Spirit of adoption" who simultaneously "seals the witness of the gospel in our hearts, raises up our spirits to dare show forth to God their desires, to stir up unspeakable groanings, and confidently cry, 'Abba! Father!'" (*Inst.* 3.20.1).[39] In other words, the Spirit ties the human desire *for* God with the sign, or name, of its legitimacy. As the prayer cries to the Father, God has effectively "again begun to be our Father" (see *Inst.* 2.6.1).[40] It is the Spirit's activity that produces the self-referential sign.

Across earlier chapters of Book Three, Calvin draws from the Pauline logic of adoption to narrate the shift from learning through mimesis to active participation. In theology as much as in the contemporary legal

---

[39] For more on the significance of adoption in Calvin's thought, see Partee, *Theology*, especially 173–175, and Canlis, 130*ff*.

[40] As will be clear presently, Calvin links this to the very grammar of the Lord's Prayer (see 3.20.37).

system, adoption is, again, a legal fiction: a claim, untrue or unproven, about a person's legal origin and privileges that confers real rights and privileges upon a particular living body. When an adoption is authorized, it restructures the social relationships and responsibilities that define and locate that living body within its broader context. Theologically, when ordinary persons are adopted, they are claimed by God (a) providentially, across "genetic" or ontological difference and (b) redemptively, granted participation under the signs and patterns of Christ's own life. The justified believer may live through Christ, "as if [her] innocence were confirmed" (*Inst.* 3.11.3). This shift in signification reconstitutes a person *not by removing him from his created origin* (any more than an adopted person can or should want to change his genetic origin), but by refiguring the possibilities for living meaningfully within the reality of his own created context.

In Calvin's words, adoption allows human lives to "represent" [*repraesentare*]·Christ (*Inst.* 3.6.3).[41] Adoption also moves from the individual to the collective, because it is a status given not only to the self but to the humanity whom Christ represents. It is the prayer *of* Christ – the Lord's prayer, which invokes "Our Father" – a grammar that resists solipsism: "We are not so instructed that each one of us should individually call him his Father, but rather that all of us in common should call him our Father. From this fact we are warned how great a feeling of brotherly love ought to be among us, since by the same right of mercy and free liberality we are equally children of such a father" (*Inst.* 3.20.37). This, rather than the incarnation itself, signals the fictive logic from which the community of the church will emerge (*Inst.* 3.20.38). By including the believer under the name of Christ, adoption also facilitates the logic through which knowledge of self becomes knowledge of *ourselves*.

If prayer is seeking, then election is the modicum of understanding that is granted to an individual in the moment of illumination. Election, or predestination, is Calvin's most infamous and hated teaching – for some good reasons. While it is often inaccurately treated as Calvin's singular obsession and central doctrine, Calvin's teaching on election involves claims that are hard to defend in their own terms: "All are not created in equal condition; rather, eternal life is foreordained for some, eternal

---

[41] Battles renders this "express," though I prefer the cognate. In any case, this is a significant term that helps to underscore the sense in which participation, for Calvin, is an inscription into a fictive account of concretely existing life. In another place, Calvin writes that the one who obeys the law "expresses" the will of God (*Inst.* 2.8.51).

damnation for others." "But by his just and irreprehensible judgment [God] has barred the door of life to those whom he has given over to damnation" (*Inst.* 3.21.5, 7). Even when read in the context of Calvin's teaching, fully attuned to his uses of rhetoric and accommodation, these claims are morally and intellectually troubling. They suggest that Calvin is breaching his own warnings against large-scale, God's-eye speculation, and in doing so they crack open the possibility – or at least the temptation – for human beings to claim cognitive access to these secret divine judgments. They also appear to contradict what is otherwise a fairly prominent theme of the *Institutio* – that, in spite of fears and perceptions to the contrary, God in fact loves God's creation.

Calvin seems at least somewhat aware of the danger of the doctrine, even re-invoking the labyrinth metaphor to describe what the doctrine does to the unassuming reader's mind:

> Let them remember that when they inquire into predestination they are penetrating the sacred precincts of divine wisdom. If anyone with carefree assurance breaks into this place, he will not succeed in satisfying his curiosity and he will enter a labyrinth from which he can find no exit ... He has set forth by his Word the secrets of his will that he has decided to reveal to us. These he decided to reveal in so far as he foresaw that they would concern us and benefit us (*Inst.* 3.21.1).

As with his earlier use of the labyrinth, the thread of the Word is needed to lead to use and benefit. But for most of the discussion, that thread is hard to discern. Calvin in fact reiterates the dangers of the doctrine repeatedly, referring to it not just as a labyrinth, but also as an abyss, and later as a stormy sea on which one must sail in order to find those calmest of waters.

This raises the obvious and fair question: Is the upshot of the doctrine worth the danger it presents? As far as I can tell, Calvin puts forward not less than four – and perhaps five – reasons for promoting the strong and troubling teaching of double predestination. The first is simple empirical realism: As a matter of "fact," some reject the call while others embrace it (*Inst.* 3.21.1). The second is scripture, noting that whether we like it or not, scripture teaches election, and this legitimizes its usefulness (*Inst.* 3.21.3). The third is logical: If salvific grace is to be conceived as specially given grace and not a general feature of the universe as such, then it follows that some must not receive it. Otherwise, God's love would be tautological with human experience, and Christian teaching would be both needless and useless (*Inst.* 3.21.7, 10). Fourth, there is the moral reason, which Calvin cites more than any other. Election renders humanity utterly humble before God, cutting off any logic by which a person might impudently demand grace or demand to understand what God has not seen fit to reveal. In some ways, Calvin's radical assertiveness on double predestination seems to merely defend the fact that God *could* justly elect some and damn others if God so chose – and who are we to say otherwise, and thus assume a position of moral authority over God? (*Inst.* 3.21.1, 3.23.11).

There is something instructive about considering all of these reasons, because they speak to a pervasive, frustrating, but also compelling feature of Calvin's thinking: a stubborn realism that refuses easy answers. This, I think, is where a fifth and more subtle reason can be gleaned. Calvin repeatedly shows a general willingness to preserve God's active relationship to realities that challenge and repulse ordinary readers. We've seen this before. Calvin is characteristically unwavering when it comes to difficult arguments. This was apparent in his discussion of providence, when he was willing to admit that God "creates evil" rather than compromise the scope and activity of a divine will that affirms the world. Or in his discussion of atonement, when he was willing to promote the narrative that God's wrath demanded that Christ suffer such that, "from the fierceness of his torment, drops of blood flowed from his face" (*Inst.* 2.16.12).

But as was also apparent in both of these cases, this unflinching quality of Calvin's arguments also grants them rhetorical depth and strategic complexity. By challenging and even offending the reader, they reveal something of the reader's assumptions and emotions *to* the reader. And by revealing what was previously unconscious or hidden in the self, these arguments present the possibility that given assumptions and emotions can be explored, redirected, and even transformed. Something similar happens with the doctrine of election. After arguing many difficult things across chapters 21, 22, and 23, Calvin finally arrives at the use and benefit of the doctrine at the end of chapter 24. And this time, the thread of the Word runs straight to the interiority of the human person. Calvin writes that the call of the Word and the illumination of the Spirit produce an "inner call" that "is a pledge of salvation that cannot deceive us" (*Inst.* 3.24.2). This inner call describes what is otherwise termed desire, but desire of a specific kind: the desire that is expressed in prayer, which is a desire that responds to the call and wants to taste and become resignified by that which the call promises: God's providential and redemptive care (*Inst.* 3.24.3).

If the inner call *is* the pledge of salvation that cannot deceive us, then the structure of certainty amounts to the simple proof that if one yearns to be elect, then one can then be certain that one *is* elect. A "reprobate" person would not desire divine resignification to begin with. *I desire, therefore I am.* Here is the key passage, which I provide in full, where Calvin articulates the logic surrounding this proof of certainty:

Rare indeed is the mind that is not repeatedly struck with this thought: whence comes your salvation but from God's election? Now, what revelation do you have of your election? This thought, if it has impressed itself upon him, either continually strikes him in his misery with harsh torments or utterly overwhelms him. Truly, I should desire no surer argument to confirm how basely persons of this sort imagine predestination than that very experience, because the mind could not be infected with a more pestilential error than that which overwhelms and unsettles the conscience from its peace and tranquillity toward God. Consequently, if we fear shipwreck, we must carefully avoid this rock, against which no one is ever dashed without destruction. Even though discussion about predestination is likened to a dangerous sea, still, in traversing it, one finds safe and calm—I also add pleasant sailing unless he willfully desire to endanger himself. For just as those engulf themselves in a deadly abyss who, to make their election more certain, investigate God's eternal plan apart from his Word, so those who rightly and duly examine it as it is contained in his Word reap the inestimable fruit of comfort. Let this, therefore, be the way of our inquiry: *to begin with God's call, and to end with it* (*Inst.* 3.24.4, emphases mine).

Here is a fairly clear account of what I've been calling the interpretive crossroads. Calvin argues that if someone is in search of a "revelation" – a sign coming into the cognitive field from the outside that proves one's election – they're doing it wrong.[42] The urge to grasp for cognitive mastery by knowing the character of external signs with rigid certainty is an iteration of that self-flattering human pride that wants to assume sovereignty over other things, deciding their meaning in isolation. Calvin rejects that form of knowledge, arguing that such a posture will only perpetuate the initial phenomenological effects of fallen faculties: misery and dread. The mode of certainty he recommends is the simpler one:

---

[42] There is a longstanding debate over whether Calvin rejects the "practical syllogism," a later name for the idea that assurance of salvation is provided by the presence of a special mark in an individual life. I've argued here that the ground of assurance is found in the orientation to the call and the actions that follow from it, which I take to be more or less in line with the position that Calvin does allow the syllogism not as a syllogism per se, but as a set of movements that connect Christology to call, justification, and sanctification. For a recent discussion, see Muller, *Calvin and the Reformed Tradition* (Grand Rapids, MI: Baker Academic, 2012), chapter 8.

"to begin with God's call and to end with it." When the call is received merely as a call, it generates the desire that responds to the call. In this activity, *cognitio Dei et mei* – knowledge of God and myself – is comprehended. The desire is the sign of the call, and it presents to the believer that which it signifies.[43]

CONCLUSION

Let me conclude this chapter with some reflections on how the movement from creation to redemption to election relates teaching to the body of the believer in a holistic sense. I've argued that within Calvin's itinerary, election is the moment when the subject is turned. It is the moment when Christian teaching begins no longer outside as objects of faith, but known within. This could be read as a moment of incarnational shattering: the moment of incorrigible certainty on which the edifice of knowledge is built and oriented around the site of the elect body. It's clear that Calvin's doctrine of election has been read this way.[44] And if this reading is allowed, it is easy to see how the metaphor of a collective body can reemerge from that site of incarnational shattering as an ordering principle for society, one that regulates who belongs and who doesn't. If the refugee community can come to know itself as elect, then it is not hard to see how the logic of sovereignty can be reoriented around the site of that body rather than disrupted by it. Knowing that Calvin's itinerary is not completed yet – that he will move from this moment of *cognitio Dei et mui* to *cognitio Dei et nostri* by considering church and state – one might expect just such a move. One might expect Calvin to theorize

---

[43] It should also be noted that despite all the apparent speculation Calvin allows himself, he ultimately triangulates the certainty of election strictly around the interiority of the self. With regard to all others, "We know not who belongs to the number of the predestined or who does not belong, so we ought to be so minded as to wish that all men be saved" (*Inst.* 3.23.14). This is a citation from Augustine's *De Correptione et Gratia*, chapter 46.

[44] For some more popular examples that argue for this correlation, see James W. Perkinson, *White Theology: Outing Supremacy in Modernity* (New York: Palgrave Macmillan, 2004), especially 58–60; Alana Massey, "The White Protestant Roots of American Racism" in *The New Republic* (May 26, 2015). Available at https://newrepublic.com/article/121901/white-protestant-roots-american-racism (accessed 5/3/2018). For the best scholarly account of how Christian theologies have been racialized and nationalized, see Willie James Jennings, *The Christian Imagination* (New Haven, CT: Yale University Press, 2016) and Paul R. Griffin, "Protestantism and Racism" in *The Blackwell Companion to Protestantism*, ed. Alister E. McGrath and Darren C. Marks (Malden, MA: Blackwell, 2004), 357–372.

church and state as collective bodies modeled on the elect body of the individual believer.

For this reason, it's important to take stock of what that elected body is like: what election enables it to know, and what election demands that it *not* know. Election is the moment of illumination for an individual believer. But as with the *Proslogion*, illumination gestures toward understanding while also deferring it, because it comes at a cost. When Anselm is turned by the realization that "that than which a greater cannot be conceived" refers to a being that also exists, this turning also unseats him as the kind of knower who can fully understand the being referenced. What he *does* know is that language is invested in being, and that a faith that seeks understanding is not a vain endeavor. In fact, the argument enables Anselm to seek understanding by placing himself in the world of signs and things that all refer, in an Augustinian fashion, to that being in which language is primordially invested.

Similarly, the kind of cognition Calvin achieves does not reify the isolation of the subject nor the rationality of the subject. Calvin's argument secures the subject's identity by relating the subject to a call that precedes and exceeds it, and it certifies that identity through desire, not cognition. The peculiar *cognitio* that the argument achieves, in fact, calls back to the earliest sentences of the *Institutio* as a kind of knowledge that is always already related to other things: to the self's own affections and perceptions and to the God who exceeds them. Recall that at the beginning of the *Institutio*, "piety" is defined as "that reverence joined with love of God which the knowledge of his benefits induces" (*Inst.* 1.2.1). When introducing election, Calvin writes that God would have us "revere" what we do not understand (*Inst.* 3.21.1). Later, he writes that more than any other doctrine, election demands that humanity accept our cognitive and intellective limitations: "Let us not be ashamed to submit our understanding to God's boundless wisdom so far as to yield before its many secrets. For, of those things which it is neither given nor lawful to know, ignorance is learned; the craving to know, a kind of madness" (*Inst.* 3.23.8). If election grants self-knowledge, that knowledge involves knowing the right way to be ignorant.

If Calvin's election grants understanding, it also does so at a cost – and that cost is precisely the ability to render judgments about others. If the reader bears in mind all the layers of teaching that have preceded and abides by the restrictions Calvin places on predestination as an object of knowledge (*Inst.* 3.24.4–5), then the doctrine demands that the believer suspend forming decisive judgments about the relative good or evil of other people and things that she encounters, and in so doing honor what I've called the transcendence of materiality – the fact that material things have qualities that are excessive to linguistic and rational judgments, and that language and reason ought to be responsible to that excess. Election does not admit any human being to execute, or even intimate the judgments that belong to divine sovereignty. Rather, it grants an individual the experiential confidence to "will against her own will": to live and act in union with Christological signification by treating everyone else *as if* elect. In the following and final chapter, I examine how this alternate rendering of Calvin's election informs the way he theorizes the signification proper to "ourselves."

7

Calvin against Political Theology

By art is created that great leviathan called a commonwealth, or state (in Latin *civitas*), which is but an artificial man; though of greater stature and strength than the natural, for whose protection and defense it was intended.

–Thomas Hobbes[1]

"I've often wondered what the point of taking pictures of something like the Eiffel Tower is. I mean, this certainly isn't the best picture of the Eiffel Tower, and everyone has already seen a picture of the Eiffel Tower, so really what's the point of taking it?"
"To show that you were there," she said.
"Yes, but I'm not even in the picture," he said.
And to that she didn't really know what to say because it was true.

–Jana Casale[2]

EXCURSIS

Dietrich Bonhoeffer seems to cite a famous scene from Thus Spoke Zarathustra *in one of the many discussions of Christ and reality that take place across his* Ethics *essays. As Bonhoeffer uses the term, "reality" refers to the active unity of interpreted existence. He insists that the "reality of God" is disclosed only in relation to the "reality of the world," meaning that worldly action should not be theorized as responsibility to a transcendent principle to be imposed on an unruly world. Rather, action must ask "how life is to be lived" in*

---

[1] Thomas Hobbes, *Leviathan* (New York: Oxford University Press, 1998), 7.
[2] Jana Casale, *The Girl Who Never Read Noam Chomsky* (New York: Knopf, 2018), 157.

the context of a reality constituted by the relation between God and the world. Peter Dabrock argues that Bonhoeffer's conception of "reality" [Wirklichkeit] can be recast in phenomenological terms as the claim that reality is constituted by "significative difference" – "something as something." The "as," here, represents a gap that refuses to consign reality either to the "unstructured plenitude of data" or to the "descending function of an a priori ideatum.*"[3] When Bonhoeffer writes that reality is as Christ-reality, this is not because Christ ideologically determines the real. It is because in Christ, all worldly data is approached as "borne, accepted, and reconciled in the reality of God."[4]*

Bonhoeffer alludes to Nietzsche numerous times across the Ethics *essays, sometimes approvingly, as when he repeatedly cites that commitment to reality does not mean taking a "servile attitude toward the facts."[5] More often, his allusions assume the posture a carefully considered response to Nietzsche's forceful critiques of Christian morality. Like Nietzsche, Bonhoeffer is critical of the way Christian ethics is often structured as a collision between two realms – a structure that, according to Nietzsche, elicits resentment against the world and punishment against the body. Bonhoeffer also agrees with Nietzsche that ethical thinking in the world needs to begin with saying "Yes" to the world, its materiality, and its historicity. For Bonhoeffer, however, that "Yes" is cast as participation in the Christological "Yes" of the incarnation by which God comprehends the world as the world: "The world remains the world because it is the world that in Christ is loved, judged, and reconciled." For that reason, he continues,*

No one is commissioned to leap over the world and turn it into the kingdom of God. However, this does not lend legitimacy to the kind of pious indolence that only preserves its own virtue and abandons the evil world to its fate. Instead, human beings are placed in the position of concrete and limited, i.e., created

---

[3] Peter Dabrock, "Responding to *Wirklichkeit*" in *Mysteries in the Theology of Dietrich Bonhoeffer: A Copenhagen Bonhoeffer Symposium*, eds. Kirsten Busch Nielsen, Ulrik Nissen, Christiane Tietz (Göttingen: Vandenhoeck & Ruprecht: 2007), 57–59.

[4] Bonhoeffer, "Christ, Reality, and Good" in *Ethics*, ed. Clifford J. Green (Minneapolis, MN: Fortress Press, 2009): 47–75, 55.

[5] Bonhoeffer, "History and Good [1]" in *Ethics*, ed. Clifford J. Green (Minneapolis, MN: Fortress Press, 2009): 219–245, 223; "History and Good [2]" in *Ethics*, ed. Clifford J. Green (Minneapolis, MN: Fortress Press, 2009): 246–298, 261–262.

responsibility that recognizes the world as loved, judged, and reconciled by God, and acts accordingly within it.[6]

The "leap" image of course has many echoes in the modern philosophical archive, but in the context of Bonhoeffer's discussion about the nature of Christian action in the world, the usage recalls the striking opening to Thus Spoke Zarathustra *when a devilish jester leaps over a sincere tightrope walker and sends him plummeting to his death. Zarathustra, fresh from ten years in seclusion, has come down from the mountain to preach to the mob in the marketplace about a new meaning for the earth. Standing under a tightrope strung between two towers, he proclaims that the earth's meaning must proceed from a "faithfulness to the earth" that refuses to look for understanding in "extraterrestrial hope," or for truth in a soul "gaunt, ghastly, and starved."*[7] *The meaning of what shall be – the will of the creator that stretches forward – must also be tied back to the world.*

The structure of the scene is interesting, because what follows is a series of misrecognitions. The mob hears Zarathustra's words and laughs, mockingly demanding that Zarathustra stop talking about the tightrope walker and produce him. Meanwhile, the tightrope walker hears the commotion and "believing these words concerned him, got down to his work."[8] *And Zarathustra, in what might best be interpreted as a stubborn act of intentional misrecognition, keeps on preaching. As the tightrope walker begins his walk, Zarathustra continues, "Humankind is a rope fastened between animal and overman—a rope over an abyss. A dangerous crossing, a dangerous on-the-way, a dangerous looking back, a dangerous shuddering and standing still." Then comes the fateful leap:*

Just as [the tightrope walker] was at the midpoint of his way, the little door opened once again and a colorful fellow resembling a jester leaped forth and hurried after the first man with quick steps ... But when he was only one step behind him, the terrible thing occurred that struck every mouth silent and forced all eyes to stare: – he let out a yell like a devil and leaped over the man who was in his way. This man, seeing his rival triumph in this manner, lost his head and the rope. He threw away his pole and plunged into the depths even faster than his pole, like a whirlwind of arms and legs.[9]

---

[6] Bonhoeffer, "History and Good [2]," 266–267.
[7] Nietzsche, *Thus Spoke Zarathustra* (Cambridge: Cambridge University Press, 2006), 5–6.
[8] Nietzsche, 7.   [9] Nietzsche, 11.

Zarathustra's sermon was about the precariousness of suspended humanity. The pursuit of self-transcendence must involve a shattering of values that is nevertheless responsible to not only what is, but everything that has been – an abyss, indeed. The sincere-to-a-fault tightrope walker makes his way forward gingerly, striving to balance above the abyss while tied by gravity to it. Meanwhile, the leap of the jester – perhaps also trying to demonstrate something of the overman [Übermensch] *being preached below – literally leaps over the human being and accomplishes nothing more than sending him to his death.*

Out of this tragicomic scene of misrecognition, however, a moment of true recognition occurs, generated by the juxtaposition of the sermon with the body of the man who heard the cacophony of words and believed they referred to him. After the tightrope walker hits the ground, the preacher goes to him and receives his last confession – a fear that the same devilish lightness that sent him to his death will now pull him down to torment. Zarathustra gently counters this, telling the man, "You made your vocation out of danger, and there is nothing contemptible about that. Now you perish of your vocation, and for that I will bury you with my own hands." We are told that "when Zarathustra said this the dying man answered no more, but he moved his hand as if seeking Zarathustra's hand in gratitude."[10] *Through an apparent misrecognition, the tightrope walker began the dangerous journey that led him to death. But Zarathustra recognizes the journey across the rope as the nearest demonstration of his message: "Indeed, a nice catch of fish Zarathustra has today! No human being did he catch, but a corpse instead."*[11]

For Bonhoeffer, to live as a Christian in reality means living in the "as" – suspended in the ongoing responsiveness between experience and interpretation. Pursuing a meaning for the earth experienced as the earth means reaching for an interpretation of the earth as loved, judged, and reconciled by God. To interpret the earth merely as earth – or, more precisely, through whatever set of spheres and oppositions we mobilize to make meaning out of the earth – is to misrecognize it for what it is. To interpret the earth as loved, judged, and reconciled by God means misrecognizing what

---

[10] Nietzsche, 8.   [11] Nietzsche, 8.

the experience of the earth, taken in isolation or according to other systemic metrics, may seem to represent. True recognition, according to Bonhoeffer, happens when faithful action holds the reach of the will of God to the world as the world, an endeavor that is always muddled in context, occurring one careful step at a time, refusing the temptation of the leap.

This is only possible if the human mind commits to preserving a gap between sign and signified, preserving the space for the world to signify the will of God in unexpected ways. Anything short of that is a leap from idea to idea that not only passes over, but has the potential to destroy what is human in humanity. As in the tightrope scene, when recognition occurs it is not mediated by an idea. No one, arguably, gets what Zarathustra is talking about. Recognition occurs through the gap of signification that allows a body to take signs up and bear them in time. Misrecognition – a body taking up signs that, to others, were not meant for him – paradoxically renders the doomed tightrope walker the true disciple.

MISRECOGNITION

Calvin's account of the mediations of divine power facilitates a drama of recognition through misrecognition.[12] The account is fueled by Calvin's own contextually grounded criticisms of the relationship between the Mass and the French *Corpus Christiananum* as he knew them. Conceptually, the Mass legitimizes the authority of the church by miraculously tying the presence of the substance of the divine body to the church's particular historical lineage and priestly institutional infrastructure. By the centuries closely preceding the emergence of reform movements, that logic provided an anchor of stability not only for church but also for society. Among other things, the sacramental system granted legibility to ordinary people and their actions.[13] Not surprisingly, the effectiveness of this sacramental logic would prove useful as an enabling analogy for state

---

[12] In *Image and Word in the Theology of John Calvin* (Notre Dame, IN: University of Notre Dame Press, 2009), Randall Zachman argues that Calvin's theological thinking is fundamentally structured by the relationship between knowledge and experience, or seeing self-manifestation. This gives a role to the initial misrecognition of what is real, for example in providence (79–81) and in the incarnation (262–265, 297), to which ordinary perceivers are initially blind.

[13] See, for example, the case of Piers Plowman as discussed in Katherine Little's essay, "Protestantism and the Piers Plowman Tradition" *in Journal of Medieval and Early Modern Studies* 43:3(2010).

power, a power similarly invested in governing the stability and legibility of a "people." Nicholas Terpstra has argued that by the fifteenth century, the social imaginary of the state as Christian body was well in place.[14] In the French context especially, this imaginary flourished by borrowing from the Mass the claim that sacramental presence runs in and through the presence of a divine body who represents the people and enables recognition.

From his 1536 "Prefatory Address to King Francis," Calvin takes this slippage as his point of departure. He argues that the true recognition of the church is not observable per se – it is not marked by either visible stability or legibility.[15] This, in fact, is the definition Calvin reserves for idols. The fallen mind is a "veritable factory of idols" precisely because it seeks stability and legibility in worldly places that flatter the mastery of the human faculties (*Inst.* 1.11.7). The logic undergirding this position comes into greater relief in Book Four of the 1559 *Institutio* where Calvin rearticulates his account of the church's worldly existence through his own theory of sacramental signification. Calvin's theory borrows heavily from Augustine. His sacramental theory is fundamentally a semiotic theory. In a way that should now be seen as characteristic, however, Calvin also insists – more earnestly than Augustine – that the sacramental sign must be held distinct from that which it signifies. The reason is so that the sign can *mediate*: It can tie together the divine signified to the worldly signified, and place the two in an active relation to one another by means of the sign. Calvin is not after an account of ontological participation. He is after participation in a choreography of signing by which God affirms the world and inscribes it, as the world, with the marks of divine glory.

For Augustine, Christian teaching takes the reality of the "subjunctive" (the rule of faith) as its point of departure and submission to mediating practices (the rule of love) as a mode of training. Together, these both presume and facilitate the recognition of sacramental reality.[16] Calvin's doctrine of providence both breaks from and reoccupies this account by insisting on an ontological gap between Creator and creation. Recognition is still the matter at hand. The discourse on providence is designed to allow the reader to "recognize" [*agnitio*] that every good comes from God, to "recognize this special care" surrounding what might otherwise seem explicable merely as ordinary events, to live and make deliberations

---

[14] Nicholas Terpstra, *Religious Refugees in the Early Modern World* (New York: Cambridge University Press, 2015), chapter 1.
[15] Calvin, "Prefatory," 24.   [16] See Chapter 5.

accordingly (*Inst.* 1.1.1–2; 1.17.6). In fact, because of the *sensus divini-tatis*, creation itself entices human beings to desire a recognition of that which is beyond the obvious. But this desire is also what leads fallen faculties, in the absence of the Word, to claim to recognize God in privileged sites within creation – locating a "figment" in which to "find solace" (*Inst.* 1.5.10; 1.11.7).

This means that, from the perspective of the fallen creature, true recognition can only happen through the experience of misrecognition and destabilization. The eyes accommodated by providential teaching first *misrecognize* the limited definition imposed on created things and respond, instead, to the call to see reality as constituted by significative difference, addressed by a divine will that affirms its created reality while also exceeding it.[17] So Calvin will claim that clouds are really water vapor but they are also really the sign of the divine chariot (*Inst.* 1.5.1). This is the peculiar kind of recognition that comes through the use of the Word that does not define or replace but deepens one's understanding of the reality of things (*Inst.* 1.6.1). Calvin's providential arguments, in part by their very radicality, stage an exercise of seeing that asks believers to recognize the relation of divine signification even to things that might be ordinarily recognizable as merely evil, ugly, or painful (*Inst.* 1.14.22; 1.17.6; 3.9.3).

The teaching proper to the incarnation follows with the "person of the Mediator as the Redeemer" to show what reason cannot: "who the true God is or what sort of God he wishes to be toward us" (*Inst.* 2.2.18). The Mediator addresses the student as an acting and speaking body whose words and deeds represent both the divine will and the fully human mode of existence. Furthermore, the signing actions of the Redeemer mark a pattern of life in which the Spirit can enable human participation (*Inst.* 1.6.1; 1.9.1; 2.6.4; 3.17.6). The faith that grasps and embraces this pattern is, for Calvin, also self-recognition. More specifically, it is the recognition that one, in one's own particularity, is also renamed and loved *as* a child of God (*Inst.* 3.2.14).

In the fourth book of the 1559 *Institutio*, Calvin draws his reader to the itinerary's last stage: life on earth conceived socially. Nineteen of the book's twenty chapters are addressed to the church, articulating a

---

[17] This drama of recognition is particularly salient in John Bunyan's early modern itinerary, *The Pilgrim's Progress* (Oxford: Oxford University Press, 2003), when a series of artificial devices including the roll enable the pilgrim to misrecognize ordinary surroundings in order to recognize them more fully.

reformist approach to its existence, function, and operation. For Calvin, like Augustine, the church supplies a special location for Christian formation. Yet Calvin's ontological commitments mean that he more deliberately distinguishes the invisible church (the spiritual body of the elect) from the visible church (the church physically gathered on earth). The former is comprised of those who are sewn together in one body with Christ through the activity of the Word and the Spirit (*Inst.* 4.1.2). The invisible church is unrecognizable on earth, yet the visible church exists to signify the reality of that which is unrecognizable. The gap between the invisible and the visible frustrates ordinary patterns of recognition in order to enable practices of displaced recognition.[18] For a refugee community, in particular, this might well be rephrased as enabling the recognition of, and by, the displaced. The visible church, therefore, performs the function of enabling this exercise of non-idolatrous recognition.

In what follows, I retrace Calvin's argument for the kind of existence peculiar to the visible church, examine how his sacramental theory supports that existence theoretically, and then consider the political *scopus* to which this sacramental ecclesiology leads. Throughout, I'll be focused – as I have been so far – on Calvin's pedagogical aims. Specifically, how the apparatuses of church and state are theorized to protect and facilitate participation in the way God providentially and redemptively recognizes the things God has created, enabling *cognitio Dei et nostri*.

SIGNIFYING "OURSELVES": THE APPARATUS OF THE VISIBLE CHURCH

In the opening chapters of Book Four, when Calvin is introducing the nature of the true church, he tends to reserve the Pauline language of the "body of Christ" for the invisible church comprised of the elect. It is, for him, a thing that faith deems real, rather than an object in which faith rests.[19] Later, in the chapters on the sacraments, the "body of Christ" is used almost exclusively to refer to the physical and local body of Christ

---

[18] The logic of the church's existence thus follows that of the Christian subject's emergence, only *writ large*. If the moments of prayer and election generate knowledge of God and myself as an ordinary person, the moments of proclamation and sacrament generate knowledge of God and *ourselves* as ordinary people.

[19] Calvin suggests that it is inappropriate, grammatically, to parrot the creedal claim that "I believe in the church." One ought to believe *in* God and, in turn, *believe* the church in much the same way one believes the reality of forgiveness or resurrection (*Inst.* 4.1.2).

represented by bread and wine. There is an important connection here. For believers to assume participation in the invisible and spiritual body of Christ, it was necessary that Christ first come to believers as fully human. To be sure, participation is made possible because it is the *Word* that becomes flesh, and the invisible church is the participation of believers in the Word through the Spirit. But just as Christ's particular human body makes such participation possible, the semiotics of the Word also address and involve the particular human bodies of living believers. This is the work of the visible church.[20]

When Calvin introduces the visible church, he prefers the Cyprianic and Augustinian characterization of the church as the "mother of believers." As mother, the worldly infrastructure of the church ushers believers into life – conceiving, birthing, nourishing, and caring for human beings until their death. According to Calvin, "Our weakness does not allow us to be dismissed from her school until we have been pupils all our lives" (*Inst.* 4.1.4). His use of this metaphor is interesting for two reasons. For one, it underscores the particularity of the human lives who join the visible church. Christian training cannot skip straight to the spiritual unity of believers without birthing and addressing individuals as embodied persons. Along these lines, part of what the visible church teaches is how to recognize other members as legitimate members merely by virtue of their participation – participation that evidences their desire to be elect and suggests, across other dissimilarities, a common birth. This, according to Calvin, should elicit from others a "charitable judgment" (*Inst.* 4.1.4). This judgment must hold even if one harbors doubts about another person: "For it may happen that we ought to treat like brothers and count as believers those whom we think unworthy of the fellowship of the godly, because of the common agreement of the church by which they are borne and tolerated in the body of Christ" (*Inst.* 4.1.8). Much as Christ's human form accommodates our weakness to teach how God wills, the visible form of the church – and the visible form of those individuals who comprise it – accommodates our weakness to teach us how to will concerning one another (*Inst.* 4.1.8).

Second, the metaphor emphasizes the dynamic nature of the visible church as an institution whose legitimacy is lodged in its dynamic activity. This becomes clearer when Calvin suggests that a legitimate church on earth should be recognized by two distinguishing marks: (1) the

---

[20] See also Zachman, 401f.

pure preaching of the Word and (2) the administration of the sacraments according to Christ's institution (*Inst.* 4.1.9). These marks are actions more than static features. It is possible to read them with a polemical valence as refusing other traditional ways for recognizing the church's legitimacy – for example, its continuity of presence either by genetic (apostolic) lineage or by performing the miracle of making the substance of Christ's body present.[21] Calvin's two marks reoccupy the question of legitimacy and recognizability by reframing the church's presence as a performative presence, or a kind of existence that obtains only through the ritualizing activity that relates Word to thing and thing to Word.[22]

Tellingly, on one of the rare occasions when Calvin may be referring to the visible church as a body, he writes that this activity of human ministry is the "sinew" holding "the church together in one body" (*Inst.* 4.3.2). He later makes a similar claim about the church's discipline to which I'll return shortly (*Inst.* 4.12.1). In both cases, Calvin is following the well-trod path of building a case for the church's mode of teaching modeled on the incarnation's mode of teaching. Because for Calvin it is crucial that Christ teaches both through his full humanity and through a representative way of life that is followable as a living narrative; the church similarly teaches by facilitating exercises that refer ordinary humans to that narrative and vice versa. As the Spirit works in this process, the invisible church is built up by those who participate in the *memoria* of the life, death, and resurrection of Christ that comes to signify the life of every believer as elect. At one point, he resists the sacrificial valence of the Roman Catholic Mass on the grounds that it defers from the memory of the historicity and physicality of Christ's singular death, thereby deferring believers from the mode of representation that is tied to that singular body (*Inst.* 4.18.5). When the Lord's Supper remembers the sacrifice, it does so in view of the fact that the perception of divine wrath has been rendered inoperative and

[21] Calvin discusses these two options in lengthy sections of Book Four, particularly in chapters 2 and 18. It's also worth noting that Calvin's rearticulation of the church's legitimacy follows from his prior assertions that scripture is prior to the church (see *Inst.* 1.7).

[22] As might be expected, Calvin also explicitly ties the marks of Word and Sacraments to the pedagogical-epistemic rubric of use and benefit, such that "we who have experienced them feel [them] to be highly useful aids to foster and strengthen faith" (*Inst.* 4.1.1; see 4.1.6).

that believers now share in Christ's life as a sign of their own adopted status (*Inst.* 4.18.16).[23]

The sacraments Calvin acknowledges are the two he sees instituted explicitly by Christ in scripture: baptism and the Lord's Supper. Both refer the Word of Christ to the shared, noncognitive features of human life – birth, cleansing, digestion. In baptism, the originary gesture of Christ's earthly ministry is analogically tied to a child's entry into a spiritual family through the material sign of water. The church gathered around the sacrament collectively performs the "body of Christ" by pledging the providential and redemptive signs of care and forgiveness to the person being baptized. In the supper, the power of Christ's own vitality is analogically tied to the power by which bread nourishes the internal organs of the body (see *Inst.* 1.2.1; 4.17.37, 40, 44). It is important that the sign of bread refer in two directions: both to bread itself, according to its natural use by humans; and to the physical body of Christ, whose atoning life anchors the spiritual body through which believers are nourished.[24]

While Calvin does not treat discipline as a third mark (which later Reformed denominations would come to do), the logic of discipline he forwards helps to develop the active relationship he envisions between the invisible body and the visible apparatus of the church.[25] He writes that the discipline falls into three general areas. First, as with prayer, discipline refers to the orderliness of the performances themselves without which they fail to signify (*Inst.* 4.12.1).[26] A performance – say, a marriage – is

---

[23] See chapter 6 for the argument about the relationship between the atonement and adoption.

[24] This performative reading of Calvin's notion of the church as an apparatus for materialization accords with Joshua Ralston's description of Calvin's church as that which *makes* the reformation of the church by the Spirit visible. See Ralston, "Preaching Makes the Church: Recovering a Missing Ecclesial Mark" in *John Calvin's Ecclesiology: Ecumenical Perspectives*, eds. Eddy van der Borght and Gerard Mannion (New York: T&T Clark, 2011), 126.

[25] Gottfried Wilhelm Lochner writes that "Calvin defines church discipline more as a natural consequence of the preached word than as a prerequisite of the true Church." See Gottfried Wilhelm Locher, *Sign of the Advent: A Study in Protestant Ecclesiology* (Fribourg: Academic Press Fribourg), 79.

[26] Calvin gives a clear account of disrupted signification when he glosses Paul's warnings in 1 Corinthians that those who eat and drink unworthily will become sick or even die. In 4.16.30, he argues that in the Lord's Supper, the Word joined to Flesh in Christ establishes the pattern through which human flesh participates in Word through the sacrament. Following this logic, partaking of the sacrament without faith in the Word (or promise) does not activate a curse in any magical sense, but rather a deliberate and deleterious failure of signification. That is, to return to Augustine's language, partaking of

enacted by an iterative choreography of bodily activity attached to and enabled by linguistic conventions.[27] If the visible church's existence is generated through its performances, the church must require a level of discipline among those gathered.[28] Second, discipline is tied to the responsibility of the church to govern the "moral" lives of citizens more broadly. The church ought to promote the moral patterning given by the Word in which believers participate by addressing ordinary human lives both extra-ecclesially and extra-politically.[29] In this regard, private moral matters occupy the work of the church, but they threaten neither church membership nor political citizenship (*Inst.* 4.12.11). In fact, Calvin glosses the famous "keys of the kingdom" passage (Matt. 16:19) by arguing that the concrete exercise of forgiveness is central to the task of the visible church (*Inst.* 4.1.22). Third, Calvin argues that the church also has a duty to exercise excommunication. It is interesting, however, that the grounds for removal from the community are neither moral peccadillos nor private sins, but persistent public refusals to submit one's body to the rule and guidance of the Word and Sacrament (*Inst.* 4.12.3). The logic, here, is that the visible church can withstand sins that are in the process of being forgiven. This is, after all, central to its task. It cannot withstand the refusal to

the Lord's Supper without faith amounts to a denial of the rule of faith (faith in the coincidence of signs and things through creation and incarnation) without which the rule of love (enactment of the coincidence of signs and things) can take no effect. In Calvin's view, such an eating reenacts the refractive separation of the divine will from immanent life, a movement which corresponds to Calvin's understanding of sin. Taken in faith, however, the Lord's Supper works to return the believing youth or adult to her flesh as the location in which God's glory shines, from which she can learn to live into her adoption through participation.

[27] See *Inst.* 3.20.5; 4.10.29.

[28] Calvin does, of course, make the point that the church cannot be defined by the surface appearance of discipline or mere bodily exercise. See 4.10.11. This accords with his later claim that the physicality of the sacraments requires being adjoined to the Word (4.17.36), though he also argues that the sacraments cannot be merely thought but must be physically observed (4.17.7).

[29] To underscore that the church is responsible and addressed to the whole world, Calvin at one point cites Cyprian: "So also the church, bathed in the light of the Lord, extends its rays over the whole earth: yet there is one light diffused everywhere. Nor is the unity of the body severed; it spreads its branches through the whole earth; it pours forth its overflowing streams; yet there is one head and one source." See *Inst.* 4.6.17 and Cyprian, *On the Unity of the Catholic Church* iii, v, vi.

perform the exercises of signification that generate its very mode of existence.[30]

The basic structure of the sacraments and discipline articulate a church that exists in the world to refer actively ordinary bodies to Christ's representative body collectively through exercises of scriptural signification. And when Calvin finally discusses how the sacraments themselves work, this is exactly the process he theorizes.[31] For Calvin, sacraments are

---

[30] Importantly, excommunication is never viewed as final from a worldly point of view. Such a view would trespass over Calvin's injunction in Book Three to hope that everyone is elect. According to Calvin, the church "should deal mildly with the lapsed and should not punish with extreme rigor, but rather, according to Paul's injunction, confirm its love toward them. Similarly, each layman ought to temper himself to this mildness and gentleness. It is, therefore, not our task to erase from the number of the elect those who have been expelled from the church, or to despair as if they were already lost. It is lawful to regard them as estranged from the church, and thus, from Christ—but only for such time as they remain separated. However, if they also display more stubbornness than gentleness, we should still commend them to the Lord's judgment, hoping for better things of them in the future than we see in the present. Nor should we on this account cease to call upon God in their behalf" (*Inst.* 4.12.9). This comports with Calvin's previous citation of Augustine that a Christian making proper use of the doctrine of election ought to "hope that everyone is elect" (3.23.14). See Augustine, *De Correptione et Gratia*, chapter 46

[31] Historically, Calvin's treatment of the Eucharist is particularly interesting as one that emerged toward the end of a period of unprecedented anxiety and argumentation concerning the metaphysical mechanics of the Lord's Supper. While the ongoing celebration of the Eucharist is among the most ancient of Christian rituals, it would remain surprisingly un-polemicized throughout the first millennium of Christianity. Even in the third part of Thomas Aquinas' *Summa Theologica* (thirteenth century), we see the sacrament of the Eucharist enjoy a treatment relatively unmarked by polemic. Thomas, for example, easily recognizes that this one sacrament carries a threefold significance, corresponding to past, present, and future: first, as a memorial of Christ's last supper with his disciples; second, as an enactment of the Ecclesiastical unity through which the individual members are united in their participation with the body of Christ; and third, as a foretaste of "Divine fruition," when the grace of God will be realized in life everlasting (*Summa Theologica*, III, 73, 4).

In contrast, the Institutes' treatment of the sacrament follows not only after the technical term "transubstantiation" had entered Church vocabulary in the early thirteenth century during the Fourth Lateran Council, but also after this term had come under attack from early sixteenth century reformers who then proceeded to fight about the meaning of the supper amongst themselves. Calvin's writing on the topic, as it appears in the 1559 Institutes, follows some thirty years after the public Luther-Zwingli dispute which carried high stakes for subsequent relations between the Lutheran churches, the Swiss Federation, and proliferating Anabaptist groups. In certain respects, then, Calvin's discussion is rich with a theoretical precision not available to earlier treatments of the Eucharist. In other ways, however, Calvin's treatment sometimes feels overextended in its attempt to bridge the polarization resulting from the disagreement between Luther and Zwingli: Luther, who rejected the metaphysical trappings of transubstantiation while maintaining the real physical presence of the body of Christ in the meal ("sacramental

central to performing the resignification of ourselves in the world because they facilitate the relational signification that obtains between the real body of Christ and the real bodies of ourselves, performing a spiritual unity rooted in real physical particularity. The meaning generated by the sacraments obtains by drawing attention to the differentiation of created matter while also constellating material parts such that their spiritual significance can be represented and recognized. It is important on every level for Calvin that the sacraments not be understood as transubstantiation. The qualities of bread are not a mask for divine substance (*Inst.* 4.17.13). The qualities of bread play an active role in teaching human beings about realities that elude sight, allowing human bodies to experience what providence sets out to teach about God's affirmation of, and engagement in, the world.[32]

Here is a passage where Calvin describes the usefulness of the sacraments:

As our faith is slight and feeble unless it be propped on all sides and sustained by every means, it trembles, wavers, totters, and at last gives way. Here our merciful Lord, according to his infinite kindness, so tempers himself to our capacity that, since we are creatures who always creep on the ground, cleave to the flesh, and, do not think about or even conceive of anything spiritual, he condescends to lead us to himself even by these earthly elements, and to set before us in the flesh a mirror of spiritual blessings. For if we were incorporeal (as Chrysostom says), he would give us these very things naked and incorporeal. Now, because we have souls engrafted in bodies, he imparts spiritual things under visible ones. Not that the gifts set before us in the sacraments are bestowed with the natures of the things, but that they have been marked with this signification by God (*Inst.* 4.14.3).

If providential teaching works by counteracting normative habits of worldly recognition; if the faith of Christ teaches a new mode of worldly recognition; and if the spiritual cycle of prayer and election set out to confirm and enable that mode of recognition at the level of the individual

---

unity"), and Zwingli, who insisted upon the Lord's Supper as a memorial meal aimed to foster the unity of the community. For a more extended treatment of the origin of these Reformation debates and their historical impact, see Amy Nelson Burnett, *Karlstadt and the Origins of the Eucharistic Controversy* (Oxford: Oxford University Press, 2011).

[32] For other related accounts of how Calvin understands that the elements themselves teach in concert with the Word, see Thomas J. Davis, *This Is My Body: The Presence of Christ in Reformation Thought* (Grand Rapids, MI: Baker Academic, 2008), 74; Zachman 333–336. Both accounts note that Calvin draws an analogy between the ordinary reality of the elements as they relate to human life, but do not emphasize the extent to which this implies attention to the reality of bread and wine themselves. This, however, is logically necessary for the relation between the Word and the thing to obtain.

self; then the sacramental cycle is given to teach human beings how to live together in a world *as* addressed by God through all of these means. Put another way, if providence teaches *that* God's will is directed toward the world's continuation and care and the incarnation teaches *how* God's will performs that continuation and care; then election assures a believer *that* God loves her while the sacraments show believers *how* God loves them.

It is crucial, then, that the sacrament is material. Calvin writes that you can't merely "think" the sacraments (*Inst.* 4.17.7). At the same time, a sacrament becomes a sacrament when Word is joined to flesh. And because the Word encounters us in flesh, it is by virtue of that appearance that the Word can also encounter us as "word" – as fictive mediation capable of recasting the terms through which we recognized ourselves.[33] Here is one passage where Calvin narrates this kind of dynamic:

> In this Sacrament we have such full witness of all these things that we must certainly consider them *as if* Christ here present were himself set before our eyes and touched by our hands. For his word cannot lie or deceive us: "Take, eat, drink: this is my body, which is given for you; this is my blood, which is shed for forgiveness of sins." By bidding us take, he indicates that it is ours; by bidding us eat, that it is made one substance with us; by declaring that his body is given for us and his blood shed for us, he teaches that both are not so much his as ours. For he took up and laid down both, not for his own advantage but for our salvation (*Inst.* 4.17.3).[34]

The artifactual quality of Christ's words – not the words only, but the scene in which words and gestures are contextualized to generate meaning – enables the force through which the sacrament can address "ourselves," *as if* Christ were performing that relation himself – which is, of course, how faith reads what is happening.

But for this to obtain, the details of Christ's signs must first encounter the physical sign of the bread as a particular to a particular. Bread, according to Calvin, is chosen for its peculiar properties, because it nourishes. By virtue of the words that are attached by narrative gesture

---

[33] In using the term "fictive", I want to resist the impulse to locate the meaning of the Word either in a transcendent world or in a merely projected phantasm. If the Word addresses us with fictive qualities, it is because these qualities supply a tool useful for differentiating, relating, and exploring the mysterious depths of ordinary lives that nevertheless carry their own material integrity. Meaning, as I discussed in the chapters on providence, is once again lodged in "significance" rather than "intention." Calvin's ontological distinction between God and the world resists any collapse between the two. In so doing, it both becomes misrecognized and then recognized again in relation to each other. See, again, Zachman's account in *Image and Word*.

[34] Emphasis mine.

to bread, Calvin writes that we can experience the spiritual force that these signs signify:

> Now, that sacred partaking of his flesh and blood, by which Christ pours his life into us, *as if* it penetrated into our bones and marrow, he also testifies and seals in the Supper—not by presenting a vain and empty sign, but by manifesting there the effectiveness of his Spirit to fulfill what he promises. And truly he offers and shows the reality there signified to all who sit at that spiritual banquet, although it is received with benefit by believers alone, who accept such great generosity with true faith and gratefulness of heart ... I indeed admit that the breaking of bread is a symbol [*symbolum*];[35] it is not the thing itself. But, having admitted this, we shall nevertheless duly infer that by the showing of the symbol the thing itself is also shown (*Inst.* 4.17.10).[36]

This account relies on a fundamental analogy between the way bread is constructed to signify in relation to human beings according to a natural, even scientific account; and the way Christ's life is narratively constructed to signify in relation to human beings in a real spiritual sense. The bread and Christ's embodied life both signify by generating words and gestures that *make* a followable account of nourishment. In other words, they share a life-giving signature.[37]

But this making is ineffectual unless the thing that is made is also given and received. This is where the particularity of bodies plays a role in the structure of the Supper. On the one side, Jesus' representative life refers to Jesus' singular body. One of Calvin's critical points of departure from transubstantiation is his insistence that Jesus' body continues to be real, material, and local, even as it has attained immortal flesh (*Inst.* 4.17.9, 12, 30). On the other side, the representational qualities of bread refer to the life of human bodies. It is only because these figures refer to really existing material things that the signature of the sacrament can perform a relation between Jesus and believers. According to Calvin:

> [Sacramental] signification would have no fitness if the truth there represented had no living image in the outward sign. Christ's purpose was to witness by the outward symbol that his flesh is food; if he had put forward only the empty

---

[35] *Symbolum* is the Latin transliteration of a Greek cognate that originally referred to an identification made by virtue of two separate halves being rejoined. While Calvin seems to use *symbolum* alongside *signa* in his Eucharistic discussions, he does not often refer to *symbolum* outside of this context. For more on this, see Elwood 1991: 7–8; G. R. Evans, "Calvin on Signs: An Augustinian Dilemma"; and Gerhart B. Ladner, "Medieval and Modern Understanding of Symbolism: A Comparison" in *Speculum* 54:2 (April 1979): 223–256.

[36] Emphasis mine.   [37] See my discussion of Agamben's theory of signatures in chapter 4.

appearance of bread and not true bread, where would be the analogy or comparison needed to lead us from the visible thing to the invisible? For, to be perfectly consistent, the signification extends no farther than that we are fed by the form of Christ's flesh. For instance, if in baptism the figure of water were to deceive our eyes, we would have no sure pledge of our washing; indeed, that false show would give us occasion to hesitate. The nature of the Sacrament is therefore canceled, unless, in the mode of signifying, the earthly sign corresponds to the heavenly thing. And the truth of this mystery accordingly perishes for us unless true bread represents the true body of Christ ... Now by what reason would Paul infer that we are all one bread and one body who partake together of one bread, if only the appearance of bread, and not rather the true nature of bread, remained? (*Inst.* 4.17.14).

In this passage, Calvin is willing to admit that the bread "is" the body of Christ in much the same way that he was willing to permit the claim that "nature is God" – provided that the identification be made with a "reverent mind" that takes this identification to imply the "order prescribed by God" (see *Inst.* 1.5.5; see 4.17.22). The reverent mind is one that has submitted to training by means of the mediating Word – a technology that effects a relationship between ontologically distinct particulars. Calvin explicitly writes that this is equally conceived as training in the use of metaphors (*Inst.* 4.17.20).

Within the apparatus of the church, the sacraments are the focal point for training in "reading" ourselves together in relation to God. Calvin's account thus continues to resonate with Augustine, who recommended the church as the maternal incubator for practicing Christian teaching.[38] For Calvin, however, the church exists only insofar as its practices are directed toward the world that it reads *as* created, redeemed, and renamed. In this vein, Calvin continues to retheorize the visible church as an institution that belongs properly to the world and that is fully subject to the reform of the world enabled by scripture more generally. In fact, because the church only exists performatively – in its obedient exercise of Word and Sacrament – the church literally exists *as* perpetual reform. The reformist question of "how could the church go so wrong?" is in this sense identical to the providential question of "how could the world go so wrong?" The response is likewise the same: through the fallen urge to imagine that the source of stability and legibility can be recognized in one worldly body or location.

---

[38] See my discussion of Augustine's claim that the church is the domain of habituation in chapter 5.

If the whole project is an account of how God addresses that fallen condition through both justifying grace and aids to sanctification, then it is also an account of how divine power disrupts competing attempts at establishing sovereign regimes of intelligibility and order.[39] Yet, there is also a way of reading Calvin's account that resonates exactly with Agamben's account of a divine economy that enacts sovereignty on earth by generating practices of differentiation, resignification, and glorification – or that plays into a much older reading of Calvinism as a virulent mode of religious asceticism that proceeds from church discipline to further a more general posture of disciplinary mastery over the conditions of worldly life.

I'll return to this again, but specify at the moment that part of my aim is to reconstruct a conceptual blueprint for how Calvin's thinking could have been employed to reinforce the disciplinary apparatuses of national sovereignty. But in doing so, I am also shining a light on the precise interpretive decisions on which those outcomes depend – and, as such, on alternate interpretive decisions that might facilitate the critique of those outcomes. Such interpretive decisions can be summarized according to the shorthand of representational versus participatory grammar, which I discussed back in Chapter 1. Calvin's sacramental theory is important in this vein because it so frustrates efforts at easy summary. It makes little sense as a representation. To say that in the Lord's Supper Christ is "spiritually present" can easily be reduced to the claim that the supper is a mere memorial – or an imposition of ideas onto material circumstances – which Calvin refuses. The fuller complexity of Calvin's account resounds much more when it is approached as a grammar of participation, designed to lead one into a fully ontological relationship to others through the use of mediations. When Calvin's theory is read in a way that involves the reader in the kind of contextual interpretive practice that I've suggested the 1559 *Institutio* invites, it does offer mechanisms for challenging the decisionist structure of sovereignty and the political theology that underwrites it. To draw those mechanisms out, the next section returns to the matter of political theology and leads, finally, to the end of Calvin's itinerary.

---

[39] Divine power is able to do this, for Calvin, because divine power is itself a remembering of the order of the world as known by not just divine power but divine goodness, justice, and the other divine attributes. See Zachman 75 and Susan Schreiner, *Where Shall Wisdom Be Found? Calvin's Exegesis of Job from Medieval and Modern Perspectives* (Chicago: University of Chicago Press, 1994), 119.

CALVIN'S TWO BODIES AND THE QUESTION
OF POLITICAL THEOLOGY

At several points, I've noted my interest in Victoria Kahn's claim that poiesis is the missing third term in discussions of whether modernity remains perniciously beholden to a theological past.[40] Kahn suggests that it is possible to defend an authentically secular politics by recalling the early modern *verum factum* principle, advanced by Hobbes and Vico, that "we can only know what we make ourselves."[41] If politics is such a making, then it is possible to both know and improve our political institutions by reconceiving them as revisable products of human art. Kahn thinks that attention to poiesis can supply critical tools for resisting the "permanence of political theology" and reconceiving it under the broader banner of metaphor.[42]

I'm interested in whether *theology itself* can undermine the "permanence of political theology" – at least to the extent that "political theology" is understood in the Schmittian sense as the claim that politics is rooted in mystical claims to transcendent authority. I have argued that theology has long privileged the artifactual and fictive qualities of writing in order to address itself to human beings and facilitate practices of both attention and critique. Certainly, theology does so while referring to metaphysical entities. Yet these references can be read primarily as representational propositional claims or primarily as claims designed to generate a posture of responsibility to the conditions of immanent life – even to the transcendent dimensions of a materiality that exceeds conceptual grasp.[43]

---

[40] Portions of the following section also appear in my article, "Calvin and the Two Bodies of Christ: Fiction and Power in Dogmatic Theology, Political Theology" in *Political Theology*, online March 9, 2018. DOI: 10.1080/1462317X.2018.1440157. Forthcoming in press.

[41] Kahn, xii.

[42] Kahn, 4, 7, 8of. As noted in the Introduction, this refers both to a broader posture held by a number of theorists and to the particular title of an essay by Claude Lefort: "The Permanence of the Theologico-Political?" in *Democracy and Political Theory*, trans. David Macey (Cambridge: Cambridge University Press, 1988): 213–255. For more on Lefort, see also Warren Breckman's analysis in *The Adventures of the Symbolic.: Post-Marxism and Radical Democracy* (New York: Columbia University Press, 2013).

[43] The argument that follows, put succinctly, is that for Calvin the sovereignty of God is indexed primarily to creation rather than to political infrastructure. Drawing on Walter Benjamin and others in conversation with Schmittian political theology, Ted A. Smith's recent book, *Weird John Brown* (Redwood City, CA: Stanford University Press, 2014) argues that the witness of divine violence signals a necessary theological distinction between divine sovereignty and political sovereignty. Smith's argument is congenial to the position I am articulating here, sharing many of my own concerns. Though I do not develop the conversation here, I anticipate that a more deliberate indexing of divine

Along the way, I've argued that the form and content of Calvin's 1559 *Institutio* make evident use of the artifactual qualities of theological writing to effect new relationships among immanent things. Most recently, I've shown how Calvin's understanding of the church – a corporate entity – relies itself on a certain use of signifying representations. Specifically, Calvin gives an account of how the concrete, fleshly body of Christ gives itself to be narrated in order to generate a fictive "body of Christ" that is received, through Word and Sacrament, among elect believers gathered on earth. This account differs from what Kahn is looking for in a number of ways – not least because the "authorship" of the narrative is itself undecidable, and given to be received as if from a divine origin. This is not the poetics of *verum factum*, in the sense that it is not conceived as made by and responsible to a strict conception of immanence. Yet it is also not a notion of transcendence beholden in strict terms to mystical authority. The narrative retains qualities of an object made for specifically human use. And insofar as the narrative manifests not just by enabling self-knowledge but also worldly activity, its proclamation assumes the form of a legal fiction. It is an account, either factually untrue or (in this case) merely unproven, that nevertheless enables relational activities.

Calvin's account of Christ's two bodies is furthermore legible alongside one important strand of scholarship on political theology from the twentieth century that follows the work of Ernst Kantorowicz who was, himself, offering an oblique critique of Schmitt. Kantorowicz's 1957 *The King's Two Bodies* asks whether and how the Western political institutions were shaped by a series of metaphorical exchanges between theology and jurisprudence precisely over how to theorize the relationship between, say, the Pope and the mystical body of the church, or the monarch and the dignity of the "crown" he or she represents. Kantorowicz shows how Christology and sacramental theory were important sources for ecclesial and political jurists. In this section, I will briefly trace Kantorowicz's account of how slippages between Christology, ecclesiology, and monarchical theory enabled the theory of the modern state as a sovereign body politic – or, in Hobbes' terms, an "artificial man" who replaces, and is unbeholden to, divine sovereignty. I expect this will

sovereignty to creation would help to strengthen Smith's case for theorizing a mode of divine sovereignty capable of underwriting critiques of political sovereignty.

help to draw out some of the more subtle political implications of Calvin's sacramental version of the two body problematic.

According to the narrative Kantorowicz traces through the archive, the fundamentally theological tenor of Christological debates over the relationship between Christ's humanity and divinity took on a more explicit metaphorical quality as the church's peculiar existence came to be theorized as the *corpus Christi mysticum*. For centuries, the church understood itself to exist insofar as it referred the mystical sacramental effects of Christ's "mysterious materiality" to the immanent community through the Mass. As the church took on an increasingly political role in the world, however, the record shows that church documents began to conceive the church as a *corpus mysticum* with its own distinct *mystica persona*: a "personality" distinct from Christ's sacrificial body.[44] Here is Kantorowicz's most concise summary of this shift, which I provide at length:

Hitherto it had been the custom to talk about the Church as the "mystical body of Christ" (*corpus Christi mysticum*) which sacramentally alone makes sense. Now, however, the Church, which had been the mystical body of Christ, became a mystical body in its own right. That is, the Church organism became a "mystical body" in an almost juristic sense: a mystical corporation. The change in terminology was not haphazardly introduced. It signified just another step in the direction of allowing the clerical corporational institution of the *corpus ecclesiae iuridicum* to coincide with the *corpus ecclesiae mysticum* and thereby to "secularize" the notion of "mystical body." The term *corpus mysticum*, despite all the sociological and organological connotations it had acquired, nevertheless preserved its definitely sacramental ring simply because the word "body" still recalled the consecrated sacrifice. That last link to the sphere of the altar, however, was severed when Aquinas wrote: "It may be said that head and limbs together are as though one mystical person." Nothing could be more striking than this bona fide replacement of *corpus mysticum* by *persona mystica*. Here the mysterious materiality which the term *corpus mysticum*—whatever its connotations may have been—still harbored, has been abandoned: The *corpus Christi* has been changed to a corporation of Christ. It has been exchanged for a juristic abstraction, the "mystical person," a notion reminiscent of, indeed synonymous with, the "fictitious person," the *persona repraesentata* or *ficta*.[45]

[44] Reformation reformulations of Eucharistic theology generally reflect a rejection of the Eucharist as sacrifice in favor of gift or commemoration. This, however, does not equate to a rejection of the Eucharist as a relation to Christ's material body.

[45] Kantorowicz, 201–202. For a critical view of this claim, see Jennifer Rust, "Political Theologies of the *Corpus Mysticum*: Schmitt, Kantorowicz, and de Lubac."

Theoretically, this shift constitutes the structural emergence of later (generally Hobbesian) conceptions of sovereignty by which the body politic is brought into being artificially, through a putative contractual agreement that limits individual freedoms in order to decisively organize immanent bodies into a "*corpus repraesentatum.*" According to Kantorowicz, it was key that "the pope could be the head of the 'mystical body of the Church' as a corporation or polity or *regnum* more easily than head of the 'mystical body of Christ.'"[46] And while there were still important shifts that had to occur for this metaphor to move fully into the political domain – for the *persona mystica* to become "the Crown" or "royal dignity," and ultimately the democratic "body politic" – the basic structure of modern sovereignty is legible in the move from sacrificial to representative body.[47]

The crucial shift involves the deliberate use of poiesis to constitute a collective. When the *corpus mysticum* became abstracted from the *corpus Christi mysticum*, it assumed the fundamental structure of a fiction: a fabricated imaginative device. A *persona mystica* may purport to be more. It may, in fact, retain all of the theological imaginative force that Schmitt would argue continues to haunt liberal sovereignty. But for Kantorowicz, a *persona mystica* shares the same basic structure as a *persona repraesentata* or *ficta*. As an imaginative body that organizes the use of decisive force – deciding friend and enemy – it is also a literary entity, theoretically capable of being unmade or resignified. What is key, then, is not the presence or absence of the *persona*, but how that *persona* is made responsible to concrete human lives and immanent material conditions. Kahn helpfully unpacks this as follows:

Kantorowicz's understanding of the juristic person is key to understanding his idea of political theology ... Where Schmitt insists on a Catholic, personalist notion of representation, which he clearly distinguishes from a joint stock company, Kantorowicz argues that the Roman-canon juristic person is compatible with the legal notion of a corporation. This, in turn, means that Kantorowicz sees the juridical person or corporation as an enabling fiction rather than a "real being." Kantorowicz then suggests that juristic fictions may have some relation to nominalist intellectual fictions. And he goes on to argue that the fact "that this corporate person was a fictitious person detracted nothing from its value, especially its heuristic value ... Aquinas, actually following Augustine, could define 'fiction' in a signally positive sense as *figura veritatis* [figure of truth]. And Baldus, elaborating glosses of Accursius and Bartolus, finally declared, with a slight twist

---

[46] Kantorowicz, 203.   [47] Kantorowicz, *The King's Two Bodies*, 207; 271-ff.

of an Aristotelian tenet: '*Fiction imitates nature*. Therefore, fiction has a place only where truth can have a place.'"[48]

The conceptual conditions that allow slippage between the abstract mystical body [*corpus mysticum*] and the abstract person of the corporation [*persona mystica*] underscore the fundamental linguistic "made-ness" of both: the sense in which both are artistic imitations of nature whose truth is accountable to the nature they imitate.

As Kantorowicz tells it, the fictionality of sovereignty is first explicit in Dante's *Divine Comedy*, when Virgil crowns Dante the poet with the words, "I crown and mitre you over yourself." Kahn notes that Kantorowicz also mentions this scene in the essay "The Sovereignty of the Artist" as the moment when Dante, an individual man [*homo*] is invested with the dignity of the office of humanity [*humanitas*] which "never dies." According to Kahn, "in Kantorowicz's genealogy of the dignity of man, dignity refers less to the individual's intrinsic nobility than to an office, a notion of representation, whereby the individual comes to stand for the mystical body of mankind."[49] In the hands of the poet – the artist – the metaphysical trappings of the mystical body finally give way to the concrete, mortal individual who assumes the full dignity of the office of *humanitas*. Kahn concludes as follows:

Strikingly, in Kantorowicz's history of the king's two bodies, the body falls away to be replaced, ultimately, by fiction or … by the distinction between symbolic and real power. Whereas fascism and religious fundamentalism attempt to give society a body, the usefulness of the category of fiction is that it complicates any attempt to locate power in one particular body or one particular place. This displacement of the body is, ironically, the message of *The King's Two Bodies*, which, in pointing us to the role of legal fiction in bringing about the emergence of the constitutional state, may be thought of as a secular version of negative theology or as the tragedy of political theology averted.[50]

This account offers a critical lens for better understanding – and resisting – the shared logic of both theological and political absolutisms that operate by asserting a privileged identification of sign and thing, fashioning a sociopolitical or national imaginary around a specific kind of body.[51] The importance of the Dante scene is that it makes explicit something like the embarrassing secret of any political theology: that there is a perpetual difference conserved between representations and the real conditions that they clarify and organize. To the extent that the power of sovereignty is tied to the "persona" who represents sovereignty, sovereignty itself is subject to strategies of revision and accountability.

For Kahn and Kantorowicz, this makes the artist, as individual, sovereign over the representation, because the artist's office stands at the undecidable threshold of fiction and nature. It's a little different for Calvin. Calvin reads the concrete individual of the Redeemer as supplying a divinely or self- written *persona repraesentata* or *persona ficta*: an accommodation through which humanity is persuaded to reconceive God and ourselves (*Inst.* 2.16.2). According to Calvin, "The Word itself, however it be imparted to us, is like a mirror in which faith may contemplate God. Whether, therefore, God makes use of human help in this or works by his own power alone, he always represents himself [*se repraesentat*] through his Word to those whom he wills to draw to himself" (*Inst.* 3.2.6). This representation, as we've seen, enables human beings through the Spirit to "represent [*repraesentare*]" Christ (*Inst.* 3.6.3). Yet, although the representation encounters human beings as from God, it also hinges on the Redeemer's claim to real humanity – that "he fashioned for himself a body from our body, flesh from our flesh, bones from our bones" (*Inst.* 2.12.2), suggesting that a real human being must stand in for the office of humanity.

Later, when Calvin theorizes the apparatus of the visible church as one that refers the Word of Christ to the context of those gathered, he is suggesting that the "mystical body" (of the always-invisible church) is recognized by the actual community's participatory relation to the fictive representation of Christ – by a community adopted and renamed as "children of God." Yet, just as the sacrament is said to be nothing if it is not truly bread, the representation of Christ is nothing if it is not truly referring to that really existing, material human body. This means that, for Calvin, the visible church on earth never becomes "a mystical body in its own right."[52] The visible polity exists dynamically only as the nexus of relational signification enabled by Christ's *persona ficta* but obtaining only as particular bodies learn to recognize one another's particularity through Christ's particularity.

Calvin's unquestionably theological iteration of the two-body problematic therefore adds a layer of complexity to Kantorowicz's account. On the one hand, the representative body of Christ enables Christ and

---

[52] Kantorowicz 1957: 201.

human beings to recognize one another under the covenant of adoption. On the other hand, because Calvin insists that the local body of Christ exists really and perpetually in its "immortal flesh" at the right hand of God, the relationship between this local body and the church is grounded not in the fiction itself, but in the real material existence of Christ and those who are renamed under Christ (*Inst.* 4.17.32). In the context of the 1559 *Institutio*, this is both the pedagogical end and practical beginning of a more holistic providential resignification that accomplishes an important desideratum of Calvin's.[53] It allows him to reconceive the church as existing both by virtue of, and to facilitate, a perpetual activity of world reform that does not rely on the stable apparatus of an ecclesial or political corporation. The church that exists through its performance of Word and Sacrament also exists *to enable* God to "once more" become our Father, and the world to "once more" be the "frame in which we were to learn piety" through an accommodated sense of the divine (*Inst.* 2.6.1; 1.3–5). It exists to place humans in a direct relation to other humans and to the world as creation.

When Calvin makes the choice to theorize the church in this way, he makes use of Christian writing (scripture but also theology) as a particular thing to be used and moreover inhabited in a particular way, according to a particular choreography. He is recommending that writing operate in a domain of shared practice to trigger memory and combat what he takes to be fundamental effects of the fall into sin: the oblivion

---

[53] It's worth pausing here to consider the relationship between Calvin's program of teaching and the situation of the reader who would be likely to read it. For an ordinary reader of the *Institutio* of the kind that Calvin might have had in mind – a student of theology, or an educated, literate lay person – the practice of the Eucharist would have been likely to precede the deliberate formation of the *duplex cognitio*. The liturgical practice of the Eucharist would come *before* the decision to embark on Calvin's itinerary. It is important, then, that all the preceding layers of teaching lead up to this point of symbolic coincidence between the properties of Christ and ordinary bread, and that the resignification of the world can itself be comprehended in that very act of observance. This is all the more important for the illiterate and undereducated participant in the church, for whom a life turned by Christian signs will continue to revolve around the life of the church. The Eucharist comprehends all the layers of teaching for all of "the pious" – teachings that the *Institutio* itself can only claim to refine:

> This must be the rule of the pious [*Atque omnino isthaec piis tenenda regula est*]: whenever they see symbols appointed by the Lord, to think and be persuaded that the truth of the thing signified is surely present there. For why should the Lord put in your hand the symbol of his body, except to assure you of a true participation in it? But if it is true that a visible sign is given us to seal the gift of a thing invisible, when we have received the symbol of the body, let us no less surely trust that the body itself is also given to us (*Inst.* 4.17.10).

and dread that tempt one to construct and rely on comforting idols. From the earliest pages of the *Institutio*, Calvin's work is addressed to the deleterious and positive effects of idolatry, understood as the confused and compounding tendency to treat "things" as their own "signs," or to give abstractions a body. I've noted already that the critique of idolatry was central to the French reform movement in which Calvin became embroiled as a young man. It is also what, in my view, leads Calvin to refuse the move of theorizing civil government in terms of a body at all.

The French reformers who were expelled from France in 1534 had plastered Paris with pamphlets calling the Mass an abomination. Tellingly, this critique was received not just as heretical, but as seditious.[54] Christopher Elwood gives some insight into why this would have been the case. According to Elwood, the early reformist critiques of the Mass were part and parcel of a more general rejection of any "embodiment of God and the sacred in physical media, events, and institutions."[55] These reformers were particularly anxious about the close semiotic relationship between the late-medieval Catholic *corpus Christi mysticum* and the *Corpus Christianum* governed by the French crown. Here's how Elwood unpacks the logic:

> What does it mean to speak of a physical object becoming the sign of something else? . . . In what sense can a sign be said to make its referent present, and what kind of presence might such signification entail? . . . This language and these questions furnished the means by which people determined and specified the nature of their access to God and their participation in the redeeming and sanctifying power that mediated salvation. Laypeople had a large stake in the outcome of this kind of questioning. But the interests of ordinary people in the question of the sacrament's symbolizing capacity extended also into the realm of social or political affairs. The Eucharistic symbol, after all, had served to represent the unity and the ordered and integrated wholeness of both the Christian and the political community as it established and reinforced social and political hierarchies. As a social symbol reflecting as well as governing the social disposition of power, the Eucharist was likely to become the focus of practically every member of society with an interest in negotiating her role within the social network of power (Elwood 1991: 166).[56]

---

[54] Bruce Gordon, *Calvin* (New Haven, CT: Yale University Press, 2009), 181.

[55] Christopher Elwood, *The Body Broken: The Calvinist Doctrine of the Eucharist and the Symbolization of Power in France, 1530–1570* (New York: Oxford University Press, 1999), 9.

[56] While Elwood does not think that this association had to be explicit in the minds of French subjects in order for it to have been operative (167), he argues for this association historically in several ways, including the following: an analysis of how the Corpus Christi parades reinforced a logic of absolutism (21–26); the practice of the royal touch

As this particular construal of the Eucharist came to govern the imaginary of social life in concert with the crown, it allowed the crown itself to promise both stability and legibility to an obedient body politic, thereby governing the terms of recognition and exclusion. If the Mass were called idolatrous, so would the logic of the crown. They would not be idolatrous by virtue of any overt claim to divinity, but because they rely on a mode of recognition that privileges the coincidence of sign and thing in some worldly places over others.

Elwood points out that a number of specific public ceremonies reinforced what Calvin may have seen as a pernicious logic of recognition that trained ordinary people to semiotically associate the body of Christ with the body of the king. From the fourteenth to the sixteenth centuries, these ceremonies would have included the existence of parallel cults linking the Eucharist with the holy order of French society. The pageantry of *corpus Christi* feasts and parades sometimes placed the Eucharistic Host and the king side-by-side. At other times, such parades were staged for the king alone, such that "an observer of one of these processions would then most likely recognize that here was nothing other than a *Corpus Christi* procession except for the significant fact that the body of the king had replaced the body of Christ hidden in the sacred host."[57] This semiotic merger would have been further reinforced by traditions of royal healing that attributed sacred power to the king's blood, including the "royal touch" that healed scrofula.[58]

In this context, Calvin's performative theorization of the church and sacraments is legible as a simultaneous refusal to theorize the state as *Corpus Christianum*. If Calvin denies the church its own distinct *mystica persona*, arguing that the church exists only when staging collective performances of scriptural resignification that refer simultaneously to the really existing body of Christ and the worldly bodies of believers, then he is also denying that the state has any share in the body of Christ that does not first run through the bodies of individuals *as* creations. If the church exists only to facilitate the resignification of the world such that the universe is once more "the frame in which we were to learn piety," then divine power addresses the world as a whole from a site of onto-logical difference. As an institutional apparatus, the state can no more

and the rhetoric around Henry of Navarre (170); and the easy symbolic reciprocity that developed (when unchallenged) between the acclamation of God as king and the king as the absolute authority (158).
[57] Elwood, 25.   [58] Elwood, 15–26.

claim sovereignty than any other created thing can claim sovereignty. In fact, Calvin writes that the state should be understood analogous to "food, water, sun, and air" – worldly things that also nourish and enable human life (*Inst.* 4.20.3).[59] Any attempt to fix divine semiotics to one privileged earthly referent, or to identify the body of Christ with one particular kind of institutional or imagined body, signals idolatrous phantasm.[60]

When Calvin finally leads his reader to the consideration of civil government as the end of the itinerary, he delimits its authority and task just as one might expect a refugee to do. The reader is placed in the world in general, conceived *in societate*, and equipped with general instructions for how to critically navigate the ordinary context of civic life using the same posture of world- and self-reform that had been developed throughout the *Institutio* as a whole. Unlike the *Institutio*'s generic forbears and successors – Augustine, Bonaventure, Dante, even John Bunyan – the city at the end of the *Institutio* is not transcendent, heavenly, or even spiritual. Calvin doesn't even offer any suggestions for the best form of government. His city boasts no distinctly shaped "body." In fact, the term does not appear with a political valence anywhere in that final chapter. Any gesture to an ideal or eternal character for the civic sphere would risk idolatrous collapse between sign and signified and defer attention away

---

[59] It is perhaps here that government is most closely linked to providential care – to the things God provides to sustain life. Derek S. Jeffreys argues that Calvin's thinking on civil government is directly informed by his concern over the paranoia induced by disorder. Divine sovereignty is not the proper analogy for government itself, but government should be understood as one of the many intermediary apparatuses useful for bringing about conditions through which grace can enable the recognition of the divine. Jeffreys writes, for example:

> Limiting the power of the nation-state, educating people properly, developing a world community, all such policies may reduce disorder, but cannot repair our defection from divine goodness. Instead, they channel unfaithfulness into different institutional or cultural contexts, in which pride, mistrust and cruelty appear in new guises. However, retrieving Calvin's thought does not lead to a passive acceptance of the status quo. Nor, does it allow us to wallow in stern warnings about anarchy, tyranny or the dangers of utopia. On the contrary, with a clear understanding of unfaithfulness, we can identify and promote those forces that mitigate disorder (129).

See Jeffreys, "'It's a Miracle of God That There Is Any Common Weal among Us': Unfaithfulness and Disorder in John Calvin's *Political Thought*" in *The Review of Politics* 62/1 (2000): 107–129.

[60] According to Elwood, "For the convert to Calvin's sacramental view, the social world ceased to be organized by the idea of an immanental power proceeding from the presence of God's body in the Eucharist" (Elwood 1999: 75; see also 166–169).

from the bodies that matter: those of Christ and the people.[61] Yet, if the city's wings are clipped, it is nevertheless given a providentially given temporal task: to preserve worldly order, bring about justice for the poor, and pursue virtue and wellbeing so that human beings are able to live peaceably (*Inst.* 4.20.1, 6, 9, 20).[62]

---

[61] Matthew Tuininga argues that Calvin consistently rejected approaches to government that were overly elided with a strict moral vision or that sought to bring about the Kingdom of God on earth. Calvin "explicitly defended religious liberty for Muslims and Jews, and he clarified that while it is government's task to enforce God's moral law as much as possible, this does not require government to enforce or to conform to the laws of Moses. The appropriate laws and polity for a Christian commonwealth are to be determined in accord with natural law, the rule of love, and the virtue of prudence." See *Calvin's Political Theology and the Public Engagement of the Church: Christ's Two Kingdoms* (New York: Cambridge University Press, 2017), 359. He argues that this approach gives good reasons for contemporary Calvinists to support the consensus-aims of liberalism. Tuininga, like other recent Calvin scholars, bases this on a positive reading of Calvin's approach to natural law – one with which I agree, to a point. I agree that Calvin places an enormous amount of weight on the fact that creation is engraved with divine marks and endowed with receptors for divine glory. I do not find that Calvin prefers a lexical imaginary to describe the way natural life responds to divinity. As I've shown across this book, at times he uses legal language – but more often he will speak of sense, conscience, and affection as the human sites addressed by, and made responsive to, divine revelation. For other interpretations of natural law in Calvin, see Stephen J. Grabill, *Rediscovering the Natural Law in Reformed Theological Ethics* (Grand Rapids, MI: Eerdmans, 2006); Susan Schreiner, "Calvin's Use of Natural Law" in *A Preserving Grace: Protestants, Catholics, and Natural Law*, ed. Michael Comartie (Grand Rapids, MI: Eerdmans, 1997); C. Scott Prior, "God's Bridle: John Calvin's Application of Natural Law" in *Journal of Law and Religion* 22/1 (2006/2007): 225–254.

[62] Sheldon Wolin is right when he argues that Calvin's city must be understood as having aims that exceed those of the church in the care of life – that the city cultivates the life that is addressed by the operation of the Word through the church. According to Wolin:

> The charge that Calvin was intent on stamping society with a Christian image, or on purging it of its distinctively political attributes, does less than justice to his basic intent. If the matter is analyzed merely in terms of certain "higher" and "lower" values, then there can be no denying that Calvin believed political society ought to promote the "higher" ends of Christianity—*ad majorem Dei gloriam*. To be a good citizen was not an end in itself; one became a good citizen in order to be a better believer. Nevertheless, the ends of political society were not exhausted by its Christian mission. Government existed to promote "decency" as well as "godliness," "peace" as well as "piety," "moderation" as well as "reverence." In other words, government existed to promote values that were not necessarily Christian, even though they might be given a Christian coloration; they were values that were necessary for order and, as such, a precondition for human existence (163).

See Wolin, *Politics and Vision* (Princeton, NJ: Princeton University Press, 2004), chapter 6.

Accordingly, it's striking to see the extent to which Calvin's sketch of a Christian's responsibility to civil government is both tied to, and imitative of, the providential God he describes at the conclusion of Book One. First, Calvin's reader is instructed to will the continued existence of rulers as a necessary component of life, even if that means willing against one's own will.[63] Second, the reader is asked to accept the importance of intermediaries: "Here are revealed his goodness, his power, and his providence. For sometimes he raises up open avengers from among his servants, and arms them with his command to punish the wicked government and deliver his people, oppressed in unjust ways, from miserable calamity" (*Inst.* 4.20.30). Finally, the reader is called to bridle political power that is openly subverting the signification of the divine Word. Near the conclusion of the *Institutio*, Calvin writes, "In that obedience which we have shown to be due the authority of rulers, we are always to make this exception, indeed, to observe it as primary, that such obedience is never to lead us away from obedience to [God], to whose will the desires of all kings ought to be subject ... to whose majesty their scepters ought to be submitted" (*Inst.* 4.20.32). Divine sovereignty does not secure an analogy for political sovereignty. Because divine sovereignty runs through the affirmation of created life, it constitutes the ground for resistance to political governance.[64]

Though Calvin is famously hesitant to authorize resistance, he ultimately argues for its legitimacy on grounds consistent with those that required excommunication from the visible church: the open obfuscation of the Word such that the church cannot facilitate the resignification of the world. The last words of the 1559 *Institutio* are as follows: "If [rulers] command anything against [God], let it go unesteemed ... That we have been redeemed by Christ at so great a price as our redemption cost him, so that we should not enslave ourselves to the wicked desires of men—much less be subject to their impiety. GOD BE PRAISED [*Laus Deo*]" (*Inst.* 4.20.32). Across the *Institutio*, the glory of God is tied to the right perception of the world under the signature of its author. When the recognition commanded by the sovereign state demands the misrecognition of created life as inglorious, then normative misrecognition becomes the only genuine recognition.

---

[63] According to Calvin, "We owe this attitude of reverence and therefore of piety toward all our rulers in the highest degree, whatever they may be like" (*Inst.* 4.20.29).

[64] For an account of Calvin's historical attitudes toward questions of sedition and resistance in the last years of his life, see Tuininga, 87–91.

CONCLUSION

The activity that Calvin portrays as proper to civic life follows from the chain of significations that began, in the first chapter, with the *duplex cognitio*. In these last lines of text, it is as if Calvin has pressed the rewind button: impious rulers should go unesteemed because *we* are redeemed by Christ to be renamed children of God, knowing ourselves as we refer back in our very existence to the Creator whose glory permeates that relationship. The grounds for resisting a temporal government are the same as those that enable the desire for a non-idolatrous way of living. Refusing idolatry means refusing to cling to imaginary securities and instead to risk willing the fullness of creation – refusing nothing less than a knowledge of God that is also knowledge of ourselves as we refer back to God and God wills us. The only bodies that participate in this relationship are real bodies. Representations can be useful aids to render us attentive and responsible to God and each other. But reality is lodged in God and each other.

Calvin's version of the two bodies of Christ centers the particular, concrete body over (or under) the body of the office – echoing, to a degree, Dante's crowning as the individual Artist over the abstract idea of "humanity." Christ teaches not only by existing but by accommodating: providing a narrative. Recall, for a moment, the place in Book Two where Calvin addresses the role of that narrative, juxtaposing one spare account of Christ's atonement with a more dramatic and persuasive version (*Inst.* 2.16.3). The first version is, strictly speaking, closer to what he takes to be the "facts," even the stricter language of scripture itself. But he prefers the rhetorically elaborate second version for the way it is crafted as a fictive tool of effective (and affective) persuasion. It is not that Calvin does not think that theological representations should refer to realities. But the grammar being privileged in the way he approaches representations privileges the craftedness of language for its ability to enable fuller participation in and with realities, rather than merely representing them. After all, the fallen person is not the kind of thing that can receive transparent representations. Fallen persons need accommodation – specifically, accommodation that graciously positions them to see, feel, and know in a different way. This kind of poiesis may not enable the knowledge of "what we have made ourselves," but it does approach language as capable of being made and unmade in ways that are accountable to created life.

Attention to the artistic dimensions of redemptive mediation may enable a critique of versions of incarnational sovereignty that posit a world-shattering assemblage of word and flesh. According to Calvin's account of the sacraments, Christ's unique body entered and then left the immanent world, though it remains locally existent. If the narratives generated by that body and others' relation to it have fictive qualities that allow them to be attentive to context – in other words, through ongoing productions of theological writing and preaching – then Christ's body stands in tension with the urge to imagine the incarnation as an event-like shattering of immanent space and time. For Calvin, Christ encounters the world as "flesh from our flesh, bones from our bones" (*Inst.* 2.12.2). In linguistic terms, this suggests that the artistic dimensions of the incarnation must also be read as the language of our language and grammar of our grammar – effective not because they either reify or destroy, but continually engage the patterns of signification by which the world is rendered intelligible. According to this account, any world-shattering coincidence of word and flesh signals an idol, not an incarnation, and this is why I find it telling that Calvin rethinks the existence of the church in performative (rather than representative) terms.

But a performative church raises yet more questions about the political potential of Calvin's thinking, particularly in relation to the emerging disciplinary society of modernity. Recall that Gorski links Calvinism to modern statecraft because of its role in crafting technologies of the self-congenial to bottom-up tactics of management. Agamben makes a similar point not only about the fundamentally disciplinary structure of modern sovereignty but about Christian theology's series of exchanges with it: "Christian theology is, from its beginning, economic-managerial, and not politico-statal."[65] If Calvin's church reconstitutes power in terms of activity rather than being, and directs that activity to the world at large rather than referring the activity back to the church as a transcendently grounded body, this might not challenge but rather further reinforce why Calvinism seems to have played such an outsized role in techniques of power that govern through the bipolar structure of differentiating knowledge and rationalizing production.

Indeed, I expect that dimensions of my own study shed further light on that which Max Weber termed an elective affinity between Calvinism and capitalism, or between Calvinism and the managerial techniques that organize overlapping spheres of life in the modern West. If Calvin's theology is read as an ideal pattern to be realized at the level of material life, this is the result. But there are also elements of Calvin's logic that

---

[65] Agamben, *The Kingdom and the Glory* (Stanford, CA: Stanford University Press, 2011), 66.

destabilize such an affinity by asking readers to grant an active role to material life itself in casting and shaping the use of signs. Take, for example, the precise consistency with which Calvin theorizes glory and glorification, from the locus on providence right to the last two words of the book. According to Agamben, the function of glorification is to cover the failure of governmentality to take full command over the life it manages. In Trinitarian terms, glory refers to the inoperativity of the sovereign Father who is putatively glorified by the praxis of the Son – the Father who rules but does not reign. Calvin's account differs precisely at this point. When he reframes the world as "the frame in which we were to learn piety" and the Father as actively willing every aspect of creation in order to govern it with care, he describes an activity peculiar to God the Creator by which God becomes recognized as Father. Glory emerges from this primal recognition – a recognition that exceeds all other rendered judgments and refers something akin to Agamben's account of the "pure potentiality" of matter to the hidden transcendence of the divine.

Glory is therefore not a product of glorification. It is a feature of the significative difference that is reality-as-creation-willed-by-God-as-recognized-by-faith. So Calvin can claim, near the beginning of the *Institutio*, that "wherever you cast your eyes, there is no spot in the universe wherein you cannot discern at least some sparks of God's glory" (*Inst.* 1.5.1). He is not referring here to the result of an exercise of glorification, but what he takes to be a persistent feature of fallen faculties in which the sense of the divine is not entirely defaced. As a result of fallenness, however, "most people, immersed in their own errors, are struck blind in such a dazzling theater ... and certainly however much the glory of God shines forth, scarcely one person in a hundred is a true spectator of it!" (*Inst.* 1.5.8). Glorification compounds these errors, preferring imaginative figments to the glory of ordinary life (*Inst.* 1.11.7).

This reading of glory that cuts all the way back to the first 1536 edition is also visible in the way Calvin the refugee challenges Francis I:

It will then be for you, most serene King, not to close your ears or your mind to such just defense, especially when a very great question is at stake: how God's glory may be kept safe on earth, how God's truth may retain its place of honor, how Christ's Kingdom may be kept in good repair among us ... But our doctrine must tower unvanquished above all the glory and above all the might of the world, for it is not of us, but of the living God and his Christ whom the Father has appointed King to "rule from sea to sea, and from the rivers even to the ends of the earth."[66]

[66] Calvin, *Inst.*, 11–12.

When the church performs its task of resignification through preaching and the observance of the sacraments, it reenacts a chain of significations that address and reorient those gathered to refer all the way back to God the Creator who in turn cares for creation as Father. This is where Calvin locates glory – beyond the narratives and the practices that relate them to bodies. Glory refers to a creation that cannot be leapt over. Glory refers to the life that exceeds other tactics of mastery and production because it recognizes itself loved by virtue of its existence.

Conclusion

Holy God, the breath of life, we give you thanks for this day. We give you thanks for this people. We give you thanks for this life, and we lean today into it. And lean today into you. And lean today into the fullness of life, knowing well that that life includes hurt and pain and tears. But God, remembering today the promise you made so long ago to Sarah and to Abraham; remembering the promise we saw embodied in the Christ; remembering your faithfulness when we take time to be grateful; we lean today, God, into you. You have heard, God, many, many prayer requests. We give them all to you and do so grateful for the gift and the time to name and talk and share and weep. And we do this, God, grateful for the blessing we find when we pause long enough ... to notice. Thank you for that, God. Thank you. In Jesus's name, Amen.

–Heard at a Presbyterian church in South Boston on February 25, 2018[1]

The reformed movements that coalesced in sixteenth-century Europe continue to be widely linked to modern disenchantment – to a feeling of loss, or perhaps open-eyed maturity, that now lingers over the way the West understands its own history. For people like Blumenberg who theorize modern legitimacy as a break with a socio-temporal past beholden to transcendent authority, modernity brings the demand to evacuate ontologically robust notions of the sacred or the mysterious and to approach the immanent world as a domain to be theorized, deconstructed, and reconstructed in immanent terms. This inevitably directs and shapes the category of religion along one or several catar-acts. Religion can signal a dangerous resurgence of the mystical; it can

---

[1] Rev. Burns Stanfield, prayer over congregational celebrations and concerns. Fourth Presbyterian Church, South Boston, MA. (February 25, 2018. Recording available.)

be safely privatized for personal edification alongside aesthetic pursuits and hobbies, or it can serve the broader rational and disciplinary aims of modernity. It is through this kind of gesture that (Protestant) Christianity was renamed as Religion, and Religion was renamed as Secular.[2]

This kind of account is freighted with implicit yet highly particularized notions of transcendence and immanence and their relation to language. If theological language is immediately suspected to assume a referential relation to unwieldy mystical-metaphysical realities, then this implies that disenchanted or demythologized language will refer more stably to immanent realities. Yet the ability to mark a difference in these two registers of language relies on a sovereign gesture: a gesture rooted in an approach to reality that proceeds from an implicit decision over the nature of reality in order to enable the control and organization of that reality. The structure of this power play is especially visible in the politics of temporality, or in the attempt to periodize the "modern" over and against a "past" in which language putatively worked differently. If modern "secular" language is presumed to assume an inherently more natural relation to the things it signifies, this claim first renders the modern world as the kind of object that can be presented through its rejection of non-secular language.

Such a claim relies on a sovereign gesture, one that decisively excises dimensions of human life and experience from "the present" as well as "the past." The management of so-called good and bad religion into the aforementioned cataracts depends on this gesture, but attention to historical and material details disrupts this gesture. Attention – close reading with attention to marginalized details – has the ability to recover evidence of "modern" data in times and places we're taught not to expect it. It also has the ability to confront us with the extent to which "religious metaphysics" continue to haunt the very structure of modern societies themselves. When social-textual anomalies are allowed to enter the data pool, their presence raises fundamental questions about the ways that uses of language have already been disciplined – predetermined, as it were – by the methodological ideology of modern sovereignty that wants to exclude contravening aspects of particularity in the name of achieving a stable unity. Resisting this must involve recasting the question of language itself in a way that eschews the presumption that language is either

---

[2] See Gil Anidjar, "Secularism" in *Critical Inquiry* 33 (2006): 55–77, which I discussed in Chapter 5.

metaphysically beholden or subject to rational revision. It means, in short, asking about the fuller embodied strategies and techniques through which language that *looks* mystical, or that *looks* rational, is made responsible to that which exceeds it.

Calvin's 1559 *Institutio Christianae Religionis* is an example of an early modern writing that upsets overly rigid binaries between metaphysics and poiesis, transcendence and immanence, theology and enabling literature – the very binaries on which the narrative of disenchantment and modern legitimacy often rely. In its form and texture as well as content, Calvin's writing asks that theological arguments be placed in relation to the contours of the existing world and offers strategies for doing so in real, rather than ideal, time. Attention to the details of this text invites the reader not to focus on whether it is theological or secular, or whether it is medieval or modern, but on what are the key turning points through which exercises of reading and writing are made responsible to the reality of the world.

Some version of this question is certainly close to the heart of the Enlightenment's putative values, as well as the values that inform defenses of secularity for its fundamental revisability. Whether in Francis Bacon's defense of induction, Kant's reason, Blumenberg's curiosity, or Kahn's poiesis, there is a consistent element that advocates of the "modern" seem to desire: a use of language that puts human beings better in touch with what we are and with what we need to live well. If theology is cast as a threat to immanent responsibility, it is because theology is perceived and received as a form of discourse that answers such questions by asserting given metaphysical confines. This, in turn, suggests furtive authoritarian allegiances to a set of transcendent goods that are not revisable, not responsive to discovery, not amenable to creativity and difference. Yet, as a substantial body of critical and postcolonial research over the last several decades has shown, the values of Western modernity have always been bound up with interpretive practices that give reason a certain kind of body, imagining it to have a specific relationship to the time and place of its own European emergence. The patterns of meaning that flow from and reinforce the legitimacy of this modern "decision" continue to resignify bodies as abject or as threats to privileged regimes of intelligibility.

Protestant histories, communities, and individuals have reinforced and colluded in the logic of modern sovereignty. Many scholars have noted this for decades, and I take this to be beyond controversy. But these same histories, communities, and individuals have also been subject to the violence of its operation. When Protestantism is identified as a religious tradition defined by "beliefs over practices," this affects the erasure of strategies of signification through which such binaries have been historically and even presently challenged. For Calvinists in particular, exercises of resignification rely on the critical capacity of texts to interface with existing conditions. This doubtless makes Reformed thinking vulnerable to logocentrism and its violent effects. Yet these exercises also demand attention to the reality of existing conditions "to which scripture refers." This means remembering the materiality of the bodies who carry and turn the signs directed to them. It also means remembering the complexity of the textual bodies that facilitate this work, aiding in the exercise of resignification. It means remembering that the generic and argumentative features of texts do things as well as say things, and in order to do things, they need to conserve the space between signs and things.

This is why I find value in approaches to secularization, modernity, and political theology that refuse to abide by categorical distinctions like theology versus literature, medieval versus modern, or even transcendence versus immanence. Foucault, Agamben, Derrida, and their better readers – whatever their respective disagreements and limitations – foreground two things: not only the perpetual slippages between words and things, a position for which the so-called postmodernists are probably most known; but also the positive force of language in making things that interface with a world that exceeds our grasp, enabling us to ask questions about reality and ourselves from a different vantage. This sets up a posture through which a reader is taught to pay attention to the aesthetic details and differentiating strategies of language in order to appreciate the forms of life they can enable in their address, all while remaining ever mindful of what is perpetually absent: the total context of possible materializations.

Such a posture might look for any writing to both perform and rely on contingent relationships between particulars, while never taking the appearance of one such relationship to be definitive or final. The spell cast by a signature might not generate the same outcome in one context as the same spell in a different context, although the results may nevertheless generate the semblance of useful repetition if attention is paid to the ritual or experimental context. For me, and I think for Agamben, this speaks to a structural similarity between theology, the conditions of a scientific experiment, and the efficacy of a legal fiction. It is also an echo of the structure of the claim that the Holy Spirit works through preaching and sacrament to accommodate the meaning of divine signs to the particular needs and conditions of the community gathered.[3]

I'm sure that all of the doctrinal *loci* I've discussed in these chapters have explicitly or implicitly reinforced a range of political effects and ethical dispositions over centuries. I don't take this multiplicity to mean that questions about the ethical and political implications of theology overextended to the point of irrelevance. On the contrary, when Löwith, Davis, or Kahn worry about the sovereign logic that attaches to the Christian incarnation, or when Nietzsche, Weber, Foucault, and Agamben worry about whether the secularized providential logic of modern rationalization and governmentality can be responsible to life, they fine-tune and complicate our understanding of the variety of interpretive strategies through which theological-sociopolitical signatures differentiate and dispose the world as a site of activity. This underscores all the more that readers of theology – whether self-described insiders or outsiders – should remain mindful of the way that the writing shapes and disposes the world of the reader. This means resisting the temptation to read as if metaphysically intoned claims are offering something in the way of cognitive certainty or transcendent insight that they cannot, in fact, deliver – and for which the delivery would, in theological terms, be idolatrous.[4]

While it might be easier in some ways for both confessional and non-confessional readings to catalog and assess the meaning of theological claims according to their abstract content, such a practice nevertheless defers an abundance of potential data pointing to the multiple ways that theological texts not only can, but *have* shaped the lives and communities who practice living and facing their difficulties through this mediating lens. If there are definite features of Calvin's writing that present theology and scripture as tools for fine-tuning attention to the details of the world and relating the self to them, it is not surprising when Calvinists choose to rebuild sovereignty around the conditions of their own wandering bodies.

---

[3] Gottfried Wilhelm Locher also emphasizes this aspect of Calvin's argument, writing, "Calvin maintains that the Church is the form in which the Incarnate Son of God is present among Christians. God makes use of the human mouth and tongue to proclaim his Word, even if those who hear it are unworthy of it. He does so in order to communicate with us according to our abilities and without frightening us. Rather than intimidating us by addressing us directly, God speaks his Word to us through our fellow man." See *Sign of the Advent: A Study in Protestant Ecclesiology* (Fribourg: Academic Press Fribourg), 75.

[4] This language of "world of the reader" is theoretically indebted to Paul Ricoeur, *Time and Narrative*, Vol. 1, trans. Kathleen McLaughlin and David Pellauer (Chicago: University of Chicago Press, 1984).

But it is also not surprising to notice that Calvinist communities have also been leading advocates for racial justice, gender and sexuality inclusion, anti-poverty work, and the need for strong systems of social welfare.[5] If the sign is understood not to determine but rather to underscore the peculiar details of the things to which it is addressed, these ethical postures must be entertained as both biblically and ethically serious.

* * *

For Calvin, the very logic of church reform is geared at making the church's signifying practices responsible to the context of the world more generally – asking, in turn, for a social world that tolerates these signifying practices. Is it so surprising, then, if Calvinist churches have incubated subjects who were attentive to the details of things, interested in worldly engagement, and motivated to improve conditions for the habitation of life? Or that Calvinist communities might have been especially interested in how the deliberate use of signs and signatures can reveal new productive capacities for ordering life? Certainly, this kind of account walks the razor's edge when it comes to reinforcing disciplinary effects through worldly asceticism. But, as Foucault and others have taught us, the relationship between technologies of governmentality and technologies of the self is a very close one, one that turns on the extent to which the

---

[5] What I want to suggest, here, is a slow rhetoric that undergirds a persistent correlation between Calvin's mode of reading that treats the world as an active and crucial referent for signification; and a call to activism that does not merely impose the Word *a priori*, but rather cultivates a responsive posture before the details of worldly conditions. For a fuller account of the diversity of Calvinism on matters of activism, policy, and progressivism, see my Introduction, note 18.

But here are some additional resources that focus more acutely on socially responsible progressivism. See Dale Edward Soden, *The Reverend Mark Matthews: An Activist in the Progressive Era* (Seattle: University of Washington Press, 2000); Kenneth J. Stewart, *Ten Myths about Calvinism: Recovering the Breadth of the Reformed Tradition* (Downers Grove, IL: Intervarsity Press Academic, 2011); Robert Vosloo, "Calvin and Anti-Apartheid Memory in the Dutch-Reformed Families of South Africa" in *Sober, Strict and Scriptural: Collective Memories of John Calvin: 1800–2000*, eds. Johan de Neit, Herman Paul, and Bart Wallet (Leiden: Brill, 2009); chapter 10 of Bruce Gordon, *John Calvin's Institutes of the Christian Religion: A Biography* (Princeton, NJ: Princeton University Press, 2016); Albert J. Raboteau's discussion of A. J. Muste (who left the Reformed tradition eventually) in *American Prophets: Seven Religious Radicals and Their Struggle for Social and Political Justice* (Princeton, NJ: Princeton University Press, 2016), 27–62. Finally, a recent episode of the 99% Invisible podcast discusses how the "sanctuary city" movement was started by Presbyterian pastor John Fife. See http://99percentinvisible.org/episode/church-sanctuary-part-1/.

subject comes to actively know and work on herself by means of these technologies.[6]

Because any scholar's analysis will necessarily hit up against the opacity of reader reception, it is the text that we can analyze with the greatest care. And it is clear that the 1559 *Institutio* prioritizes not only the domain of the world and the content of the Christological narrative, but also a series of deliberate practices through which that narrative becomes one's own through the Spirit. In this way, the text is legible not only as a technology of a situated immanent self but as a technology to facilitate the concrete memory of the life of a community. We should expect, then, that some in the vast network of churches who trace the history of their practices to or through Calvin might very well have implemented these kinds of responsible reading practices with a degree of self-awareness, and thus generated a different range of ethical affective postures toward the world than those who read theology as strict propositions of adherence. The distinct features of the "left" side of Calvin's ethical and political legacy might be no more an aberration than the better-known "right" side, and no less "biblical" in its orientation.[7]

[6] See, for example, Michael Foucault, "Technologies of the Self" in *Technologies of the Self: A Seminar with Michel Foucault*, eds. Luther H. Martin, Huck Gutman, Patrick H. Hutton (Amherst: The University of Massachusetts Press, 1988), 16–49; Giorgio Agamben, *The Use of Bodies*, trans. Adam Kotsko (Stanford, CA: Stanford University Press, 2016); Mark Jordan, *Convulsing Bodies* (Stanford, CA: Stanford University Press, 2014); Judith Butler, *Bodies That Matter: On the Discursive Limits of "Sex"* (New York: Routledge, 1993); Talal Asad, *Genealogies of Religion: Discipline and Reasons of Power in Christianity and Islam* (Baltimore: The Johns Hopkins University Press, 1993); Catherine Bell, *Ritual Theory Ritual Practice* (New York: Oxford University Press, 2009).

[7] For a wider reading or demonstration of Calvin's intellectual impact, see the following array of works: Heather White, *Reforming Sodom: Protestants and Gay Rights* (Chapel Hill: University of North Carolina Press, 2015); Marilynne Robinson's body of work, including *The Death of Adam: Essays on Modern Thought* (New York: Picador, 1998), *Gilead* (New York: Farrar, Straus and Giroux, 2004); and *The Givenness of Things* (New York: Farrar, Straus and Giroux, 2015); Richard R. Niebuhr, *Experiential Religion* (New York: Harper and Row Publishers, 1972); Hans Frei, *Eclipse of Biblical Narrative: A Study in Eighteenth and Nineteenth Century Hermeneutics* (New Haven, CT: Yale University Press, 1974) and *Types of Christian Theology* (New Haven, CT: Yale University Press, 1992); Roland Boer, *Political Grace: The Revolutionary Theology of John Calvin* (Louisville, KY: Westminster John Knox Press, 2009); John Dewey, *A Common Faith* (New Haven, CT: Yale University Press, 1934) and *The Quest for Certainty: A Study of the Relation of Knowledge and Action* (New York: Minton Blach and Co., 1929). See also Laube, Stefan, "Calvin in Germany: A Marginalized Memory" in *Sober, Strict and Scriptural: Collective Memories of John Calvin: 1800–2000* edited by

In order to give a fuller account of what I take to be the postures of responsibility invited by Calvin's writing, my readings have strived to inhabit the seriousness of his self-evident claims about divine revelation. With him, I've privileged Christological and scriptural narratives over all others. I've allowed, for the sake of the text's argument, the particular constitution of the fallen human person that he presumes. I have done this to study how Calvin's strategies of writing work in both narrowing but also acknowledging the inevitable distance between the reader, the world of her life, and the claims of the text. When Calvin lays out his mode and order of teaching, he anticipates that the ordinary "fallen" reader will bring a range of interpretations concerning her relationship to God, the state, the world, other people, and the traditional sources of Christian faith. Even if the text evidences a structure that entices the reader to inhabit its convictions, the text can never do more than assert that the practice of reading and relating things to the world will, in fact, be useful to the reader and bring her insight, clarity, forbearance, enjoyment, and the feeling of special care. Even the moment of illumination on which these signs turn – for Calvin, the certainty of election – is tied to the evidence supplied by the reader's own desire. If the desire is not elicited, the teaching loses its usefulness. If the reader is embodied, the text cannot have meaning without some living end to which it is directed, and from which it conserves a measure of distance.

In this way, Calvin's writing demonstrates its own inability to achieve, much less to present, the fusion of sign and thing. In all of the clearest examples of resignification, understanding occurs not through the writing or the reading, but the unharnessable glimpse, a kind of spiritual magic, that one prays to occur through the faithful use of the sign. With the use of the right argument, the world might become perceptible as "the visible splendor of [divine] apparel," or the "insignia whereby he shows his glory to us, whenever and wherever we cast our gaze." The sky might be seen as the "royal tent" of God, while never ceasing to be nitrogen and oxygen; clouds might be "his chariot" while continuing to also be water vapor; the wind will be "the wings" of his "swift messengers," while also cooling the body (*Inst.* 1.5.1). To know by means of these resignifications is not to redefine, but to more fully perceive significatory depths. Under the sign of providence, God's will affirms created intermediaries while also reminding us of their limitations. Under the sign of divinity, the humanity

Johan de Neit, Herman Paul, and Bart Wallet (Leiden: Brill, 2009). See the Introduction for a more exhaustive discussion.

of Christ lives and advocates for other humans. Under the sign of the sacrament, bread is spiritual food and the life of Christ without ceasing to be nourishing to ordinary bodies. These signs do not uncover or redefine the things they reference but change the dimensions through which we see them.

Certainly, Calvin treats these privileged signs as true – *as true*. To appreciate the performative technology of Calvin's resignification, it is important to hold both parts of the signature together in the tightest possible oscillation. On the one hand, these signs are revealed, which means they are unverifiable. The words that present them to the imaginative faculties of the reader do so through the operation of a language that is also fully ordinary and unable to shed itself of its vulnerability to context in which truth claims can never be more than "as if." As one response, the reader could jettison that little modifier on the grounds of a confessional allegiance that demands deference to authority and thereby gives propositional metaphysical language its own body. But this would also strip the textual body of the *Institutio* – indeed, of a number of premodern texts – of the very features through which they address readers as bodies. From Epictetus' *Enchiridion* to Augustine's *De Doctrina Christiana*, from Boethius' *Consolation* to Anselm's *Proslogion*, the needs and persuasive requirements of the text's constructed reader are not only foregrounded in the text, they are presumed to play a role in casting the receptive force of the iterable arguments.

On the other hand, all of these texts proceed with a seriousness that could very well be described as life-or-death. It's a seriousness that might seem to contrast with the more playful and creative tone of modern literature, although I would proceed cautiously before calling Nietzsche's *Zarathustra*, Camus' *The Plague*, James Baldwin's *Go Tell It on the Mountain*, or Toni Morrison's *Beloved* anything but serious. Nor do I think that anyone should incautiously treat legal and political fictions – for example, corporate personhood, probable cause, American exceptionalism – as anything but deadly serious in their force and scope.[8] All of these fictions are life-or-death because life relies on them to constitute its intelligibility and disposition in community. Yet, the posture of responsibility to life would mean foregrounding the memory that fictions are something, but they are not everything, and they should never be treated as more than what they are. Their distance from excessive

---

[8] See, for example, William Cavanaugh, *Migrations of the Holy: God, State and the Political Meaning of the Church* (Grand Rapids, MI: Eerdmans, 2011).

materiality should be conserved. Much like Calvin thinks the state must be resisted when it encroaches on the proper operation of God's Word in the world, remembering both the necessity and the limits of the operation of fiction serves as a tool for remembering the limits of any sovereign apparatus that assumes the right to define and circumscribe life.

Certainly, the conventional features of theological writing will render it more vulnerable to a sovereign posture (or to rejection by other sovereign postures) because of the scope and sheer ambition of the discourse itself. The "as if" of a theological truth-claim confronts a reader *as if* metaphysically decisive, suggesting that saying yes to it means inhabiting that mode of materialization by acceding to a mode of differentiating the world through such a narrative. But the "as if" also asks the reader to remain open to the narrative's re-materialization in new contexts. The "decision" of the self to read the world in a certain way is paradoxically both fused with and refused by the putative decisiveness of the narrative itself. What is key is how the self relates to this paradox – and the extent to which a text conveys its own mechanisms for acknowledging the conservation of distance between signs and things. Such mechanisms include accommodations, exercises, persuasions, prayers, calls for faith, and elicitations of desire to remind the reader of what the "as if" actually enables: a mode for performing possible relationships between things in order to know them and ourselves better.

This also means that, unlike governmental technologies that reinforce the paradigm of sovereignty, writings that are approached as technologies of "selves" don't claim to exhaust the body of the self on which they work, nor can they be fully determined by the decision of the individual. Among other things, such texts need not be read as competing with alternate accounts of the truth. If writing is made accountable to the needs and desires of life, the decision to believe is less relevant to the operation of the text than the mere willingness – the desire – to read, write, hear, listen, engage, contemplate, and respond. Theology is no less capable than other forms of art of eliciting the desire for these kinds of activities and of fostering attention to the transcendence of material existence itself. It may be that the modern outpouring of written genres underscores the creative capacities of writing against the backdrop of more constrained premodern genres. But this need not diminish the creative capacities of older styles and genres. When premodern theology is read alongside modern writing, what stands out is the way that literary devices more visibly work through relational structures of teaching and tradition, attention and memory, therefore rendering the "sovereignty of the artist" undecidable. If the artist attains sovereignty in modernity, that sovereignty is always haunted by the specters of materializations excluded by the momentary decision to embrace or reject what is deemed past.

***

This leads me to one final, more open-ended consideration: the question of Calvin's more general relation to life – his own life, the life addressed in his writing, and our conceptions of what life is now. I've noted, many times by now, the generally accepted and well-substantiated accounts of Calvinist disciplinary and legal practices.[9] While the best of these accounts focus on data other than Calvin's own theological writing, these effects are nevertheless intelligible alongside what is distinctive about the role providence plays in Calvin's larger project of reform. If the world replaces the church as the scene of habituation in teaching, the world becomes the site of ongoing differentiation and resignification. The world is legible as a site of activity, which means it is also legible as a domain of perpetual disciplinary management. By the time critics like Nietzsche, Weber, and Agamben worry about the sources for attending to the meaning of life in the face of rationalization, mechanization, and bureaucratization, they rightly recognize that it is not good enough to simply remember or make space for some transcendent meaning. What is needed is some strategy of meaning that begins and ends with what is transcendent and inoperative about the force of immanent life itself.

That's why, for me, one of the more astonishing features of Calvin's 1559 *Institutio* is found in the extent to which he anticipates the structure of what seems a uniquely "counter-modern" approach to the question of theodicy – one that is modern to the extent that it self-consciously responds to both the novel conditions of a post-scientific and post-industrial world, but one that also self-consciously responds to the perceived shortcomings of modernity's claims to superiority over the past. This approach to suffering emphasizes the importance of facing its reality rather than turning away from its reality through either consolation or resentment. I've noted that the contours of a gesture that responds to

<hr/>

[9] For example, John Witte Jr. and Robert M. Kingdon, *Sex, Marriage, and Family in John Calvin's Geneva*, three vols. (Grand Rapids, MI: Eerdmans, 2005); Pamela A. Mason, "The Communion of Citizens: Calvinist Themes in Rousseau's Theory of the State" in *Polity* 26: 1 (Autumn, 1993): 25–49; and Philip S. Gorski, "Calvinism and State-Formation in Early Modern Europe" in *State/Culture: State-Formation after the Cultural Turn*, ed. George Steinmetz (Ithaca, NY: Cornell University Press, 1999), 147–181.

suffering through affirmation appears in a range of authors from Dostoevsky and Camus to Weil, with anterior echoes in biblical sources like Job. But this posture may find no clearer narration than in Nietzsche's writing on suffering.

When Nietzsche's Zarathustra, the figure of the immanent Creator, faces suffering by affirming life eternally, this is a response to suffering that refuses both the "comforts" of Christian theodicy and the futurism of a modernity that promises to overcome pain. Nietzsche sees both of these as channeling resentment toward the reality of life – as manifestations of the same ascetic ideal that Weber traces so magnetically to Calvinism: one that wills the subjection of present conditions to generate some future good. At the same time, Nietzsche also refuses to simply return to pre-Christian sources such as the Stoics to advocate for the acclimation of the self to the natural necessities of life. His response to suffering wants to self-consciously reoccupy the position of both servile claims to worldly necessity and otherworldly escapes via transcendence. So he retains a more-or-less Christian structure of the will – a will that wills a transcendent future – but he *ties* that will to the earth. Overcoming resentment against what the world has been, while also willing a better future, requires first looking at all that the world has been, and saying "yes" to its existence.

Nietzschean affirmation choreographs a response to suffering and injustice that prioritizes the medium of affect over cognition. What is on offer is not an explanation, but the management and direction of the desire *for* an explanation. By willing the resignification of things past *as things willed*, the will cultivates what is more fundamental to creativity: a love for life itself in all of its sometimes-crooked details; a desire that life be, and continue, and continue eternally. Affirmation, here, means willing the conditions of *this* life, *our* life – willing even the suffering, because without it there would be no life, no creation, and no joy. This is no easy gesture. It is, in fact, one of immense difficulty. But it approaches living as involving the complex negotiation of willing and learning, of facing and resignifying all that has been, precisely in order to draw forth something new from the wellspring of what is.

When Calvin makes the shocking claim that God wills everything, even suffering, even evil, this marks a posture to the problem of evil that runs through and away from Calvin like a deep and cold current through warmer waters. It is as shocking to theological sensibilities as it is to those of modern progressive humanism – as disturbing, even, as the will to affirm the eternal recurrence of the same. Read as a theodicy – as a

286   *Calvin and the Resignification of the World*

reasoned explanation for suffering and program for how to overcome it – Calvin's work is every bit as unsatisfying as Nietzsche's. It verges uncomfortably on affirming suffering itself. It also recalls the longstanding perception that Calvinist "determinism" reinforces quietistic tendencies in the face of injustices by coupling the precision of its exercises at world mastery with a latent nihilism. Nietzsche, of course, is vulnerable to the same suspicions. Yet, there is a resonant logic that ties the two in an uncanny repetition of sensibilities. For both, the transcendent will to life must run through that which is, strictly speaking, against its will. To realize the glory of life, one must go through, rather than leap over, conditions of suffering. The creative will to let there be light is, for both, also the providential will that perpetually wills the existence that has been created.

For Calvin, the will to affirm is divine. For Nietzsche, it is "all too human." Yet, for Calvin, the divine will is also a will that becomes human and involves humanity. Zarathustra's affirmation says, "Was that life? One more time!" and concludes that "all joy wants itself, and therefore wants all misery too! Oh happiness, oh pain! Oh break, my heart!"[10] Calvin's account of Christian self-denial says, "The Lord so willed, therefore let us follow his will. Indeed, amid the very pricks of pain, amid groaning and tears, this thought must intervene: to incline our heart to bear cheerfully those things which have so moved it" (*Inst.* 3.8.11). In spite of so many intervening and important differences between these two pieces of writing and their authors, there is something resonant in the posture shared by Nietzsche's life-affirming asceticism and Calvin's worldly asceticism – a posture that perhaps ties atheistic uses of signs to theistic uses in a profound way. What is common, here, is not just a way of using signs to cultivate the responsibility of the self to the world. That is a posture that goes back centuries, even millennia. What they also share is the insistence that the world – not the church, not the state, not conventional norms – offers the proper domain of signification and the proper site of the emergence of glory.

Perhaps it is also not surprising that this current also flows onto the page through the body of a refugee – through someone who knew something of what it meant to be pushed to the inglorious margins of the imagined social body and to write from that position. If Calvin's hypostases continue to haunt the modern world, perhaps it is time they

---

[10] Nietzsche, *Zarathustra*, 263.

were joined by another, less familiar: one for whom the Word of God was directed to an existence that exceeds and slips beyond the artifice of human institutions, even as artifice is nevertheless crucial for enabling the care of that very existence. Despite being one of the more famous advocates of a sovereign God, Calvin also offers a radical critique of sovereignty as an organizing mechanism for worldly life. The divine secures no progressive arc to human history. The divine engages in no time-disrupting incarnation of the sovereign on earth. The divine refers itself to creation as the site of the real, as that against which institutions are to be judged and always held wanting. Sovereign power supports that creation, and human beings participate in that support by perpetual exercises of reading and writing that are also seeking and learning. Here, it is possible to glimpse a mode of divine sovereignty that meets the earth as perpetual responsibility – one that cannot help but be open to new modes of recognition if it remains attentive not just to the power of the sign, but also the material bodies that bear and exceed signification. These bodies elicit the perpetual need to resignify the world – and to rename and recognize anew what *we* can be, in, with, and through it.

Bibliography

Adams, Edward. "Calvin's View of Natural Knowledge of God." *International Journal of Systematic Theology* 3 (3) (2001): 280–292.

Adams, Marilyn McCord. "Ockham's Nominalism and Unreal Entities." *Philosophical Review* 86 (2) (1977): 144–176.

Agamben, Giorgio. *Homo Sacer: Sovereign Power and Bare Life*. Redwood City, CA: Stanford University Press, 1998.

  The Kingdom and the Glory: For a Theological Genealogy of Economy and Government. Redwood City, CA: Stanford University Press, 2011.

  The Signature of All Things. Brooklyn, NY: Zone Books, 2009.

  The Use of Bodies. Translated by Adam Kotsko. Stanford, CA: Stanford University Press, 2016.

Alighieri, Dante. *The Divine Comedy*. Oxford: Oxford University Press, 1998.

Anidjar, Gil. "Secularism." *Critical Inquiry* 33 (2006): 55–77.

Anselm. *Meditation 17*.

Anselm. *Monologion and Proslogion with the Replies of Gaunilo and Anselm*. Indianapolis, IN: Hackett Publishing, 1996.

  "On the Fall of the Devil." In *Three Philosophical Dialogues*. Translated by Thomas Williams. Indianapolis, IN: Hackett Publishing, 2002: 52–100.

  "On Freedom of Choice." In *Three Philosophical Dialogues*. Translated by Thomas Williams. Indianapolis, IN: Hackett Publishing, 2002.

  "On Truth." In *Three Philosophical Dialogues*. Translated by Thomas Williams. Indianapolis, IN: Hackett Publishing, 2002: 3–30.

Aristotle, *Economics*.

Armstrong, Brian G. "The Nature and Structure of Calvin's Theology: Another Look." In *John Calvin's "Institutes": His Opus Magnum*. Edited by B. van der Walt. Potchefstroom: Institute for Reformational Studies, 1986: 55–81.

Asad, Talal. *Formations of the Secular*. Stanford, CA: Stanford University Press, 2003.

Genealogies of Religion: Discipline and Reasons of Power in Christianity and Islam. Baltimore, MD: The Johns Hopkins University Press, 1993.

Auerbach, Erich. *Dante: Poet of the Secular World.* New York: New York Review of Books Classics, 2007.

Mimesis. Princeton, NJ: Princeton University Press, 2013.

Augé, Marc. *Oblivion.* Translated by Marjolijn de Jager. Minneapolis: University of Minnesota Press, 2004.

Augustine. *The Augustine Catechism: Enchiridion on Faith, Hope, and Charity.* Edited by Boniface Ramsey. Translated by Bruce Harbert. Hyde Park, NY: New City Press, 2009.

Confessione (Confessions).

De Civitate Dei (City of God).

De Correptione et Gratia (On Rebuke and Grace).

De Doctrina Christiana (On Christian Teaching).

De Libero Arbitrio (On the Free Choice of the Will).

De Trinitate (On the Trinity).

Epistulae (Letters).

"On Grace and Free Will." In *Basic Writings of Saint Augustine.* Grand Rapids, MI: Baker Book House, 1976.

Aune, David E. *The Westminster Dictionary of New Testament and Early Christian Literature and Rhetoric.* Louisville, KY: Westminster John Knox Press, 2003.

Austin, J. L. *How to Do Things with Words.* Oxford: Oxford University Press, 1962.

Bacon, Francis. *The New Atlantis and the Great Instauration.* Malden, MA: Wiley Blackwell, 2017.

Balibar, Etienne and Immanuel Wallerstein. *Race, Nation, Class: Ambiguous Identities.* London: Verso, 1991.

Balserak, Jon. *Divinity Compromised: A Study of Divine Accommodation in the Thought of John Calvin.* Dordrecht: Springer, 2006.

Barber, John R. *Modern European History.* New York: HarperCollins, 2006.

Barro, R. J. and R. M. McCleary. "Religion and Economic Growth across Countries." *American Sociological Review* 68 (2003): 760–781.

"Which Countries Have State Religions?" *The Quarterly Journal of Economics* 120 (4) (2005): 1331–1370.

Barth, Karl. *The Church Dogmatics.* Edinburgh: T&T Clark, 1956–1975.

The Epistle to the Romans. Oxford: Oxford University Press, 1968.

Fides Quaerens Intellectum. Pittsburgh, PA: Wipf and Stock Publishing, 1975.

The Theology of John Calvin. Grand Rapids, MI: Eerdmans Publishing Company, 1995.

Battenhouse, Roy W. "The Doctrine of Man in Calvin and in Renaissance Platonism." *Journal of the History of Ideas* 9 (4) (1948): 447–471.

Bayer, Osward and Benjamin Gleede, eds. *Creator est Creatura: Luthers Christologie als Lehre von der Idiomenkommunikation.* Berlin: Walter de Gruyter, 2007.

Beeke, Joel R. "Calvin on Sovereignty, Providence, and Predestination." *Puritan Reformed Journal* 2 (2) (2010): 79–107.

Bell, Catherine. *Ritual Theory Ritual Practice.* New York: Oxford University Press, 2009.

Benedetto, Robert, ed. *Interpreting John Calvin.* Grand Rapids, MI: Baker Books, 1996.

Berger, Peter. *The Desecularization of the World.* Grand Rapids, MI: Eerdmans, 1999.

Berkhof, Louis. *Systematic Theology.* Grand Rapids, MI: Eerdmans, 1932.

Berkouwer, G. C. *The Providence of God.* Grand Rapids, MI: Eerdmans, 1952.

Bhargava, Rajeev. *Secularism and Its Critics.* New York: Oxford University Press, 1998.

Biale, David. *Not in the Heavens: The Tradition of Jewish Secular Thought.* Princeton, NJ: Princeton University Press, 2011.

Billings, J. Todd. *Calvin, Participation, and the Gift.* New York: Oxford University Press, 2007.

"United to God through Christ: Assessing Calvin on the Question of Deification." *The Harvard Theological Review* 98 (3) (2005): 315–334.

Billings, J. Todd and I. John Hesselink, eds. *Calvin's Theology and Its Reception: Disputes, Developments, and New Possibilities.* Louisville, KY: Westminster John Knox, 2012.

Blacketer, Raymond A. *The School of God Pedagogy and Rhetoric in Calvin's Interpretation of Deuteronomy.* Dordrecht: Springer, 2006.

Blackwood, Stephen. *The Consolation of Boethius as Poetic Liturgy.* New York: Oxford University Press, 2015.

Blaisdell, Charmarie Jenkins. "Calvin's Letters to Women: The Courting of Ladies in High Places." *The Sixteenth Century Journal* 13 (3) (1982): 67–84.

Blanco, María del Pilar and Esther Peeren, eds. *The Spectralities Reader: Ghosts and Haunting in Contemporary Cultural Theory.* London: Bloomsbury, 2013.

Blumenberg, Hans. *The Legitimacy of the Modern Age.* Cambridge, MA: MIT Press, 1983.

Boer, Roland. *Political Grace: The Revolutionary Theology of John Calvin.* Louisville, KY: Westminster John Knox Press, 2009.

Boesak, Allan A. *Black and Reformed: Apartheid, Liberation, and the Calvinist Tradition.* Eugene, OR: Wipf and Stock, 1984.

Boethius, *Consolation of Philosophy.* Translated by W. V. Cooper. Midlothian, TX: Alacrity Press, 2013.

Bohatec, Josef. *Budé und Calvin: Studien zur Gedankenwelt des französischen Frühhumanismus.* 1950.

Calvin und das Recht. 1934.

ed. *Calvinstudien. Festschrift zum 400. Geburtsage Johann Calvins.* 1909.

Bonaventure. *Itinerarium Mentis in Deum, or The Soul's Journey into God.* Edited by Ewart Cousins. Mahwah, NJ: Paulist Press, 1978.

Bonhoeffer, Dietrich. "Christ, Reality, and Good." In *Ethics.* Edited by Clifford J. Green. Minneapolis, MN: Fortress Press, 2009: 47–75.

"History and Good [1]." In *Ethics.* Edited by Clifford J. Green. Minneapolis, MN: Fortress Press, 2009: 47–75.

"History and Good [2]." In *Ethics.* Edited by Clifford J. Green. Minneapolis, MN: Fortress Press, 2009: 246–298.

Bosco, David. "Conscience as Court and Worm: Calvin and the Three Elements of Conscience." *Journal of Religious Ethics* 14 (1986): 331–355

Boulton, Matthew Myer. *Life in God: John Calvin, Practical Formation, and the Future of Protestant Theology.* Grand Rapids, MI: Eerdmans, 2011.

Bouwsma, William J. *John Calvin: A Sixteenth Century Portrait.* New York: Oxford University Press, 1988.

Bowles, M. J. "The Practice of Meaning in Nietzsche and Wittgenstein." *Journal of Nietzsche Studies,* 26 (2003): 12–24.

Bowlman, Matthew. "Sin, Spirituality, and Primitivism: The Theologies of the American Social Gospel, 1885–1917." *Religion and American Culture: A Journal of Interpretation* 17 (1) (2007): 95–126.

Bowman, Glenn. "A Textual Landscape: The Mapping of a Holy Land in the Fourth-Century *Itinerarium* of the Bourdeaux Pilgrim." In *Unfolding the Orient: Travellers in Egypt and the Near East.* Edited by Paul and Janet Starkey. Reading: Ithaca Press, 2001.

Brady, Thomas A. and Elisabeth Müller-Luckner, eds. *Die deutsche Reformation zwischen Spätmittelalter und Früher Neuzeit.* Berlin: Oldenbourg, 2001.

Brady, Thomas A., Heiko A. Oberman, and James D. Tracy. *Handbook of European History, 1400–1600. Late Middle Ages, Renaissance, Reformation,* 2 vols. Grand Rapids, MI: Eerdmans, 1996.

Breckman, Warren. *The Adventures of the Symbolic: Post-Marxism and Radical Democracy.* New York: Columbia University Press, 2013.

Brown, Peter. *Augustine: A Biography,* 2nd edition. Berkeley: University of California Press, 2000.

Authority and the Sacred: Aspects of the Christianisation of the Roman World. Cambridge: Cambridge University Press, 1995.

Brown, Wendy. *Walled States, Waning Sovereignty.* Brooklyn, NY: Zone Books, 2010.

Brunt, P. A. *Studies in Stoicism.* Oxford: Oxford University Press, 2013.

Bunyan, John. *The Pilgrim's Progress.* Oxford: Oxford University Press, 2003.

Burger, Christoph. "Calvin and the Humanists." Translated by Judith J. Guder. In *The Calvin Handbook.* Edited by Herman J. Selderhuis. Grand Rapids, MI: Eerdmans, 2009: 137–142.

Burnett, Amy Nelson. *Karlstadt and the Origins of the Eucharistic Controversy.* Oxford: Oxford University Press, 2011.

Burnett, Richard. "John Calvin and the *Sensus Literalis.*" *Scottish Journal of Theology* 57 (1) (2004): 1–13.

Burton, Simon J. G. *The Hallowing of Logic.* Leiden: Brill, 2012.

Buse, Peter and Andrew Stott, eds. *Ghosts: Deconstruction, Psychoanalysis, History.* Basingstoke: Palgrave Macmillan, 1999.

Butler, Judith. *Bodies That Matter: On the Discursive Limits of "Sex."* New York: Routledge, 1993.

Giving an Account of Oneself. New York: Fordham University Press, 2005.

Calhoun, Craig, Mark Juergensmeyer, and Jonathan VanAntwerpen, eds. *Rethinking Secularism*. Oxford: Oxford University Press, 2011.

Calvin, John. *Calvin Commentaries*. Grand Rapids, MI: Baker Press, 2009.

　The Institutes of the Christian Religion. Edited by John T. McNeill. Translated by Battles. Louisville, KY: Westminster John Knox Press, 1960.

　Ionnis Calvini opera quae supersunt omni. Edited by Wilhelm Baum, Edward Cunitz, and Edward Reuss. Brunsvigae: Corpus reformatorum, 1863: 29–89.

　Writings on Pastoral Piety. Edited by Elsie Anne McKee. Mahwah, NJ: Paulist Press, 2001.

Calvin, John and Elijah Waterman. *The Catechism of the Church of Geneva*. Hartford, CT: Sheldon and Goodwin, 1815.

Cameron, Euan. *Enchanting Europe*. New York: Oxford University Press, 2010.

Camus, Albert. *The Plague*. New York: Vintage, 1999.

Candler, Peter. *Theology, Rhetoric, Manuduction, or Reading Scripture Together on the Path to God*. Grand Rapids, MI: Eerdmans, 2006.

Canlis, Julie. *Calvin's Ladder*. Grand Rapids, MI: Eerdmans, 2010.

Carpenter, Angela. "Sanctification as a Human Process: Reading Calvin Alongside Child Development Theory." *Journal of the Society of Christian Ethics* 35 (1) (2015): 103–119.

Carter, J. Kameron. "An Unlikely Convergence: W. E. B. Du Bois, Karl Barth, and the Problem of the Imperial God-Man." *The New Centennial Review* 11 (3) (2011): 167–224.

　"The Inglorious." *Political Theology* 14 (1) (2013): 77–87.

　"The Politics of the Atonement." *The Immanent Frame* (2011). Available at https://tif.ssrc.org/2011/07/18/the-politics-of-the-atonement/ (accessed 5/1/2018).

Casale, Jana. *The Girl Who Never Read Noam Chomsky*. New York: Knopf, 2018.

Castricano, Jodey. *Cryptomimesis: The Gothic and Jacques Derrida's Ghost Writing*. Montreal: McGill-Queen's University Press, 2001.

Cavanaugh, William T., Jeffrey W. Baily, and Craig Hovey, eds. *An Eerdmans Reader in Contemporary Political Theology*. Grand Rapids, MI: Eerdmans, 2012.

Chakrabarty, Dipesh. *Provincializing Europe: Postcolonial Thought and Historical Difference*. Princeton, NJ: Princeton University Press, 2000.

Chow, Rey. *The Protestant Ethnic and the Spirit of Capitalism*. New York: Columbia University Press, 2003.

Chupungco, Anscar J. *Handbook for Liturgical Studies: Liturgical Time and Space*. Collegeville, MN: The Liturgical Press, 2000.

Ciaffa, Jay A. *Max Weber and the Problems of Value-Free Social Science*. Cranbury, NJ: Associated University Presses, 1998.

Cicero. In *M. Tulli Ciceronis Rhetorica*, vol. 1. Edited by A. S. Wilkins. Oxford: Clarendon Press, 1902–1903.

　De natura Deorum.

　De officiis. Edited by Michael Winterbottom. Oxford: Clarendon Press, 1994.

Clark, Maudmarie. *Nietzsche on Truth and Philosophy*. Cambridge: Cambridge University Press, 1990.

Claxton, Guy. *Intelligence in the Flesh: Why Your Mind Needs Your Body Much More Than It Thinks.* New Haven, CT: Yale University Press, 2015.

Cleanthes. "Hymn to Zeus." In *Stoic Theology.* Edited by P. A. Meijer. Delft: Eburon, 2008: 209–228.

Coetzee, C. F. C. "The Doctrine of Providence in the Institutes of Calvin – Still Relevant?" In *John Calvin, 1509–2009: A South African Perspective.* Edited by C. J. Smit, W. A. Dreyer, and J. J. Gerber, supplement, *In die Skriflig* 44 (S3) (2010): S145–S166.

Cohen, H. *Floris. The Scientific Revolution: A Historiographical Inquiry.* Chicago: University of Chicago Press, 1994.

Cone, James. *God of the Oppressed.* Maryknoll, NY: Orbis, 1975.

Connerton, Paul. *How Societies Remember.* Cambridge: Cambridge University Press, 1999.

Cranach, Lucas the Elder. An Allegory of Melancholy, 1528. Oil on panel. National Gallery of Scotland.

　　Die Melancholie, 1532. Oil on panel. Musée d'Unterlinden, Colmar, France.

　　Melancholie, 1532. Oil on panel. Statens Museum for Kunst, Copenhagen, Denmark.

Curtis, David Ames, ed. *World in Fragments: Writings on Politics, Society, Psychoanalysis, and the Imagination.* Stanford, CA: Stanford University Press, 1997.

Cyprian, *On the Unity of the Catholic Church.*

Czapkay Sudduth, Michael L. "The Prospects for 'Mediate' Natural Theology in John Calvin." *Religious Studies* 31 (1) (1995): 53–68.

Dabrock, Peter. "Responding to *Wirklichkeit.*" In *Mysteries in the Theology of Dietrich Bonhoeffer: A Copenhagen Bonhoeffer Symposium.* Edited by Kirsten Busch Nielsen, Ulrik Nissen, and Christiane Tietz. Göttingen: Vandenhoeck & Ruprecht, 2007: 49–80.

Daggers, Jenny. "Thinking 'Religion': The Christian Past and Interreligious Future of Religious Studies and Theology." *Journal of the American Academy of Religion* 78 (4) (2010): 961–990.

Davis, Kathleen. *Periodization and Sovereignty.* Philadelphia: University of Pennsylvania Press, 2008.

　　"The Sense of an Epoch: Periodization, Sovereignty, and the Limits of Secularization." In *The Legitimacy of the Middle Ages: On the Unwritten History of Theory.* Durham, NC: Duke University Press, 2010: 77–102.

Davis, Thomas J. *John Calvin's American Legacy.* New York: Oxford University Press, 2010.

　　This Is My Body: The Presence of Christ in Reformation Thought. Grand Rapids, MI: Baker Academic, 2008.

De Certeau, Michel. *The Practice of Everyday Life.* Translated by Stephen Rendall. Berkeley: University of California Press, 1984.

　　The Writing of History. Translated by Tom Conley. New York: Columbia University Press, 1988.

De Man, Paul. "Literary History and Literary Modernity." *Daedelus* 99 (2) (1970): 384–404.

Derrida, Jacques. "*Before the Law*." Translated by Avital Ronell. In *Acts of Literature*. Edited by Derek Attridge. New York: Routledge, 1991: 181–220.

"Différance." In *Margins of Philosophy*. Translated by Alan Bass. Chicago: University of Chicago Press, 1985.

The Gift of Death. Translated by David Wills. Chicago: University of Chicago Press, 2007.

Given Time: Counterfeit Money. Translated by Peggy Kamuf. Chicago: University of Chicago Press, 1992.

Of Grammatology. Translated by Gyatri Chakravorty Spivak. Baltimore, MD: Johns Hopkins University Press, 1997.

"How to Avoid Speaking: Denials." Translated by Ken Frieden. In *Languages of the Unsayable*. Edited by Sanford Budick and Wolfgang Iser. New York: Columbia University Press, 1989: 3–70.

On the Name. Edited by Thomas Dutoit. Stanford, CA: Stanford University Press, 1995.

"Plato's Pharmacy." In *Dissemination*. Translated by Barbara Johnson. London: The Athlone Press, 1981: 61–172.

"Signature Event Context." In *Margins of Philosophy*. Chicago: University of Chicago Press, 1985.

Derrida, Jacques. *Specters of Marx*. Translated by Peggy Kamuf. New York: Routledge, 1994.

Writing and Difference. Translated by Alan Bass. London: Routledge, 1978.

Del Caro, Adrian. *Grounding the Nietzsche Rhetoric of Earth*. Berlin: Walter de Gruyter, 2004.

Dewey, John. *A Common Faith*. New Haven, CT: Yale University Press, 1934.

The Quest for Certainty: A Study of the Relation of Knowledge and Action. New York: Minton Blach and Co., 1929.

De Vries, Hent and Lawrence E. Sullivan, eds. *Political Theologies: Public Religions in a Post-Secular World*. New York: Fordham University Press, 2006.

De Vries, Hent and Samuel Weber, eds. *Religion and Media*. Redwood City, CA: Stanford University Press, 2001.

Dixon, C. Scott. *Contesting the Reformation*. Oxford: Wiley-Blackwell, 2012.

Donato, Antonio. *Boethius' Consolation of Philosophy as a Product of Late Antiquity*. London: Bloomsbury Academic, 2013.

Doob, Penelope Reed. *The Idea of the Labyrinth from Classical Antiquity through the Middle Ages*. Ithaca, NY: Cornell University Press, 1990.

Dostoevsky, Fyodor. *The Brothers Karamazov*. Translated by Peaver and Volokhonsky. New York: Farrar, Straus, Giroux, 2002.

Dowey, Edward A., Jr. "Law in Luther and Calvin." *Theology Today* 41 (2) (1984): 146–153.

The Knowledge of God in Calvin's Theology. New York: Columbia University Press, 1952.

"The Structure of Calvin's Theological Thought as Influenced by the Two-Fold Knowledge of God." In *Calvinus Ecclesiae Genevensis Custos: Die Referate des Internationalen Kongressesfur Calvinforschung*. Edited by W. H. Neuser. Frankfurt am Main: Peter Lang, 1984: 135–48.

Dupré, Louis. *Passage to Modernity: An Essay in the Hermeneutics of Nature and Culture.* New Haven, CT: Yale University Press, 1995.

Dürer, Albrecht. Melancholia I, 1514. Copperplate. Frankfurt: Städelsches Kunstinstitut und Städtische Galerie.

Durkheim, Émile. *The Elementary Forms of the Religious Life.* Translated by Carol Cosman. Oxford: Oxford University Press, 2001.

Edwards, Jonathan. *A Dissertation concerning the End for Which God Created the World,* 1765.

Elrod, John W. "The Self in Kierkegaard's Pseudonyms." *International Journal for Philosophy of Religion* 4 (4) (1973): 218–240.

Elwood, Christopher. *The Body Broken: The Calvinist Doctrine of the Eucharist and the Symbolization of Power in France, 1530–1570.* New York: Oxford University Press, 1999.

Engel, Mary Potter. *John Calvin's Perspectival Anthropology.* Atlanta, GA: Scholars Press, 1988.

Epictetus. *Discourses and Other Writings.* London: Penguin Books, 2008.

Erasmus. "Enchiridion." In *Collected Works of Erasmus: Spiritualia.* Toronto: University of Toronto Press, 1988.

Evans, G. R. "Calvin on Signs: An Augustinian Dilemma." *Renaissance Studies* 3 (1989): 35–45.

Etzrodt, Christian. "Weber's Protestant-Ethic Thesis, the Critics, and Adam Smith." *Max Weber Studies* 8 (1) (2008): 49–78.

Farrell, John. *Paranoia and Modernity: Cervantes to Rousseau.* Ithaca, NY: Cornell University Press, 2006.

Febvre, Lucien. *The Problem of Unbelief in the 16th Century.* Cambridge, MA: Harvard University Press, 1985.

Fedler, Kyle. "Calvin's Burning Heart: Calvin and the Stoics on the Emotions." *Journal of the Society of Christian Ethics* 22 (2002): 133–162.

Ferretter, Luke. "The Trace and the Trinity: Christ and Difference in Augustine's Theory of Language." *Literature & Theology* 12 (3) (1998): 256–267.

Fesko, John. *Beyond Calvin: Union with Christ and Justification in Early Modern Reformed Theology (1517–1700).* Gottingen: Vandenhoeck & Ruprecht, 2012.

Fine, Gail. *The Possibility of Inquiry: Meno's Paradox from Socrates to Sextus.* Oxford: Oxford University Press, 2014.

Fiskesjö, Magnus. "Critical Reflections on Agamben's *Homo Sacer.*" *Journal of Ethnographic Theory* 2 (1) (2012): 161–180.

Fiorenza, Francis Schüssler. "Political Theology and the Critique of Modernity." *Distinktion: Scandinavian Journal of Social Theory* 6 (2005): 87–105.

Foucault, Michel. *Abnormal.* London: Verso, 2003.

Archeology of Knowledge. Abingdon: Routledge, 2002.

"About the Beginning of the Hermeneutics of the Self." In *Religion and Culture.* Edited by Jeremy Carrette. New York: Routledge, 1999: 158–181.

Discipline and Punish. New York: Vintage Books, 1995.

The Hermeneutics of the Subject: Lectures at the Collège de France, 1981–1982. Translated by Graham Burchell. New York: Picador, 2001.

History of Sexuality 1: The Will to Knowledge. New York: Vintage, 1978,

History of Sexuality 2: The Use of Pleasure. New York: Vintage, 1985.
"Nietzsche, Genealogy, History." In *Language, Counter-Memory, Practice: Selected Essays and Interviews by Michel Foucault.* Edited by Donald F. Bouchard. Ithaca, NY: Cornell University Press, 1977: 139–164.
Power/Knowledge: Selected Interviews and Other Writings 1972–1977. Edited by Colin Gordon. Translated by Colin Gordon, Leo Marshall, John Mepham, and Kate Soper. New York: Pantheon Books, 1980.
"The Subject and Power." *Critical Inquiry* 8 (4) (1982): 777–795.
"Technologies of the Self." In *Technologies of the Self: A Seminar with Michel Foucault.* Edited by Luther H. Martin, Huck Gutman, and Patrich H. Hutton. Amherst: The University of Massachusetts Press, 1988: 16–49
Frantz, Nadine Pence. "Material Culture, Understanding, and Meaning: Writing and Picturing." *Journal of the American Academy of Religion* 66 (4) (1998): 791–816.
Frei, Hans. *Eclipse of Biblical Narrative: A Study in Eighteenth and Nineteenth Century Hermeneutics.* New Haven, CT: Yale University Press, 1974.
Types of Christian Theology. New Haven, CT: Yale University Press, 1992.
Freud, Sigmund. "Mourning and Melancholia." In *The Standard Edition of the Complete Psychological Works of Sigmund Freud, Volume XIV (1914–1916): On the History of the Psycho-Analytic Movement, Papers on Metapsychology and Other Works.* London: Hogarth Press and the Institute of Psychoanalysis, 1968: 237–258.
Funkenstein, Amos. *Theology and the Scientific Imagination from the Middle Ages to the Seventeenth Century.* Princeton, NJ: Princeton University Press, 1986.
Furey, Constance M. "Body, Society, and Subjectivity in Religious Studies." *Journal of the American Academy of Religion* 80 (1) (2012): 7–33.
Erasmus, Contarini, and the Religious Republic of Letters. New York: Cambridge University Press, 2006.
Garrison, James D. *Pietas from Vergil to Dryden.* University Park: The Pennsylvania State University Press, 1992.
Gauchet, Marcel. *The Disenchantment of the World: A Political History of Religion.* Princeton, NJ: Princeton University Press, 2007.
Le Débat 50 (1988).
Geréby, György. "Political Theology versus Theological Politics: Erik Peterson and Carl Schmitt." *New German Critique* 105 (2008): 7–33.
Gerhart, Mary. "Generic Studies: Their Renewed Importance in Religious and Literary Interpretation." *Journal of the American Academy of Religion* 55 (3) (1977): 309–325.
Gerrish, B. A. *Grace and Gratitude: The Eucharistic Theology of John Calvin.* Minneapolis, MN: Fortress Press, 1973.
"'To the Unknown God': Luther and Calvin on the Hiddenness of God." *The Journal of Religion* 53 (3) (1973): 263–292.
Gibson, David. *Reading the Decree: Exegesis, Election, and Christology in Calvin and Barth.* New York: T&T Clark, 2009.
Giddens, Anthony. *Sociology.* Malden, MA: Polity Press, 2006.

The Theological Origins of Modernity. Chicago: University of Chicago Press, 2008.

Gleeson-White, Jane. *Double Entry: How the Merchants of Venice Created Modern Finance.* New York: W. W. Norton and Company, 2012.

Goodloe, James. "The Body in Calvin's Theology." In *Calvin Studies V.* Edited by John H. Leith. Davidson, NC: Davidson College, 1990: 103–117.

Gordon, Bruce. *Calvin.* New Haven, CT: Yale University Press, 2009.

John Calvin's Institutes of the Christian Religion: A Biography. Princeton, NJ: Princeton University Press, 2016.

Gordon, Peter. "The Place of the Sacred in the Absence of God." *Journal of the History of Ideas* 69 (4) (2008): 647–673.

Gorski, Philip S. "Calvinism and State-Formation in Early Modern Europe." In *State/Culture: State-Formation after the Cultural Turn*, ed. George Steinmetz. Ithaca, NY: Cornell University Press, 1999.

The Disciplinary Revolution: Calvinism and the Rise of the State in Early Modern Europe. Chicago: University of Chicago Press, 2003.

Gorski, Philip S. and Ateş Altınordu. "After Secularization?" *Annual Review of Sociology* 34 (2008): 55–85.

Grabill, Stephen J. *Rediscovering the Natural Law in Reformed Theological Ethics.* Grand Rapids, MI: Eerdmans, 2006.

Grant, Edward. "Cosmology." In *Science in the Middle Ages.* Edited by David C. Lindberg. Chicago: University of Chicago Press, 1978: 275–279.

Grayston, Kenneth. *The Johannine Epistles.* Grand Rapids, MI: Eerdmans, 1984.

Gregory, Brad S. *The Unintended Reformation.* Cambridge: Harvard University Press, 2012.

Griffin, Paul R. "Protestantism and Racism." In *The Blackwell Companion to Protestantism.* Edited by Alister E. McGrath and Darren C. Marks. Malden, MA: Blackwell, 2004: 357–372.

Gronewoller, Brian. "God the Author: Augustine's Early Incorporation of the Rhetorical Concept of Oeconomia into His Scriptural Hermeneutic." *Augustinian Studies* 47 (1) (2016): 65–77.

Guthrie, Shirley C. "Human Suffering, Human Liberation, and the Sovereignty of God." *Theology Today* 53 (1) (1996): 23–34.

Habermas, Jürgen. "What Is Meant by a 'Post-Secular Society?' A Discussion on Islam in Europe." In *Europe: The Faltering Project.* Malden, MA: Polity Press, 2009.

Hadot, Pierre. *Philosophy as a Way of Life.* Malden, MA: Wiley-Blackwell, 1995.

Hall, David M. *A Reforming People: Puritanism and the Transformation of Public Life in New England.* New York: Alfred A. Knopf, 2011.

Hammill, Graham. "Blumenberg and Schmitt on the Rhetoric of Political Theology." In *Political Theology and Early Modernity.* Edited by Graham Hammill and Julia Reinhard Lupton. Chicago: Chicago University Press, 2012: 84–101.

Hankins, Barry. *Francis Schaeffer and the Shaping of Evangelical America.* Grand Rapids, MI: Eerdmans, 2008.

Hartvelt, G. P. *Verum corpus: een studie over een centraal hoofdstuk uit de avondmaalsleer van Calvijn.* Delft: Meinema, 1960.

Headley, John M., Hans J. Hillerbrand, and Anthony J. Papalas, eds. *Confessionalization in Europe, 1555–1700: Essays in Honor of Bodo Nischan.* Burlington, VT: Ashgate Publishing, 2004.

Hegel, G. W. F. *Lectures on the Philosophy of Religion: The Lectures of 1827.* Edited by Peter C. Hodgson. Oxford: Oxford University Press, 2006.

Heim, S. Mark. *Saved from Sacrifice: A Theology of the Cross.* Grand Rapids, MI: Eerdman's, 2006.

Helm, Paul. "John Calvin, the *sensus divinitatis*, and the noetic effects of sin." *International Journal for Philosophy of Religion* 43 (1998): 87–107.

John Calvin's Ideas. New York: Oxford University Press, 2004.

Helseth, Paul Kjoss. "God Causes All Things." In *Four Views on Divine Providence.* Edited by Dennis W. Jowers. Grand Rapids, MI: Zondervan, 2011: 25–52.

Henry, John. *The Scientific Revolution and the Origins of Modern Science.* New York: Palgrave Macmillan, 2008.

Hillerbrand, Hans J., ed. *The Protestant Reformation.* New York: Perennial, 2009.

Hobbes, Thomas. *Leviathan.* New York: Oxford University Press, 1998.

Hochschild, Paige E. *Memory in Augustine's Theological Anthropology.* Oxford: Oxford University Press, 2012.

Hodge, Charles. *Systematic Theology.* London: Thomas Nelson and Sons, 1872.

Holder, R. Ward. *Calvin and the Grounding of Interpretation.* Leiden: Brill, 2006.

Hollywood, Amy. *Acute Melancholia and Other Essays: Mysticism, History, and the Study of Religion.* New York: Columbia University Press, 2016.

"Performativity, Citationality, Ritualization." *History of Religions* 42 (2) (2002): 93–115.

Sensible Ecstasy. Chicago: University of Chicago Press, 2006.

Howell, Kenneth J. *God's Two Books: Copernican Cosmology and Biblical Interpretation in Early Modern Science.* Notre Dame, IN: University of Notre Dame Press, 2002.

Hsia, R. Po-Chia and Henk Van Nierop, eds. *Calvinism and Religious Toleration in the Dutch Golden Age.* Cambridge: Cambridge University Press, 2010.

Huff, Toby E. *Intellectual Curiosity and the Scientific Revolution: A Global Perspective.* New York: Cambridge University Press, 2011.

Hughley, Michael. "The Idea of Secularization in the Works of Max Weber: A Theoretical Outline." *Qualitative Sociology* 2 (1) (1979): 85–111.

Huijgen, Arnold. *Divine Accommodation in John Calvin's Theology: Analysis and Assessment.* Göttingen: Vandenhoeck & Ruprecht, 2011.

Hutson, Lorna. "Imagining Justice: Kantorowicz and Shakespeare." *Representations* 106 (2009): 118–142.

Ifergan, Pini. "Cutting to the Chase: Carl Schmitt and Hans Blumenberg on Political Theology and Secularization." *New German Critique* 37 (3) (2010): 149–171.

Jackson, B. Darrell. "The Theory if Signs in St. Augustine's *De doctrina christiana.*" *Revue des études augustiniennes* 15 (1969): 9–49.

Jackson-McCabe, Matt. "The Stoic Theory of Implanted Preconceptions." *Phronesis* 49 (4) (2004): 323–347.

Jeffreys, Derek S. "How Reformed Is Reformed Epistemology? Alvin Plantinga and Calvin's 'Sensus Divinitatis.'" *Religious Studies* 33 (4) (1997): 419–431.

"'It's a Miracle of God That There Is Any Common Weal among Us': Unfaithfulness and Disorder in John Calvin's Political Thought." *The Review of Politics* 62 (1) (2000): 107–129.

Jennings, Willie James. *The Christian Imagination*. New Haven, CT: Yale University Press, 2016.

Johnson, Henry M. *Sociology: A Systematic Introduction*. New York: Routledge, 1963.

Johnson, Scott Fitzgerald. "Travel, Cartography, and Cosmology." In *Oxford Handbook of Late Antiquity*. Edited by Scott Fitzgerald Johnson. Oxford: Oxford University Press, 2012: 562–594.

Jonas, Hans. *The Gnostic Religion*. Boston: Beacon Press, 2001.

"Gnosticism and Modern Nihilism." *Social Research* 19 (4) (1952): 430–452.

Jones, Serene. *Calvin and the Rhetoric of Piety*. Louisville, KY: John Knox Press, 1995.

Jones, Serene and Amy Plantinga Pauw, eds. *Feminist and Womanist Essays in Reformed Dogmatics*. Louisville, KY: Westminster John Knox, 2006.

Jordan, Mark D. "Aquinas the *Aesthetics* of Incarnation." In *Image and Incarnation: The Early Modern Doctrine of the Pictorial Image*. Edited Walter S. Melion and Lee Palmer Wandel. Leiden: Brill, 2015: 161–172.

"Cicero, Ambrose, and Aquinas 'On Duties' or the Limits of Genre in Morals." *The Journal of Religious Ethics* 33 (3) (2005): 485–502.

Convulsing Bodies. Stanford, CA: Stanford University Press, 2014.

"Missing Scenes: Forgotten Forms of Teaching Need to Be Restored to Christian Ethics." *Harvard Divinity Bulletin* 38 (3 and 4) (2010).

Rewritten Theology: Aquinas After His Readers. Oxford: Wiley-Blackwell, 2005.

"The Word, His Body." In *Seducing Augustine: Bodies, Desires, Confessions*. New York: Fordham University Press, 2010.

"Words and Word: Incarnation and Signification in Augustine's *De Doctrina Christiana*." *Augustinian Studies* 11 (1980): 177–196.

Jorink, Eric. *Reading the Book of Nature in the Dutch Golden Age, 1575–1715*. Leiden: Brill, 2010.

Kahn, Paul W. *Political Theology: Four New Chapters on the Concept of Sovereignty*. New York: Columbia University Press, 2011.

Kahn, Victoria. *The Future of Illusion: Political Theology and Early Modern Texts*. Chicago: University of Chicago Press, 2013.

"Political Theology and Fiction in *The King's Two Bodies*." *Representations* 106 (1) (2009): 77–101.

Kaiser, Christopher. "Calvin's Understanding of Aristotelian Natural Philosophy: Its Extent and Possible Origins." In *Calviniana: Ideas and Influence of Jean Calvin*, ed. Robert V. Schnucker. Kirksville, MO: Sixteenth Century Journal Publishers, 1988: 77–92.

Kant, Immanuel. *Critique of Pure Reason*. Cambridge: Cambridge University Press, 1998.
　Religion within the Boundaries of Reason Alone. Cambridge: Cambridge University Press, 1998.
Kantorowicz, Ernst H. *The King's Two Bodies: A Study in Medieval Political Theology*. Princeton, NJ: Princeton University Press, 1985.
　"The Sovereignty of the Artist: A Note on Legal Maxims and Renaissance Theories of Art." In *De Artibus Opuscula XL: Essays in Honor of Erwin Panofsky*. Edited by Millard Meiss. New York: New York University Press, 1961: 267–279.
Kennedy, George A. *Classical Rhetoric and Its Christian and Secular Tradition: From Ancient to Modern Times*, 2nd edition Chapel Hill: University of North Carolina Press, 1999.
King, Karen. *What Is Gnosticism?* Cambridge, MA: Harvard University Press, 2003.
Kingdon, Robert M. *Adultery and Divorce in Calvin's Geneva*. Cambridge: Harvard University Press, 1995.
　"International Calvinism." In *The Handbook of European History, Volume 2: Visions, Outcomes, Programs*. Edited by Thomas A. Brady, Heiko A. Oberman, and James D. Tracy. Leiden: E. J. Brill, 1995: 158–172.
　"Social Welfare in Calvin's Geneva." *The American Historical Review* 76 (1) (1971): 50–69.
　ed. *Registers of the Consistory of Geneva in the Time of Calvin, Volume 1*. Grand Rapids, MI:William B. Eerdmans Publishing company, 1996: 1542–1544.
Kristeller, Paul Oskar, Thomas A. Brady, and Heiko Augustinus Oberman. *Itinerarium Italicum: The Profile of the Italian Renaissance in the Mirror of Its European Transformations: Studies in Medieval and Reformation Thought, No 14*. Leiden: Brill Academic Publishers, 1975.
Laclau, Ernesto and Chantal Mouffe. *Hegemony and Socialist Strategy: Towards a Radical Democratic Politics*. New York: Verso, 1985.
　"Post-Marxism without Apologies." In *New Reflections on the Revolutions of Our Time*. Edited by Ernesto Laclau. London: Verso, 1990: 97–132.
Ladner, Gerhart B. "Medieval and Modern Understanding of Symbolism: A Comparison." *Speculum* 54 (2) (1979): 223–256.
Langston, Douglas C. "Did Scotus Embrace Anselm's Notion of Freedom?" *Medieval Philosophy and Theology* 5 (1996): 145–159.
Laube, Stefan, "Calvin in Germany: A Marginalized Memory." In *Sober, Strict and Scriptural: Collective Memories of John Calvin: 1800–2000*. Edited Johan de Neit, Herman Paul, and Bart Wallet. Leiden: Brill, 2009.
Lazier, Benjamin. "Overcoming Gnosticism: Hans Jonas, Hans Blumenberg, and the Legitimacy of the Natural World." *Journal of the History of Ideas* 64 (4) (2003): 619–637.
Lefort, Claude. "The Permanence of the Theologico-Political?" In *Democracy and Political Theory*. Translated by David Macey. Cambridge: Cambridge University Press, 1988: 213–255.
Leibniz, Gottfried. *Theodicy*. New York: Cosimo Books, 2009.

Little, David. "Religion and Human Rights: A Personal Testament." *Journal of Law and Religion* 18 (1) (2002–2003): 57–77.

Little, Katherine, "Protestantism and the Piers Plowman Tradition." *Journal of Medieval and Early Modern Studies* 43 (3) (2010): 497–526.

Lloyd, Genevieve. *Providence Lost*. Cambridge, MA: Harvard University Press, 2008.

Locher, Gottfried Wilhelm. *Sign of the Advent: A Study in Protestant Ecclesiology*. Fribourg: Academic Press Fribourg.

Loevlie, Elisabeth M. "Faith in the Ghosts of Literature: Poetic Hauntology in Derrida, Blanchot and Morrison's *Beloved*." *Religions* 4 (2013): 336–350.

Lofton, Kathryn. *Oprah: The Gospel of an Icon*. Berkeley: University of California Press, 2011.

Lootens, Matthew R. "Augustine." In *The Spiritual Senses: Perceiving God in Western Christianity*. Edited Paul L. Gavrilyuk and Sarah Coakley. Cambridge: Cambridge University Press, 2011.

Löwith, Karl. *Meaning in History*. Chicago: University of Chicago Press, 1949.

"Nietzsche's Doctrine of Eternal Recurrence." *Journal of the History of Ideas* 6 (1/4) (1945): 273-f.

Nietzsche's Philosophy of the Eternal Recurrence of the Same. Translated by J. Harvey Lomax. Berkeley: University of California Press, 1997.

Lupton, Julia Reinhard. *Citizen-Saints: Shakespeare and Political Theology*. Chicago: University of Chicago Press, 2005.

Luther, Martin. "The Babylonian Captivity of the Church." In *Luther's Works Volume 36: Word and Sacrament II*. Edited by Helmut T. Lehmann and Abdel Ross Wentz. Translated by Frederick C. Ahrens. Minneapolis, MN: Fortress Press, 1959: 3–126.

Formula of Concord.

Heidelberg Disputations.

"On the Bondage of the Will." In *Luther and Erasmus: Free Will and Salvation*. Edited and translated by Rupp et al. Louisville, KY: Westminster John Knox, 1969: 101–334.

MacCulloch, Diarmaid. "A House Divided (1517–1660)." In *Christianity: The First Three Thousand Years*. New York: Viking, 2009: 604–654.

Mackey, Louis. *Peregrinations of the Word*. Ann Arbor: University of Michigan Press, 1997.

MacKinnon, Malcolm H. "Part I: Calvinism and the Infallible Assurance of Grace: The Weber Thesis Reconsidered." *The British Journal of Sociology* 39 (2) (1988): 143–177

Mahmood, Saba. "Secularism, Hermeneutics, and Empire: The Politics of Islamic Reformation." *Public Culture* 18 (2) (2006): 323–347.

Marcus Aurelius. *Meditations*.

Massey, Alana. "The White Protestant Roots of American Racism." In *The New Republic* (May 26, 2015). Available at https://newrepublic.com/article/121901/white-protestant-roots-american-racism (accessed 5/3/2018).

Masuzawa, Tomoko. *The Invention of World Religions, Or, How European Universalism Was Preserved in the Language of Pluralism*. Chicago: Chicago University Press, 2005.

Mason, Pamela A. "The Communion of Citizens: Calvinist Themes in Rousseau's Theory of the State." *Polity* 26 (1) (1993): 25–49.

Mauss, Marcel. *On Prayer: Text and Commentary*. Oxford: Berghahn Books: 2003.

McCormick, John P. "Transcending Weber's Categories of Modernity? The Early Lukács and Schmitt on the Rationalization Thesis." *New German Critique* 75 (1998): 133–177.

McCurry, Jeffrey. "Towards a Poetics of Theological Creativity: Rowan Williams Reads Augustine's *De Doctrina* After Derrida." *Modern Theology* 23 (3) (2007): 415–433.

McCutcheon, Russell. "Words, Words, Words." *Journal of the American Academy of Religion* 75 (4) (2007): 952–987.

McGrath, Alister E. "The Shaping of Reality: Calvin and the Formation of Theological Vision." *Toronto Journal of Theology* 25 (2) (2009): 187–204.

McKenzie, D. F. *Bibliography and the Sociology of Texts*. Cambridge: Cambridge University Press, 1999.

McLaren, Brian. *A New Kind of Christian*. San Francisco, CA: Jossey-Bass, 2001. *The Story We Find Ourselves In*. San Francisco, CA: Jossey-Bass, 2003.

McLoughlin, Daniel. "On Political and Economic Theology." *Angelaki* 20 (4) (2015): 53–69.

McMahon, Robert. *Understanding the Medieval Meditation Ascent: Augustine, Anselm, Boethius & Dante*. Washington, DC: Catholic University of America Press, 2006.

McNeill, John T. *The History and Character of Calvinism*. Oxford: Oxford University Press, 1954.

Meeks, Douglas. *God the Economist: The Doctrine of God and Political Economy*. Minneapolis, MN: Fortress Press, 1989.

Melanchthon, Philipp. *Loci Communes*.

Melion, Walter S. Melion and Lee Palmer Wandel, eds. *Image and Incarnation: The Early Modern Doctrine of the Pictorial Image*. Leiden: Brill, 2015.

Merleau-Ponty, Maurice. *L'Institution dans l'histoire personnelle et publique: Le problème de la passivité. Le sommeil, l'inconscient, la mémoire. Notes de cours au Collège de France (1954–1955)*. Paris: Belin, 2003.

Meyer, Thomas F., ed. *Reforming Reformation*. London: Ashgate, 2012.

Milbank, John and Slavoj Zizek. *The Monstrosity of Christ*. Cambridge, MA: MIT Press, 2011.

Miles, Margaret. "Theology, Anthropology, and the Human Body in Calvin's *Institutes of the Christian Religion*." *The Harvard Theological Review* 74 (3) (1981): 303–323.

Millet, Olivier. *Calvin et la dynamique de la parole: Etude de rhétorique réformée*. Paris: Librairie Honoré Champion, 1992.

Montag, Warren. "Spirits Armed and Unarmed: Derrida's *Specters of Marx*." In *Ghostly Demarcations: A Symposium on Jacques Derrida's Specters of Marx*. Edited by Michael Sprinker. New York: Verso, 1999: 68–82.

Monter, E. William. "Women in Calvinist Geneva (1550–1800)." *Signs* 6 (2) (1980): 189–209.

Morton, Bethany. *To Serve God and Wal-Mart: The Making of Christian Free Enterprise.* Cambridge, MA: Harvard University Press, 2010.

Moyn, Samuel. "Amos Funkenstein on the Theological Origins of Historicism." *Journal of the History of Ideas* **64** (4) (2003): 639–657.

Muller, Richard A. *Calvin and the Reformed Tradition: On the Work of Christ and the Order of Salvation.* Grand Rapids, MI: Baker Academic, 2012.

"Calvin on Sacramental Presence, in the Shadow of Marburg and Zurich." *Lutheran Quarterly* **23** (2009): 147–67.

"Calvin's 'Argument du livre' (1541): An Erratum to the McNeill and Battles Institutes." *The Sixteenth Century Journal* **29** (1) (1998): 35–38.

"'Duplex cognitio dei' in the Theology of Early Reformed Orthodoxy." *The Sixteenth Century Journal* 10 (2) (1979): 51–62.

The Unaccommodated Calvin: Studies in the Foundation of a Theological Tradition. New York: Oxford University Press, 2001.

Murray, John. *Redemption Accomplished and Applied.* Grand Rapids, MI: Eerdmans, 1955.

Naphy, William G. *Calvin and the Consolidation of the Genevan Reformation.* Louisville, KY: Westminster John Knox Press, 2003.

"Calvin's Geneva." In *The Cambridge Companion to John Calvin.* Edited by Donald K. McKim. Cambridge: Cambridge University Press, 2004: 25–37.

"Geneva II." In *The Calvin Handbook.* Edited by Herman J. Selderhuis. Translated by Henry J. Baron, Judith J. Guder, Randi H. Lundell, and Gerrit W. Sheeres. Grand Rapids, MI: Eerdmans, 2009: 44–56.

Nevin, John W. *The Mystical Presence: A Vindication of the Reformed or Calvinistic Doctrine of the Holy Eucharist.* Philadelphia: S. R. Fisher & Co., 1867.

Niebuhr, Richard R. *Experiential Religion.* New York: Harper and Row Publishers, 1972.

Nietzsche, Friedrich. *On the Genealogy of Morals.* Cambridge: Cambridge University Press, 2006.

The Use and Abuse of History. New York: Cosimo Books, 2010.

Thus Spoke Zarathustra. Cambridge: Cambridge University Press, 2006.

Noll, Mark. *The Civil War as a Theological Crisis.* Chapel Hill: University of North Carolina Press, 2006.

The Scandal of the Evangelical Mind. Grand Rapids, MI: Eerdmans, 1994.

Oberman, Heiko A. *The Dawn of the Reformation.* Grand Rapids, MI: Eerdmans, 1992.

"Fourteenth-Century Religious Thought: A Premature Profile." *Speculum* **53** (1) (1978): 80–93.

The Harvest of Medieval Theology: Gabriel Biel and Late Medieval Nominalism. Grand Rapids, MI: Baker Academic, 2001.

"Europa Afflica." In *John Calvin and the Reformation of the Refugees.* Geneva: Librairie Droz S. A., 2009.

Luther: Man between God and the Devil. New Haven, CT: Yale University Press, 1989.

"The Pursuit of Happiness: John Calvin between Humanism and Reformation." In *Humanity and Divinity in Renaissance and Reformation: Essays in Honor of Charles Trinkaus.* Edited by John W. O'Malley. Leiden: Brill, 1993: 251–83.

Olmsted, Wendy Raudenbush. "Philosophical Inquiry and Religious Transformation in Boethius's 'The Consolation of Philosophy' and Augustine's 'Confessions.'" *The Journal of Religion* 69 (1) (1989): 14–35.

O'Malley, John W. "Introduction." In *Collected Works of Erasmus: Spiritualia.* Toronto: University of Toronto Press, 1988.

O'Mally, John W., ed. *Humanity and Divinity in Renaissance and Reformation: Essays in Honor of Charles Trinkaus.* Leiden: Brill, 1993.

Ong, Walter. *Ramus, Method, and the Decay of Dialogue: From the Art of Discourse to the Art of Reason.* Chicago: University of Chicago Press, 2004.

Orsi, Robert. *History and Presence.* Cambridge, MA: Harvard University Press, 2016.

Osler, Margaret. *Reconfiguring the World: Nature, God, and Human Understanding from the Middle Ages to Early Modern Europe.* Baltimore, MD: Johns Hopkins University Press, 2013.

Outler, Albert C. "Theodosius' Horse: Reflections on the Predicament of the Church Historian." *Church History* 34 (1965): 251–261.

Ozment, Steven. *The Age of Reform, 1250–1550: An Intellectual and Religious History of Late Medieval and Reformation Europe.* New Haven, CT: Yale University Press, 1981.

Parish, Helen and William G. Naphy, eds. *Religion and Superstition in Reformation Europe.* Manchester: Manchester University Press, 2002.

Parker, Charles H. and Jerry H. Bentley, eds. *Between the Middle Ages and Modernity: Individual and Community in the Early Modern World.* Lanham, MD: Rowman and Littlefield, 2007.

Parker, T. H. L. *The Doctrine of the Knowledge of God: A Study in the Theology of John Calvin.* London: Lutterworth, 1962.

Partee, Charles. *Calvin and Classical Philosophy.* Louisville, KY: Westminster John Knox Press, 2005.

"Calvin and Determinism." *Christian Scholar's Review* 5 (2) (1975): 123–128.

"The Soul in Plato, Platonism, and Calvin." *The Scottish Journal of Theology* 22 (1969): 278–295.

The Theology of John Calvin. Louisville, KY: Westminster John Knox, 2008.

Pascal, Blaise. *Pensées.* New York, NY: Penguin Classics, 1995.

Pecknold, C. C. "Migrations of the Host: Fugitive Democracy and the Corpus Mysticum." *Political Theology* 11 (1) (2010): 77–101.

Perkinson, James W. *White Theology: Outing Supremacy in Modernity.* New York: Palgrave Macmillan, 2004.

Peterson, Erik. "Monotheism as a Political Problem." In *Theological Tractates.* Translated by M. Hollerich. Redwood City, CA: Stanford University Press, 2011: 68–105.

Pini, Giorgio. "Signification of Names in Duns Scotus and Some of His Contemporaries." *Vivarium* 39 (1) (2001): 20–51.

Pitkin, Barbara. *What Pure Eyes Could See: Calvin's Doctrine of Faith in its Exegetical Context* Oxford: Oxford University Press, 1999.

Plato. *Meno. Phaedo.*
  Symposium.
  Timaeus.
Porter, Ray and Mikuláš Teich, eds. *The Scientific Revolution in National Context.* New York: Cambridge University Press, 1991.
Porterfield, Amanda. "Leaving Providence Behind." *Church History* 80 (2) (2011): 366–368.
Potts, Matthew. "Preaching in the Subjunctive." *Practical Matters* 7 (2014): 27–45.
Preus, J. Samuel. "Zwingli, Calvin and the Origin of Religion." *Church History* 46 (2) (1977): 186–202.
Prior, C. Scott. "God's Bridle: John Calvin's Application of Natural Law." *Journal of Law and Religion* 22 (1) (2006/2007): 225–254.
Pseudo-Dionysius. "*The Mystical Theology.*" In *Pseudo-Dionysius: The Complete Works.* Mahwah, NJ: Paulist Press, 1987.
Quintilian. *Institutiones oratoriae, The Orator's Education.* Translated by Donald A. Russell. Cambridge, MA: Harvard University Press, 2001.
Ralston, Joshua, "Preaching Makes the Church: Recovering a Missing Ecclesial Mark." In *John Calvin's Ecclesiology: Ecumenical Perspectives.* Edited by Eddy van der Borght and Gerard Mannion. New York: T&T Clark, 2011: 125–142.
Rancière, Jacques. *Disagreement: Politics and Philosophy.* Translated by Julie Rose. Minneapolis: University of Minnesota Press, 1999.
Renick, Timothy M. "From Apartheid to Liberation: Calvinism and the Shaping of Ethical Belief in South Africa." *Sociological Focus* 24 (2) (1991): 129–143.
Reynolds, David S. *John Brown, Abolitionist: The Man Who Killed Slavery, Sparked the Civil War, and Seeded Civil Rights.* New York: Vintage, 2006.
Ricoeur, Paul. *Time and Narrative Volume 1.* Translated by Kathleen McLaughlin and David Pellauer. Chicago: University of Chicago Press, 1984.
Roberts, Tyler T. *Contesting Spirit: Nietzsche, Affirmation, Religion.* Princeton, NJ: Princeton University Press, 1998.
  Encountering Religion: Responsibility and Criticism after Secularism. New York: Columbia University Press, 2013.
Robinson, Marilynne. *Absence of Mind: The Dispelling of Inwardness from the Modern Myth of the Self.* New Haven, CT: Yale University Press, 2011.
  The Death of Adam: Essays on Modern Thought. New York: Picador, 1998.
  Gilead. New York: Farrar, Straus and Giroux, 2004.
  The Givenness of Things. New York: Farrar, Straus and Giroux, 2015.
  "Preface." In *John Calvin: Steward of God's Covenant.* Edited by John F. Thornton and Susan B. Varenne. New York: Random House, 2006.
  When I Was a Child I Read Books. New York: Farrar, Straus and Giroux, 2012.
Roth, Randolph A. "The First Radical Abolitionists: The Reverend James Milligan and the Reformed Presbyterians of Vermont." In *Abolitionism and American Religion.* Edited by John R. McKivigan. New York: Garland, 1999: 540–63.

Ross, James Bruce and Mary M. McLaughlin, eds. *The Portable Renaissance Reader*. New York: Penguin Books, 1981.

Rust, Jennifer. "Political Theologies of the Corpus Mysticum: Schmitt, Kantorowicz, and de Lubac." In *Political Theology and Early Modernity*. Chicago: University of Chicago Press, 2012.

Salles, Ricardo. *God and Cosmos in Stoicism*. New York: Oxford University Press, 2009.

Sanchez, Michelle C. "Ritualized Doctrine: Protestant Ritual, Genre, and the Case of Calvin's *Institutes*." *Journal of the American Academy of Religion* 85 (3) (2017): 746–774

"Calvin and the Two Bodies of Christ: Fiction and Power in Dogmatic Theology, Political Theology." In *Political Theology*. DOI: 10.1080/1462317X.2018.1440157 (2018).

Santner, Eric L. *The Royal Remains: The People's Two Bodies and the Endgames of Sovereignty*. Chicago: University of Chicago Press, 2011.

Schäfer, Christian. "The Anonymous Naming of Names: Pseudonymity and Philosophical Program in Dionysius the Areopagite." *American Catholic Philosophical Quarterly* 82 (4) (2008): 561–580.

Seligman, Adam B., Robert P. Weller, Michael Puett, and Bennett Simon. *Ritual and Its Consequences*. Oxford: Oxford University Press, 2008.

Seneca. *De Providentia*.

Epistle 117.

Schildgen, Brenda Deen. *Divine Providence: A History: The Bible, Virgil, Osorius, Augustine, and Dante*. New York: Bloomsbury Academic, 2012.

Schleiermacher, Georg Freidrich Daniel Erst. *Glaubenslehre*.

Schmitt, Carl. *The Leviathon in the State Theory of Thomas Hobbes: Meaning and Failure of a Political Symbol*. Translated by George Schwab and Erna Hilfstein. Chicago: University of Chicago Press, 1996.

Political Theology: Four Chapters on the Concept of Sovereignty. Translated by George Schwab. Cambridge, MA: MIT Press, 2010.

Schreiner, Susan. "Calvin's Use of Natural Law." In *A Preserving Grace: Protestants, Catholics, and Natural Law*. Edited by Michael Comartie. Grand Rapids, MI: Eerdmans, 1997: 51–76.

Are You Alone Wise? The Search for Certainty in the Early Modern Era. New York: Oxford University Press, 2011.

The Theater of His Glory: Nature and Natural Order in the Thought of John Calvin. Durham, NC: The Labyrinth Press, 1991.

Where Shall Wisdom Be Found? Calvin's Exegesis of Job from Medieval and Modern Perspectives. Chicago: University of Chicago Press, 1994.

Scribner, Robert. "Ritual and Reformation." In *R. Po-chia Hsia: The German People and the Reformation*. Ithaca, NY: Cornell University Press, 1988.

Seidman, Steven. "Modernity, Meaning, and Cultural Pessimism in Max Weber." *Sociological Analysis* 44 (4) (1983): 267–78.

Selderhuis, Herman J., ed. *The Calvin Handbook*. Translated by Henry J. Baron, Judith J. Guder, Randi H. Lundell, and Gerrit W. Sheeres. Grand Rapids, MI: Eerdmans, 2009.

John Calvin: A Pilgrim's Life. Downers Grove, IL: IVP Academic 2009.

Seneca. *De Providentia.*

Shapin, Steven. *The Scientific Revolution.* Chicago: University of Chicago Press, 1996.

Shaw, Bret D. "African Christianity: Disputes, Defintiions, and Donatists." In *Orthodoxy and Heresy in Religious Movements: Discipline and Dissent.* Edited by M. R. Greenshields and T. R. Robinsons, 5–34. Lampeter: The Edwin Mellen Press, 1992: 5–34.

Shaw, Ian J. *High Calvinists in Action: Calvinism and the City, Manchester and London, 1810–1860.* New York: Oxford University Press, 2002.

Shulman, George. "White Supremacy and Black Insurgency as Political Theology." In *Race and Secularism in America.* Edited by Jonathan S. Kahn and Vincent W. Lloyd. New York: Columbia University Press, 2016: 23–42.

Sica, Alan. "Weberian Theory Today." In *Handbook of Sociological Theory.* Edited by Jonathan H. Turner. New York: Springer, 2006: 487–507.

Singh, Devin. "Anarchy, Void, Signature: Agamben's Trinity among Orthodoxy's Remains." *Political Theology* 17 (1) (2016): 27–46.

Smith, Jonathan Z. *Drudgery Divine: On the Comparison of Early Christianities and the Religions of Late Antiquity.* Chicago: Chicago University Press, 1990.

Smith, Ted A. *Weird John Brown.* Redwood City, CA: Stanford University Press, 2014.

Smyth, Thomas. *Calvin and His Enemies: A Memoir of the Life, Character, and Principles of Calvin.* Bellingham, WA: Logos Research Systems, Inc., 2009.

Socher, Abraham. "Funkenstein on the Theological Origins of Historicism: A Critical Note." *Journal of the History of Ideas* 67 (2) (2006): 401–408.

Sprinker, Michael, ed. *Ghostly Demarcations: A Symposium on Jacques Derrida's Specters of Marx.* New York: Verso, 1999.

Spivak, Gayatri. *An Aesthetic Education in the Era of Globalization.* Cambridge, MA: Harvard University Press, 2012.

Stachiewski, John. *The Persecutory Imagination: English Puritanism and the Literature of Religious Despair.* Oxford: Clarendon Press, 1991.

Stang, Charles M. *Apophasis and Pseudonymity in Dionysius the Areopagite: "No Longer I."* New York: Oxford University Press, 2012.

Steinmetz, David. "Calvin and the Natural Knowledge of God." In *Via Augustini: Augustine in the Later Middle Ages, Renaissance and Reformation, Essays in Honor of Damasus Trapp, OSA.* Edited by Heiko A. Oberman and Frank A. James III. Leiden: E. J. Brill, 1991: 142–156.

Calvin in Context. Oxford: Oxford University Press, 2010.

Stewart-Kroeker, Sarah. *Pilgrimage as Moral and Aesthetic Formation in Augustine's Thought.* New York: Oxford University Press, 2017.

Stock, Brian. *Augustine the Reader: Mediation, Self-Knowledge, and the Ethics of Interpretation.* Cambridge, MA: Harvard University Press, 1996.

Stout, Jeffrey. "Secularization and Resentment." In *Democracy and Tradition.* Princeton, NJ: Princeton University Press, 2004.

Sytsma, David S. "Calvin, Daneau, and *Physica Mosaica*: Neglected Continuities at the Origins of an Early Modern Tradition." *Church History and Religious Culture* 95 (2015): 457–476.

Szabari, Antonia. *Less Rightly Said: Scandals and Readers in Sixteenth-Century France*. Stanford, CA: Stanford University Press, 2009.

Talay, Zeynep. "A Dialogue with Nietzsche: Blumenberg and Löwith on History and Progress." *History of European Ideas* 37 (3) (2011): 376–381.

Tanner, Kathryn. *God and Creation in Christian Theology*. Oxford: Blackwell, 1988.

Taves, Ann. "The Camp Meeting and Paradoxes of Evangelical Protestant Ritual." In *Teaching Ritual*. AAR Teaching Religious Studies Series. Edited by Catherine Bell. Oxford: Oxford University Press, 2007.

Tawney, R. H. *Religion and the Rise of Capitalism*. New Brunswick, NJ: Transaction Publishers, 1998.

Taylor, Charles. *A Secular Age*. Cambridge, MA: Harvard University Press, 2007. *Modern Social Imaginaries*. Durham, NC: Duke University Press, 2004.

Taylor, Mark C. "*Itinerarium Mentis in Deum*: Hegel's Proofs of God's Existence." *The Journal of Religion* 57 (3) (1977): 211–231.

Thiemann', Ronald F. *The Humble Sublime*. London: IB Taurus, 2013.

Thomas Aquinas. *Summa Theologica*.

Thompson, John Lee. *John Calvin and the Daughters of Sarah*. Geneva: Librairie Droz, 1992.

Thuesen, Peter J. *Predestination: The American Career of a Contentious Doctrine*. New York: Oxford University Press, 2009.

Thomas Aquinas. Summa *Theologica*.

Tilley, Maureen A. "Redefining Donatism: Moving Forward." *Augustinian Studies* 42 (1) (2011): 21–32.

Torrance, T. F. *Calvin's Doctrine of Man*. Grand Rapids, MI: Eerdman's, 1957.

Torrance, Thomas. *Atonement: The Person and Work of Christ*. Downers Grove, IL: Intervarsity Press, 2009.

Trinkaus, Charles. *In Our Image and Likeness: Humanity and Divinity in Italian Humanist Thought*. Chicago: University of Chicago Press, 1970.

Trueman, Carl R. and R. Scott Clark, eds. *Protestant Scholasticism: Studies in Reassessment*. Eugene, OR: Wipf and Stock, 2005.

Turretin, Francis. Institutes *of Elenctic Theology*.

Valeri, Mark. "Religion, Discipline, and the Economy in Calvin's Geneva." *The Sixteenth Century Journal* 28 (1) (1997): 123–142.

Van Dken, Tamara. "Always Reforming? Evangelical Feminism and the Committee for Women in the Christian Reformed Church, 1975–1995." *Church History and Religious Culture* 95 (4) (2015): 495–522.

Vasquez, Manuel. *More Than Belief: A Materialist Theory of Religion*. New York: Oxford University Press, 2011.

Vattimo, Gianni. *Belief*. Redwood City, CA: Stanford University Press, 1996.

Vico, Giambattista. *New Science*. Ithaca, NY: Cornell University Press, 1984.

Voltaire, *Candide*. London: Penguin Books, 1947.

von Trier, Lars. *Melancholia*. Film. Directed by Lars von Trier. Denmark: Meta Louise Foldager, Louise Vesth, 2011.

Vosloo, Robert. "Calvin and Anti-Apartheid Memory in the Dutch-Reformed Families of South Africa." In *Sober, Strict and Scriptural: Collective Memories of John Calvin: 1800–2000*. Edited by Johan de Neit, Herman Paul, and Bart Wallet. Leiden: Brill, 2009: 217–244.

Walker, Henry J. *Theseus and Athens*. New York: Oxford University Press, 1995.

Wallace, Robert M. "Progress, Secularization and Modernity: The Lowith-Blumenberg Debate." *New German Critique* 8 (1) (1981): 63–79.

Walsh, James P. *Divine Providence and Human Suffering*. Wilmington, DE: Michael Glazier, 1985.

Walzer, Michael. *The Revolution of the Saints: A Study in the Origins of Radical Politics*. Cambridge: Harvard University Press, 1965.

Wandel, Lee Palmer. "John Calvin and Michel de Montaigne on the Eye." In *Early Modern Eyes*. Edited by Walter S. Melion and Lee Palmer Wandel. Leiden: Brill, 2010: 135–155.

"Incarnation, Image, and Sign: John Calvin's *Institutes of the Christian Religion* & Late Medieval Visual Culture." In *Image and Incarnation: The Early Modern Doctrine of the Pictorial Image*. Edited by Walter S. Melion and Lee Palmer Wandel. Leiden: Brill, 2015: 187–203.

Warfield, Benjamin B. "Predestination." In *Biblical Doctrines: Volume 2 of the Works of Benjamin B. Warfield*. Grand Rapids, MI: Baker, 1991.

"Some Thoughts on Predestination." In *Shorter Writings*. Edited by John E. Meeter. Phillipsburg, NJ: P&R, 2001: 1:15.

Waswo, Richard. *Language and Meaning in the Renaissance*. Princeton, NJ: Princeton University Press, 1987.

Webb, Stephen H. "The Theo-Economics of God." In *The Gifting God: A Trinitarian Ethics of Excess*. New York: Oxford University Press, 1996. 83–120.

Weber, Max. "Science as Vocation." In *Essays in Sociology*. Edited and translated by H. H. Gerth and C. Wright Mills. Oxford: Oxford University Press, 1946. 129–156.

The Protestant Ethic and the Spirit of Capitalism. Translated by Peter Baehr and Gordon C. Wells. New York: Penguin, 2002.

Weil, Simone. *Gravity and Grace*. New York: Routledge, 1999.

Weinrich, Harold. *Lethe: The Art and Critique of Forgetting*. Translated by Steven Rendall. Ithaca, NY: Cornell University Press, 2004.

Wendell, Francois. *Calvin: The Origins and Development of His Religious Thought*. Translated by Philip Mairet. New York: Harper & Row, 1963.

Wesner, Merry E. *Early Modern Europe, 1450–1789*. New York: Cambridge University Press, 2006.

The Westminster Confession of Faith. 3rd edition. Lawrenceville, GA: Committee for Christian Education and Publications, 1990.

White, Hayden. *Metahistory: The Historical Imagination in Nineteenth-Century Europe*. Baltimore, MD: The Johns Hopkins University Press, 1973.

White, Heather. *Reforming Sodom: Protestants and Gay Rights*. Chapel Hill: University of North Carolina Press, 2015.

Widder, Nathan. "On Abuses in the Uses of History: Blumenberg on Nietzsche; Nietzsche on Genealogy." *History of Political Thought* 21 (2) (2000): 308–326.

Williams, Rowan. "Language, Reality and Desire in Augustine's *De Doctrina.*" *Journal of Theology and Literature* 3 (2) (1989): 138–150.

On Augustine. London: Bloomsbury, 2016.

Willis, E. David. "Rhetoric and Responsibility in Calvin's Theology." In *The Context of Contemporary Theology: Essays in Honor of Paul Lehmann.* Edited by Alexander J. McKelway and E. David Willis. Atlanta: John Knox Press, 1974: 43–63.

Wimsatt, W. K., Jr., and Monroe C. Beardsley. "The Intentional Fallacy." In *The Verbal Icon: Studies in the Meaning of Poetry.* Lexington: University of Kentucky Press, 1967.

Wilkinson, Iain. "The Problem of Suffering As a Driving Force of Rationalization and Social Change." *The British Journal of Sociology* 64 (1) (2013): 123–141.

Wintrobe, Ronald and Mario Ferrero, eds. *The Political Economy of Theocracy.* New York: Palgrave Macmillan, 2009.

Witte, John Jr. *The Reformation of Rights.* New York: Cambridge University Press, 2007.

and Robert M. Kingdon, *Sex, Marriage, and Family in John Calvin's Geneva.* Grand Rapids, MI: Eerdman's, 2005.

Wolin, Richard. *Heidegger's Children: Hannah Arendt, Karl Löwith, Hans Jonas, and Herbert Marcuse.* Princeton, NJ: Princeton University Press, 2001.

Wolin, Sheldon. *Politics and Vision.* Princeton, NJ: Princeton University Press, 2004.

Worthen, Molly. *Apostles of Reason: The Crisis of Authority in American Evangelicalism.* New York: Oxford University Press, 2013.

"The Chalcedon Problem: Rousas John Rushdoony and the Origins of Christian Reconstructionism." *Church History* 77 (2) (2008): 399–437.

Wright, David F. "Calvin's Accommodating God." In *Calvinus Sincerioris Religionis Vindex.* Edited by W. H. Neuser and B. G. Armstrong. Kirksville, MO: Sixteenth Century Journal Publishers, 1997: 3–20.

Zachman, Randall. "Gathering Meaning from the Context: Calvin's Exegetical Method." *The Journal of Religion* 82 (1) (2002): 1–26.

Image and Word in the Theology of John Calvin. Notre Dame, IN: University of Notre Dame Press, 2009.

John Calvin as Pastor, Teacher, and Theologian. Grand Rapids, MI: Baker Academic, 2006.

Zafirovski, Milan. *The Destiny of Modern Societies: The Calvinist Predestination of a New Society.* Leiden: Brill, 2009.

Ziegler, Philip G. and Francesca Aran Murphy. *The Providence of God: Deus habet concilium.* Edinburgh: T&T Clark, 2009.

Zwingli, Ulrich. *On the Doctrine of Providence and Other Essays.* Durham, NC: Labyrinth Press, 1922.

"*On the Lord's Supper.*" In *Zwingli and Bullinger.* Translated by G. W. Bromiley. Philadelphia: Westminster Press, 1953: 185–238.

Index

abject, 5, 162, 276
accommodation, 44, 58, 69, 132, 145, 208, 223, 246, 263, 270, 278
Adams, Edward, 57
adoption. *See* covenant of adoption
affect, emotion, 100, 121, 148, 173, 226, 229
affirmation, 6, 110, 112, 121, 201, 226, 285
Agamben, Giorgio, 3, 151–61, 168, 183, 257, 272
Agricola, Rudolf, 52
Anidjar, Gil, 179–80, 193
Anselm of Canterbury, 212–16, 229, 238
Apostles' Creed, 126, 163
Aquinas, Thomas, 50, 53, 109, 127, 151, 260–61
argument, logos, 85, 91, 94–95, 101, 104
Aristotle, 170
Arius, 157
  Calvin's view of, 164, 168
art, 1, 15, 17, 57, 104, 119, 122, 183, 254, 263, 270, *See* poiesis
  horror, 134
  Nietzsche's view of, 122
as if, 101, 171, 224, 241, 282–83
Asad, Talal, 22, 26, 193
ascent, 63, 68, 104
ascetic ideal, 120, 285
ataraxia, 110, 173–74
atonement, 222–27
Aufklärung, 112
Augustine, 61, 109, 137
  Calvin's relationship to, 23

and the church, 202, 205, 229
and incarnation, 205, 211, 229
and pedagogy, 29, 59–61, 66, 186–97, 211, 245
and providence, 107–9, 158
theory of signification, 188–94, 201–3
Austin, J. L., 24

Bacon, Francis, 114, 276
Baldwin, James, 282
Balibar, Etienne, 182
being, 168, 188, 245, 251, 273
  Anselm's ontology, 213
  Calvin's ontology, 195, 229, 256
Bell, Catherine, 22, 26, 90, 193
belonging, 210
biopower, 4, 152–59, 162, 171, 183
bios. *See* life, political
Blumenberg, Hans, 13, 112, 115, 117, 143, 153, 274
body. *See* embodiment
  collective, 3, 9, 11–12, 129, 160, 237, 248, 286
  human, 3, 38, 119, 181, 220, 263, 281
  interplay between human and collective, 2, 182, 259, 270
Boethius, 102–7, 125, 174
Bonaventure, 66, 76
Bonhoeffer, Dietrich, 240
Bourdieu, Pierre, 24–25
Bowman, Glenn, 64
Brown, Wendy, 181–83

Bunyan, John, 66
Butler, Judith, 25

Calvin, Jean
 as abject figure, 6
 as doctor of the church, 125, 129
 physical suffering, 32
 as refugee, 5, 116, 126, 129, 163
 as teacher, 67, 77, 116, 127, 144, 150,
  184, 235
 as writer, 5, 33, 43, 50, 53, 67, 84, 116,
  147, 220, 280–81
Calvinism, 33–36, 148–51, 278, 280, 285
Camus, Albert, 285
Candler, Peter, 29, 53, 65, 75
care, 95–96, 102, 105, 287
 in Calvin's providence, 130, 133, 169,
  218
Carter, J. Kameron, 3, 182–84
causality, 101, 133–34
Christ, 74
 human body of, 174, 248
 humanity of, 226
 as mediator, 221
Christology, 1, 62, 157, 165–66
church, 1, 192
 Calvin's view, 263
 as corpus mysticum, 260, 263
 visible and invisible, 149, 247–50, 256, 263
Cicero, 50, 58
civic life, 50, 70–71, 77, 129, 146, 150, 181,
  185, 203, 263, 267–69, 279
 of Geneva, 8
Cleanthes, 91
clothing
 as metaphor, 103, 105, 132, 138–39, 141
colonization, 17, 180, 276
commonplaces, 52
communucatio idiomatum, 194
Connerton, Paul, 203
Corpus Christianum, 2–3, 5–6, 23, 36, 110,
  128, 149–50, 244
covenant, 33, 36, 73
 of adoption, 232, 264
creation, 8, 56, 126, 147, 163, 208
 Augustine's view of, 188
 as primary site of divine activity, 38, 169,
  199, 203
creativity
 human, 112, 117, *See* poiesis
 and theological writing, 282–84

critique, 5, 26, 110, 163, 183, 185, 257, 270
 of fascism, 150
 of idolatry, 208, 265
 of institutions, 116
 of Protestantism, 26
Cyprian, 251

Dante, 15, 66, 262
Davis, Kathleen, 17, 19, 180, 278
de Certeau, Michel, 118
death, 74, 83, 85, 118, 124
 of Christ, 222–27, 249
 and modernity, 89, 117–20
 and providence, 94–107
decision, sovereign, 19, 112, 119, 160, 275
democracy, 11, 152, 261
depravity, 57
Derrida, Jacques, 24–25
Descartes, Rene, 89
desire, 56, 67, 190, 230–31, 235, 281
determinism, 24, 130, 286
discipline, 7, 152, 159, 257
 church, 149, 249–53
 of prayer, 231
disenchantment, 7, 87, 116, 274
doctrine, use of, 11, 32, 36, 43, 45, 94, 104,
  163–64, 186, 195, 217, 231, 234, 281
Dostoevsky, Fyodor, 285
DuBois, W.E.B., 4, 182
Duns Scotus, 135

ecclesiology, 1
economic theology, 4, 156, 170, 180, 271,
  275
Edwards, Jonathan, 160
elect, the, 6, 237, 247
 metaphor of, 2
election
 certainty of, 229, 236, 281
election, doctrine of, 143, 217, 229, 233–37
 knowledge of, 238
Elwood, Christopher, 265–66
embodiment, 10, 88, 125, 192, 226, 248,
  See body
enchiridion, 53–55, 108
Epictetus, 55
Erasmus of Rotterdam, 52, 140
eristic paradox, 187, 203, 222
eternal recurrence, 121–23, 285
Eucharist, 77, 184, 244, 248–50, 264–65
 Calvin's view of, 244–57

Luther's view of, 194
Zwingli's view of, 253
evil, 98, 105, 129, 134, 235, 285
and Calvin's providence, 134–46
exception, 2, 7, 27, 148, 162

faith, 60, 109, 126, 196, 199, 203, 226,
    231, *See* rule of faith
of Christ, 217, 219, 253
and language, 212, 215
and prayer, 230–31
and recognition, 246–47, 253–54, 272
seeking understanding, 210, 217, 231,
    237
fascism, 3, 16, 38, 110, 183
feudalism
Davis' view of, 17
fiction, fictive representation, 15–16, 194,
    254, 282
Calvin's view of, 263
ethnicity, 3
and history, 17–20
Kantorowicz's view of, 15, 261
legal, 233
and sovereignty, 9
and theology, 218–27, 283
Foucault, Michel, 4, 21, 148, 151, 161, 183,
    278–79
Francis I of France, 185, 272
freedom, 89, 105
Freud, Sigmund, 117

Gauchet, Marcel, 11, 179
Gaunilo of Marmoutiers, 216
Geneva, 5, 7, 150
glory, 4, 56, 68, 77, 146, 159–61, 266, 272
Gordon, Bruce, 1, 35
Gorski, Philip, 148–49, 271
governance, 125, 226
as discourse, 130
grace, 38, 137, 172, 198, 215, 234
grammar, 213, 229, 233
of participation, 53, 73, 257
of representation, 54

habituation, 29, 46, 203–8
habitus, 25, 53
Hadot, Pierre, 53
hermeneutics, 186, 192, 203
hiddenness, 115, 135, 138–46, 169
history, 19

Heilgeschehen, 18, 180
Heilsgeschehen, 151
historical method, 3, 20, 118
and progress, 13, 18, 114, 180
and providence, 86
Weltgeschichte, 18, 180
Hobbes, Thomas, 11, 114, 181, 258–59
Hollywood, Amy, 26–27
homo sacer, 3, 162, 170
inglorious, 5, 9, 36, 269
hope, 124, 215
and providence, 107, 120, 129

idolatry, 9, 71, 202, 270
illumination, 229, 281
imitation, 91, 98, 156, 262
immanence, 13, 16, 18, 57, 78, 110, 138,
    172, 275
incarnation, 10, 59
and Augustine, 205
for Augustine, 59, 187
for Calvin, 197–201, 219–27, 237, 246,
    249
and pedagogy, 10, 62, 186, 190–97, 208,
    254, 271
as pedagogy, 203
as poesis, 184
as poiesis, 17
secularization of, 179–82
and signification, 193
and sovereignty, 3–4, 182, 184, 270
Institutes of the Christian Religion (1559)
genre of, 36, 51, 77, 276, 280
sources of influence, 47
structure of, 45, 48, 63, 68, 125,
    227, 246
institutions, 77, 128, 186, 287
as art, 149, 258
intention, 24, 34, 87, 200
and providence, 37
and signification, 87, 188
interpretive crossroads, 6, 16, 39, 146, 216,
    236, 257, 283
itinerarium, 53, 62–67
Itinerarium Burdigalense, 64

Jonas, Hans, 115
Jordan, Mark D., 29, 129, 192, 202, 211
journey, 6, 8, 63, 66, 70, 73, 190, 217
joy, 121–24, 129, 174, 285
justification, 124, 145, 197, 225, 227

Kahn, Victoria, 14, 183, 258, 261, 278
Kant, Immanuel, 213
Kantorowicz, Ernst, 1, 15, 205, 259, 263
knowledge, 238
  Calvin's theory of, 55
  of God and ourselves (*cognitio Dei et nostri*), 37, 56, 72, 77, 125, 142, 148, 186, 198, 229, 237
  of God as Creator (*cognitio Dei creatoris*), 200, 218
  of God as Mediator, 246
  of God as Redeemer (*cognitio Dei redemptoris*), 200, 220
  of God as spirit (*cognitio Dei spiritus*), 227
  modern approaches to, 113
  of self, 68
  twofold knowledge of God (*duplex cognitio*), 37, 68, 161, 198, 217

labyrinth, 6, 70–73, 234
language, 28, 113, 188, 214, 217, 224
law, 10
  Calvin's view of, 145, 219, 268
  of the home, 152, 168, 170
  natural, 115, 198, 268
  and providence, 100
  of the state, 152
Lazier, Benjamin, 115
learning. *See* pedagogy
Lefort, Claude, 11
Leibniz, Gottfried Wilhelm, 112
liberalism, 10, 268
life, 118, 152–54, 284–87
  bare life, 4, 153, 171
  biological, 152, 161, 170
  eternal, 154, 170–71
  natural life of Jesus, 171
  political, 152, 161, 170
  political life of Jesus, 171
  worldly, 74, 112, 126, 168, 171, 201, 206, 222, 257, 287
Lloyd, Genevieve, 86, 88, 92
loci communes. See commonplaces
logos. See argument, *logos*; Word, Divine
loss, 87, 117–19, 123
  as site of divine revelation, 174
love, 56, 194, 200, 202, 205, 226, 233, 254, *See* rule of love
  for life, 110, 117, 144, 173, 285
Löwith, Karl, 12, 16, 110, 115, 117, 180, 278
Luther, Martin, 140, 194, 201

Mackey, Louis, 29, 211, 215
Manifest Destiny, 7
Marcus Aurelius, 101–2
Mason, Pamela A., 8
Mass. *See* Eucharist
mastery, 113–15, 174, 214, 245
  and Calvinism, 33, 257, 286
materiality, 18, 22, 56, 88
  excessive, 183, 210, 212, 258, 277, 283
  and Protestantism, 193
materialization, 24, 74, 145, 147, 183, 194, 277, 283
  Butler's view of, 25
  and Calvin, 29, 149
McCutcheon, Russell, 20
meaning, 23–26, 87, 184, 190, 193–97, 213, 284
  for Calvin, 201
  and incarnation, 190
  as intention, 87
  and providence, 101, 116, 172
  sacramental, 253
  as significance, 87
  of suffering, 37, 119–23
mediation, 60–61, 182, 211, 222, 270, 278
  Augustine's view of, 107, 202
  Calvin's view of, 37, 58, 195, 244
  of Christ, 62, 74, 146, 199, 220
  textual, 24, 78, 165, 254
melamncholia, 83–84
Melanchthon, Philipp, 52
memory, 73, 203, 264
  Calvin's view of, 208
metaphor, 74, 113, 248, 281
  Calvin's use of, 256
  and political theology, 1–2, 206, 258
Milbank, John, 180
modernity, concept of, 13, 87, 112, 119, 276
  Blumeberg's view of, 117
Morrison, Toni, 282
Muller, Richard A., 50, 52, 70
myth, 95, 101, 118
  and political theology, 11

nationalism, 33
nature, 57, 89, 101
  Greek valuation of, 115
necessity, 89
Neoplatonism, 66, 76
Niebuhr, Richard R., 88

Nietzsche, Friedrich, 6, 14, 110, 113, 117, 119, 129, 174, 241, 278, 282, 285
as writer, 124
Thus Spoke Zarathustra, 121, 242–43
obedience, 219, 224, 269
Oberman, Heiko, 129, 164
occasionalism, 129
oikonomia. See law, of the home
omnipotence, divine, 8, 10, 89, 116, 160, 165–69, 185, 244
against sovereignty, 257, 266
and secularization, 13
ontological argument, 212–16
ontology. *See* being
order, 95, 99, 156–59, 267, 279
Orsi, Robert, 22

paranoia, 200, 219
participation, 11, 37, 106, 196, 232
in Christ, 145, 166, 171, 227, 248
grammar of, 53, 73, 257
ontological, 92, 99, 245
textual, 23, 65, 270
pedagogy, 58, 60, 67–68, 74, 79, 107, 126, 184, 202, 228
Augustinian, 184, 190–97, 203
and text, 54, 62
perception, 56
and materialization, 68, 85, 204
and mediation, 62, 75, 218, 225, 249
and providence, 99, 104–10, 139
performative, 24–27, 250
church as, 185, 208, 249, 256, 271
and the divine Word, 146, 168
and providence, 85, 144
periodization, 19, 116, 275
and secularization, 18
Peterson, Erik, 151
piety, 49–50, 60, 125, 195, 238
pilgrimage. *See* journey
Plato, 76–77, 92
poiesis
and church, 149
and modernity, 14–17, 112–15, 258
and theology, 144, 146, 183–86, 270, 276
political. *See* civic life; political theology
political theology, 10–19, 149–50, 154, 262, *See* civic life
Calvin's view of, 258–69
Potts, Matthew, 29, 193

power, techniques of, 167, 271
practice, performance
and Anselm's *Proslogion,* 215
and Augustine's writing, 61, 187, 192, 203–6
and Calvin's writing, 230
and Calvinism, 7, 127, 148, 277, 279
and Calvin's writing, 44–48, 58, 147, 208, 264, 273, 280
and providence, 84–90, 103–7, 119–24
and ritual, 23
and signification, 17, 27, 36, 43, 53, 120, 230, 281
prayer, 92, 229–33
preaching, 201, 208, 249, 271, 277
predestination. *See* election, doctrine of
Protestant Reformations, context of, 192, 206, 265
Protestantism, 19, 22–23
and modernity, 193, 275
and the study of religion, 26, 275
providence, 6, 8, 201, 226, 230
affective dimensions of, 124, 174
and Agamben, 151–61
and Augustine, 107–9
and Boethius, 102–7
and Calvin, 146, 175
and Cleanthes, 91
and governmentality, 151–59, 169–75
and Marcus Aurelius, 101
and method, 86–90
and modernity, 111–17
and Nietzsche, 124
and Plato, 92–97
and Seneca, 98–101
and Weber, 119
Pseudo-Dionysius, 76

Ramus, Peter, 52
reality, 211
Bonhoeffer's view of, 243
constitution of, 240, 253
and language, 24
and materialization, 102, 245, 275
recognition, misrecognition, 36, 182, 244–47, 253, 266, 269
reform, 208, 256, 267
refugee, 1–3, 23, 116, 125–29, 136, 146, 152, 162, 237, 286
relationality, 15, 18, 50, 59–60, 71, 74, 90, 127, 190

religion
  concept of, 50, 275
  study of, 19, 22, 26
representation, 233, 252, *See* fiction, fictive
    representation
  artifactual, 101, 183
  and Christ, 173, 225, 249, 258–63
  Eucharistic, 255
  grammar of, 54, 143
  and language, 30
  political, 15, 182, 261–63
  and responsibility, 270
  and theology, 184
resentment, 6, 120–21
resistance, 77, 170, 269, 275
responsibility, 16–18, 36, 275–87
  and affirmation, 124
  and Bonhoeffer, 240
  to materiality, 230, 238, 258, 261
  and Nietzsche, 243
  and providence, 112, 114, 126
  and text, 39, 54, 183, 270
revelation, 69, 175
  and accommodation, 145
  and creation, 56, 142, 218
  and election, 236
  and Luther, 140
  and modern sovereignty, 180
  and the ontological argument, 214
  and pedagogy, 22, 46, 219
ritual, 22–28, 192, 203
  and Bell, 26, 90
  and the church, 249
  and De Certeau, 118
  and providence, 89–97, 101–2, 106,
    119
  and theology, 184
Roberts, Tyler, 124
rule
  of faith, 60, 187, 191, 202, 245
  of love, 49, 60, 192, 195, 245

Sabbath, 170
sacramental theology, 1, *See* Eucharist
  and Augustine, 193
  and Calvin, 244–57
  and political theology, 2, 9
sanctification, 197, 227
Schildgen, Brenda Deen, 20, 108
Schmitt, Carl, 1, 10–11, 258
  political theology, 150–52

Schreiner, Susan, 125, 133, 135
scripture, 8, 58, 62, 67, 199, 203, 224, 234
secularism, 115, 193
secularization, 10–19, 87, 109, 117, 154,
    179–86, 277
Selderhuis, Herman, 6
semiotics, 159, 193, 245, 266
Seneca, 58, 98–101, 165
sense of the divine (*sensus divinitatis*),
    56–58, 62, 69, 72, 126, 170, 198, 200,
    207
signature, 17–18, 24, 115, 282
  for Agamben, 89, 154–61
  for Calvin, 217
  of political theology, 160
  and sacrament, 255
signification, 23–29, 57
  Augustinian, 109, 188–94, 201–3
  and Calvin, 185–86, 206–9, 269, 271,
    277, 282
  Christological, 146, 185, 228, 239
  and the church, 252, 263, 266
  and the constitution of reality, 246
  and intention, 87
  as mode of participation, 167, 172, 188,
    228, 245–47, 273
  and Nietzsche, 121
  as practice, 36, 139, 149
  and providence, 92, 107, 109, 116, 126,
    132, 226, 264, 285
  sacramental, 145, 244–57
  of self, 232, 236, 239
  and theology, 211–18
  and the use of text, 58, 67–70, 75, 78,
    186, 196, 266, 281
sin, 57, 71, 74, 140
  affective dimensions of, 32, 57, 207, 236,
    265
  and divine accommodation, 168, 196,
    218, 257, 270
  and idolatry, 207, 245, 265
  and misrecognition, 36, 57, 211, 218,
    246, 256
Socrates, 93
sovereignty, 3–5, 10, 55, 119, 122, 159,
    181, 267, *See* poiesis, *See* political
    theology
  of the artist, 17, 262, 283
  and Calvin, 257, 267, 269, 276, 287
  decision, sovereign, 19
  and language, 29, 54, 162, 275, 283

logic of, 10, 17, 148, 150, 152, 180, 237, 275
and the natural world, 114, 116, 129, 162
and temporality, 19, 275
speculation, 168, 234
Spinoza, Baruch, 89
Spirit, 166, 227–28, 246, 249, 277
Calvin's view of the, 227
Stoics, 55, 97–102, 173, 285
influence on Calvin, 128
subjunctive, 194, 196, 245
suffering, 74
and Calvin, 126, 129, 146, 172–75
and interpretation, 47
and modernity, 111, 120, 284
and Nietzsche, 120–21, 285–86
and providence, 96–108, 124
meaning of, 37, 172

technology, 200, 280, 283
argumentative, 187, 231
of self or selves, 186, 203, 221, 256
temporality, 17, 31, 118, 156
Terpstra, Nicholas, 1
Tertullian, 151
theodicy, 124, 284–85
Thiemann, Ronald F., 194
transcendence
and Blumenberg, 112
within immanence, 129, 138, 146, 172, 212, 238, 283
and Calvin, 57, 78, 169
and Löwith, 13, 109
and Nietzsche, 16
and politics, 18, 275
and providence, 97

trinity
and Agamben, 157–59
for Calvin, 163–69
Calvin's view of, 163–69

Valla, Lorenzo, 52
Vattimo, Gianni, 179
Vermigli, Peter Matyr, 52
verum factum, principle of, 15, 114, 172, 181, 258
Vico, Giambattista, 112, 114, 258

Walzer, Michael, 7
Weber, Max, 119, 150, 278, 285
Weil, Simone, 285
Westminster Confession of Faith, 88
White, Hayden, 20
Wilkinson, Iain, 111
will, 16, 88, 103, 115, 121, 127, 132, 219–20, 285
Calvin's view of divine, 131–38
Williams, Rowan, 29, 191, 194
Wolin, Sheldon, 149
Word, Divine, 8, 62, 74, 78, 146, 165–66, 187, 230, 235, 246, 269
writing, 27
as art. *See poiesis*
and Calvin, 5, 33, 43, 116, 147, 220, 259, 281
complexity of, 20, 112
and embodiment, 220
as practice, 102, 119, 264

Zachman, Randall, 8, 30, 141, 244
Zizek, Slavoj, 180
zoe. See life, biological
zoe aionios. See life, eternal
Zwingli, Ulrich, 88, 109